Pro .NET Oracle Programming

MARK A. WILLIAMS

Apress®

Pro .NET Oracle Programming

Copyright © 2005 by Mark A. Williams

ISBN (pbk): 1-59059-425-8

Printed and bound in the United States of America 9 8 7 6 5 4 3 2 1

Lead Editor: Tony Davis
Technical Reviewer: Neeraj Gupta and Niall Litchfield
Editorial Board: Steve Anglin, Dan Appleman, Ewan Buckingham, Gary Cornell, Tony Davis, John Franklin, Jason Gilmore, Chris Mills, Dominic Shakeshaft, Jim Sumser
Project Manager: Beth Christmas
Copy Edit Manager: Nicole LeClerc
Copy Editor: Rebecca Rider
Production Manager: Kari Brooks-Copony
Production Editor: Kelly Winquist
Compositor: Diana Van Winkle, Van Winkle Design
Proofreaders: Patrick Vincent, April Eddy
Indexer: John Collin
Artist: Kari Brooks-Copony
Interior Designer: Diana Van Winkle, Van Winkle Design
Cover Designer: Kurt Krames
Manufacturing Manager: Tom Debolski

Distributed to the book trade in the United States by Springer-Verlag New York, Inc., 233 Spring Street, 6th Floor, New York, NY 10013, and outside the United States by Springer-Verlag GmbH & Co. KG, Tiergartenstr. 17, 69112 Heidelberg, Germany.

In the United States: phone 1-800-SPRINGER, fax 201-348-4505, e-mail orders@springer-ny.com, or visit http://www.springer-ny.com. Outside the United States: fax +49 6221 345229, e-mail orders@springer.de, or visit http://www.springer.de.

For information on translations, please contact Apress directly at 2560 Ninth Street, Suite 219, Berkeley, CA 94710. Phone 510-549-5930, fax 510-549-5939, e-mail info@apress.com, or visit http://www.apress.com.

The source code for this book is available to readers at http://www.apress.com in the Downloads section.

This book is dedicated to my parents Lee and Margy (1946–2003) Williams.
It was following my father's footsteps that led me into computers and computing; without
those footsteps, I might still be mixing apples and oranges in algebraic equations.
My mother never truly understood what Oracle is, but she knew it was important to me.
She is greatly missed. I would like to thank them both for their love, support, guidance, and
encouragement over the years—they were right more often than they ever got credit for.

Contents at a Glance

Contents

About the Author

MARK WILLIAMS currently works as a production Oracle DBA. He has worked with Oracle since database version 7.0.1.16 and holds Oracle Certified Professional certifications for versions 7, 8, 8i, and 9i. Prior to becoming a DBA, Mark developed corporate software applications that used the Oracle database as a back end. Over the years, he has worked as both an employee and as an independent contractor on a variety of Oracle projects.

About the
Technical Reviewers

NEERAJ GUPTA is a Senior Development Manager with Oracle Corporation. He specializes in data access products and manages a number of renowned Oracle data access products on Microsoft Windows platforms, including Oracle Data Provider for .NET, Oracle Provider for OLE DB, and Oracle Objects for OLE.

Neeraj has been involved in the design and development of Oracle Data Provider for .NET since its inception. He has more than 11 years of professional experience in the software industry, and he has extensive hands-on experience with C, C++, C#, COM, DCOM, OLE DB, ADO, ASP, ADO.NET, ASP.NET, .NET, Windows, and Oracle.

Neeraj holds a BS in Computer Science. He recently moved from the US to India and lives in Bangalore with his wife Ritu and son Aaryan. His spends his spare time playing cricket and golf.

NIALL LITCHFIELD started out life as an economist. Unfortunately, his tendency to seek evidence for an argument wasn't a great help there. He vividly recalls analyzing the two competing macroeconomic theories that were prevalent in the 1980s, each seeking to explain the economic performance of the Irish economy at that time, and concluding that both explained it equally well, and that neither explained it adequately. He followed this with a short spell at KPMG as a trainee chartered accountant, which he now says taught him an awful lot about managing businesses and that the sooner he stopped auditing things the better, for everyone.

Niall is now a Senior Software Engineer at a large UK public sector regulator, though he admits to this title only grudgingly as his father was a *real* engineer, with big machines and everything. His work largely entails implementing new database-driven applications on the Microsoft Windows platform. He is that rare animal—an Oracle DBA who considers that, if done right, the Microsoft platform is an excellent platform for the strategic implementation of Oracle-centric applications. He fervently hopes that this book helps you do it right.

Acknowledgments

First and foremost, I want to thank the top-drawer team at Apress—especially Tony Davis, Beth Christmas, Rebecca Rider, and Kelly Winquist. They are all truly a pleasure to work with and exemplify the qualities and professionalism on which Apress is founded.

It was also a great pleasure to work with my technical reviewers, Niall Litchfield and Neeraj Gupta. I thank them both for their respective insights, corrections, and criticisms. These have all made this book better than it would have been otherwise. The only CKI (that's for Chair Keyboard Interface) was me, however, so any omissions, typographical errors, or inaccuracies rest with me alone.

I am also fortunate to work with a group of talented and dedicated individuals on a daily basis. In particular, I want to thank Tonya Rosenberry, Rick Ours, Corrie Bumps, Tammy Reuter, Karen Martin, Cris Ingalls, Mike Ratcliff, Bob Rothrock, Bill Miller, Chris Williams, Joel Grannan (when you absolutely, positively…), Jason Small, Tom Conley, Aaron Head, Gerry Schlundt, Jay Truesdel, Carl Pfrang, Tom Fugate, Dale Cardoza, Brian Needham, Tanja Wilson, Barry Vinard, Charlie Poynter, David Valiyi, Kevin Cusimano, Kate Cekirge, Ben Buckland, Jeff Hunter, Todd Louden, Ron Ginder, Doug Tedder, Ledger Heavilon, Bruce Painter, Rita O'Connor, Ben Mason, Peter VanVleet, Jason Sinicropi, Bill Walters, and a whole host of others. I hope that I haven't offended anyone by not being able to include them in this list.

Within the Oracle community, I would like to express thanks to Tom Kyte, Cary Millsap, Jeff Holt, Jonathan Lewis, Steve Adams, Alex Keh, Scott Urman, Graham Wood, Pete Sharman, Bryn Llewellyn, Christopher Racicot, Joel Kallman, Tyler Muth, Raj Mattamal, Sean Dillon, Connor McDonald, Jonathan Gennick, Wolfgang Breitling, and Anjo Kolk. Then, of course, there are three guys named Larry Ellison, Bob Miner, and Ed Oates.

Over the years, the lives of several individuals have influenced me; here are some of them: Brian Vargus, George Screes, Don Gaucher, Rosalie Vermette, Gordon Gish, Gene Dobrzynski, Charlie Harp, Lisa York, Dan Cook, David Campbell, Kathleen Redding, John Kearney, Mike Haas, Barbara Lawrence, Connie Torrance, Tom Foster, Tony Wilkinson, Clark Sayers, Rob Edwards, Viren Kavia, and John, Paul, George, and Ringo.

Many thanks are also due to my immediate and extended families: Lee and Pat Williams; Chris, Ginny, Jacob, Isaac, and Peter Williams; Amy, Tim, Sam, Will, and Thomas Noblitt; Wilbur and Lossie Hammel; Bill and Darlene Williams; Dale Huggins; Lance Williams; Laura Williams; John and Betty Sapp; David and Hazel Warren; and Pete, Michelle, and Rebecca Ward.

Underneath it all is the support of my wonderful wife Lynda. Thank you for everything that you do. To our two children, David (my #1 man) and Elizabeth (my #1 girl), Daddy loves you, and yes, Daddy can come out to play now.

Introduction

I work with Oracle software, and in particular, the Oracle database, on a daily basis. I also work with people who are either writing software or implementing software from a vendor or other third party that interacts with those databases. One of the more popular development environments used to develop these pieces of software is Microsoft Visual Studio .NET.

Although other languages and development environments certainly have a strong and loyal following, the Visual Studio .NET developer base doesn't appear to be in danger of imminent extinction. On the contrary, with the recent releases of the .NET Framework and Visual Studio .NET, I've witnessed a renewed interest in using Visual Studio .NET.

NOTE From time to time, I shorten the official name of Microsoft Visual Studio .NET to simply Visual Studio. So, when you see the term Visual Studio, read Microsoft Visual Studio .NET.

However, a paradox of sorts has emerged from my experience working with people who use both Oracle and Visual Studio. Today, the Oracle database is one of the (if not *the*) most widely used databases, and Visual Studio .NET is also one of the most widely used development environments. Yet often, when you're working on a development project, you'll find that a knowledge or experience gap exists between these two products. How can this be? Surely the intersection of the set of Visual Studio .NET developers with the set of Oracle database-backed projects isn't so narrow as to preclude any overlap between the two? As I am sure you know from your own experiences, that the answer to this question is, "No, it isn't." As a database administrator, I see this overlap on many projects.

But overlap alone isn't sufficient. Unfortunately, no cross-technology osmosis exists, and most application systems are complex and involve many components and technologies. Oracle has always been a feature-rich database, and recent releases continue to push that envelope. The Visual Studio .NET Integrated Development Environment (IDE) and supported languages have undergone their own metamorphosis since their initial release. Perhaps database administrators have spent all their energies just maintaining fluency with Oracle features and releases. Perhaps Visual Studio .NET developers have been concentrating on becoming masters of their environment and languages. Or perhaps some anachronistic workplace rules or procedures have precluded "boundary crossing" or have forced some artificial separation between the two areas of expertise. Regardless of the reasons, I believe that these application systems can be better than what they are today, and that if you use Oracle proficiently, you'll get an almost exponential return on your investment.

It shouldn't surprise you to find out that what works well in another database may not work well (or at all) in Oracle. Not all databases are created equal, and Oracle has a distinct personality. The depth and breadth of the Oracle database software is truly amazing. As a result, Oracle is sometimes unfairly judged as being too complicated or overly difficult to use.

It is true that with increased functionality (and there is a lot of functionality in Oracle), comes additional choice. However, once you understand the choices Oracle provides, what you previously viewed as complex becomes elegant, powerful, and natural. I remember my first encounter with the UNIX utility vi. Maybe you too have used it. Perhaps you, like me, felt that it was the most esoteric, obscure, and non-intuitive thing in the world. How on earth could anyone use, let alone actually *like,* such a complicated utility just to edit a simple text file? Even trying to exit the program after you abandon an editing session in frustration can be an exercise in the arcane—escape-shift-colon-q-bang, who knew? Well, today I use VIM (a vi variant) for Windows when I need to work with a text file. My point is, of course, that once I took the time to understand how vi worked, I was able to view it in a different light.

What This Book Covers (and What It Does Not)

Beyond the broad topics of Oracle and Visual Studio, what can you expect to find inside this book? My primary goal is to provide you, the Visual Studio programmer, with the knowledge and techniques you need to begin to take full advantage of what the Oracle database has to offer. To that end, I address topic such as these:

- Exploring the Oracle database server and networking architecture

- Learning about .NET data providers (Oracle Data Provider for .NET in particular)

- Integrating with Oracle and Visual Studio .NET

- Managing connections to the database

- Becoming familiar with how Oracle implements locking, concurrency, and transactions

- Learning why bind variables and parsing are crucial to success

- Working with PL/SQL

- Using large objects

- Performing common tasks using Oracle features

- Working with code instrumentation and SQL tracing

Naturally, I can't cover every topic related to Oracle and Visual Studio .NET in this book. The Oracle-supplied documentation contains more than 20,000 pages and covers most areas I haven't included here. In addition, I've weeded out some topics that though interesting, aren't really programming related.

Here are a few examples of some topics that are beyond the scope of this book:

- Database administration

- Backup and recovery

- High-availability solutions

- Integration with Directory Services

- Virtual Private Databases

These topics, although important, typically fall into the domain of your system's administrator. However, I encourage you to read the Oracle documentation for further information if you are interested in these (or other) topics. (The "Oracle Concepts" guide is a particularly valuable resource included with the Oracle documentation set.) My goal is to stay focused on topics relevant to programming Oracle from the Visual Studio .NET environment.

What You Need to Know to Use This Book

This isn't a book about learning Visual C# or Visual Basic programming languages. Although you may gain some knowledge about their workings from the text, I don't discuss the syntax, keywords, and so on of either language per se. However, you do need a working knowledge of Visual C# to get the most from this book. I use Visual C# as the base language for the book; however, Visual Basic versions of the code are available from the Downloads section of the Apress website (www.apress.com). If you have prior programming experience, especially in languages such as C, C++, or Java, you shouldn't find the material in this book overly difficult.

You also need to understand general database concepts, SQL, Microsoft data access technologies, and Visual Studio .NET. Although I concentrate on Oracle specifically, you should be comfortable with more general items, such as SQL statements, tables, result sets, stored procedures, ADO.NET, data grids, and so forth. If you have written applications using Visual Studio .NET (or a previous version) for other database servers (such as Microsoft SQL Server), then you should be comfortable with this material.

Oracle's Relationship with Microsoft

At times, using products from Oracle and Microsoft on a project may seem like juxtaposition. Certainly, there can be no doubt that, on one level, Oracle and Microsoft are fierce competitors. However, the Windows platform is a Tier 1 platform for Oracle, and actually, teams at the two companies cooperate and communicate quite a bit. For instance, Oracle recently sponsored several sessions at the Microsoft Professional Developer's Conference, and Microsoft has included more and more support for Oracle in recent releases of Visual Studio. In addition, in early 2004, Oracle became a Visual Studio Industry Partner (VSIP).

The Oracle database is available on every major platform available today, and I don't foresee Oracle devoting itself solely to the Windows platform. Nor do I foresee Microsoft discarding SQL Server and becoming an Oracle reseller, but I do believe that Oracle and Microsoft will continue to cooperate at a level that makes sense, particularly when it comes to platform and tool integration. Since the initial release of the Oracle database product on Windows in 1993, Oracle has continued to innovate and take advantage of the features specific to the Windows operating system. Although no specific requirement says that an Oracle database must be hosted on the Windows platform to be accessible from a Windows client, I do believe the continued cooperation and integration is beneficial for Oracle developers using the Windows platform.

The Tools and Environment

Aside from access to Visual Studio .NET (with Visual C# installed), you need access to an Oracle database server. The database server can be on the same machine where you have Visual Studio .NET installed or you can have it on a separate machine. If the machine that has Visual Studio .NET installed is separate from the machine hosting the Oracle database, you need to have the Oracle client software installed on the machine hosting Visual Studio .NET. Both the Oracle database and client can be downloaded for free under a Developer's License from the Oracle Technology Network (www.oracle.com/technology/index.html). I've included a complete walk-through for installing the client software and the server software in this book's appendix. The Oracle Universal Installer (OUI) contains preconfigured and custom install types for the database server. If you choose a preconfigured install type, it will provide you with everything you need as you work through the sample code. The appendix also walks you through how to use a custom installation.

As a reference, the primary tools and environment used to create all the code used in this book are as follows:

- Oracle 10g Database Release 1, Enterprise Edition

- The Oracle Data Provider for .NET, version 10.1.0.200

- Microsoft Windows XP Professional

- Microsoft Internet Information Services 5.1

- Microsoft Visual Studio .NET 2003 Enterprise, Architect Edition

To maintain as consistent an environment as possible throughout the book, I've installed all the software on a single laptop computer. On occasion, I use the sample schemas shipped with the database in addition to the custom schema you will develop. Please see the "Oracle Database Sample Schemas" document in the Oracle documentation or your system administrator set if you need to install these schemas.

The Sample Code

I created the sample code in the text in C#, SQL, and Oracle's PL/SQL. The code download available from the Apress website (www.apress.com) includes four versions of the samples:

- C# projects using the Oracle Data Provider for .NET (ODP.NET)

- C# projects using the Microsoft Oracle .NET data provider

- VB.NET projects using the Oracle Data Provider for .NET (ODP.NET)

- VB.NET projects using the Microsoft Oracle .NET data provider

Whatever development strategy or language you choose, you should be able to find the project code that you can use and adapt it for your environment. The `README.txt` file I include in the sample code download contains details about the project and folder structure.

In all cases, I've endeavored to keep the code as simple as possible. I did this so that I could focus solely on the core aspect or concept you're exploring in a particular section of code. As a result, I've implemented a number of samples as console applications. Therefore, the core code present in these samples is the same regardless of your deployment choice (Windows Forms or web forms, for example). Where the deployment choice you make does matter, I use the appropriate technology.

For the majority of code that deals with database issues, whether a label has left-aligned text or what font is used are of little consequence. All of the sample code requires a reference to the `Oracle.DataAccess.dll` assembly. In addition, I implement a using (or Imports for Visual Basic) directive for the `Oracle.DataAccess.Client` and `System.Data` namespaces in the source code files. For more advanced operations that use the Oracle Data Provider for .NET, I also use the `Oracle.DataAccess.Types` namespace.

CHAPTER 1

■ ■ ■

Oracle Architecture and Connectivity

As a .NET programmer, one of your first concerns is to establish a connection to the database server so that you can get at your data. In order to do this effectively, however, you need to do a little bit of legwork to understand the main building blocks of the Oracle server architecture with which you interact. This chapter contains important foundational information that explains not only *how* to interact with the Oracle database, but *why* you need to perform tasks in a certain manner. Of course, in this chapter, I concentrate on the aspects of the server architecture that are relevant to us as application developers. Specifically, I cover the following:

- The concept of the Oracle Home. The Oracle Home can be confusing if you are new to the Oracle database. In a nutshell, the *Oracle Home* is a location where software is installed. Make sure you're familiar with this concept since Oracle uses the Oracle Home as a base location for locating configuration files by default.

- The fundamental building blocks of the Oracle server architecture. As a database *user*, you connect to a specified *schema* on a specific database *instance*. All of the objects for that schema are stored in a specific *tablespace.* I explain all of these terms in this chapter.

- The Oracle network architecture. Oracle uses a specific connectivity architecture, which you must understand to correctly configure and use. In this chapter, you learn how to use this architecture to connect to the database from .NET applications. You get to see the major components of this architecture and then create a standard configuration that allows you to connect to Oracle in a version-neutral manner.

I then move on to discuss the client tools that you'll use to connect to an Oracle database instance. Although in this book, you're primarily concerned with writing .NET code that interacts with an Oracle database, it's often very useful to be able to just enter and execute ad-hoc SQL statements directly against the database. You'll do this fairly regularly throughout the book, so in this chapter, you'll start by looking at the command-line interface that Oracle provides for this purpose, namely SQL*Plus.

When you do write .NET code, you connect to the database through a .NET data provider. I'll briefly discuss the providers supplied by Oracle and Microsoft and explain why I chose the Oracle data provider (ODP.NET) as the standard for this book.

Finally, I'll cover the integration available for Oracle in the Visual Studio IDE and conclude by writing a small application to connect to the database and display an informational message. This little application serves as a sanity check to verify that everything is installed and working correctly.

Let's begin with an overview of the Oracle server architecture.

Exploring the Oracle Server Architecture

The Oracle database server software is available for every platform of significance today. Of course, this software is implemented in a platform-specific manner each time, but from a client perspective, these differences are invisible. The Oracle server software operates in a similar manner from platform to platform, and this transparency to the client is one of Oracle's greatest strengths. "Oracle is Oracle," as the saying goes.

As a developer, you definitely are not required to have an in-depth knowledge of the low-level details of Oracle's platform-specific implementation. However, grasping the basic elements of an Oracle system helps you understand the bigger picture, and also aids you when you communicate with the administrator of the database you are using.

What I would like to do in the following sections is provide you with enough of a foundation so that you are familiar with the basic concepts or principles. I am not trying to make you an expert on the internals of Oracle's architecture in this section. However, as I touched on in the Introduction, you should not treat the database as a mere black box or bit bucket. Taking such an approach negatively impacts a project's chances for success and is detrimental to fostering teamwork and knowledge sharing. The database is a major component in a database-backed application. That may seem like an obvious statement, but chances are, you've been around for one or two projects where this has been the case.

The Oracle Home

The Oracle Home is basically a name associated with a directory where Oracle products are installed. There are two components to the Oracle Home: the logical name and the physical operating system directory. Both the name and the physical operating system directory are defined very early in the installation process. The operating system directory defines the physical location of the software. One purpose of the Oracle Home is to allow multiple versions of the Oracle software to be installed on a single host—each version is installed in its own Oracle Home. The Oracle Home also allows you to install multiple Oracle products on a machine more easily by separating each installation into its own directory. Each Oracle Home must have a distinct name and point to a single directory path. There is a one-to-one relationship between the Oracle Home name and the operating system directory. That is, two Oracle Home names can't point to the same directory path.

■**NOTE** Beginning with the Oracle10g release, all Oracle products are multi-home aware; however, if you are using a release prior to 10g, a few products may be installed into a single home only. Although you won't be working with any of these products in this book, if you are performing a preconfigured installation on a host with an existing Oracle installation and encounter a product collision, you need to be aware of this trait.

Like most Windows-based software, Oracle software utilizes the Windows registry. As you create Oracle Homes, the homes are registered in the Windows registry. The manner in which this occurs is slightly different between versions. For versions of Oracle prior to 10g, the registry hive HKLM\Software\Oracle\All_Homes enumerates the existing Oracle Homes on a system. The mapping of home names to operating system directories takes place in the IDn keys under the All_Homes key. The IDn keys are simply keys where n is an integer counter that is incremented for each new key. You can find parameters specific to an individual Oracle Home in HKLM\Software\Oracle\HomeN where N is simply an integer counter that is incremented for each new home. For Oracle 10g, the registry hive HKLM\Software\Oracle\KEY_OracleHomeName is used. The functionality of the keys and values under this hive are the same as in the old-style homes.

■**TIP** If you chose to specify values for variables using the Environment Variable dialog, those values may override values specified in the registry.

If multiple Oracle Homes are on a particular system, one is the default home. The default home is simply the Oracle Home directory path that occurs first in the PATH environment variable. This has two consequences: Since the default Oracle Home is the one that appears first in the PATH variable, this is the version of Oracle software that runs by default; and this is the default location where Oracle looks for configuration files. If you need to, you can change this simply by altering the PATH environment variable. For versions prior to 10g, Oracle has a graphical utility (called Home Selector), located in the Oracle Installation Products Start Menu folder, that performs this task for you as well. For version 10g of the database, this functionality is part of the Oracle Universal Installer and is accessible via the Environment tab. In order to view or change the Oracle Home information on a 10g system, start the Oracle Universal Installer, click the Installed Products button, and select the Environment tab. Figure 1-1 illustrates what this looks like on my system.

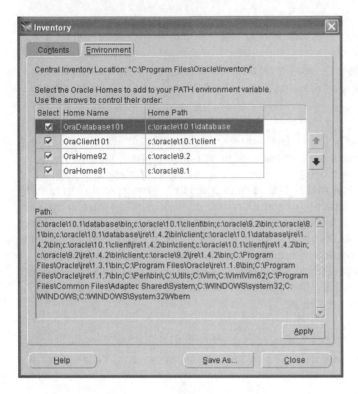

Figure 1-1. *The Oracle Universal Installer Environment tab*

The Difference Between a Database and an Instance

When you examine the Oracle architecture, you'll come across two terms that often cause confusion: *database* and *instance*. These two terms are also the primary building blocks you use to develop your macroscopic view of the Oracle server architecture. One of the contributing factors to the confusion surrounding these two terms is that they are quite often used interchangeably, sometimes even within the same sentence. The two terms actually represent distinct concepts or entities, though there is also a close relationship between them.

A variety of physical operating system files make up the components in an Oracle system. In simple terms, the database is the collection of permanent, physical files that reside on disk. However, a set of files sitting around on disk can't really do much on its own. This is where the instance comes into play. In contrast to the physical nature of the database, the instance exists solely in memory and is, therefore, transitory in nature. For example, if you shut down or restart the host server, the instance will go away, whereas the database will remain intact. Figure 1-2 illustrates the relationship between a database and an instance.

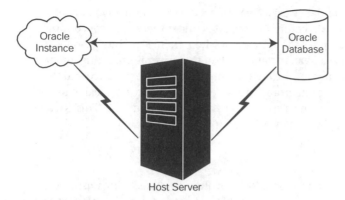

Figure 1-2. *A simple representation of a database and an instance*

So, fundamentally, a database is the collection of physical files on disk and an instance is an area of memory. The instance, of course, is not just a bunch of empty memory taking up space. To be a little more precise, the instance is a collection of processes and structures inside that memory space.

The term *processes* is a slight misnomer when you're discussing an Oracle server installation on the Windows platform. On Windows, the processes are really threads inside a single, main process. Even though, from a physical architecture standpoint, the processes are really threads, I refer to them as processes for the sake of consistency. The processes (commonly called *background processes*) that belong to an instance are what actually operate on the database files, doing such things as reading and sorting data on behalf of the user, for example. In Oracle, the user doesn't directly interact with the database itself. When a connection from a client (such as a .NET data provider) is established, the connection is a pathway to the instance. The instance works as a broker between the client and the database, with the structures inside the instance providing a common area of memory used by the various processes. As a .NET programmer, you do not need to do anything special in your code to accommodate this. I am just examining the process here to establish what occurs when a connection is made.

CONNECTION MODES

One feature Oracle provides allows a client to obtain a connection to the database in one of two modes. These two modes are known as dedicated mode or shared mode. In a nutshell, dedicated mode means that an Oracle process on the server is dedicated (hence the name) to serving your connection and your connection only. In contrast to dedicated mode, shared mode means that the process on the Oracle server is capable of serving multiple connections. In this mode, the process is shared among multiple connections. This is a resource-saving scheme for a database server that serves a large number of connections. The dedicated mode is by far the most common mode and is the default. The connection mode is largely transparent to us as developers. However, in an application that employs .NET connection pooling, you may not want to use a shared connection mode to the database. If you have any questions about which mode you are using, consult with your administrator.

Typically a one-to-one correspondence exists between a database and an instance, though this is not the case under certain configurations. It is under these types of configurations (Oracle Parallel Server or Real Application Clusters) where there is no one-to-one correspondence between a database and an instance. When the server is operating under one of these configurations, there is a many-to-one relationship between the instance and the database. In a Real Application Clusters environment, for example, many physical machines with their own instance are attached to and are operating on a single database. This is a specialized configuration and, as such, you won't work with it in this book.

The Schema

Much like the terms database and instance, the *schema* is often confused with a *user*. Again, part of this confusion may arise from the interchangeable use of the two terms. The schema is simply the collection of objects owned by a database user. In other words, a schema *belongs* to a user; it isn't actually the user. If a database user doesn't own any objects, the user's schema is said to be empty. A database user can own exactly one schema, though the same user may have access to multiple schemas. A database user may grant access on its schema to another database user, for example. There is a special schema called Public to which all database users have access. A variety of objects may be part of a schema. Basic schema objects include tables, indexes, and views; these objects are common to virtually all database systems.

Included in the database are two important users/schemas. These are the SYS and SYSTEM users. The SYS user/schema contains, among other things, the data dictionary for the database. The Oracle data dictionary, like those in other databases, comprises various tables and views and can be viewed as the repository that contains all the metadata for the rest of the database. One of the more important aspects of the data dictionary that is relevant to application developers is that it contains the definitions for all of the objects in a schema (as well as the database as a whole). For example, the USER_TABLES view contains a great deal of information about each of the tables in the schema for the current user. Occasionally, you may need to look up information about objects in the database such as size, location, or creation date, for example, and the data dictionary is the place to do it. You access the information in the data dictionary the same way you access any other information in the database. However, since the data dictionary is read-only, only SELECT statements are permitted. Of course the data dictionary is fully documented in the Oracle-supplied documentation.

■**NOTE** See the "Oracle Concepts Guide" or the "Oracle Database Reference" in the Oracle-supplied documentation for complete details on the tables and views in the data dictionary.

The SYS user is the highest-privileged user in an Oracle database and may be viewed as the database equivalent of the Administrator or root operating system account. Second in command to the SYS user is the SYSTEM user. This user contains important schema objects that are used internally by Oracle in much the same way as those belonging to the SYS schema. Under normal circumstances, these users should not be used for anything other than database administration tasks. Certainly, you won't be using them for any of the code you develop.

The Tablespace

A tablespace is simply an organizational convenience. It is a logical structure rather than a physical one. You cannot, for example, open up Windows Explorer, navigate to a directory containing Oracle files, and "see" a tablespace. Tablespaces are commonly used to group functionally related schema objects. For example, the system tablespace (a very important tablespace) contains all the objects for the SYS and SYSTEM schemas by default. Tablespaces can be treated as distinct units. You can, for example, place Tablespace A in an offline state (make it unavailable) and not affect any of the other tablespaces in the database.

A schema object that requires physical storage must belong to a tablespace. You can't create such a schema object if no tablespace is assigned. When you create a schema object, you may specify a tablespace in which to create the object, or you may allow it to be created in the default tablespace for that user. You define the default tablespace when you create the user initially, and you may alter it after the user has been created if you need to or want to. If you alter the default tablespace for a user after you create it, any objects you previously created for the user won't automatically move or migrate to the new default tablespace—only new objects you create after you have assigned the new default tablespace will be created in that tablespace.

■**TIP** You should *never* specify the system tablespace as the default tablespace for a normal user. As discussed in the previous section, the SYS and SYSTEM users utilize the system tablespace. The system tablespace belongs to Oracle—consider it off limits.

The Oracle Network Architecture

As we discussed in the "The Oracle Server Architecture" section, the Oracle database is available on a wide variety of platforms, yet the actual platform is, for the most part, invisible to the client. The Oracle network architecture is what allows for this transparency. In this section, I examine the typical network architecture and show you how to create a common network configuration that allows you to connect to the target database in a consistent manner throughout the remainder of the book. Along the way, I also dispel a few points of confusion that crop up from time to time.

By now, your head may be swimming with all the different terms and concepts that I have been discussing. If you try to digest all of the concepts, processes (or threads), terms, and so on, as one single entity, you may be a bit overwhelmed. Before I move on to discussing the Oracle network components, I'll develop a graphic representation of what a typical connection to Oracle looks like. This allows me to approach the topic from a slightly different perspective, and perhaps it will help clear up any confusion you may have about these topics. Keep in mind that this represents the concepts more than the actual underlying details, and it is a simplified view of what takes place in a typical, dedicated mode scenario. Figure 1-3 illustrates the processes and files I discuss in relation to the Oracle network architecture. It gives a graphic representation of the following steps:

1. An application generates a request for a database connection from a client machine, and if the request is for a valid connection as defined by the network configuration (typically the sqlnet.ora and tnsnames.ora files), the Oracle networking layer submits a request for a new connection to the server listener process.

2. The server listener process receives the request and gets a port for the spawned server process.

3. The listener process returns the port information to the client.

4. The client processes the information returned from the listener process and creates a redirected connection to the Oracle server process via the port returned from the listener process.

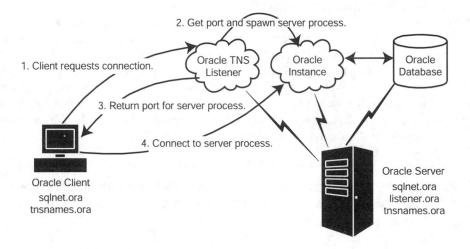

Figure 1-3. *A simple representation of the Oracle network components*

In the following section, you get to examine the server process (the listener) and the three configuration files represented in Figure 1-3.

Oracle Network Components

Depending on how the Oracle server and/or the Oracle client software has been installed, the three configuration files may or may not all be present on your workstation. These are the files that I cover in this section (as illustrated in Figure 1-3):

The listener.ora file: This file contains configuration information for the database listener.

The tnsnames.ora file: This file contains what are known as TNS aliases and spells out the configuration information for connecting to a database.

The sqlnet.ora file: This file contains configuration or profile information for the Oracle networking environment.

For this book, I chose to install the Oracle server software on my laptop; therefore, all the files in question are on my system. If you are working in an environment where the Oracle server software is installed on a separate machine, you may not have appropriate privileges to view or change the files on that machine. If this is the case, be sure to consult with your database administrator for any questions you have regarding these files. Also, though you are working with a typical configuration, your configuration may vary from mine depending on your actual setup. The configuration here is based on the installation I present in the Appendix.

The Listener

The listener is considered a server component, even if you installed the server software on a client workstation. The Oracle software doesn't know if it has been installed on a workstation, of course. The function performed by the listener is very simple. When a client would like a new connection to the database, it contacts the listener and requests a new connection. The listener spends virtually all of its time (ideally) waiting for connection requests. Once it receives a connection request, it finds a free port that the client software can use to communicate with the database server process. It then sends a reply (a tcp redirect) to the client indicating what port it should use to communicate with the server process that has been spawned in anticipation of the incoming connection. After handing off the connection request, the listener returns to waiting for another connection request.

The listener.ora File

In order for the listener process to listen on the correct port, it must be configured to do so. The listener.ora file is the file that contains the configuration information used by the listener process. The listener.ora file created by the installation process is very similar for Oracle8i, Oracle9i, and Oracle10g installations. Listing 1-1 contains a typical listener.ora file. The file was created during the Oracle10g server installation as outlined in the Appendix.

Listing 1-1. *A Typical listener.ora File*

```
# listener.ora Network Configuration File:
# c:\oracle\10.1\database\network\admin\listener.ora
# Generated by Oracle configuration tools.

LISTENER =
  (DESCRIPTION_LIST =
    (DESCRIPTION =
      (ADDRESS_LIST =
        (ADDRESS = (PROTOCOL = IPC)(KEY = EXTPROC))
      )
      (ADDRESS_LIST =
        (ADDRESS = (PROTOCOL = TCP)(HOST = ridmrwillim1801)(PORT = 1521))
      )
    )
  )

SID_LIST_LISTENER =
  (SID_LIST =
    (SID_DESC =
      (GLOBAL_DBNAME = LT10G.SAND)
      (ORACLE_HOME = C:\oracle\10.1\database)
      (SID_NAME = LT10G)
    )
```

```
  (SID_DESC =
    (SID_NAME = PLSExtProc)
    (ORACLE_HOME = C:\oracle\10.1\database)
    (PROGRAM = extproc)
  )

)
```

You can see here that the entries made during the installation process (included in the Appendix) are directly incorporated into the configuration file. The HOST (ridmrwillim1801) and PORT (1521) entries define the listener's endpoint. This is how the listener listens on the correct port and knows the name of its host. You can also see that the listener knows the global database name (GLOBAL_DBNAME), the Oracle Home (ORACLE_HOME), and the system ID (SID) for each database in its list. The global database name is composed of the database name, which is defined during database creation, and the database domain. (We will discuss the database domain when we examine the sqlnet.ora file.) The SID matches the database name. You don't need to make any modifications to the listener.ora file for our purposes. In addition, the database can automatically register itself as a service with the listener when the database is started rather than creating "hard coded" entries in the listener.ora file.

The tnsnames.ora File

The tnsnames.ora file contains the TNS aliases, which are similar to a DSN that ODBC uses. A TNS alias is a symbolic name like a moniker that represents the configuration information required to connect to a database. In contrast to the listener.ora file, which is used in conjunction with a server process, the tnsnames.ora file is used in conjunction with the client. Since the Oracle server software includes the client components, this file is part of both a server and a client installation. Only one copy of the file is used for an Oracle Home, so for a server installation, only one copy of the file is created or needed. That is, the client component of a server installation doesn't motivate the need for an additional tnsnames.ora file. Listing 1-2 contains the tnsnames.ora file from my machine.

Listing 1-2. *The tnsnames.ora File*

```
# tnsnames.ora Network Configuration File:
# c:\oracle\10.1\database\network\admin\tnsnames.ora
# Generated by Oracle configuration tools.

EXTPROC_CONNECTION_DATA =
  (DESCRIPTION =
    (ADDRESS_LIST =
      (ADDRESS = (PROTOCOL = IPC)(KEY = EXTPROC))
    )
    (CONNECT_DATA =
      (SID = PLSExtProc)
      (PRESENTATION = RO)
    )
  )
```

```
LT10G =
  (DESCRIPTION =
    (ADDRESS = (PROTOCOL = TCP)(HOST = ridmrwillim1801)(PORT = 1521))
    (CONNECT_DATA =
      (SERVER = DEDICATED)
      (SERVICE_NAME = LT10G.SAND)
    )
  )
```

The default tnsnames.ora file created during the installation process contains two entries: LT10G, and EXTPROC_CONNECTION_DATA. At this point, you are only concerned with the LT10G entry or TNS Alias. You can see here how the choices I made during the installation process are implemented in the LT10G entry. The HOST (ridmrwillim1801) and SERVICE_NAME (LT10G.SAND) entries have been completed with the entries I made. The EXTPROC_CONNECTION_DATA entry is used for external procedures. You can also see that this connection uses a dedicated mode connection to the database by the SERVER = DEDICATED entry. You'll be adding a new entry to this file (the common entry we discussed earlier) in a later step.

The sqlnet.ora File

Rounding out the trio of configuration files is the sqlnet.ora file. This file determines or influences the profile or environment of the Oracle network components. It is an optional file, but it's created as a part of the preconfigured installation types. If this file isn't present, default values as specified in the Oracle networking documentation are used. Your administrator knows if your environment requires this file. Listing 1-3 contains the sqlnet.ora file from my laptop

Listing 1-3. *The sqlnet.ora File*

```
# sqlnet.ora Network Configuration File: ↵
 c:\oracle\10.1\database\network\admin\sqlnet.ora↵
 Generated by Oracle configuration tools.

SQLNET.AUTHENTICATION_SERVICES= (NTS)

NAMES.DIRECTORY_PATH= (TNSNAMES, EZCONNECT)
```

The sqlnet.ora file in Listing 1-3 has two entries. The SQLNET.AUTHENTICATION_SERVICES= (NTS) entry enables Windows-based authentication for database connections. Another common value for this entry is NONE, which allows Oracle-based authentication only. I discuss this in more detail later in the book. The second entry tells the Oracle network client how it should resolve a symbolic name that is passed in a connection request. The TNSNAMES entry indicates that Oracle attempts to resolve a symbolic name by using the tnsnames.ora file first, and if it can't do so, it attempts to use the EZCONNECT method. The EZCONNECT method is new with the 10g release. You will only work with TNSNAMES as a resolver for your names. The other entry is for a new connection method with Oracle10g. When you use TNSNAMES as a resolver, Oracle looks in the tnsnames.ora file to locate information for the requested connection.

If you install the Oracle software onto a machine that is part of a DNS domain, then you have an additional entry in the sqlnet.ora file. That entry is names.default_domain and has a value of your DNS domain. In addition, that domain is appended to the entries in the tnsnames.ora file. Because my laptop is a stand-alone machine, the names.default_domain entry is absent from my configuration files.

The influence that the names.default_domain entry has often causes confusion; however, the influence this parameter has is really straightforward. This parameter has two characteristics that are important. First, if this parameter is present, then *every* entry in the tnsnames.ora file *must* have a domain name specified, or it will be ignored. The domain name (also referred to as the *suffix*) doesn't need to be the same as this entry, but one *must* be present. If the domain specified in the tnsnames.ora file is different from the default, it needs to be specified in the connection request. The domain is specified as a "." followed by one or more entries (including additional "." entries).

Second, this parameter specifies a *default* value. This means that if an application requests a connection, and the TNS alias symbolic name doesn't have a domain specified, the domain this parameter specifies is *automatically* appended. This is what causes entries without a domain name specified in the tnsnames.ora file to be effectively ignored. If the names.default_domain parameter isn't specified, you may still use domain names in the tnsnames.ora file, it just means that you won't have a default domain name. Also, the domain name doesn't need to be an actual Windows domain or DNS domain. You could, for example, have domains of Sandbox, Development, Test, Stage, Production, and so on.

Perhaps I can give you several examples (Listings 1-4 through 1-9) that will help clarify the influence of the sqlnet.ora file and the names.default_domain parameter.

Listing 1-4. *sqlnet.ora File Scenario 1*

```
sqlnet.ora file:
  names.default_domain is NOT specified

tnsnames.ora file:
  lt8i
  lt9i

connection request:
  lt8i
```

In this scenario, the connection request succeeds because the names.default_domain isn't specified and the connection request lt8i matches the net service name entry (another name for the TNS alias) lt8i in the tnsnames.ora file.

Listing 1-5. *sqlnet.ora File Scenario 2*

```
sqlnet.ora file:
  names.default_domain is NOT specified

tnsnames.ora file:
  lt8i
  lt8i.us.company.com
  lt9i
```

```
connection request:
  lt8i.us.company.com
```

In this scenario, the connection request succeeds because the names.default_domain isn't specified and the connection request lt8i.us.company.com matches the net service name entry lt8i.us.company.com in the tnsnames.ora file.

Listing 1-6. *sqlnet.ora File Scenario 3*

```
sqlnet.ora file:
  names.default_domain= us.company.com

tnsnames.ora file:
  lt8i
  lt8i.us.company.com
  lt9i

connection request:
  lt8i
```

In this scenario, the connection request succeeds because the names.default_domain is specified as us.company.com and the connection request lt8i matches the net service name entry lt8i.us.company.com in the tnsnames.ora file. The domain of us.company.com is automatically appended to the request even though the entry of lt8i also exists in the tnsnames.ora file.

■NOTE Even though the stand-alone entry of lt8i exists in the tnsnames.ora file, it isn't used because the names.default_domain parameter is specified in the sqlnet.ora file.

Listing 1-7. *sqlnet.ora File Scenario 4*

```
sqlnet.ora file:
  names.default_domain= us.company.com

tnsnames.ora file:
  lt8i
  lt8i.us.company.com
  lt9i

connection request:
  lt8i.us.company.com
```

In this scenario, the connection request succeeds because the connection request lt8i.us.company.com matches the net service name entry lt8i.us.company.com in the tnsnames.ora file. The names.default_domain of us.company.com isn't automatically appended to the request because a domain is specified in the request.

Listing 1-8. *sqlnet.ora File Scenario 5*

```
sqlnet.ora file:
  names.default_domain= us.company.com

tnsnames.ora file:
  lt8i
  lt8i.us.company.com
  lt9i

connection request:
  lt9i
```

In this scenario, the connection request fails because the connection request lt9i has the names.default_domain of us.company.com automatically appended to the requested value of lt9i. There is no entry lt9i.us.company.com in the tnsnames.ora file.

Listing 1-9. *sqlnet.ora File Scenario 6*

```
sqlnet.ora file:
  names.default_domain= us.company.com

tnsnames.ora file:
  lt8i
  lt8i.us.company.com
  lt9i

connection request:
  lt9i.does.not.exist
```

In this scenario, the connection request fails because the connection request lt9i.does.not.exist doesn't match any entries in the tnsnames.ora file. The names.default_domain of us.company.com aren't automatically appended to the request because a domain is specified as part of the request (even though it's a "bad" domain).

Of course, Oracle also provides error messages if things aren't correctly configured to help you resolve any issues. For example, if a default domain name is specified in a sqlnet.ora file, but the domain isn't included in the tnsnames.ora file or in the requested TNS alias, you receive a "Failed to resolve name" error indicating that Oracle can't find the correct name in the tnsnames.ora file.

Creating the Standard Configuration

To keep the naming consistent in this section, I create a standard configuration that provides a layer of abstraction, which makes the use of the 8i, 9i, or 10g Oracle server software fairly transparent. Rather than using the TNS alias that Oracle created during database creation (LT10G in my case), I use this new entry. This enables me to refer to a single TNS alias. After I create the new tnsnames.ora entry, I examine a few pitfalls that you may encounter when you configure the tnsnames.ora file; then I show how to create database users. This is where you'll start to pull together all the concepts I've been discussing up to this point.

Creating a New tnsnames.ora Entry

Because the tnsnames.ora file is simply a text file, you could edit it with your favorite text editor and create a new entry manually or by copying an existing entry and making the relevant changes. However, this file is sensitive to unmatched parentheses and other syntactical errors; therefore, I use the Oracle-supplied graphical tool known as the Net Manager to accomplish this task.

■**NOTE** These steps assume you have installed the Oracle10g software by following the steps in the Appendix. However, if you installed another version of the software or installed the software in a different manner, the steps will be similar to these.

---

1. Start the Oracle Net Manager utility (see Figure 1-4) located in the Configuration and Migration Tools Start Menu folder.

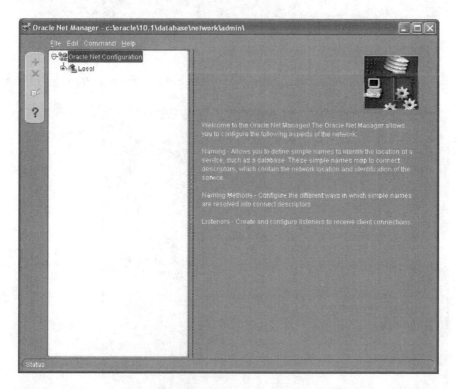

Figure 1-4. *The Oracle Net Manager utility*

2. Select and expand the Local node under the Oracle Net Configuration main node (see Figure 1-5).

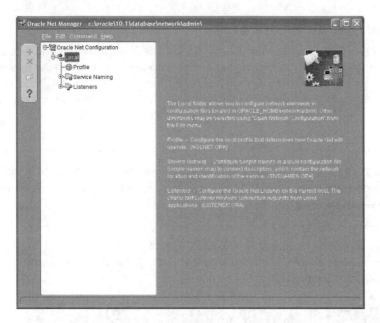

Figure 1-5. *The expanded Local node*

3. Select and expand the Service Naming node under the Local node (see Figure 1-6).

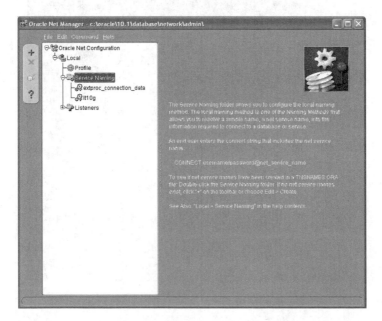

Figure 1-6. *The expanded Service Naming node*

4. Click the green plus sign (+) to create a new entry (see Figure 1-7). This launches the Net Service Name Wizard.

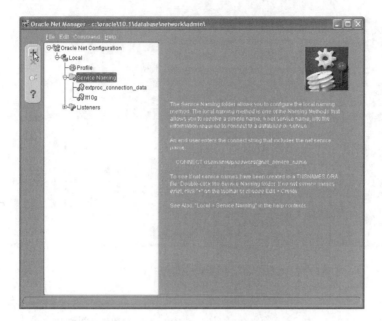

Figure 1-7. *Launching the Net Service Name Wizard*

5. Enter the new net service name that you'll be creating (see Figure 1-8). This is the TNS alias that you'll create in the `tnsnames.ora` file. I entered ORANET here and will use this TNS alias for the remainder of the book. Click Next after you enter your new net service name.

Figure 1-8. *The Net Service Name Wizard Welcome dialog*

6. Select TCP/IP (Internet Protocol) as the network protocol (see Figure 1-9) and click Next to continue.

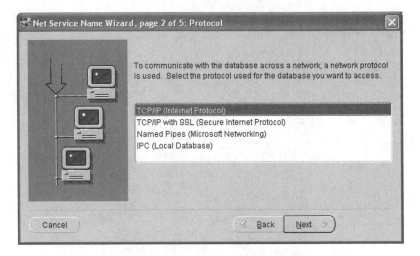

Figure 1-9. *The Net Service Name Wizard Protocol dialog*

7. Enter the appropriate host name and port number for the machine that is hosting the Oracle database (see Figure 1-10). If you followed the installation walkthrough in the Appendix, you should accept the default port of 1521. Click Next to continue.

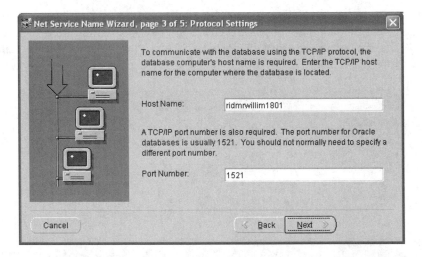

Figure 1-10. *The Net Service Name Wizard Protocol Settings dialog*

8. If you are using an Oracle8i or later database, enter the service name for the database (see Figure 1-11). If you are using an Oracle8 or earlier release, enter the database's SID. If you installed the database by using the walkthrough in the Appendix, use the service name that was specified during that process. See your administrator for the appropriate value to enter here if you are using a previously created database. Accept the default value of Database Default for the Connection Type. Click Next to continue.

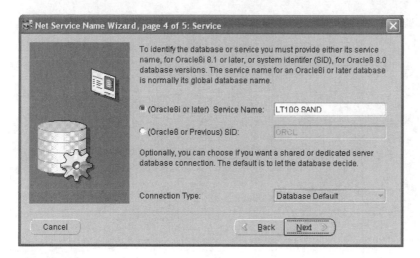

Figure 1-11. *The Net Service Name Wizard Service dialog*

9. Click the Test button to test the connection as you have defined it (see Figure 1-12). Depending on how your database was set up, the test may fail initially. The test process attempts to connect to the database as a sample user known as SCOTT. If your database doesn't have this user, the test fails.

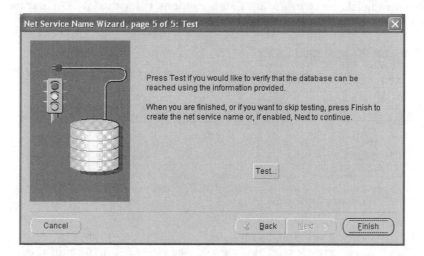

Figure 1-12. *The Net Service Name Wizard Test dialog*

10. If the test fails (see Figure 1-13) because the user SCOTT doesn't exist, you can simply use another user and retry the test.

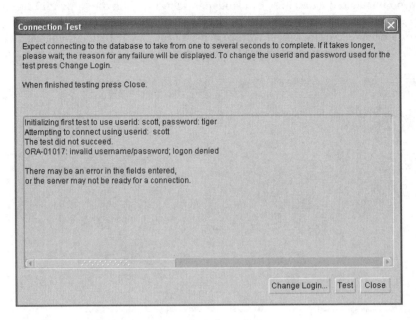

Figure 1-13. *The Connection Test failure dialog*

11. To retry the test with a different user, click the Change Login button. In the resulting Change Login dialog (see Figure 1-14), enter the username and password for a user that you know exists.

    I am using the SYSTEM user to perform this test. Because this test only connects to the database and doesn't perform any data operations, using the SYSTEM user for this operation is safe. Click OK after you enter the information.

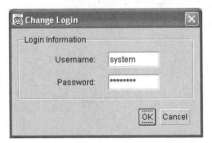

Figure 1-14. *The Change Login dialog*

12. Click the Test button if necessary to retry the test with the new username and password. The connection test should now succeed (see Figure 1-15). Click the Close button followed by the Finish button to return to the Net Manager.

The Oracle Net Manager utility now shows the entry in the Service Naming node (see Figure 1-16).

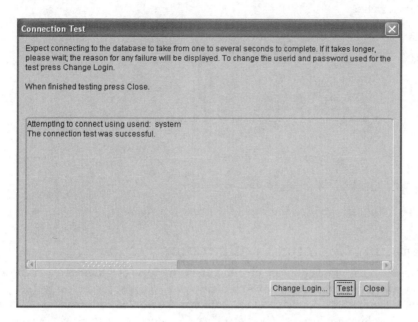

Figure 1-15. *The Connect Test success dialog*

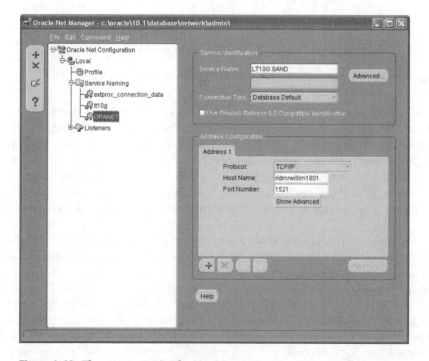

Figure 1-16. *The new entry in the Net Manager*

13. Select File ➢ Exit from the menu. You're presented with the Changed Configuration Confirmation dialog (see Figure 1-17). Click the Save button to save the entry in the `tnsnames.ora` file.

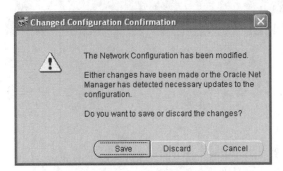

Figure 1-17. *The Changed Configuration Confirmation dialog*

Troubleshooting Common Configuration Errors

As mentioned earlier, the Oracle software provides an error message if there is a configuration error in the network files. Three preventative measures go a long way toward protecting you from configuration errors. The configuration files that you've worked with so far are relatively small and reasonably uncomplicated. However, on a real system, you can expect the files to be much larger with many more entries (mostly in the `tnsnames.ora` file). Here are the three preventative measures that I recommend using:

- Make a copy of your configuration files before making changes.

- Use the Oracle-supplied tools for making configuration changes.

- Use the Test functionality inside the tools before saving changes.

One of the most common error messages related to configuring the Oracle networking components is "TNS-12154 TNS:could not resolve service name." This error is frequently caused by a mismatch between the `sqlnet.ora` file and the `tnsnames.ora` file. For example, this may happen if `names.default_domain` is specified in `sqlnet.ora`, but when a new entry is added (usually manually) to `tnsnames.ora`, the suffix is somehow overlooked. It can be very frustrating to look at a `tnsnames.ora` file and never realize that the only problem is that the entry is missing the proper suffix (or has a different suffix not specified in the connection request).

Another common error message is "TNS-12560 TNS:protocol adapter error". This message is almost invariably due to an improperly configured Oracle network file. Again, this usually occurs when one of the files is edited manually.

By following these simple recommendations, you'll prevent virtually all configuration errors in your Oracle network files. Of course, doing something like specifying an incorrect host name will result in a syntactically correct and well-formed file, but any connection using that entry won't connect properly (or worse, you'll connect to a different database than you intended). Prudent naming aids you in avoiding this sort of error. The "Oracle Database Error Messages" guide lists most of the error messages (and some possible resolutions) you are likely to encounter. This documentation is also available online through the Oracle Technology Network (www.oracle.com/technology/index.html).

Creating Users

In this section, I walk you through how to create a typical-privileged user and an administrative-privileged user. Although you can use the built-in Oracle accounts, it is not a good idea to do so. In fact, I strongly discourage this practice. Instead, think of the built-in accounts (SYSTEM and SYS in particular) as belonging to Oracle and don't use them for any routine application development tasks. Database administrators frequently use the SYSTEM account for the sole purpose of performing database administration tasks; however, they usually leave the SYS schema alone. Certainly you won't want to use either account for your application schema.

When you go to create a typical-privileged user, you'll give the user only the rights it needs to perform the tasks that you'll be performing in the remainder of the book. Often a typical-privileged user is simply granted database roles (CONNECT and RESOURCE in particular), which results in a somewhat over-privileged user. For example, the CONNECT role allows users to create what is known as a database link. Because you won't be using database links in any of the samples in the book, you don't need this privilege. However, you will grant the DBA role, which is a highly privileged role, to your administrative-privileged user. This is because you expressly desire that user to have elevated privileges in the database. A *role* is simply a named group of privileges; granting a role to a user grants the privileges represented by that role to the user. The privileges you'll grant to your typical-privileged user are as follows:

alter session: The ability to change attributes of your session in the database.

create procedure: The ability to create stored procedures and functions.

create sequence: The ability to create a sequence object.

create session: The ability to connect to the database and create a session.

create table: The ability to create tables.

create trigger: The ability to create a trigger on a table.

■**NOTE** This walkthrough uses the Oracle Enterprise Manager Console to create the users. If you would prefer to use SQL*Plus or do not have Oracle Enterprise Manager (OEM) installed or available, I've provided a SQL script to create the users in the code download for the book. You can find this script in the Create Users subfolder of this chapter's folder in the Downloads section of the Apress website (www.apress.com).

You'll use Oracle's graphical Enterprise Manager Console to create your users. If you are using Oracle 10g, you can find the Enterprise Manager Console on the Client software CD and on the Server CD in previous versions. If you've installed both the 10g Server and the 10g Client software on your machine, ensure that the Client Oracle Home is configured to correctly access the database by following these steps.

1. Start the Enterprise Manager Console, which is located in the main Oracle Start Menu folder.

   If this is the first time you've started the Enterprise Manager Console, you'll be presented with the Add Databases To Tree dialog (see Figure 1-18).

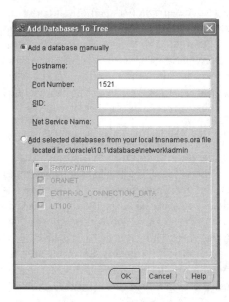

Figure 1-18. *The Add Databases To Tree dialog*

2. Select the "Add selected databases from your local tnsnames.ora file located in *<your path>*" radio button (see Figure 1-19).

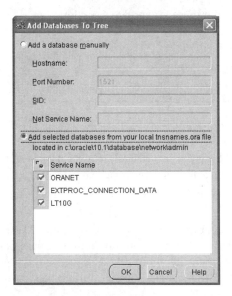

Figure 1-19. *The Add Databases To Tree dialog, continued*

3. Click OK to continue.

This adds the entries from the `tnsnames.ora` file into the Databases node in the Enterprise Manager Console. After the databases have been added to the Databases node, you will be returned to the Enterprise Manager Console (see Figure 1-20).

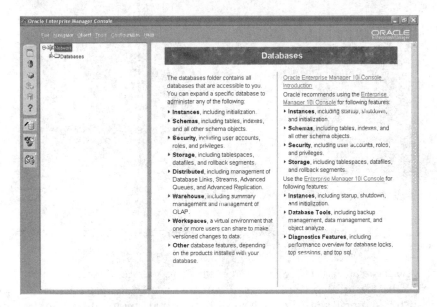

Figure 1-20. *The Oracle Enterprise Manager Console*

4. Expand the Databases node to reveal the new database entries (see Figure 1-21).

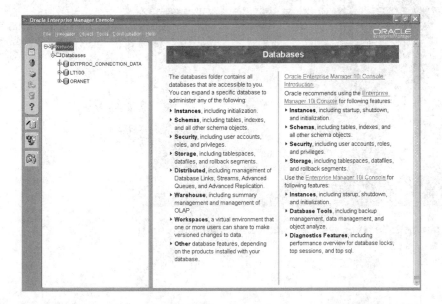

Figure 1-21. *The expanded Databases node in the Oracle Enterprise Manager Console*

5. Select the ORANET entry, and then right-click and select Connect from the pop-up menu to produce the Database Connect Information dialog (see Figure 1-22).

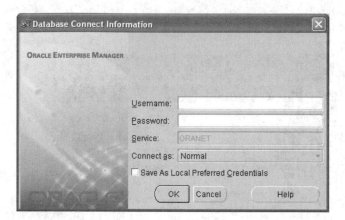

Figure 1-22. *The Database Connect Information dialog*

6. Complete the Username and Password fields and ensure that the Connect as drop-down list displays Normal (see Figure 1-23).

In this case, you are using the SYSTEM user to create your new users. You need to use an appropriately privileged user to create your new users. After you have created your administrative-privileged user, you'll be able to use that user for future administration tasks.

7. Click OK to connect to the database and return to the Enterprise Manager Console.

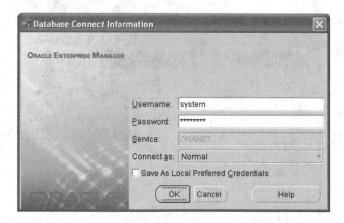

Figure 1-23. *The completed Database Connect Information dialog*

8. In the Enterprise Manager Console, select and expand the Security node under the ORANET node (see Figure 1-24).

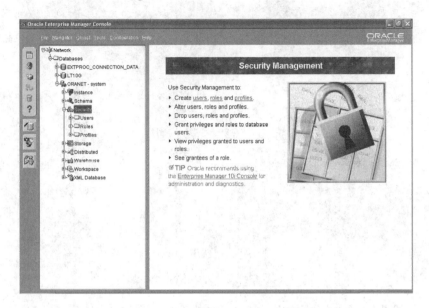

Figure 1-24. *The Security node in the Oracle Enterprise Manager Console*

9. Select the Users node, then right-click and select Create from the pop-up menu (see Figure 1-25). The Create User dialog opens.

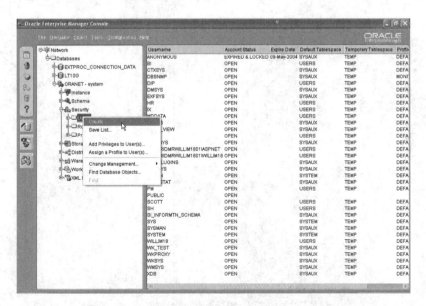

Figure 1-25. *Selecting Create to create a new user in the Oracle Enterprise Manager Console*

10. Complete the General tab in the Create User dialog (see Figure 1-26).

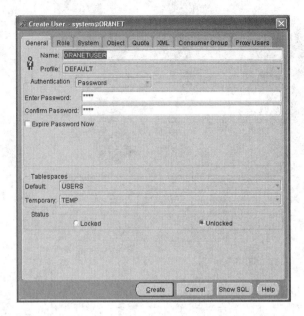

Figure 1-26. *The General tab in the Create User dialog*

11. To remove the CONNECT role, select it in the Granted list and click the up arrow button.

Figure 1-27 illustrates what the dialog looks like after you've removed the role.

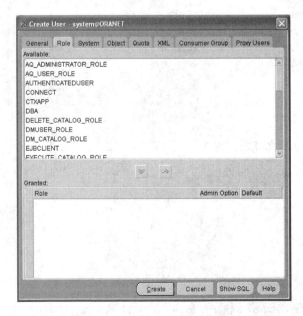

Figure 1-27. *The Role tab in the Create User dialog*

12. Select the System tab and assign the privileges in the bulleted list at the beginning of this section (see Figure 1-28).

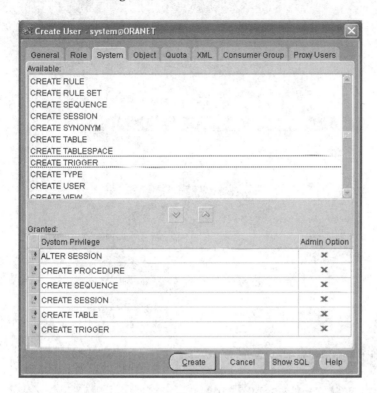

Figure 1-28. *The System tab in the Create User dialog*

13. Now, select the Quota tab, select the USERS tablespace, and then select the Unlimited radio button. Leave the other tablespace selections at the default value of <none> (see Figure 1-29).

You have now specified that the user you're creating has an unlimited quota on the USERS tablespace. In other words, you aren't limiting the amount of space that this user can use in this tablespace. If you're working in a shared environment and wish to make sure that the user doesn't exceed a space-use threshold, or if you have any questions about the appropriate value for this field, consult with your database administrator.

You don't have to grant any quota on the TEMP tablespace because the user doesn't directly create any objects in this tablespace.

Figure 1-29. *The Quota tab in the Create User dialog*

14. Now click the Create button to create the user.

When the user has been created, you'll see a dialog that says the user was created successfully (see Figure 1-30).

Figure 1-30. *The User Created Successfully dialog*

15. Simply click OK to return to the Enterprise Manager Console (see Figure 1-31).

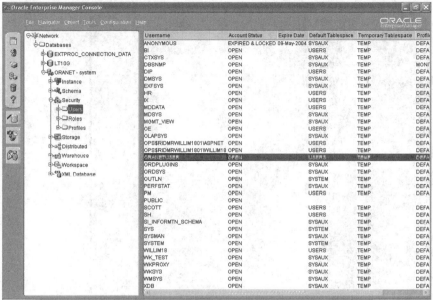

Figure 1-31. *The Users node in the Oracle Enterprise Manager Console*

16. Select and right-click the Users node to create your administrative-privileged user as you did for your typical-privileged user. Click Create (see Figure 1-32).

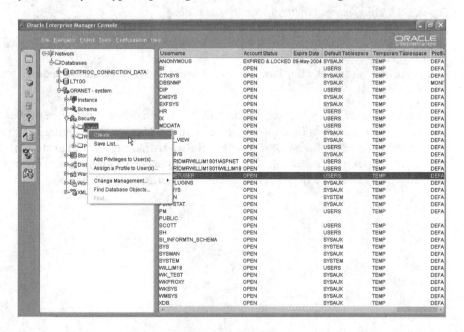

Figure 1-32. *Selecting Create to create a new user in the Oracle Enterprise Manager Console*

17. Complete the General tab in the same manner as you did for your typical-privileged user using the new username (see Figure 1-33).

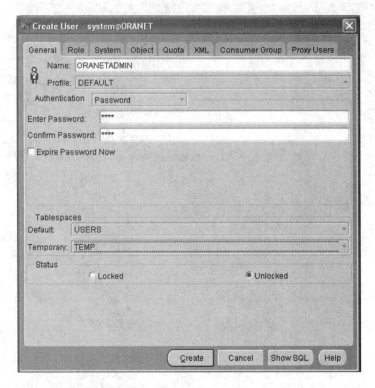

Figure 1-33. *The General tab in the Create User dialog*

18. Click the Role tab.

19. Grant the DBA role by selecting it in the Available list and then clicking the down arrow (see Figure 1-34).

It is not strictly necessary to leave the CONNECT role in the Granted list since the DBA role contains all the privileges (and more) that are in the CONNECT role. In Figure 1-34, you can see that I've removed the CONNECT role in the same manner as I did in step 11. Because this user has the DBA role, you don't need to explicitly grant quotas on any tablespace. This user is a highly privileged user by virtue of their DBA role.

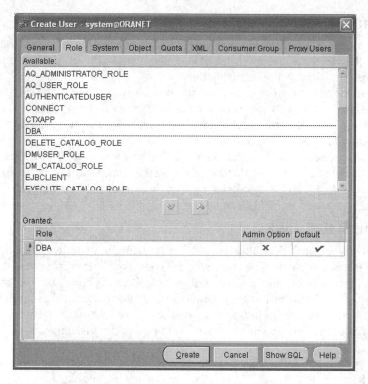

Figure 1-34. *The Role tab in the Create User dialog*

20. Click the Create button to create the user, and then click OK to dismiss the informational message dialog.

Examining SQL*Plus

Up to this point, you've been using Oracle's graphical tools to perform all of your tasks. In contrast to these graphical tools, SQL*Plus is a character-based utility that provides a command-line interface to an Oracle database. Perhaps the primary attribute that best describes SQL*Plus is a single word: ubiquitous. SQL*Plus is a near universal truth in an Oracle server installation. It would be highly unusual for an Oracle server installation to be missing SQL*Plus, though for security reasons, you may find that it has not been installed on a client workstation. A typical end user doesn't need to act interactively with the database through a facility such as SQL*Plus under normal circumstances. However, you'll use SQL*Plus from time to time as you work through the material in this book. In this section, I'll briefly examine some of its main features.

SQL*Plus Variants

On the Windows platform, there are typically three variations of the SQL*Plus utility: a Windows variation, a command-line variation, and a web-based variation. Each has its own characteristics, but they all, for the most part, provide the same functionality.

The web-based variation is known as iSQL*Plus, and it is fully described in the "SQL*Plus Getting Started" guide included in the Oracle documentation. You won't be using iSQL*Plus in this book, and therefore, I won't discuss it. If you wish to learn more about iSQL*Plus, I encourage you to explore the Oracle documentation.

Oracle Corporation has recently hinted that the Windows-based version of SQL*Plus will be deprecated in a future release. However, this won't impact the command-line version of the utility. Therefore, I'll focus the SQL*Plus discussion around the command-line version.

Command-Line SQL*Plus

If you are accustomed to working with applications and utilities on the Windows platform, a command-line utility may seem out of place. However, the command-line version of SQL*Plus provides a great deal of functionality and is easily configurable. Perhaps one of the most basic uses of SQL*Plus is to act as a litmus test of sorts. That is, SQL*Plus is often used to verify connectivity, correct SQL syntax in a query, and so on. I often hear the question, "Does it work in SQL*Plus?" In short, you'll always find being able to connect directly to a database via SQL*Plus useful.

By default, when you start SQL*Plus, you're prompted for a username and a password. You can override this behavior in a couple of ways. You can specify the /nolog switch or you can specify either the username or the username and password. Listing 1-10 illustrates how you'd connect to your standard TNS alias using the ORANETUSER user.

Listing 1-10. *Starting SQL*Plus in Command-Line Mode*

```
C:\>sqlplus

SQL*Plus: Release 10.1.0.2.0 - Production on Fri Jul 30 22:40:50 2004

Copyright (c) 1982, 2004, Oracle.  All rights reserved.

Enter user-name: oranetuser@oranet
Enter password:

Connected to:
Oracle Database 10g Enterprise Edition Release 10.1.0.2.0 - Production
With the Partitioning, Oracle Label Security, OLAP and Data Mining options

SQL> exit
Disconnected from Oracle Database 10g Enterprise Edition Release 10.1.0.2.0↵
    - Production
With the Partitioning, Oracle Label Security, OLAP and Data Mining options

C:\>
```

The format for connecting to a TNS alias is simply username@tns_alias. If you choose to specify a password in your connect string, it's displayed in plain text. For this reason, I typically don't specify the password as part of the connect string. However, if you wish to do so, the format is simply username/password@tns_alias. As you can see in Listing 1-10, you're prompted for the password if it isn't specified. You may specify the username and TNS alias as parameters to sqlplus.exe if you wish. Listing 1-11 illustrates how to do this.

Listing 1-11. *Passing the Username and TNS Alias as Command-Line Parameters*

```
C:\>sqlplus oranetuser@oranet

SQL*Plus: Release 10.1.0.2.0 - Production on Fri Jul 30 22:43:04 2004

Copyright (c) 1982, 2004, Oracle.  All rights reserved.

Enter password:

Connected to:
Oracle Database 10g Enterprise Edition Release 10.1.0.2.0 - Production
With the Partitioning, Oracle Label Security, OLAP and Data Mining options

SQL> exit
Disconnected from Oracle Database 10g Enterprise Edition Release 10.1.0.2.0↵
  - Production
With the Partitioning, Oracle Label Security, OLAP and Data Mining options

C:\>
```

As mentioned earlier, you can use the /nolog switch to suppress being prompted for a user name and password. This is useful in situations where you may want to start SQL*Plus, but you don't want to establish a database connection at that same time. Listing 1-12 illustrates how to use the /nolog switch.

Listing 1-12. *Using the /nolog Command-Line Switch to SQL*Plus*

```
C:\>sqlplus /nolog

SQL*Plus: Release 10.1.0.2.0 - Production on Fri Jul 30 22:45:30 2004

Copyright (c) 1982, 2004, Oracle.  All rights reserved.

SQL> exit

C:\>
```

I'll complete this short discussion of methods to start the command-line version of SQL*Plus with an example of how to connect to the default database. In order for this connection type to work, you must start SQL*Plus from the machine that is hosting the database.

Earlier in the chapter, I discussed the Oracle Home and the registry hive where this key lives. One of the keys that may exist under the Oracle Home has a value name of ORACLE_SID. The value that this key holds represents the default database on the machine. This key/value pair doesn't have to be present but typically is.

■**TIP** The value specified for the ORACLE_SID registry key must be a SID, as specified when the database was created. You can't use a TNS alias name here.

Recall from the earlier discussion that values in the registry may be overridden by values specified at the environment level. From this, it follows that if the key/value pair is not present, you may simply set it in the environment. You could also, of course, add the value to the registry if you so desire.

■**CAUTION** Be careful when editing the registry directly. It is possible to corrupt the registry or enter keys that are invalid, thus causing issues such and rendering the registry hive unreadable.

On my machine, the Oracle Home for the 10g database created in the Appendix is located at HKLM\SOFTWARE\ORACLE\KEY_OraDatabase101 in the registry. The registry key ORACLE_SID has the value of LT10G because that is what I specified in the Database Creation Assistant during the database creation process. Therefore, if I omit a TNS alias from the SQL*Plus connect string, SQL*Plus attempts to connect to the LT10G database on my local machine. Listing 1-13 illustrates how a connection to the default database looks when you're using SQL*Plus.

Listing 1-13. *Using the Default Database When Connecting via SQL*Plus*

```
C:\>sqlplus oranetuser

SQL*Plus: Release 10.1.0.2.0 - Production on Fri Jul 30 22:48:43 2004

Copyright (c) 1982, 2004, Oracle.  All rights reserved.

Enter password:

Connected to:
Oracle Database 10g Enterprise Edition Release 10.1.0.2.0 - Production
With the Partitioning, Oracle Label Security, OLAP and Data Mining options

SQL> exit
Disconnected from Oracle Database 10g Enterprise Edition Release 10.1.0.2.0↵
 - Production
With the Partitioning, Oracle Label Security, OLAP and Data Mining options

C:\>
```

In general, you'll connect to the database via the TNS alias you created earlier. As you recall, the primary purpose for creating that alias was to enable a consistent naming pattern. If you are connecting to a remote database, that is, a database not on your local machine, then you'll need to use the TNS alias to connect. You will, however, use the default database method of connecting as you explore more advanced topics later in the book.

The SQL*Plus Profile Files

In the beginning of this section, I mentioned that SQL*Plus can be easily configured. Two files called profiles can be used to configure various aspects of the SQL*Plus environment. These files are named `glogin.sql` and `login.sql`. The `glogin.sql` file is known as the site profile, and the `login.sql` file is known as the user profile. The distinction between the two is fairly obvious—the site profile is meant to contain settings common to the entire site, or machine, whereas the user profile holds settings intended for a single user. Aside from the intended scope of the items in these files, another characteristic is important. In versions of Oracle prior to 10g, by default, the files are read only once during the lifetime of a SQL*Plus session. In version 10g of the database, both files are read at each connection. The `glogin.sql` file is located in the `sqlplus\admin` folder underneath the directory where Oracle was installed. For example, if you use the Oracle installation highlighted in the Appendix, `glogin.sql` is located in the `c:\oracle\10.1\database\sqlplus\admin` folder. The `glogin.sql` file, like the `login.sql` file, is a text file, so you can easily view or edit its contents.

Unlike `glogin.sql`, which is created during the software installation process, you must create `login.sql` manually. This file is an optional file, but I typically create it. The `glogin.sql` file is always installed in the same location underneath the Oracle Home, so Oracle always knows where to find this file when it needs to read it. On the other hand, `login.sql` may not even exist, so Oracle has no advanced knowledge of where this file might be. You can solve this using a technique similar to the way the operating system searches for commands. The algorithm for searching for `login.sql` is quite simple. Oracle first looks in the current directory for the user, and if it doesn't find the file in that directory, it searches all the directories listed in the SQLPATH environment variable. Like the ORACLE_SID environment variable, you can set this in the registry under the Oracle Home hive. The SQLPATH variable is simply a listing of operating system directories with the appropriate operating system path separator token. I have a Windows folder that contains a set of common scripts (including my `login.sql` file) I use in SQL*Plus. I have added that folder to the SQLPATH variable in the registry. The SQLPATH variable in my registry has this value:

```
c:\oracle\orascripts;c:\oracle\10.1\database\rdbms\admin; ⏎
c:\oracle\10.1\database\dbs
```

This allows me to start SQL*Plus from any folder on my system and be able to execute my scripts without having to specify the full directory path.

■TIP Once Oracle finds a copy of `login.sql`, it stops searching. If you have a `login.sql` file in your current directory as well as another copy in a directory specified in your SQLPATH environment, Oracle only reads the `login.sql` file in your current directory.

I typically use the login.sql file for two purposes: I specify my editor (a VI variant known as VIM), and I occasionally include a small bit of script to set the prompt within SQL*Plus. Listing 1-14 represents a login.sql file that accomplishes these two tasks.

Listing 1-14. *A login.sql File*

```
define _editor=c:\vim\vim62\gvim.exe

column global_name new_value g_name
set termout off
select user || '@' || global_name as global_name from global_name;
set termout on
set sqlprompt '&g_name> '
```

The little script in the login.sql file is based on a script usually attributed to Tom Kyte (http://asktom.oracle.com) of Oracle Corporation. I encourage you to visit Tom's website; it has a wealth of Oracle information. The other entry defines (logically enough) what editor I want to use when editing files from within SQL*Plus. By default, on the Windows platform, the editor is Notepad. If you wish to change the editor, this is where you do it. A side effect of the login.sql file being read once per SQL*Plus session is that if you choose to include the script that sets the prompt in SQL*Plus, if you change database connections, the prompt doesn't automatically change. Also, SQL*Plus reads the script during start up, so if you use the /nolog option, the script fails. This makes sense because the /nolog option explicitly bypasses connecting to a database. Listing 1-15 illustrates one method of refreshing the SQL*Plus prompt if you choose to include the script in your login.sql file.

Listing 1-15. *Refreshing the SQL*Plus Prompt Using the 9i Version of SQL*Plus*

```
C:\>\oracle\9.2\bin\sqlplus oranetuser@oranet

SQL*Plus: Release 9.2.0.5.0 - Production on Fri Jul 30 23:03:13 2004

Copyright (c) 1982, 2002, Oracle Corporation.  All rights reserved.

Enter password:

Connected to:
Oracle Database 10g Enterprise Edition Release 10.1.0.2.0 - Production
With the Partitioning, Oracle Label Security, OLAP and Data Mining options

ORANETUSER@LT10G.SAND> connect system@lt9i
Enter password:
Connected.
ORANETUSER@LT10G.SAND> @login.sql
SYSTEM@LT9I.SAND> exit
Disconnected from Oracle9i Enterprise Edition Release 9.2.0.5.0 - Production
With the Partitioning, Oracle Label Security, OLAP and Oracle Data Mining options
JServer Release 9.2.0.5.0 - Production

C:\>
```

As you can see in Listing 1-15, my initial connection sets the SQL*Plus prompt correctly. However, when I connected to another database on my laptop, the SQL*Plus prompt didn't change. By manually running the login.sql script, I was able to refresh my SQL*Plus prompt.

■**TIP** Using the @ symbol is one method of running scripts from within SQL*Plus. Consult the "SQL*Plus User's Guide" or your system administrator for more information.

This concludes my initial examination of the SQL*Plus utility. As you make additional use of the utility, you'll examine other aspects of the utility as necessary. I encourage you to review the "SQL*Plus User's Guide" in the Oracle documentation. The utility is quite powerful once you learn its basic usage.

Selecting a .NET Data Provider

If you have programmed using any of the Windows-based data access mechanisms in the past, you are probably familiar with acronyms such as ODBC, DAO, RDO, ADO, OLE DB, OO4O, and so on. I view these technologies as belonging to the same class or lineage, whereas I view the .NET data access mechanism as representing a new class of data access technology. It's easy to see a progression from one technology to the next in the "old" data access technologies. Like the rest of the .NET technology stack, the data access layer represents a fresh start of sorts.

Most people discover that they have two primary choices when it comes to selecting a data provider vendor. These two providers, of course, are Oracle Corporation and Microsoft. Though other vendors provide .NET-compatible data access providers for the Oracle database, in all likelihood, you'll be deciding between the Oracle Corporation provider and the Microsoft provider. Both of these providers are offered free of charge, whereas other providers are typically on a purchase basis.

One feature of the .NET Framework is that data provider implementers have a greater ability to expose product-specific features through a .NET Framework data provider. Although a technology like ODBC was designed to provide a homogenized data access viewpoint through a least-common-denominator approach, a .NET Framework data provider allows for a deeper integration and expression of the back-end database. Rather than making the database back-end choice irrelevant by hiding database-specific features, .NET allows database-specific features to be used. Both the Oracle and the Microsoft data providers expose the basic functionality you'd expect to be present in the providers such as connection, command, and reader objects. In fact, there is a fairly consistent one-to-one mapping of the functionality present in each provider.

The Oracle provider exposes more features of the database than does the Microsoft provider. The other primary difference between these two relates to the Oracle client software requirements. Keep in mind that if you have installed the Oracle server software on your workstation, the client is included in that installation, though it is certainly possible to install the client as a separate component. Currently, the Oracle provider requires either the Oracle9i Release 2 (9.2.0) or the Oracle10g Release 1 (10.1.0) client software. The Oracle provider can work with any database the client software supports. For the 10g provider, those versions include Oracle8i, Oracle9i, and Oracle10g. Although the Oracle data provider works with the

9i Release 2 or later client, the Microsoft data provider works with the Oracle8i Release 3 (8.1.7) or later client. However, the Oracle 8i Release 3 software will no longer be supported as of the end of 2004.

In summary, these are the primary characteristics that drive our data provider decision:

The Oracle data provider

- Exposes more Oracle functionality than the Microsoft provider

- Works with the Oracle9i Release 2 and higher client

The Microsoft data provider

- Exposes less Oracle functionality than does the Oracle data provider

- Works with the Oracle8i Release 3 and higher client

Taking the above factors into consideration, I chose to use the Oracle data provider for .NET. The primary reason for this choice is the additional functionality exposed by the Oracle provider. Later in the book, you'll perform tasks that are simply not exposed through the Microsoft provider.

Integrating Visual Studio and Oracle

As I briefly discussed in the Introduction, the integration of Oracle in the Visual Studio environment has increased with recent releases of Visual Studio. I think it is best to think of this integration as a work in progress—it is definitely improving, but some pieces are not yet implemented. You may be wondering if it is possible to rely solely on Visual Studio to develop an application that uses Oracle. My answer, at this stage, is that it is *possible*, but perhaps it isn't the best idea to rely solely on Visual Studio. However, I do believe that this is one area that will continue to improve in future releases of Visual Studio.

Now I'll show you how to create a connection to your Oracle database in the Visual Studio .NET Server Explorer, and then you'll look at the objects that are available to you through that connection.

Server Explorer Database Connection

You may be somewhat surprised to hear that the connections you'll make from the Visual Studio .NET Server Explorer to your Oracle database do not use .NET as the underlying connection layer. This is because the hooks in the Visual Studio environment use OLEDB as the underlying protocol. Therefore, you'll use OLEDB for your connections in the Server Explorer. You can use either the Oracle OLEDB provider or the Microsoft OLEDB provider, which is installed as a part of Visual Studio.

To begin creating our connections, follow these steps:

1. Right-click the Data Connections node item in the Server Explorer tab, and select Add Connection from the pop-up menu (see Figure 1-35).

   The Data Link Properties dialog opens with the Connection tab active by default (see Figure 1-36).

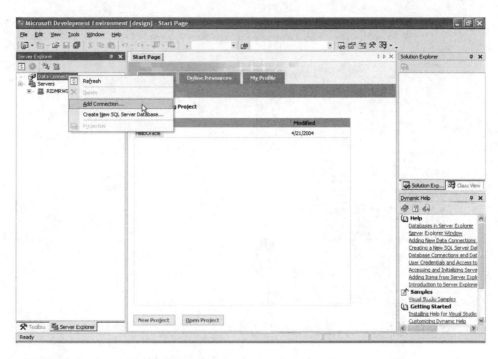

Figure 1-35. *The Visual Studio IDE Data Connection node*

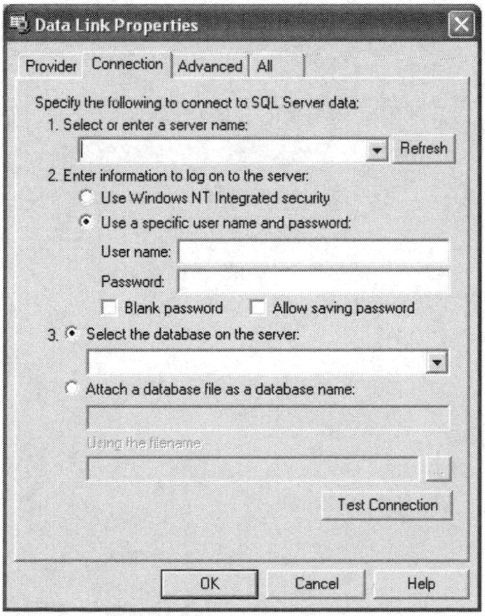

Figure 1-36. *The Data Link Properties dialog's Connection tab*

2. To change the provider from the default, click the Provider tab and select Microsoft OLE DB Provider for Oracle as the provider (see Figure 1-37).

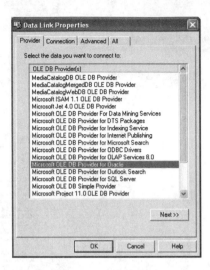

Figure 1-37. *Selecting the provider*

3. Select the Connection tab again and complete the fields with the information for your database (see Figure 1-38).

Again, you'll use the information used to create the database in the Appendix. The server name is the TNS alias from your tnsnames.ora file.

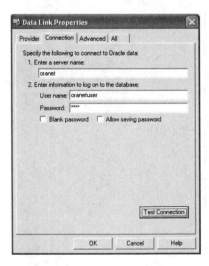

Figure 1-38. *The completed Connection tab*

4. Click the Test Connection button to ensure that you've entered your information correctly (see Figure 1-39).

Figure 1-39. *The successful connection dialog*

5. Click OK to dismiss the informational dialog that informs you that the connection succeeded.

You'll find yourself back at the Data Link Properties dialog.

6. Click OK to close this dialog.

This brings up the Microsoft OLE DB for Oracle Connect dialog (see Figure 1-40).

Figure 1-40. *The OLE DB Oracle Connection dialog*

7. Enter the password and click OK to complete the configuration of your new data connection.

In order to add a connection for your ORANETADMIN user, simply complete the above steps substituting values as appropriate. When you've finished, your Server Explorer window should contain the two new connections (see Figure 1-41).

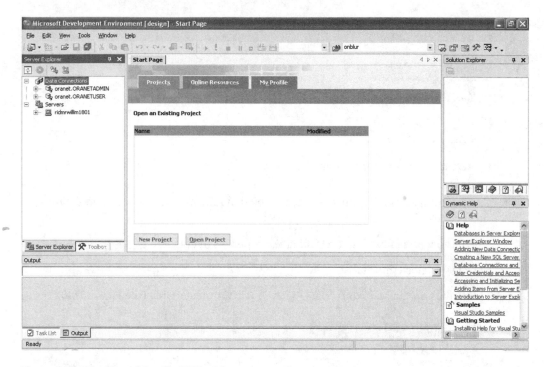

Figure 1-41. *The Visual Studio IDE with your new data connections*

Types of Oracle Objects Available

When you expand the data connection node, you'll see the set of basic Oracle database objects exposed through the Microsoft OLE DB connection that you established in the last section. Though the Database Diagrams node also appears, it is not part of this set because it is a Visual Studio object rather than an Oracle object. When you expand each node, you'll be presented with a list of objects of that type to which you have access. For example, if you followed the instructions in the Appendix to create a database, by expanding the Tables node under the ORANETUSER connection, you'll see a list of tables even though you haven't yet created any tables for that user. This is because those tables are accessible to a special user known as public. This user represents a global user, and any privileges or rights granted to this user apply to all users in the database.

■NOTE If you choose to use the Oracle OLEDB provider rather than the Microsoft OLEDB provider, the type and number of objects exposed through the Server Explorer is reduced.

You should be familiar with most of the Oracle database object types represented in the data connection node. Two possible exceptions are synonym and package specifications/bodies. I'll discuss the package types later in the book. In brief, they are like code modules in some respects. They can hold variables and code units much like a code module in Visual Basic would. The synonym type represents an alias for another object. It is a convenience mechanism—rather than referring to an object by its fully qualified name, you can create a synonym to work as a shortcut for the full object name.

By expanding the nodes and opening the objects within each node, you are working with a live version of the object. For example, if you open a table and make changes to the data in the table, those changes are applied to the table in the database (provided the user has appropriate rights). You can also create new objects from within the Server Explorer. However, you are fairly limited in the objects that you can create. As of this writing, you cannot, for example, create a new table or view. I find it best to focus on the word Explorer in Server Explorer and use it as a way to browse objects and data rather than as a front-end for the database.

Creating a Basic Connection

In this section, you're going to move from the abstract to the concrete by creating your first connection to the Oracle database and by creating the obligatory "Hello World" program. I'll start with a brief examination of the OracleConnection class and then jump into the introductory program.

The OracleConnection Class

In the remainder of this chapter, you'll develop a basic pattern of setting properties, open a connection, perform work, and finally, close the connection in most of your code. In this section, you briefly look at the properties you set and the methods that are in virtually all the code. You'll also look at how the properties you set are related to the configuration you performed in the Oracle client software.

The OracleConnection class encapsulates your connection to the Oracle database. All the work you do in the Oracle database takes place in the context of a connection. In order to create that connection to the database, you must set some values in the OracleConnection class's ConnectionString property. This property is a public property and you'll set the Data Source, Password, and User ID item connect string attributes initially. The Data Source item in the ConnectionString property corresponds to the TNS alias entry in the tnsnames.ora file you created and configured. You'll accept the default values for the remaining attributes in the ConnectionString property in your early code. Later, you'll examine some more advanced configurations of this property.

Once you've defined your ConnectionString property, you'll create an instance of the OracleConnection class called the Open method to open your connection to the database and to display a few values, and finally, you'll call the Close method to terminate your connection and indicate that you're finished with the connection object.

The "Hello, Oracle Here!" Sanity Check

It's time to fire up Visual Studio and create the staple "Hello World" program, without which no programming book would be complete. Here, you'll create a simple console application to put into place and formalize the concepts we've discussed up to this point.

Begin by creating a new Visual C# console application; name it HelloOracle. Once Visual Studio has created the application skeleton, you need to add a reference to the Oracle Data Provider for .NET assembly. The assembly is in the file Oracle.DataAccess.dll, which was created and registered in the Global Assembly Cache (GAC) when you installed the data provider. To add the reference to the Oracle data provider, right-click the References tab in the Solution Explorer and select Add Reference, which will result in the dialog seen in Figure 1-42.

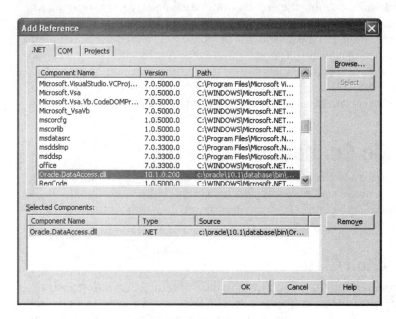

Figure 1-42. *Adding a reference to the Oracle data provider for .NET*

Because you're creating a console application, the normal visual data and design tools are not available to you. You'll simply write the code to accomplish the same tasks these tools would do for you. Begin by including the `using Oracle.DataAccess.Client` directive at the top of the code module.

Listing 1-16 is the code for our "Hello World" console application.

Listing 1-16. *The HelloOracle Code Module*

```
using System;
using Oracle.DataAccess.Client;

namespace HelloOracle
{
 /// <summary>
 /// Summary description for Class1.
 /// </summary>
 class Class1
 {
  /// <summary>
  /// The main entry point for the application.
  /// </summary>
  [STAThread]
```

```
static void Main(string[] args)
{
 String connString = "User Id=oranetuser;Password=demo;Data Source=oranet";
 OracleConnection oraConnection = new OracleConnection(connString);

 try
 {
  oraConnection.Open();

  Console.WriteLine("\nHello, Oracle Here!\n");
  Console.WriteLine("Connection String:");
  Console.WriteLine(oraConnection.ConnectionString.ToString() + "\n");
  Console.WriteLine("Current Connection State:");
  Console.WriteLine(oraConnection.State.ToString() + "\n");
  Console.WriteLine("Oracle Database Server Version:");
  Console.WriteLine(oraConnection.ServerVersion.ToString());
 }
 catch (Exception ex)
 {
  Console.WriteLine("Error occured: " + ex.Message);
 }
 finally
 {
  if (oraConnection.State == System.Data.ConnectionState.Open)
  {
   oraConnection.Close();
  }
 }
}
}
```

The code is straightforward and should be fairly familiar to you. You create an instance of the OracleConnection class using a connect string that you pass to the constructor. You simply write some connection attributes to the console and close the connection after you're done. When you have created and successfully compiled the code module, open a command prompt window, change to the project debug directory, and execute the binary. You should see output similar to that in Listing 1-17.

Listing 1-17. *The Output of the HelloOracle Program*

```
C:\My Projects\ProOraNet\Oracle\C#\Chapter01\HelloOracle\bin\Debug>HelloOracle.exe

Hello, Oracle Here!

Connection String:
User Id=oranetuser;Data Source=oranet
```

```
Current Connection State:
Open

Oracle Database Server Version:
10.1.0.2.0

C:\My Projects\ProOraNet\Oracle\C#\Chapter01\HelloOracle\bin\Debug>
```

Of course, you can also use the step-through capabilities of the Visual Studio debugger to execute your program in debug mode and explore the execution in more detail.

Chapter 1 Wrap-Up

This chapter covered a lot of abstract or theoretical ground. Nevertheless, the topics I covered should help you further your overall understanding of an Oracle system.

To sum up, you explored the Oracle server and network architectures, and learned the difference between a few key concepts that are often points of confusion. I showed you how to create standard configuration and database users and followed that with a high-level introduction to the SQL*Plus utility. I then examined the reasoning behind the use of the Oracle data provider as the primary data provider in the sample code and explored the integration of the Oracle database into the Visual Studio environment. I concluded with a traditional "Hello World" program.

CHAPTER 2

■ ■ ■

Retrieving Data

I've split our examination of data retrieval into two main sections. In this first, we examine the data provider classes typically used in the data retrieval process and their properties. These are the primary data provider classes we cover:

The `OracleConnection` **class:** Used to establish and represent the connection to the database.

The `OracleCommand` **class:** Acts as a broker between the application and the database. This class is used to pass commands to the database and to return results from the database to the application.

The `OracleParameter` **class:** Used to represent a parameter for an OracleCommand or DataSet column. You use this class a great deal, especially when you're working with bind variables.

The `OracleDataReader` **class:** Represents a forward-only, read-only result set and is returned by the `OracleCommand` class's `ExecuteReader` method.

Where appropriate, I provide self-contained examples of how to use each class using the ODP.NET provider, but I also point out any essential differences in support or behavior if you happen to be using the Microsoft provider.

■**NOTE** In this chapter, I focus on the data retrieval aspects of these classes. Chapter 3 covers the data manipulation aspects. Also, I deal with certain properties in dedicated chapters. For example, in Chapter 6, we discuss Oracle's support for large objects; properties such as the `InitialLOBFetchSize` are addressed there.

In the second section of this chapter, I put this knowledge to work with some complete examples of data retrieval that use .NET Windows Forms or console applications. You'll see some of the key data provider classes in action in working projects. I also show the important task of how to perform effective data querying for the Oracle database; I point out singularities in its architecture and explore the expected mode of operation that dictates how you should write your .NET data code.

If you're accustomed to working with database systems other than Oracle, it's important to understand that Oracle behaves, in all likelihood, differently from those systems. Its architecture is unique, and you need to program in a way that properly exploits this architecture; if you don't, you'll very quickly run into issues with code that performs poorly and doesn't scale, or with code that doesn't behave as you expect it to.

In this chapter, the architecture issue I address is using the Oracle shared pool effectively by using bind variables in your code. This is a massive factor in the drive to build scalable, high-performance Oracle .NET applications.

■**NOTE** In Chapter 3, I discuss transactions, for which you'll need to properly understand Oracle's locking model and multiversion read consistency architecture.

Using the Application Templates

Before jumping into the sample code and the data provider classes, we'll look at the templates I use to create the code in this chapter as well as the remainder of the book. I use these templates as the basis for each of the projects. You can access them and the complete projects from this chapter's folder in the Downloads section of the Apress website (`www.apress.com`).

The Console Application Template

The template I use for the console applications in this chapter is a basic console application. I added a reference to the data provider assembly, which we discussed in Chapter 1, to the project, and I included the namespaces for the data provider in the beginning of the code file.

Listing 2-1 shows the code I used for the console template.

Listing 2-1. *The Console Application Template Code*

```
using System;
using System.Data;
using Oracle.DataAccess.Client;
using Oracle.DataAccess.Types;

namespace ConsoleTemplate
{
  /// <summary>
  /// Summary description for Class1.
  /// </summary>
  class Class1
  {
    /// <summary>
    /// The main entry point for the application.
    /// </summary>
    [STAThread]
    static void Main(string[] args)
```

```
      {
        //
        // application code is inserted here
        //
      }
    }
}
```

The Windows Forms Application Template

Like the console application template, the Windows Forms application template is simply a basic Windows application. I added a reference to the data provider to the project, and I included the data provider namespaces in the form code file.

Listing 2-2 illustrates the code I used in the template. Due to the nature of a Windows Forms–based application, most of the code you'll create resides in event handlers for specific components you create on the form as you develop the samples. Of course, other than the included namespaces, this code is generated by Visual Studio.

Listing 2-2. *The Windows Forms Application Template Code*

```csharp
using System;
using System.Drawing;
using System.Collections;
using System.ComponentModel;
using System.Windows.Forms;
using System.Data;
using Oracle.DataAccess.Client;
using Oracle.DataAccess.Types;

namespace WindowsTemplate
{
  /// <summary>
  /// Summary description for Form1.
  /// </summary>
  public class Form1 : System.Windows.Forms.Form
  {
    /// <summary>
    /// Required designer variable.
    /// </summary>
    private System.ComponentModel.Container components = null;

    public Form1()
    {
      //
      // Required for Windows Form Designer support
      //
      InitializeComponent();
```

```csharp
      //
      // TODO: Add any constructor code after InitializeComponent call
      //
    }

    /// <summary>
    /// Clean up any resources being used.
    /// </summary>
    protected override void Dispose( bool disposing )
    {
      if( disposing )
      {
        if (components != null)
        {
          components.Dispose();
        }
      }
      base.Dispose( disposing );
    }

    #region Windows Form Designer generated code
    /// <summary>
    /// Required method for Designer support - do not modify
    /// the contents of this method with the code editor.
    /// </summary>
    private void InitializeComponent()
    {
      this.components = new System.ComponentModel.Container();
      this.Size = new System.Drawing.Size(300,300);
      this.Text = "Form1";
    }
    #endregion

    /// <summary>
    /// The main entry point for the application.
    /// </summary>
    [STAThread]
    static void Main()
    {
      Application.Run(new Form1());
    }
  }
}
```

The initial appearance of the Windows Forms application template in the Visual Studio designer is illustrated in Figure 2-1. As you can see, the reference to the data provider is listed under the References node in the Solution Explorer.

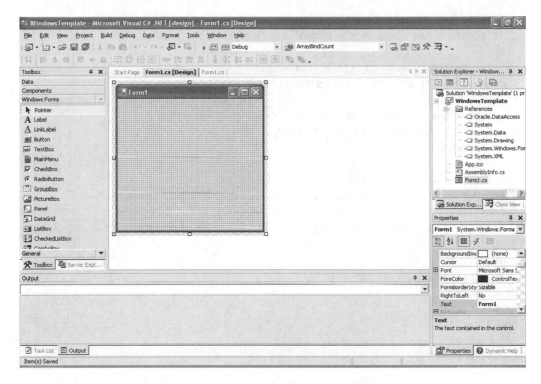

Figure 2-1. *The Windows Forms application template in the designer*

Creating the Get Employees Sample

In order to illustrate the basics of data retrieval, I've created a simple console application, based on the console application template developed in Listing 2-1, that retrieves employee information from the database. I utilize the EMP and DEPT tables from the SCOTT schema in this sample. Listing 2-3 contains the code that accomplishes this for me. Because the template contains everything I need, I only need to create the Main method.

Listing 2-3. *The Get Employees Sample Main Method*

```
static void Main(string[] args)
{
  // create and open a connection object
  string connstr = "User Id=scott; Password=tiger; Data Source=oranet";
  OracleConnection con = new OracleConnection(connstr);
  con.Open();

  // the sql statement to retrieve the data from the tables
  string sql = "select a.empno, a.ename, a.job, b.dname ";
  sql += "from emp a, dept b ";
  sql += "where a.deptno = b.deptno ";
  sql += "order by a.empno";
```

```
// create the command object
OracleCommand cmd = new OracleCommand(sql, con);

// execute the command and get a data reader
OracleDataReader dr = cmd.ExecuteReader();

// display the results to the console window
// use a tab character between the columns
while (dr.Read())
{
  Console.Write(dr[0].ToString() + "\t");
  Console.Write(dr[1].ToString() + "\t");
  Console.Write(dr[2].ToString() + "\t");
  Console.WriteLine(dr[3].ToString());
}

// close and dispose of the objects
dr.Close();
dr.Dispose();
cmd.Dispose();
con.Close();
con.Dispose();
}
```

When this application runs, it outputs the data to the console window as illustrated in Listing 2-4. Although this is a simple application, the classes and techniques I use here are used in virtually all of the sample code you develop later.

Listing 2-4. *The Get Employees Output*

```
C:\My Projects\ProOraNet\Oracle\C#\Chapter02\GetEmployees\bin\Debug>⏎
GetEmployees.exe
7369    SMITH   CLERK       RESEARCH
7499    ALLEN   SALESMAN    SALES
7521    WARD    SALESMAN    SALES
7566    JONES   MANAGER     RESEARCH
7654    MARTIN  SALESMAN    SALES
7698    BLAKE   MANAGER     SALES
7782    CLARK   MANAGER     ACCOUNTING
7788    SCOTT   ANALYST     RESEARCH
7839    KING    PRESIDENT   ACCOUNTING
7844    TURNER  SALESMAN    SALES
7876    ADAMS   CLERK       RESEARCH
7900    JAMES   CLERK       SALES
7902    FORD    ANALYST     RESEARCH
7934    MILLER  CLERK       ACCOUNTING

C:\My Projects\ProOraNet\Oracle\C#\Chapter02\GetEmployees\bin\Debug>
```

Now that you have seen a working data retrieval example, we'll step through the data provider classes and their properties in more detail.

Examining the Data Provider Classes

In this section, you examine the primary or backbone classes exposed by the data provider. You'll become very familiar with these classes because they are used in virtually every application that retrieves data from the database. Let's begin exploring with the OracleConnection class I introduced in Chapter 1.

The OracleConnection Class

In order to interact with the database, you must first establish a connection. The Oracle-Connection class is the class you use for this purpose, and you'll use it in every application you develop.

The OracleConnection class exposes two constructors: the first takes no parameters, whereas the second accepts a string parameter. This string parameter represents a database connection string. Typically you'll use this second constructor in your code since you'll pass a connection string to the constructor as you did in the Get Employees sample in the previous section.

The following code snippet illustrates how to use these two constructors. In this snippet, the connection string is passed directly to the constructor rather than a string variable being created and then passed as would be typical in an application.

```
// the parameterless constructor
OracleConnection con = new OracleConnection();

// passing the connection string to the constructor
OracleConnection = new OracleConnection("User Id=scott; Password=tiger; ⤶
 Data Source=oranet");
```

The ConnectionString Property

The ConnectionString property is a read-write string property. You can use this property to retrieve the value of the ConnectionString as you did in Chapter 1 or you can use it to set the value of the connection string.

An interesting attribute of this property is that if the connection hasn't been opened, the value for the password displays. If the connection has been opened, the value doesn't display. This is illustrated in the ConnectionString project, which is available in the code download for this chapter.

The Main method for the project is presented in Listing 2-5. In addition, in this sample, I use the default constructor and set the ConnectionString via the property instead of using the constructor. For additional details on the ConnectionString, see the data provider documentation. I use some of the more advanced features of the ConnectionString in Chapter 7, when we discuss advanced connection techniques.

Listing 2-5. *The ConnectionString Sample Main Method*

```
static void Main(string[] args)
{
  // create a connection object
  string connstr = "User Id=scott; Password=tiger; Data Source=oranet";
  OracleConnection con = new OracleConnection();

  // set the connection string
  con.ConnectionString = connstr;

  // display the ConnectionString property to the console
  // this will show the password
  Console.WriteLine("Connection String 1: {0}", con.ConnectionString);

  // open the connection
  con.Open();

  // display the ConnectionString property to the console
  // this will not show the password
  Console.WriteLine("Connection String 2: {0}", con.ConnectionString);

  // close the connection
  con.Close();

  // display the ConnectionString property to the console
  // this will not show the password
  Console.WriteLine("Connection String 3: {0}", con.ConnectionString);

  // clean up the connection object
  con.Dispose();
}
```

When this application executes, the password used in the connection string displays initially. However, once the connection opens, the password no longer displays, even if the connection is closed. Listing 2-6 contains the output for this sample illustrating this behavior.

Listing 2-6. *The ConnectionString Sample Output*

```
C:\My Projects\ProOraNet\Oracle\C#\Chapter02\ConnectionString\bin\Debug>⏎
ConnectionString.exe
Connection String 1: User Id=scott; Password=tiger; Data Source=oranet
Connection String 2: User Id=scott; Data Source=oranet
Connection String 3: User Id=scott; Data Source=oranet

C:\My Projects\ProOraNet\Oracle\C#\Chapter02\ConnectionString\bin\Debug>
```

The ConnectionTimeout Property

For connection requests that use the connection pool, this int property specifies, in seconds, the length of time that the data provider waits to acquire a connection from the connection pool. For connections that don't use pooling, this parameter has no effect. If the value of this property is set to zero, the provider should wait indefinitely. This is illustrated in the following code snippet:

```
// connection is named con
// set to wait indefinitely
con.ConnectionTimeout = 0;

// get the ConnectionTimeout property
int timeout = con.ConnectionTimeout;
```

The DataSource Property

The DataSource property is a read-only string property. The value of this property corresponds to the TNS alias (the entry in the tnsnames.ora file that we discussed in Chapter 1) used to create the connection. As you'll see in Chapter 7, it is also possible to create a connection without using the tnsnames.ora file. The following code snippet illustrates how to use this property:

```
// use the standard connect string
string connstr = "User Id=scott; Password=tiger; Data Source=oranet";
OracleConnection con = new OracleConnection(connstr);

// get the data source property
// the value will be "oranet"
string ds = con.DataSource;
```

The ServerVersion Property

This read-only string property represents the version of the Oracle server software. As you saw in Chapter 1, the value of this property on my system is 10.1.0.2.0. Of course, your system has a different value if you're using a different version of the server. The following code snippet illustrates retrieving the value of this property:

```
// assumes connection is con
string serverVersion = con.ServerVersion;
```

The State Property

The read-only State property returns a value from the ConnectionState enumeration. The returned value is either ConnectionState.Open or ConnectionState.Closed. You can use this property to detect the connection state of the `OracleConnection` object. The following code snippet illustrates a possible use of this property:

```
if (con.State == ConnectionState.Open)
{
  // perform some action
};
```

The BeginTransaction Method

By default, transactions are explicit in the data provider. That is, a transaction is started, work is performed, and then the transaction is committed. If you wish to specifically start a transaction, the `BeginTransaction` method is the method to use. The method returns an object of type `OracleTransaction`. I discuss transactions and the `OracleTransaction` class in more detail in Chapter 3.

The Close Method

When you finish using a connection, use the `Close` method to terminate it. There are two important aspects to using the `Close` method. First, if you're using connection pooling, the connection returns to the pool. If you aren't using connection pooling, the connection simply closes. If the `Connection Lifetime` attribute of the `ConnectionString` is exceeded, the connection may still close. See the data provider documentation for more details about the `Connection Lifetime` attribute.

Second, any uncommitted transactions are rolled back. This means that if you start a transaction and close the connection associated with it, any uncommitted work is discarded. The following code illustrates how to use this method:

```
// assume connection is called con
con.Close();
```

The Open Method

The `Open` method is responsible for actually creating (or opening) the connection to the database. If connection pooling is enabled, the Open method attempts to acquire the connection from the pool; otherwise a new connection is created. Calling this method is simple, as illustrated here:

```
// create a connection object
string connstr = "User Id=scott; Password=tiger; Data Source=oranet";
OracleConnection con = new OracleConnection(connstr);

// open the connection
con.Open();
```

The OpenWithNewPassword Method

Use this method to open a connection to the database with a new password, as its name suggests. You use this method when the database administrator enables password expiration. For more information on this method, see Chapter 7.

The OracleCommand Class

Like the connection class, the command class is a root class of sorts since so many operations begin with the instantiation of a command class object. All of the data retrieval operations I present involve an instance of the command class. The OracleCommand class functions as a broker, in the sense that it is responsible for passing your command to the database and returning results (if any) to your application. It typically returns the data as an OracleDataReader object. I'll highlight other return types, such as scalar values or output parameters, as I use them.

The OracleCommand class provides three constructors you can use to instantiate a new instance of the class. The most basic constructor is parameterless and simply creates an instance of the class with all default values for its properties. The second constructor allows you to specify a text parameter that is used by the command object as the command to be executed. The final constructor allows you to specify both the command text and the connection object. Listing 2-7 illustrates the basic ways to create a command object.

Listing 2-7. *The OracleCommand Constructors*

```
// create a basic connect string to connect to our standard database
string connStr = "User Id=oranetuser;Password=demo;Data Source=oranet";
OracleConnection conn1 = new OracleConnection(connStr);

// The basic constructor
OracleCommand cmd1 = new OracleCommand();

// Specifying command text in the constructor
OracleCommand cmd2 = new OracleCommand("select user from dual");

// we can assign the connection property to the command
// object even if we have not yet opened the connection
// to the database.
OracleCommand cmd3 = new OracleCommand("select user from dual",conn1);

// specifying the command text is optional
OracleCommand cmd4 = new OracleCommand(null,conn1);
```

As you can see, if you use either of the first two constructors, you aren't able to specify the connection to be used for your command object in the constructor call. When using either of these constructors, you can, however, set the connection using the Connection property, which is exposed by the command object. There are six properties of the OracleCommand class that I examine in this section:

Connection: Represents the connection to the database.

CommandType: Used to specify how the CommandText should be interpreted.

CommandText: Used to specify the actual command.

FetchSize: Used to control how much data is retrieved for each database round trip.

RowSize: Used to control how much data is retrieved for each database round trip; similar to the FetchSize property.

BindByName: Used to indicate whether bind variables are specified in order or by name.

The Connection Property

Most operations take place in the context of a connection to a database; you use the Connection property to specify or retrieve the OracleConnection object associated with the command object. Therefore, this property is read-write.

If I continue the analogy of the OracleCommand object as a broker, you can think of the connection the Connection property represents as the channel through which the command and results are passed. If the OracleCommand object hasn't yet been assigned an Oracle connection, the value of this property will be null. The value of this property may change during the lifetime of the OracleCommand object; however, the command object may assign only a single connection at any given point. This property may be assigned regardless of whether the connection state is open or closed as illustrated by the third constructor in Listing 2-7.

Listing 2-8 illustrates how to set and retrieve the OracleCommand Connection property.

Listing 2-8. *The OracleCommand Connection Property*

```
// create a connection object
string connStr = "User Id=oranetuser;Password=demo;Data Source=oranet";
OracleConnection con1 = new OracleConnection(connstr);
con1.Open();

// create a command object and set the connection property
OracleCommand cmd = new OracleCommand();
cmd.Connection = con1;

// retrieve the connection and assign it to new connection object
OracleConnection con2 = cmd.Connection;
```

You can also set the Connection property of the OracleCommand object via the Properties window in Visual Studio at design time, if you want to. In order to do this, simply drag an OracleConnection and an OracleCommand from the toolbox onto a form. Select the Oracle-Command object that was dragged onto the form and click the drop-down list box for the Connection property in the Properties window. Expand the Existing node in the drop-down list box and select the OracleConnection object. This process is illustrated in Figure 2-2.

Figure 2-2. *Setting the Connection property using the Visual Studio Properties window*

The CommandType Property

As I mentioned when I started discussing the OracleCommand class, your command can represent a table name, a SQL statement, or a stored procedure. The property you use to indicate to the data provider which type of command you'll use is the CommandType property. The following are the valid values for this read-write property:

CommandType.TableDirect: Indicates that the value of the CommandText property is the name of a table or view.

CommandType.Text: Indicates that the value of the CommandText property is a SQL statement.

CommandType.StoredProcedure: Indicates that the value of the CommandText property is a stored procedure or function.

■NOTE The CommandType.TableDirect isn't supported in the current version of the Microsoft provider.

The default value for this property is CommandType.Text, which represents a SQL statement. Therefore, you don't need to specify a value for this property if your code won't use a SQL statement to retrieve the data. Listing 2-9 illustrates the simple process of setting this property directly in code.

Listing 2-9. *Setting the CommandType Property Directly in Code*

```
// Use the basic constructor
OracleCommand cmd1 = new OracleCommand();
OracleCommand cmd2 = new OracleCommand();

// indicate that we will be retrieving a
// single table with cmd1
cmd1.CommandType = CommandType.TableDirect;

// indicate that we will be using a
// sql statement on cmd2
// this is optional since it is the default
cmd2.CommandType = CommandType.Text;
```

Of course, you can also access this property from the Visual Studio Properties window in the Windows Forms designer. Figure 2-3 illustrates how to set this property at design time using the Properties window.

Figure 2-3. *Setting the CommandType property at design time*

The CommandText Property

The actual command the `OracleCommand` object executes is defined by the `CommandText` property. This is a read-write property. The manner in which this property is interpreted is influenced by the `CommandType` property. If the `CommandType` property is set to `CommandType.Text` or left to its default, then the value of this property is interpreted as a SQL statement. This is probably the most common use of this property.

In this section, you'll learn to use this property for a SQL statement and for a table name. Chapter 5 illustrates how to use this property when you're working with stored procedures or functions.

As you saw in the Get Employees sample at the beginning of the chapter, setting this property is a simple process. Listing 2-10 illustrates a similar method of setting this property directly in code; it also explicitly sets the `CommandType` property.

Listing 2-10. *Setting the CommandText Property*

```
// create a command object
OracleCommand cmd = new OracleCommand();

// set the command type
cmd.CommandType = CommandType.Text;

// set the command text
cmd.CommandText = "select ename from emp order by ename";
```

As with the `CommandType` property, you can set this property from within the Properties window inside Visual Studio. Figure 2-4 illustrates how to set this property value to `TableDirect` at design time through the Properties window rather than directly in the code.

Figure 2-4. *Setting the CommandType property to TableDirect*

Figure 2-5 illustrates how to set the CommandText property once you've set the CommandType property to Text. You can simply type the SQL statement directly into the CommandText text box in the Properties window in the Visual Studio designer.

Figure 2-5. *Setting the CommandText property in Visual Studio*

The FetchSize Property

When data is fetched from the Oracle server, it's stored in client memory for processing. The FetchSize property determines the size of the cache used for this purpose. This read-write property specifies the size (in bytes) of the cache on the client where data fetched from the server will be stored. The default value is 65,536 bytes or 64K.

■NOTE This property isn't supported in the current version of the Microsoft provider. This value specifies the size of the cache that is used for *each* server round-trip. It doesn't specify the maximum size of data that may be returned to the client.

You use this property to tune the performance of data retrieval from the server. I explore how to use this property in detail later in the chapter.

Note that this property is specific to each `OracleCommand` object. Nothing prevents multiple `OracleCommand` objects from having different values for this property within an application, or even within the same method. The `OracleDataReader` class, which I discuss later in this chapter, inherits the value of this property. Therefore, it is possible to override this value if you also set it on the data reader object. Like the other properties of the `OracleCommand` object, you may set this property directly in code or via the visual interface provided by Visual Studio. Setting this property directly in code is illustrated by the following code snippet:

```
// Use the basic constructor
OracleCommand cmd1 = new OracleCommand();

// set the fetch size to 128K
cmd1.FetchSize = 131072;
```

Figure 2-6 illustrates how you set the value of this property at design time via the Visual Studio interface.

Figure 2-6. *Setting the FetchSize property to 128K in the Properties window*

The RowSize Property

In contrast to the other properties of the `OracleCommand` class that you've been exploring, the `RowSize` property is read-only. Initially, the value of this property is zero, and you set it after a command that returns a result set execute. For commands that don't return results, this parameter has no meaning. Like the `FetchSize` property, the value for this property is specified in bytes. You may use this parameter in conjunction with the `FetchSize` property to optimize the fetching of data from the server. Later in the chapter, you'll utilize this parameter, along with the `FetchSize` parameter, to control the number of rows retrieved from the server for each round-trip. The following code snippet illustrates how to retrieve this property after you execute a command that returns results.

```
// assume we have a valid connection
OracleCommand cmd1 = new OracleCommand();

// execute a query here...

// retrieve the rowsize after execution
long rowSize = cmd1.RowSize();
```

■**NOTE** This property isn't supported in the current version of the Microsoft provider. Since the value of this property is only meaningful after an execute call on the command object, it isn't available in the Properties window inside Visual Studio.

The BindByName Property

When parameters in a SQL statement are used instead of literal values, the BindByName property influences the manner in which this occurs. This property is a read-write Boolean property. When you substitute parameter values into variables at run time, there are two methods in which this operation may occur: you may substitute the parameter values in order or by name. The default value of false for this parameter indicates that parameters should be substituted in order at runtime. What this means is that parameters specified in the parameters collection are substituted into the SQL statement in the order in which they were added to the collection. This is the default behavior, and it's the method you'll use in virtually all of the code in this book. If you prefer to use the BindByName property set to true, by all means use it. Some people feel that binding by name makes the code more readable and easier to understand. Perhaps it is just my background, but I prefer to bind by position rather than by name. The following code snippet illustrates how to set this property.

```
// create a command object
OracleCommand cmd1 = new OracleCommand();

// indicate that we will bind using parameter
// names rather than position
// default for BindByName is false
cmd1.BindByName = true;
```

■**NOTE** This property isn't supported in the current version of the Microsoft provider.

The OracleParameter and OracleParameterCollection Classes

In the Introduction, I mentioned the importance of using bind variables in your code. In a little while, you're going to look at that in detail; it's the OracleParameter class that is the mechanism through which you accomplish this task. As its name implies, the OracleParameterCollection class is a collection class that holds the various OracleParameter objects associated with an instance of the OracleCommand class. You access the OracleParameterCollection class via the Parameters property of the command object. The parameter collection class behaves exactly like any other .NET collection class and provides the expected methods (such as Add) to work with objects in the collection. The use of this class is not limited to bind variables only. You can also use it to pass parameters to PL/SQL procedures and functions; for specifics, see Chapter 5.

The OracleParameter class provides nine constructors and 15 properties. In this section, I'll show you nine of the 15 properties; those I don't address here I cover in Chapter 3. The six properties not covered here are related to array operations. Here are those nine properties:

Direction: Indicates the parameter direction (that is, input, output, or both).

DbType: Indicates the data type of the parameter as defined by the DBType .NET Framework enumeration.

OracleDbType: Indicates the data type of the parameter as defined by the ODP.NET OracleDbType enumeration.

ParameterName: Simply indicates the name of the parameter.

Precision: Indicates the maximum number of digits in an OracleDbType.Decimal parameter.

Scale: Indicates the number of digits in the decimal portion of an OracleDbType.Decimal parameter.

Size: Specifies the maximum number of characters in a variable length data type such as varchar2.

Status: Indicates the parameter status, such as a null, was fetched from the database.

Value: Indicates the actual value of the parameter.

■**NOTE** The OracleDbType and Status properties aren't supported in the current version of the Microsoft provider.

Although the OracleParameter class provides nine constructors for you to use, typically you only need two or three of them on a regular basis. For situations in which you require values other than the default values, you'll find the other constructors are available. Of course, it's always possible to create a basic parameter and specify the nondefault property values after instantiation via the properties exposed by the class. The default values for all properties are listed in the Oracle Data Provider for .NET documentation, which is installed as part of the data provider software installation. Listing 2-11 contains a series of snippets that illustrate how to use each of the constructors available.

Listing 2-11. *The OracleParameter Class Constructors*

```
// this sample illustrates the usage of the
// constructors made available by the OracleParameter
// class

// the basic "default" constructor
OracleParameter p1 = new OracleParameter();

// this constructor allows us to specify
// the parameter name as well as the Oracle data type
OracleParameter p2 = new OracleParameter("p2", OracleDbType.Varchar2);

// this constructor allows us to specify
// the parameter name and the value
OracleParameter p3 = new OracleParameter("p3", "Parameter 3");

// this constructor allows us to specify
// the parameter name, the data type,
// and the direction of the parameter
// here we set the direction to input,
// which is the default
OracleParameter p4 = new OracleParameter("p4",
  OracleDbType.Varchar2, ParameterDirection.Input);

// this constructor allows us to specify
// the parameter name, the data type,
// the value, and the direction of the parameter
OracleParameter p5 = new OracleParameter("p5",
  OracleDbType.Varchar2, "Parameter 5",
  ParameterDirection.Input);

// this constructor allows us to specify
// the parameter name, the data type,
// and the size
OracleParameter p6 = new OracleParameter("p6",
  OracleDbType.Varchar2, 32);

// this constructor allows us to specify
// the parameter name, the data type,
// the size, and the source column
// the source column is used with the DataTable
// and DataSet objects
OracleParameter p7 = new OracleParameter("p7",
  OracleDbType.Varchar2, 32, "SourceColumn");

// this constructor allows us to specify
// the parameter name, the data type,
```

```
// the size, the direction, a null indicator,
// the precision, the scale, the source column,
// the source version, and the value
// this constructor is the "fully equipped" constructor
OracleParameter p8 = new OracleParameter("p8",
  OracleDbType.Varchar2, 32, ParameterDirection.Input,
  false, 0, 0, "SourceColumn", DataRowVersion.Current,
  "");

// this constructor allows us to specify
// the parameter name, the data type, the size,
// the value, and the direction
OracleParameter p9 = new OracleParameter("p9",
  OracleDbType.Varchar2, 32, "Parameter 9",
  ParameterDirection.Input);
```

For most code, the basic constructors are typically sufficient; however, you may encounter times when you may want to use the more verbose versions of the constructors. This is a coding style issue. Either you set the appropriate properties at instantiation or you set them after instantiation via the individual properties of the class. In this book, most of your code uses the default values, and, therefore, it mostly uses the "basic" constructors.

The properties that we discuss here are all accessible from within the Visual Studio Windows Forms designer environment. You use the OracleParameter Collection Editor to add parameters and set property values at design time from within Visual Studio. To access the editor, select an OracleCommand object and click the ellipses (…) in the Parameters property box. Once inside the editor, simply click the Add button to create a new parameter and set the property values. Figure 2-7 illustrates how to perform these tasks in Visual Studio. I'll explore using the parameter properties in more depth in the "Chapter 2 Wrap-Up" section at the end of this chapter.

Figure 2-7. *Creating a parameter and the property values in the Visual Studio designer*

The Direction Property

The Direction property is a read-write property that indicates whether the parameter is an input parameter, an input/output parameter, an output parameter, or a return value from a stored function. The default value of this parameter is ParameterDirection.Input. You can specify the value for this property as part of a constructor, or you can set it as a simple property on an existing object. Listing 2-12 illustrates the possible values for this property.

Listing 2-12. *The Direction Property Values*

```
OracleParameter p1 = new OracleParameter();

// setting the possible direction property values
p1.Direction = ParameterDirection.Input;
p1.Direction = ParameterDirection.InputOutput;
p1.Direction = ParameterDirection.Output;
p1.Direction = ParameterDirection.ReturnValue;
```

The DbType Property

The DbType property is an implementation of the System.Data.DbType property. This read-write property is the .NET representation of the parameter type. The valid values for this property are listed in the .NET Framework documentation. This property is closely related to the OracleDbType property, as you'll see shortly. The default value of this property is DbType.String. Listing 2-13 illustrates setting this property to its default value.

Listing 2-13. *Setting the DbType Property*

```
OracleParameter p1 = new OracleParameter();

// sample DbType setting
p1.DbType = DbType.String;
```

The OracleDbType Property

The OracleDbType property is the Oracle Data Provider for .NET representation of the parameter type. This read-write property is optional in the sense that if it is not specified, it is derived automatically based on the DbType property. The default value for this property is OracleDbType.Varchar2, which corresponds to the default value of DbType.String for the DbType property. The DbType property and the OracleDbType property are linked in the sense that changing one results in the other being derived to the correct type. This allows you to easily exchange data between the .NET Framework and the Oracle Data Provider. The available values for this parameter are extensive and are listed in the Oracle Data Provider for .NET documentation. Listing 2-14 illustrates how to set this property and how it is linked to the DbType property.

Listing 2-14. *Setting the OracleDbType Property*

```
OracleParameter p1 = new OracleParameter();

// set to nondefault value (date in this case)
// the default value is varchar2
p1.OracleDbType = OracleDbType.Date;
```

■**NOTE** This property isn't supported in the current version of the Microsoft provider. The Microsoft provider uses the DBType property in place of this Oracle-specific property.

The ParameterName Property

If the BindByName property of the OracleCommand object is false—the default—the Parameter-Name property is optional, though you may specify it if you want to. The default value of the ParameterName property is null. This is a read-write property and takes a String value. If the BindByName property of the OracleCommand object is true, then the value of this property must match the variable name used in the SQL statement in order for variable substitution to occur correctly. This value is also required if you use index by name when you reference a member in the Item method of the OracleParameterCollection class. The value for this property should be less than 30 characters in length. In Listing 2-15, you're setting the ParameterName property.

Listing 2-15. *Setting the ParameterName Property*

```
// create a parameter object
OracleParameter p1 = new OracleParameter();

// setting the ParameterName property
p1.ParameterName = "Parameter1";
```

The Precision Property

The precision of an Oracle numeric type indicates the maximum number of digits that may be present in the number. This property is a read-write property that has a default value of 0. The reason that the default value is 0 is that the default value of the OracleDbType property is OracleDbType.Varchar2, which is a character data type. The precision property only has meaning for the OracleDbType.Decimal data type, which is the Oracle Data Provider for .NET representation of the internal database type of NUMBER. This property may hold any integer value in the range of 0 to 38, which corresponds to the precision values for a column of type NUMBER in the database. In Listing 2-16, you set the maximum number of digits allowed to 8.

Listing 2-16. *Setting the Precision Property*

```
// create the parameter
OracleParameter p1 = new OracleParameter();
```

```
// setting the OracleDbType to decimal
p1.OracleDbType = OracleDbType.Decimal;

// set the precision property
// this sets the total number of digits allowed to 8
p1.Precision = 8;
```

The Scale Property

Like the Precision property, the Scale property is only meaningful when you're dealing with the OracleDbType.Decimal data type. You use this property to specify how many decimal places are used in the resolution of the value to which this property is applied. This read-write property has a default value of 0 for the same reason the Precision property does. This property may hold any integer value in the range of –84 to 127. It may seem bizarre that this property can have a negative value. After all, how can you have a negative number of decimal places? When this value is a negative integer, it's telling Oracle to round the value to the specified number of digits to the left of the decimal point. For example, if this value is –3, Oracle rounds the number to the nearest whole thousandth. Listing 2-17 illustrates how to set the Scale property.

Listing 2-17. *Setting the Scale Property*

```
// create a parameter
OracleParameter p1 = new OracleParameter();

// setting the OracleDbType to decimal
p1.OracleDbType = OracleDbType.Decimal;

// set the precision property
// this sets the total number of digits allowed to 8
p1.Precision = 8;

// set the scale property
// this sets the decimal places to 2
p1.Scale = 2;
```

The Size Property

In Listing 2-11, you created an OracleParameter object (p9) by specifying a size of 32 and a value of "Parameter 9". You may wonder why this is acceptable when clearly the value "Parameter 9" doesn't have a size of 32. The Size property specifies the maximum size that the Value property will be in either bytes or characters, as appropriate. This is a read-write integer property and is also mutable. After a command associated with a parameter object executes, this property holds the size of the data in the Value property. You may choose not to specify this value. If you choose not to, if it can, the data provider derives the size of the data in the Value property for you when the binding operation occurs. However, the data provider is not aware of the size of data in the database, so you should set this property when you're using out parameters in a stored function or procedure. In addition, you don't need to set this property for fixed-size data such as a date data type. Listing 2-18 illustrates setting this property.

Listing 2-18. *Setting the Size Property*

```
// create a parameter
OracleParameter p1 = new OracleParameter();

// setting the OracleDbType to Varchar2 which is a variable size type
p1.OracleDbType = OracleDbType.Varchar2;

// set the size property
p1.Size = 10;
```

The Status Property

The Status property is a bidirectional read-write property, which is of type OracleParameter-Status. You can use this property to inform the data provider that you wish to create a null in the database. I discuss this in Chapter 3. After executing a command, you can use this property to determine if your operation succeeded or fetched a null from the database. In Listing 2-19, you perform a hypothetical operation based upon the Status property.

Listing 2-19. *Using the Status Property*

```
// create a parameter
OracleParameter p1 = new OracleParameter();

// setting the OracleDbType to Varchar2
p1.OracleDbType = OracleDbType.Varchar2;

// perform an operation such as calling a stored function

// get the status
if (p1.Status == OracleParameterStatus.Success)
{
  // perform some process
}
```

■**NOTE** This property isn't supported in the current version of the Microsoft provider.

The Value Property

The Value property is a read-write property that is represented by the .NET object data type. When you're using parameters for input, this is the value substituted into your bind variable placeholder at run time. When you're using output parameters, this is how you retrieve the data from the database into your application. And when you're using input/output parameters, this property serves both purposes. You may also use the Value property to specify a null as an input parameter (see Chapter 3). Listing 2-20 illustrates using this property for an input parameter.

Listing 2-20. *Setting the Value Property*

```
// create a parameter
OracleParameter p1 = new OracleParameter();

// setting the OracleDbType to Varchar2
p1.OracleDbType = OracleDbType.Varchar2;

// set the value
// this will be passed to the database
p1.Value = "Test Value";
```

The OracleDataReader Class

When it comes to working with forward-only, read-only result sets, the OracleDataReader class is the class of choice. As opposed to the OracleDataAdapter class, which I discuss in the next chapter, this class maintains a connection to the database. Unlike the other classes we've examined, this class doesn't provide a constructor. Instead, you obtain a reference to an OracleDataReader by calling the ExecuteReader method on the OracleCommand object. The OracleDataReader class provides eight properties:

Depth: Indicates the nesting level of a row.

FetchSize: Indicates the size of the data reader cache.

FieldCount: Indicates the number of fields (columns) in the result set.

IsClosed: Indicates if the data reader is closed.

Item: Is used to retrieve the value of a column.

InitialLOBFetchSize: Specifies how much of a LOB (or large object) column is initially read by the data reader.

InitialLONGFetchSize: Specifies how much of a LONG column is initially read by the data reader.

RecordsAffected: Indicates the number of rows affected by an operation.

NOTE The FetchSize, InitialLOBFetchSize, and InitialLONGFetchSize properties aren't supported in the current version of the Microsoft provider.

The Depth Property

This property is a read-only integer property that always returns a value of 0. I've included it here for completeness; you won't be using this property.

The FetchSize Property

The initial value for this property is inherited from the `OracleCommand` object. The property behaves in the same way as the `FetchSize` property of the `OracleCommand` object. Listing 2-21 illustrates retrieving the value of this property from an `OracleDataReader` object.

Listing 2-21. *Retrieving the FetchSize Property from a Data Reader*

```
// create a command object
OracleCommand c1 = new OracleCommand();

// set OracleCommand properties such as commandtext...

// get the data reader object
OracleDataReader dataReader = c1.ExecuteReader();

// get the fetch size
// this is inherited from the OracleCommand object
long fetchSize = dataReader.FetchSize;
```

■**NOTE** This property isn't supported in the current version of the Microsoft provider.

The FieldCount Property

The `FieldCount` property is a read-only property that returns an integer. This property represents the total number of columns in the result set associated with this instance of the `OracleDataReader` class. In Listing 2-22, you get the number of fields that are in the result set, which is represented by the data reader object.

Listing 2-22. *Retrieving the FieldCount Property Value*

```
// create a command object
OracleCommand c1 = new OracleCommand();

// set OracleCommand properties...

// get a data reader
OracleDataReader dataReader = c1.ExecuteReader();

// get the number of fields in the result set
int fieldCount = dataReader.FieldCount();
```

The IsClosed Property

The `IsClosed` property is a read-only Boolean property and has a default value of true. This property, along with the `RecordsAffected` property, is available when the data reader object is either in a closed or an open state. Listing 2-23 illustrates how to perform conditional processing based on the value of this property.

Listing 2-23. *Using the IsClosed Property*

```
// create a command object
OracleCommand c1 = new OracleCommand();

// set OracleCommand properties…

// get a data reader
OracleDataReader dataReader = c1.ExecuteReader();

// if the dataReader is not closed...
if (!dataReader.IsClosed)
{
  // perform some process such as reading the data and displaying it
}
```

The Item Property

The Item property is a read-only property that returns the value of a column either by column index or column name. The object returned by the Item property is returned as a .NET Framework object rather than an Oracle Data Provider type. When you're using the column name as an indexer, the data provider attempts to perform a case-sensitive search for the supplied column name. If the case-sensitive search fails, the provider then attempts a case-insensitive search. This property is accessed via the "indexer" mechanism. Listing 2-24 illustrates how to access this property in a similar manner to that presented in the Get Employees sample.

Listing 2-24. *Accessing the Item Property*

```
// create a command object
  OracleCommand c1 = new OracleCommand();

// set OracleCommand properties…

// get a data reader
OracleDataReader dataReader = c1.ExecuteReader();

string ename = dataReader[0].ToString();
```

The InitialLOBFetchSize Property

Like the FetchSize property, the initial value for this property is inherited from the Oracle-Command object. This property specifies, in bytes or characters as appropriate, the amount of data initially fetched for a large object column. The maximum legal value for this property is 32K or 32,767 bytes or characters. You'll use this property in Chapter 6 when you explore Oracle's support for large objects.

■**NOTE** This property isn't supported in the current version of the Microsoft provider.

The InitialLONGFetchSize Property

The use of the LONG column data type is deprecated in favor of the more flexible LOB column types. Because the LONG column type has been deprecated, you won't utilize this property in this book.

■**NOTE** This property isn't supported in the current version of the Microsoft provider.

The RecordsAffected Property

This property, along with the IsClosed property, is available when the data reader object is in either a closed or an open state. The RecordsAffected property is a read-only integer type that always returns a value of –1 for SELECT statements like those you'll be using in this chapter.

The OracleDataReader Methods

You can think of the methods of the OracleDataReader class as either operating on the class object itself or on the data contained in the result set represented by the class object. That is, some methods, such as FetchSize, are related more to the data provider classes than to the data in the result set. This method doesn't change the data in a result set, for example. The methods that operate on the data typically begin with a prefix of Get, and as a result, I refer to these methods as the Get methods. Within the grouping of the Get methods, methods return data as an Oracle type or as a .NET Framework type. The GetOracle methods return data as an Oracle type, whereas the Get methods return data as a .NET Framework type. For example, the GetOracleDate method returns an OracleDate object. On the other hand, the GetDateTime method returns a .NET Framework DateTime value.

■**NOTE** The methods of the OracleDataReader class generally correspond to the Oracle column type. For a complete mapping of the Oracle database, the .NET Data Provider, and the .NET Framework type mappings, please consult the Oracle Data Provider for .NET documentation.

Implementing Data Retrieval Techniques

In this section, you'll pull together all the concepts, properties, methods, classes, and so on, that we've been discussing. The samples here go into greater depth and illustrate more features than the Get Employees sample you developed at the beginning of the chapter.

Using the TableDirect Method

Let's start with a simple example: a Windows Forms–based project that returns all the data from a specified table (the JOBS table in the HR schema), by setting the CommandType property of the OracleCommand object to a value of TableDirect.

You'll find the TableDirect method useful when you wish to simply display the data in a table. Using this method is essentially the same as issuing a select * from <table> SQL statement against the database. You don't have control over the order of the data as it is returned from the database using this method.

■**NOTE** The TableDirect method isn't supported in the current version of the Microsoft provider.

In this project, you use a list box control to display, in a read-only fashion, the complete data in the JOBS table. The OracleConnection object is created as a form-level variable and initialized in the form load event as with the first sample. In this sample, I illustrate the TableDirect method of retrieving data from the database.

In this sample, I use a non-data-bound control. In the next chapter, I investigate using a data-bound control and the OracleDataAdapter class. The form that I use in this sample is illustrated in Figure 2-8. This sample is the TableDirect sample in the code download.

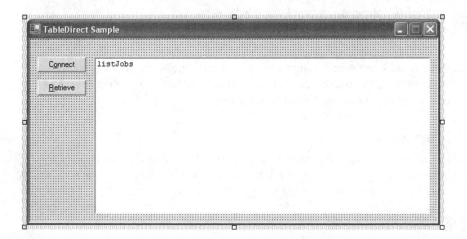

Figure 2-8. *The TableDirect sample form*

The structure of the JOBS table is illustrated in Listing 2-25.

Listing 2-25. *The JOBS Table Structure*

```
C:\>sqlplus hr@oranet

SQL*Plus: Release 10.1.0.2.0 - Production on Wed May 12 11:29:52 2004

Copyright (c) 1982, 2004, Oracle.  All rights reserved.

Enter password:

Connected to:
Oracle Database 10g Enterprise Edition Release 10.1.0.2.0 - Production
With the Partitioning, OLAP, and Data Mining options

SQL> desc jobs
 Name                                              Null?    Type
 ------------------------------------------------- -------- ------------
 JOB_ID                                            NOT NULL VARCHAR2(10)
 JOB_TITLE                                         NOT NULL VARCHAR2(35)
 MIN_SALARY                                                 NUMBER(6)
 MAX_SALARY                                                 NUMBER(6)

SQL>
```

■**NOTE** The default password for the HR schema is hr and the account is initially locked. I have unlocked the account and changed the password to demo as shown in the Appendix.

This sample uses the same mechanism to connect to the database as the first sample in this section, and it has a single point of interaction with the database. That single point of interaction occurs within the code for the Retrieve button.

The Connect Button Code

The code for the Connect button in this sample uses a variable of type `string` to assign the connection string value to the `ConnectionString` property of the `OracleConnection` rather than pass it to the connection object constructor. Listing 2-26 contains this code.

Listing 2-26. *The Connect Button Code*

```
private void btnConnect_Click(object sender, System.EventArgs e)
{
  // create a basic connection string using the sample
  // Oracle HR user the default password of hr has been changed
```

```
// to demo on my system
string connString = "User Id=hr; Password=demo; Data Source=oranet";

// only connect if we are not yet connected
if (oraConn.State != ConnectionState.Open)
{
  try
  {
    oraConn.ConnectionString = connString;

    oraConn.Open();

    MessageBox.Show(oraConn.ConnectionString, "Successful Connection");
  }
  catch (Exception ex)
  {
    MessageBox.Show(ex.Message,"Exception Caught");
  }
}
}
```

The Retrieve Button Code

All of the meaningful interaction with the database happens in the code for the Retrieve button. Because you are using the TableDirect method to retrieve data from the database, your interaction with the database is fairly brief and simple in nature. The code to retrieve the data in this fashion is contained in Listing 2-27.

Listing 2-27. *The Retrieve Button Code*

```
private void btnRetrieve_Click(object sender, System.EventArgs e)
{
  // create an OracleCommand object
  // we will use the TableDirect method
  // and the JOBS table
  OracleCommand cmdEmployees = new OracleCommand();
  cmdEmployees.Connection = oraConn;
  cmdEmployees.CommandType = CommandType.TableDirect;
  cmdEmployees.CommandText = "JOBS";

  // build a string that will make the header row
  // in the list box
  string headText = "Job".PadRight(12);
  headText += "Title".PadRight(37);
  headText += "Min Salary".PadRight(12);
  headText += "Max Salary".PadRight(12);

  // build a string that will separate the heading
```

```
    // row from the data
    string headSep = "==========  ";
    headSep += "=====================================  ";
    headSep += "==========  ";
    headSep += "==========  ";

    if (oraConn.State == ConnectionState.Open)
    {
      try
      {
        // get a data reader
        OracleDataReader dataReader = cmdEmployees.ExecuteReader();

        // add the heading and separator
        // listJobs is the list box on the form
        listJobs.Items.Add(headText);
        listJobs.Items.Add(headSep);

        // this string will represent our lines of data
        string textLine = "";

        // loop through the data reader
        // build a "line" of data
        // and add it to the list box
        while (dataReader.Read())
        {
          textLine = dataReader.GetString(0).PadRight(12);
          textLine += dataReader.GetString(1).PadRight(37);
          textLine += dataReader.GetDecimal(2).ToString().PadRight(12);
          textLine += dataReader.GetDecimal(3).ToString().PadRight(12);

          listJobs.Items.Add(textLine);
        }
      }
      catch (Exception ex)
      {
        MessageBox.Show(ex.Message,"Exception Caught");
      }
    }

    cmdEmployees.Dispose();
}
```

Your code here begins with the standard instantiation of your OracleCommand object and the setting of the basic properties. You set the CommandType property to CommandType.Table-Direct in order to enable the correct interpretation of the CommandText property. If you left the CommandType to default to CommandType.Text, you'd receive an error when you invoked the

ExecuteReader method. The CommandText property is simply assigned the name of the table you wish to use.

In order to provide a minimal header and a separator to give meaning to the data that you'll display in the list box, you create two string objects. Although you're hard-coding the values here, you'll work with a dynamic method to accomplish this later in the chapter.

You perform a simple check to verify that the database connection is in an open state by including the code to retrieve the data inside of a simple if construct. Your next step is to get a data reader from your command object. Once you have the data reader object, simply loop through the data and build a line of text to add to the list box. Figure 2-9 illustrates the form at run time.

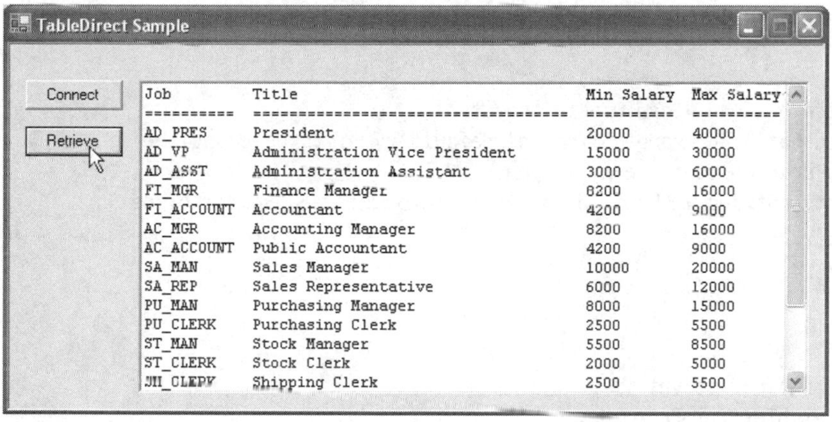

Figure 2-9. *The TableDirect form at run time*

Controlling the Number of Rows Returned

In this example, you build a console-based project that you can use to study the effect of altering the number of rows fetched during each round-trip to the database server. You do this by accessing the RowSize property and using simple multiplication to set the number of rows to be fetched. You use the sh user and the SALES table for this sample. As with the hr user, I've changed the password to demo and unlocked the account during the software installation. The SALES table is a larger table with around 1,000,000 records. The exact number of records in this table depends on the version of Oracle you're using. For example, in version 9i, there are 1,016,271 rows in the table, whereas in the 10g release, there are 918,843 rows on my system. Although it is possible to use the TableDirect method in this sample, you'll use a simple SQL statement instead. This makes the code more portable among the data providers and allows you a finer degree of control over the SQL statement you submit to the database.

The code for this sample includes a Main method and a single helper method. The helper method performs all the necessary work; it retrieves all the rows from the SALES table using different values for the FetchSize parameter. The sample code calls the helper function six times, passing a different value for the number of rows to fetch on each call. You bracket the fetch operation by a simple timing construct so you can determine the amount of time spent during this operation. You can download this sample (the FetchSize project) from this chapter's folder in the Downloads section of the Apress website (www.apress.com).

The Main Method Code

As with the other samples, the code in your Main method for this sample is responsible for creating a connection to the database. Once you've established the connection, this method simply calls your test method, passing a reference to the database connection and a value that determines the number of rows to fetch. The code for the Main method is detailed in Listing 2-28.

Listing 2-28. *The Main Method Code*

```
static void Main(string[] args)
{
  // instantiate the class to call private helper method
  // Class1 is the default class created by Visual Studio
  Class1 theClass = new Class1();

  OracleConnection oraConn = new OracleConnection();
  // the password has been changed from the default of hr to demo and the
  // account has been unlocked on my system
  oraConn.ConnectionString = "User Id=sh; Password=demo; Data Source=oranet";

  try
  {
    oraConn.Open();

    // fetch 10 rows per server trip
    theClass.doFetchTest(oraConn,10);

    // fetch 100 rows per server trip
    theClass.doFetchTest(oraConn,100);

    // fetch 1,000 rows per server trip
    theClass.doFetchTest(oraConn,1000);

    // fetch 10,000 rows per server trip
    theClass.doFetchTest(oraConn,10000);

    // fetch 100,000 rows per server trip
    theClass.doFetchTest(oraConn,100000);

    // fetch 1 row per server trip
    theClass.doFetchTest(oraConn, 1);
  }
  catch (Exception ex)
  {
    Console.WriteLine("Exception caught: {0}", ex.Message);
  }

  if (oraConn.State == ConnectionState.Open)
  {
```

```
    oraConn.Close();
  }
  oraConn.Dispose();
}
```

This code is straightforward in nature and creates the database connection, calls the test method, closes the database connection, and disposes of the database connection object. If an exception is thrown, a simple message appears in the console window. As I mentioned earlier, the test method performs the bulk of the work. In Chapter 10, you'll examine a method of creating trace files with timing information in them that allows you to see exactly where Oracle is spending its processing time.

The Test Method Code

Once the Main method has successfully created a connection to the database, this method is called in succession for a total of six executions. This method creates an OracleDataReader and an OracleCommand object and sets the properties as required. Once the code has retrieved a data reader from the command object, you're able to determine the value of the RowSize property. Your code then simply sets the number of rows to be fetched for each trip to the database by taking the product of the RowSize and the value of the numRows parameter. Although the data reader object inherits the value for the FetchSize property from the command object, you override it with the result of your number of rows calculation.

The code then reads all the data from the database server into the internal cache that the FetchSize property sized. You're using a no-op loop because you aren't particularly interested in the data itself in this sample. The total time it takes to perform the operation is calculated and informational text is written to the console window. You calculate the total time by getting the current date and time using the Now property of the DateTime object, performing the fetch operation (which is the operation to be timed), getting the current time again, and calculating the difference between the two times. You can then use the Console.WriteLine method to display the elapsed time for each test of the fetch operation. Listing 2-29 contains the code for the test method.

Listing 2-29. *The Test Method Code*

```
private void doFetchTest(OracleConnection con, long numRows)
{
  // create our command and reader objects to be
  // used in the test
  OracleCommand cmdFetchTest = new OracleCommand();
  OracleDataReader dataReader = null;

  // this will hold the time taken and the "i"
  // will simply be incremented as we read through
  // the result set
  DateTime dtStart;
  DateTime dtEnd;
  double totalSeconds = 0;
  long i = 0;
```

```csharp
    // Set the command object properties
    // the sales table is a "larger" table so we
    // will use it to test the fetch size impact
    // if using the Oracle Data Provider, this could well
    // be a TableDirect operation
    cmdFetchTest.Connection = con;
    cmdFetchTest.CommandText = "select * from sales";

    // ensure we have an open connection
    if (con.State == ConnectionState.Open)
    {
        dtStart = DateTime.Now;

        dataReader = cmdFetchTest.ExecuteReader();

        // once we have the data reader we can get the
        // row size from the command object
        // set the fetch size to the number of rows passed
        // as a parameter
        dataReader.FetchSize = cmdFetchTest.RowSize * numRows;

        // ensure we actually fetch from the result set
        // even though this is a sort of "no-op" loop
        while (dataReader.Read())
        {
            i++;
        }

        dtEnd = DateTime.Now;

        // calculate the total time it takes to fetch
        totalSeconds = dtEnd.Subtract(dtStart).TotalSeconds;

        dataReader.Close();

        // display some info about the time it takes to perform
        // the operation
        Console.WriteLine("Number of rows per fetch: {0}", numRows.ToString());
        Console.WriteLine("   Fetch time: {0} seconds.", totalSeconds.ToString());
        Console.WriteLine();

        // explicitly dispose...
        dataReader.Dispose();
        cmdFetchTest.Dispose();
    }
}
```

Running the FetchSize Sample

Because this sample is noninteractive, simply run the binary from a command-line prompt. Running the application from within the Visual Studio debugger is problematic because the console window is closed at the end of the application execution, and therefore, it's difficult to view its results. Listing 2-30 illustrates the application running and its output. Obviously, you'll see different numbers than those presented here when you run it on your own setup.

Listing 2-30. *The Fetch Time Results for Different Batch Sizes*

```
C:\My Projects\ProOraNet\Oracle\C#\Chapter02\FetchSize\bin\Debug>⏎
FetchSize.exe
Number of rows per fetch: 10
  Fetch time: 17.7054592 seconds.

Number of rows per fetch: 100
  Fetch time: 9.1431472 seconds.

Number of rows per fetch: 1000
  Fetch time: 8.1316928 seconds.

Number of rows per fetch: 10000
  Fetch time: 8.061592 seconds.

Number of rows per fetch: 100000
  Fetch time: 8.1016496 seconds.

Number of rows per fetch: 1
  Fetch time: 70.9920816 seconds.

C:\My Projects\ProOraNet\Oracle\C#\Chapter02\FetchSize\bin\Debug>
```

As you can see in the output of the application, when you use a fetch size greater than 100 rows, not much performance benefit is gained in terms of time. It is interesting to note that if you use a fetch size of 1 to save resources, the fetch time dramatically increases. In addition, the amount of memory you use isn't indicated by the output of the application itself. However, you can use the Windows Task Manager to monitor how much memory the application uses while it's executing to get a rough idea of how much memory the application is using. Table 2-1 summarizes the results, including memory usage. Again, your experiences will be different than mine, but the sample application should, in general, exhibit the same behavior.

■NOTE Don't infer that 100 is the ideal number of rows to be fetched for every result set. Each result set behaves differently depending on row size, among other factors.

Table 2-1. Fetch Size and Time vs. Memory Usage

Number of Rows	Time Spent Fetching	Memory Usage
10	17.71 secs	16,856K
100	9.14 secs	16,972K
1,000	8.13 secs	17,216K
10,000	8.06 secs	19,560K
100,000	8.10 secs	42,816K
1	70.99 secs	17,020K

As Table 2-1 illustrates, although the time to fetch is somewhat constant, the return in terms of memory consumption diminishes as the number of rows to fetch increases. Because this data represents a single user on a laptop, an application with hundreds (or more) of users on a server consumes much more memory because each and every connection uses that amount of memory. Having a system that has 1,000 clients with each asking for 42MB of server memory is probably not a good idea on many systems. As with many software construction decisions, you must determine a balance based on the context in which the activity takes place.

Bind Variables and the OracleParameter Class

You need to be aware of several major paradigms when you're working with the Oracle database; one of those is that the Oracle software is written with the expectation that you'll use bind variables in your code.

This issue is so significant with regards to the performance and scalability of your .NET Oracle code, that it's worth taking a little time to explore what bind variables are and why it's imperative that, by default, you use them in your .NET code.

Oracle Architecture: The Shared Pool

In Chapter 1, I briefly discussed the Oracle instance and indicated that certain memory structures reside inside of the instance. One of those memory structures is an important component referred to as the *Shared Pool*.

Multiple components are contained in the Shared Pool. One of the components is the *Library Cache*. Like the Shared Pool, the Library Cache contains multiple structures. The structure that you're most concerned with is known as the *Shared SQL Area*. As its name implies, the Shared SQL Area is a shared resource inside of the instance. It's an important structure because it allows Oracle to save memory and processing time.

The purpose of the Shared SQL Area is simple: it allows Oracle to reuse existing information. By being able to reuse existing information, Oracle doesn't have to re-create things such as execution plans and parse trees for every SQL statement presented to it. These are time-consuming operations, and any time you can eliminate or avoid them results in better execution times. In a multiuser application, it's likely that more than one user will want to execute the same SQL statement. If the SQL statement in question can be found in the Shared SQL Area, Oracle can efficiently use that copy of the SQL statement. If the SQL statement in question can't be located in the Shared SQL Area, Oracle must go through the process of parsing and generating an execution plan for that statement before placing it in the Shared SQL Area for potential reuse. This is where using bind variables becomes significant.

Using Bind Variables

As .NET developers, one of the simplest things we can do in our code to help enable Oracle to efficiently use the Shared SQL Area is to use *bind variables*. When you use bind variables, a SQL statement is presented to Oracle with certain pieces of information missing. In this situation, a placeholder (the bind variable) is used in place of an actual data value. When the Oracle server actually executes the SQL statement, the value of the bind variable is substituted into the placeholder location. The following simple code snippet illustrates what a SQL statement using a bind variable looks like compared to one that does not. In the snippet, the identifier :p_empno is a bind variable.

```
-- SQL with a literal
select ename from emp where empno = 7788;

-- The same SQL with a bind variable in place of the literal
select ename from emp where empno = :p_empno;
```

This is an incredibly simple thing to do, yet it can have a profound impact on the efficiency and scalability of a particular database. The reason this can have such an impact is that the act of using bind variables allows SQL statements to be much more readily shared among sessions. When you use bind variables, as far as Oracle is concerned, the SQL statements not only look the same, they *are* the same. When SQL statements are the same, Oracle has the ability to reuse them as discussed in the previous section.

This brings up an interesting point: If Oracle can reuse SQL statements that look the same, do you have to use bind variables when the values in a SQL statement never differ from execution to execution? The short answer is "No." If the values in a SQL statement absolutely remain identical from execution to execution, then using bind variables may not be necessary. It is when the Shared Pool becomes flooded with similar, but not identical, SQL statements that bind variables pay dividends. Of course, if you design an application without using bind variables because you expect SQL statements to be identical and then you find out that this assessment isn't true, you might want to redesign. It's much easier to employ bind variables from the beginning rather than retrofitting a deployed application.

You should be familiar with an important aspect of using bind variables. They may appear anywhere a text literal may appear in a SQL statement. A side effect of this is that you may not use bind variables for items such as table or column names. An easy way to think of this is to think of bind variables as placeholders for user input. Bind variables aren't limited to .NET code—you may also use them with stored procedures and functions on the server (see Chapter 5). I illustrate the proper use of bind variables in .NET code in this section.

The Traditional Approach

In many applications, a technique may be employed that appears to use bind variables, but in fact, it does not. This technique is the concatenation of values into a SQL statement at run time. The following pseudo code snippet shows an example of what code like this looks like:

```
for (int i = 0; i < 11; i++)
{
  sqlStatement = "select ename ";
  sqlStatement += "from emp ";
  sqlStatement += "where enum = " + i.toString();

  <submit and process statement>
}
```

The problem with this approach, of course, is that although the value of i isn't directly hard-coded into the SQL statement, the binding is all done before the statement is submitted to Oracle. As a result, Oracle sees only the completed statement. In this scenario, each completed statement looks different to Oracle because the value in the where clause changes as the code iterates through the loop.

The correct approach is to use the OracleParameter class with bind variables so that the binding occurs on the database side during statement processing.

Transaction Processing vs. Data Warehouse

It used to be that databases could traditionally be classified into two categories:

- Online Transaction Processing (OLTP)

- Data Warehouse (DW) or Decision Support Systems (DSS)

Because systems are growing and becoming more complex and consolidated, many systems are now mixed workload systems. However, it's still possible to classify databases as generally DW/DSS or OLTP in nature, though the line is often blurred. For the databases that are truly in the middle, you need to apply the appropriate coding techniques to the process at hand.

In general, an OLTP system is characterized by many short-duration transactions, whereas a DW or DSS system is characterized by a long runtime and fewer transactions. In OLTP systems, the chief concern may be stated as the maximum number of transactions per unit of time. In contrast, the chief concern of a DW system may be the maximum data throughput per unit of time. Transactions of less than a second would be commonplace in an OLTP system. On the other end of the spectrum, DW transactions often last minutes or hours.

Because the primary characteristics and chief concerns of these two types of systems are somewhat disparate, the subject of bind variables can often be confusing. If the system with which you are working is clearly an OLTP system, bind variables are a necessity. However, if the system is more of a pure DW system, using bind variables can actually hinder performance. This seems strange, but when you consider that the use of bind variables is all about shaving a percentage of time off an operation and resource preservation, it can make a little more sense.

In an OLTP environment, being able to reuse SQL statements can shave a significant percentage of time. For example, if a statement takes .05 seconds to process, saving only .01 of a second represents a 20-percent saving in units of time. In a DW environment, in contrast, if a statement takes 90 minutes to run, saving .01 of a second doesn't amount to a great advantage.

This is one of those areas where knowledge sharing between the development team and the database administration team is invaluable. By correctly analyzing and designing the system as a whole, you can make the right choices from the beginning.

The OracleParameter Project

In this project, you work with the basic concepts that you explored earlier in the chapter. Specifically, you look at using bind variables via the OracleParameter class and using the OracleDbType to inform the data provider directly of what type of parameters you're using. Using the OracleDbType is not strictly necessary because the data provider can derive the type from the actual parameter value. However, explicitly specifying the parameter type eliminates any possible confusion as to the parameter type. This project is implemented as a simple Windows form. The completed form in the design environment is depicted in Figure 2-10.

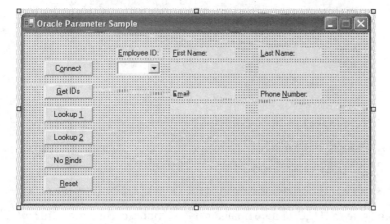

Figure 2-10. *The OracleParameter sample form*

For this sample, you use the hr user, which is an Oracle-supplied sample user. This user is created and the schema populated by following the installation process in the Appendix. If you need to create this user, consult the Oracle documentation or your database administrator.

You'll use the EMPLOYEES table to retrieve and display basic information based on the EMPLOYEE_ID, the FIRST_NAME, and the LAST_NAME columns. Listing 2-31 provides the structure of the EMPLOYEES table.

Listing 2-31. *The EMPLOYEES Table Structure*

```
C:\>sqlplus hr@oranet

SQL*Plus: Release 10.1.0.2.0 - Production on Tue May 11 10:54:50 2004
```

Enter password:

Connected to:
Oracle Database 10g Enterprise Edition Release 10.1.0.2.0 - Production
With the Partitioning, OLAP, and Data Mining options

```
SQL> desc employees
 Name                                                   Null?    Type
 ------------------------------------------------------ -------- -------------
 EMPLOYEE_ID                                            NOT NULL NUMBER(6)
 FIRST_NAME                                                      VARCHAR2(20)
 LAST_NAME                                              NOT NULL VARCHAR2(25)
 EMAIL                                                  NOT NULL VARCHAR2(25)
 PHONE_NUMBER                                                    VARCHAR2(20)
 HIRE_DATE                                              NOT NULL DATE
 JOB_ID                                                 NOT NULL VARCHAR2(10)
 SALARY                                                          NUMBER(8,2)
 COMMISSION_PCT                                                  NUMBER(2,2)
 MANAGER_ID                                                      NUMBER(6)
 DEPARTMENT_ID                                                   NUMBER(4)

SQL>
```

This sample provides five points of interaction with the database:

The Connect button: Connects to the database using the technique of creating a string variable and assigning the variable to the ConnectionString property.

The Get IDs button: Issues a SELECT statement against the database to retrieve the data.

The Lookup 1 button: Issues a SELECT statement against the database using the bind by position method.

The Lookup 2 button: Issues a SELECT statement against the database using the bind by name method.

The No Binds button: Issues a SELECT statement against the database using no bind variables.

There is a form-level variable of type OracleConnection. The variable is declared as follows:

```
private OracleConnection oraConn;
```

It is initialized in the form load event as follows:

```
oraConn = new OracleConnection();
```

All other variables are declared inside of their respective procedures. The five points of interaction with the database are represented by the button controls on the form. The Reset button
simply clears the Label controls and deselects any value in the Employee ID drop-down list

control. Now, you'll examine the functionality each button provides and then run the sample. After running the sample, you'll examine the results in SQL*Plus.

The Connect Button

Not surprisingly, this button creates your connection to the database. Listing 2-32 contains the code that accomplishes this task.

Listing 2-32. *The Connect Button Code*

```
private void btnConnect_Click(object sender, System.EventArgs e)
{
  // create a basic connection string using the sample
  // Oracle HR user
  // the password has been changed from hr to demo and the account unlocked
  string connString = "User Id=hr; Password=demo; Data Source=oranet";

  // only connect if we are not yet connected
  if (oraConn.State != ConnectionState.Open)
  {
    try
    {
      oraConn.ConnectionString = connString;

      oraConn.Open();

      MessageBox.Show(oraConn.ConnectionString, "Successful Connection");
    }
    catch (Exception ex)
    {
      MessageBox.Show(ex.Message,"Exception Caught");
    }
  }
}
```

There is nothing extravagant about this code. It simply creates a connection to the database using default attribute values and your standard TNS alias. After you've established a connection, a message box displays the connection string for your connection. In the event that an exception is thrown, you simply catch it and display a MessageBox indicating what exception occurred.

The Get IDs Button

Your first substantive activity with the database in your sample occurs within the code for the Get IDs button. The code behind this button creates an OracleCommand object and an Oracle-DataReader object. You then use these two objects to retrieve the employee_id for each row in the EMPLOYEES table. Rather than working with the Employee ID drop-down list control as a data-bound control, you simply load it with the values from the database. The code for the Get IDs button is listed in Listing 2-33.

Listing 2-33. *The Get IDs Button Code*

```
private void btnGetIDs_Click(object sender, System.EventArgs e)
{
  // get the employee ids from the database
  // we are not using the drop-down list control
  // as a databound control
  OracleCommand cmdEmpId = new OracleCommand();
  cmdEmpId.CommandText = "select employee_id from employees order by employee_id";
  cmdEmpId.Connection = oraConn;

  try
  {
    // get a data reader
    OracleDataReader dataReader = cmdEmpId.ExecuteReader();

    // simply iterate the result set and add
    // the values to the drop-down list
    while (dataReader.Read())
    {
      // cbEmpIds is the Employee ID combo box on the form
      cbEmpIds.Items.Add(dataReader.GetOracleDecimal(0));
    }

    dataReader.Dispose();
  }
  catch (Exception ex)
  {
    MessageBox.Show(ex.Message,"Exception Caught");
  }
  finally
  {
    cmdEmpId.Dispose();
  }
}
```

In this code, you instantiate an OracleCommand object and set the CommandText property to a simple SQL statement that retrieves all the employee_id values from the database. You then loop through the values and add them to the Items collection of the drop-down list control. Since you haven't set any properties other than the Connection and the CommandText, you're using the default values as described earlier in the chapter.

The Lookup 1 Button

Once the Employee ID drop-down list control has been populated with the values from the database, you can retrieve some additional information about each employee. In the code for the Lookup 1 button, you retrieve the first_name and last_name from the EMPLOYEES table using the employee_id. However, you pass the value to the database as a bind variable. Listing 2-34 contains the code for this button.

Listing 2-34. *The Lookup 1 Button Code*

```
private void btnLookup1_Click(object sender, System.EventArgs e)
{
  // get the selected item in the Employee ID
  // drop-down list
  // cbEmpIds is the combo box on the form
  object selectedItem = cbEmpIds.SelectedItem;

  if (selectedItem != null)
  {
    // get the employee name based on the employee id
    // we will pass the employee id as a bind variable
    OracleCommand cmdEmpName = new OracleCommand();

    // the :p_id is our bind variable placeholder
    cmdEmpName.CommandText = "select first_name, last_name from employees where
    employee_id = :p_id";

    // set the connection property
    cmdEmpName.Connection = oraConn;

    // create a new parameter object
    // we will use this to pass the value of the
    // employee_id to the database
    OracleParameter p_id = new OracleParameter();

    // here we are setting the OracleDbType
    // we could set this as DbType as well and
    // the Oracle provider will infer the correct
    // OracleDbType
    // by setting the type, we can avoid any confusion
    // regarding the parameter type
    p_id.OracleDbType = OracleDbType.Decimal;
    p_id.Value = Convert.ToDecimal(selectedItem.ToString());

    // add our parameter to the parameter collection
    // for the command object
    cmdEmpName.Parameters.Add(p_id);

    // get our data reader
    OracleDataReader dataReader = cmdEmpName.ExecuteReader();

    // get the results - our query will only return 1 row
    // since we are using the primary key
    if (dataReader.Read())
    {
      // lblFirstName and lblLastName are labels on the form
```

```
      lblFirstName.Text = dataReader.GetString(0);
      lblLastName.Text = dataReader.GetString(1);
    }

    dataReader.Close();

    p_id.Dispose();
    dataReader.Dispose();
    cmdEmpName.Dispose();
  }
}
```

Your code begins by verifying that you have a selected item in the drop-down list control and instantiating an OracleCommand object. You then set the CommandText and Connection properties. Your CommandText includes a bind variable placeholder indicated by the : preceding the p_id variable. This is where the parameter value is substituted into the SQL statement. The SQL statement simply selects the first_name and last_name values for a given employee_id. Because the employee_id is the primary key for the EMPLOYEES table, you won't retrieve more than one row from the database using this query.

After creating a command object, you instantiate an OracleParameter object named p_id. You aren't required to name the variable the same as the placeholder in the SQL statement. However, if you use the same name, it can serve to identify the relationship readily when you visually inspect the code. As illustrated in Listing 2-32, the employee_id column has the NUMBER data type. Therefore, you set the OracleDbType property to OracleDbType.Decimal. You assign the employee_id selected in the drop-down list control to the parameter Value property. Once you've set all the properties on the OracleParameter object, add the parameter to the parameter collection of the command object. At this point, you simply get an OracleDataReader from the command object and assign the values retrieved from the database to the label controls on the form.

The Lookup 2 Button

The code for the Lookup 2 button is similar to that of the Lookup 1 button. The primary differences in this code is that you're passing two bind variables rather than a single variable, and you're using the BindByName mechanism rather than binding by position, which is the default. Listing 2-35 contains the code you use to perform this functionality.

Listing 2-35. *The Lookup 2 Button Code*

```
private void btnLookup2_Click(object sender, System.EventArgs e)
{
  // get the employee email and phone based on the
  // first name and last name
  // there are no duplicate first name / last name
  // combinations in the table
  // we will pass the first name and last name as
  // bind variables using BindByName
  OracleCommand cmdEmpInfo = new OracleCommand();
```

```
// the :p_last and :p_first are our bind variable placeholders
cmdEmpInfo.CommandText = "select email, phone_number from employees
where first_name = :p_first and last_name = :p_last";

cmdEmpInfo.Connection = oraConn;

// we will use bind by name here
cmdEmpInfo.BindByName = true;

OracleParameter p1 = new OracleParameter();
OracleParameter p2 = new OracleParameter();

// the ParameterName value is what is used when
// binding by name, not the name of the variable
// in the code
// notice the ":" is not included as part of the
// parameter name
p1.ParameterName = "p_first";
p2.ParameterName = "p_last";

// lblFirstName and lblLastName are labels on the form
p1.Value = lblFirstName.Text;
p2.Value = lblLastName.Text;

// add our parameters to the parameter collection
// for the command object
// we will add them in "reverse" order since we are
// binding by name and not position
cmdEmpInfo.Parameters.Add(p2);
cmdEmpInfo.Parameters.Add(p1);

// get our data reader
OracleDataReader dataReader = cmdEmpInfo.ExecuteReader();

// get the results - our query will only return 1 row
// since we are using known unique values for the first
// and last names
if (dataReader.Read())
{
  // lblEmailText and lblPhoneText are labels on the form
  lblEmailText.Text = dataReader.GetString(0);
  lblPhoneText.Text = dataReader.GetString(1);
}

dataReader.Close();

p1.Dispose();
```

```
    p2.Dispose();
    dataReader.Dispose();
    cmdEmpInfo.Dispose();
}
```

This code uses the same basic process as the code for the Lookup 1 button. Rather than using the employee_id as you did in the code for the Lookup 1 button, you use the values from the first_name and last_name labels to identify your employee in the table. This is a safe operation for the data supplied in the table because no duplicate values are in the table. Because you're using two bind variables, you're able to use the BindByName property. You're able to use BindByName with a single variable; however, it doesn't make much sense because only a single position needs to be bound. The idea with BindByName is that the parameters don't need to be added to the collection in the same order because they are specified by the placeholders in the SQL statement. With only a single value, it's difficult not to get the order correct.

You've named your parameter values with more generic names in this sample as a way to illustrate that they don't need to be named the same as the placeholder values. In addition, you've added the parameters to the parameter collection in an order different from that which was used by the placeholders. This illustrates that the order is irrelevant when you use the BindByName feature. As mentioned earlier in the chapter, this feature isn't available with the Microsoft provider.

The No Binds Button

In contrast to the code in the previous two sections, the code in this section doesn't use bind variables. This illustrates what was termed the traditional approach earlier. In addition, as noted in Listing 2-36, this code carries out both of the functions performed by the Lookup 1 and Lookup 2 buttons.

Listing 2-36. *The No Binds Button Code*

```
private void btnNoBinds_Click(object sender, System.EventArgs e)
{
// this illustrates the "traditional" approach
// that does not use bind variables

// cbEmpIds is combo box on the form
object selectedItem = cbEmpIds.SelectedItem;

if (selectedItem != null)
{
  OracleCommand cmdNoBinds = new OracleCommand();
  cmdNoBinds.Connection = oraConn;
  OracleDataReader dataReader;

  cmdNoBinds.CommandText = "select first_name, last_name from employees
  where employee_id = " + selectedItem.ToString();

  // get our data reader
```

```
dataReader = cmdNoBinds.ExecuteReader();

// get the results - our query will only return 1 row
// since we are using the primary key
if (dataReader.Read())
{
  // lblFirstName and lblLastName are labels on the form
  lblFirstName.Text = dataReader.GetString(0);
  lblLastName.Text = dataReader.GetString(1);
}

dataReader.Close();

// get the data that Lookup 2 performed above
// lblFirstName and lblLastName are labels on the form
cmdNoBinds.CommandText = "select email, phone_number from employees
 where first_name = '" + lblFirstName.Text + "' and last_name = '" +
 lblLastName.Text +"'";

// get our data reader
dataReader = cmdNoBinds.ExecuteReader();

// get the results - our query will only return 1 row
// since we are using known unique values for the first
// and last names
if (dataReader.Read())
{
  // lblEmailText and lblPhoneText are labels on the form
  lblEmailText.Text = dataReader.GetString(0);
  lblPhoneText.Text = dataReader.GetString(1);
}

dataReader.Close();
dataReader.Dispose();
cmdNoBinds.Dispose();
}
```

In this code, you can clearly see that you aren't using bind variables and are, instead, concatenating the values directly into the SQL statements. You'll examine the effects this has after you run the sample code a few times.

Running the OracleParameter Project

Now that you have a good idea of what the code in this sample project does, you'll run it a few times and look at the results in SQL*Plus. You can run it either from the debugging environment, from within Visual Studio, or simply by executing the binary directly. Figure 2-11 illustrates what the form looks like after you start the application.

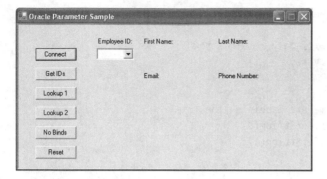

Figure 2-11. *The OracleParameter form initial state*

The following steps take you through a sample running of the application.

1. Click the Connect button to create the connection to your standard TNS alias as discussed in the code analysis. The results of this are illustrated in Figure 2-12.

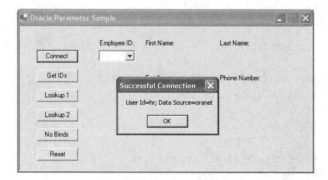

Figure 2-12. *The successful connection message*

2. After you've successfully established the database connection, click the Get IDs button to populate the Employee ID drop-down list. Figure 2-13 illustrates the results of this.

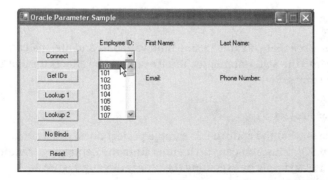

Figure 2-13. *The populated Employee ID drop-down list*

3. Select an Employee ID in the list and click the Lookup 1 button. Figure 2-14 illustrates the results of doing this for employee #100.

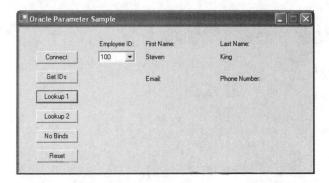

Figure 2-14. *The Lookup 1 results for employee #100*

4. In order to retrieve the first and last names, click the Lookup 2 button. The results should resemble those in Figure 2-15.

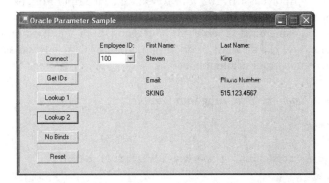

Figure 2-15. *The Lookup 2 results for employee #100*

5. In order to reset the form to a clean state, click the Reset button. This is illustrated by Figure 2-16.

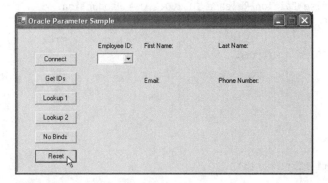

Figure 2-16. *The results of the Reset button*

6. Select employee #100 in the Employee ID drop-down list and click the No Binds button to perform the operations with no bind variables. The results of this are illustrated in Figure 2-17.

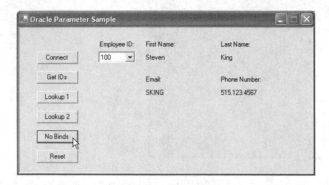

Figure 2-17. *Executing the No Binds code*

At this point, you should execute each of the operations just discussed a couple of times. I also executed each operation for employees 101, 102, and 103 so that each operation executed four times. After you have executed the operations a few times, close the form.

To see the difference between using bind variables and not using them, you'll examine the v$sql view in SQL*Plus. This view, like all views, is documented in the Oracle Database Reference. Listing 2-37 illustrates this process and the results.

Listing 2-37. *Examining the v$sql View After Executing Your Sample*

```
C:\>sqlplus oranetadmin@oranet

SQL*Plus: Release 10.1.0.2.0 - Production on Mon May 10 22:18:23 2004

Copyright (c) 1982, 2004, Oracle.  All rights reserved.

Enter password:

Connected to:
Oracle Database 10g Enterprise Edition Release 10.1.0.2.0 - Production
With the Partitioning, OLAP, and Data Mining options

SQL> col sql_text format a70 word_wrapped
SQL> select
  2    sql_text,
  3    executions
  4  from
  5    v$sql
  6  where
  7    sql_text like 'select first_name%'
  8  or
```

```
 9    sql_text like 'select email%'
10  order by
11    executions,
12    sql_text;
```

```
SQL_TEXT                                                              EXECUTIONS
---------------------------------------------------------------- ----------
select email , phone_number  from employees where  first_name =            1
'Alexander' and last_name = 'Hunold'

select email , phone_number  from employees where  first_name = 'Lex'      1
and last_name = 'De Haan'

select email , phone_number  from employees where  first_name =            1
'Neena' and last_name = 'Kochhar'

select email , phone_number  from employees where  first_name =            1
'Steven' and last_name = 'King'

select first_name , last_name  from employees where  employee_id = 100     1


select first_name , last_name  from employees where  employee_id = 101     1


select first_name , last_name  from employees where  employee_id = 102     1


select first_name , last_name  from employees where  employee_id = 103     1


select email , phone_number  from employees where  first_name =            4
:p_first and last_name = :p_last

select first_name , last_name  from employees where  employee_id =         4
:p_id


10 rows selected.

SQL>
```

After I connected via SQL*Plus as the administrative user, I issued the query in Listing 2-38 to observe the results of the sample code. As I expected, for the operations performed by the No Binds button, each SQL statement appears with the literal text and has an EXECUTIONS value of 1. This makes sense because Oracle can't reuse the SQL statement—each statement is distinct.

On the other hand, you can clearly see that Oracle was able to reuse the statements that I created with bind variables. Remember, each of my bind variable statements was executed four times. By using bind variables, I allow Oracle to more efficiently process my statements. In this simple example, I reduced the number of distinct SQL statements by using binds, and I also allowed Oracle to reuse the statements.

Using the DataReader Properties

This project is another console-based application that demonstrates how to use the FieldCount property, the IsDBNull method, and the Item access method. The application that you develop for your final sample works as a table dumper. Because you don't know the structure of the table to which the program may be asked to dump this code, you'll need to convert each column value to a string prior to displaying it in the console window. This sample program does not manipulate the data beyond that.

For this application, this is an acceptable method to employ. On the other hand, for an application that accepts user input, you need to use the correct data type for each input value. For example, you don't use a string to store a date value, don't store date data in a character column, and so forth. This application only works correctly with the basic database types; it doesn't work with LOB columns or XML types for example. Listing 2-38 contains the single method that you use to accomplish this task. You can download this project (DataReader) from this chapter's folder in the Downloads section of the Apress website (www.apress.com).

Listing 2-38. *The Main Method Code*

```
static void Main(string[] args)
{
  if (args.Length != 4)
  {
    Console.WriteLine("Incorrect number of command line parameters.");

    return;
  }

  // Build a connect string based on the command-line parameters
  string connString = "User Id=" + args[0].ToString() + ";";
  connString += "Password=" + args[1].ToString() + ";";
  connString += "Data Source=" + args[2].ToString();

  OracleConnection oraConn = new OracleConnection();
  oraConn.ConnectionString = connString;

  // build the sql statement based on the command-line parameter
  // we can't use a bind variable here
  string sqlStatement = "select * from " + args[3].ToString();

  // the number of fields in the result set
  int fieldCount = 0;
```

```csharp
// used in our counter loops
int i = 0;

try
{
  oraConn.Open();
}
catch (Exception ex)
{
  Console.WriteLine("Exception caught {0}", ex.Message);
}

if (oraConn.State == ConnectionState.Open)
{
  try
  {
    // create the command object
    OracleCommand cmdSQL = new OracleCommand(sqlStatement,oraConn);

    // get a data reader
    OracleDataReader dataReader = cmdSQL.ExecuteReader();

    // the number of fields in the result set
    fieldCount = dataReader.FieldCount;

    // output a comma separated header
    for (i = 0; i < fieldCount; i++)
    {
      Console.Write(dataReader.GetName(i));

      if (i < fieldCount - 1)
      {
        Console.Write(",");
      }
    }

    Console.WriteLine();

    // output a comma separated "line" of data
    while (dataReader.Read())
    {
      for (i = 0; i < fieldCount; i++)
      {
        // check if the data is null or not
        if (!dataReader.IsDBNull(i))
        {
          // not null, so write value
```

```
                        // we use the "item" method by
                        // specifying the index rather than
                        // using a typed accessor
                        Console.Write(dataReader[i].ToString());
                    }
                    else
                    {
                        // null value
                        Console.Write("(null)");
                    }

                    if (i < fieldCount - 1)
                    {
                        Console.Write(",");
                    }
                }

                Console.WriteLine();
            }
        }
        catch (Exception ex)
        {
            Console.WriteLine("Exception caught {0}", ex.Message);
        }
    }

    if (oraConn.State == ConnectionState.Open)
    {
        oraConn.Close();
    }

    oraConn.Dispose();
}
```

As you can see, this code is fairly basic in its error handling and capabilities. However, it demonstrates the ease with which a result set can be generically processed. The FieldCount property, IsDBNull method, and the Item access method make this simple to accomplish. The inline comments in the code indicate the important pieces of information. Listing 2-39 illustrates a sample execution of the application to create a comma-separated dump of the JOBS table you used earlier.

Listing 2-39. *Running the DataReader Project*

```
C:\My Projects\ProOraNet\Oracle\C#\Chapter02\DataReader\bin\Debug>↲
DataReader.exe hr demo oranet jobs
```

```
JOB_ID,JOB_TITLE,MIN_SALARY,MAX_SALARY
AD_PRES,President,20000,40000
AD_VP,Administration Vice President,15000,30000
AD_ASST,Administration Assistant,3000,6000
FI_MGR,Finance Manager,8200,16000
FI_ACCOUNT,Accountant,4200,9000
AC_MGR,Accounting Manager,8200,16000
AC_ACCOUNT,Public Accountant,4200,9000
SA_MAN,Sales Manager,10000,20000
SA_REP,Sales Representative,6000,12000
PU_MAN,Purchasing Manager,8000,15000
PU_CLERK,Purchasing Clerk,2500,5500
ST_MAN,Stock Manager,5500,8500
ST_CLERK,Stock Clerk,2000,5000
SH_CLERK,Shipping Clerk,2500,5500
IT_PROG,Programmer,4000,10000
MK_MAN,Marketing Manager,9000,15000
MK_REP,Marketing Representative,4000,9000
HR_REP,Human Resources Representative,4000,9000
PR_REP,Public Relations Representative,4500,10500

C:\My Projects\ProOraNet\Oracle\C#\Chapter02\DataReader\bin\Debug>
```

Using Visual Studio and the Microsoft Data Provider

For the final example in this chapter, you're going to switch to the Microsoft data provider, and you're going to use the Visual Studio design environment to create your objects and set your properties. You can access this project (MSProvider) in this chapter's folder of the Downloads section of the Apress website (www.apress.com).

You'll implement the same sample you did in the "Bind Variables and the OracleParameter Class" section. This allows me to highlight the slight differences between the two providers. For example, the BindByName property isn't directly exposed by the current Microsoft data provider, so the bindings in this sample are positional rather than by name (as was the case for the Lookup 2 button in the ODP.NET version).

■NOTE By setting the ParameterName property of an OracleParameter object in the Microsoft provider, you can implicitly use bind by name functionality.

Also, I'll be able to point out the slight code differences that arise from using the visual design tools to set most of your properties and to create your objects rather than handcrafting them.

As with the `OracleParameter` sample earlier, here I break the tasks down into a series of steps.

1. First, create a new Windows Forms project and create a form like the one you used in the ODP.NET sample (see Figure 2-10).

   Figure 2-18 illustrates what the form should look like.

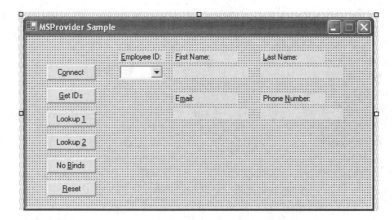

Figure 2-18. *The MSProvider form*

2. Once you've created the form, drag an `OracleConnection` from the toolbox to the form.

   This is illustrated in Figure 2-19. As you can see, I named the connection oraConn.

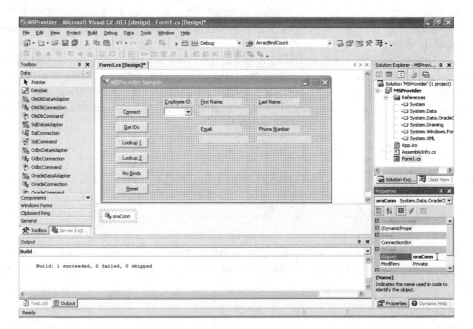

Figure 2-19. *Creating the OracleConnection object on the form*

3. To create a connection string for the connection object, you can either

   - Type it directly into the `ConnectionString` property in the Properties window, or

   - Use a wizard to create it for you.

   Use the wizard approach here because you've already seen how to type it in yourself in the console applications you have developed in this chapter.

4. To create your connection string using the wizard, select the `oraConn` connection object.

5. Once you've selected it, drop down the ConnectionString property window as illustrated in Figure 2-20.

Figure 2-20. *Starting the ConnectionString wizard*

6. Select <New Connection…> in the ConnectionString property window; the Data Link Properties window displays.

7. In the Data Link Properties window, specify the hr user, the TNS alias, and the password.

   In this case, creating a new connection is identical to the process you used in the "Server Explorer Database Connection" section of Chapter 1. When I did this, I elected to include the password because this is a simple demo.

Once you've finished creating the connection, the connection string appears in the ConnectionString property window.

Now that you have identified and created the connection, you'll create the command objects the sample application uses and set the properties of these objects.

1. First, create the command object that you'll use to retrieve the `EMPLOYEE_ID` data from the database.

2. Now drag an `OracleCommand` object from the toolbox to the form. (I've named the command object cmdGetIDs.)

3. To create the SQL statement to serve as the `CommandText` property, first assign a connection to the command object.

This process is illustrated in Figure 2-21.

Figure 2-21. *Assigning a connection to the command object*

4. Now click the ellipses (…) in the CommandText property window.

Doing so launches the Query Builder wizard. The Query Builder begins by presenting the Add Table dialog, as shown in Figure 2-22.

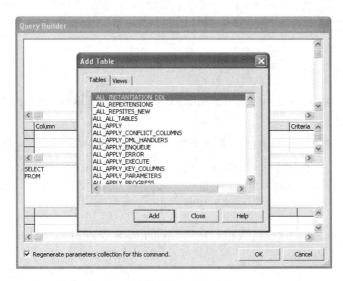

Figure 2-22. *The Query Builder wizard*

■**NOTE** In order to use the Query Builder visual tool inside of Visual Studio to graphically create your SQL statements, you need to use a separate command object for each action. This means you need to create five command objects. This isn't great for resource usage; however, if you wish to use the Visual Studio graphical designer tools, this is a side effect.

---

5. Select the EMPLOYEES table in the list and click add as illustrated in Figure 2-23.

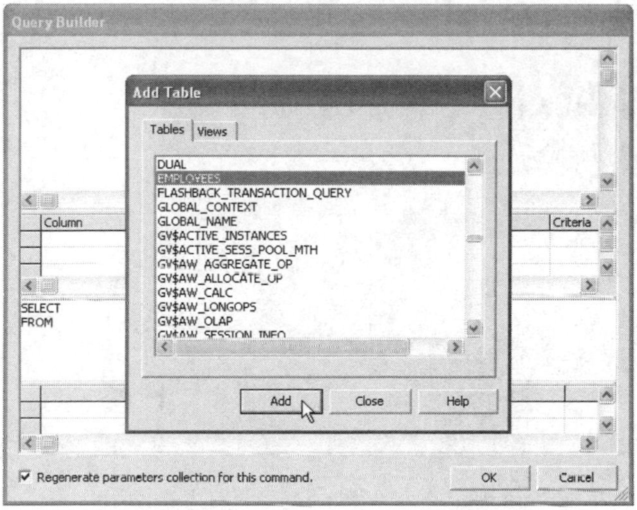

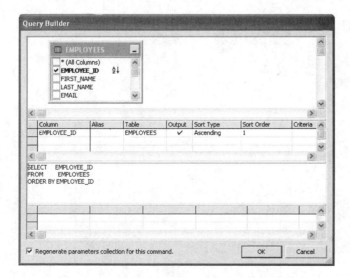

Figure 2-23. *Adding the EMPLOYEES table to the Query Builder*

6. Once you've added the EMPLOYEES table, click the Close button to dismiss the Add Table dialog.

7. Next, select the EMPLOYEE_ID column and set the Sort Order attribute to 1 (see Figure 2-24).

8. Click the OK button when you're done to return to the form designer.

Figure 2-24. *Setting the properties in the Query Builder*

9. Add four additional `OracleCommand` objects to the form and set the connection property to oraConn as you did with the cmdGetIDs command object earlier (see Figure 2-25).

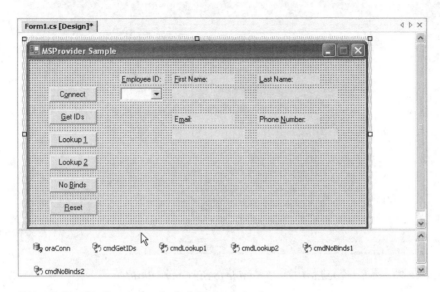

Figure 2-25. *The five command objects on the form*

10. Set the `CommandText` property for the `cmdLookup1` command object as illustrated in Figure 2-26. Click the ellipses (...) in the `CommandText` property in the Properties Window to start the Query Builder wizard. Pay particular attention to how the parameter is specified in the `Criteria` column.

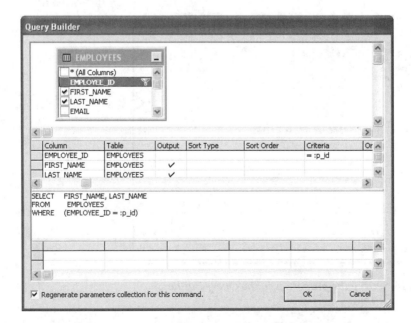

Figure 2-26. *Specifying the cmdLookup1 properties*

11. Click the OK button to close the Query Builder.

12. Click the ellipses (…) in the Parameters property window. In Figure 2-27, you can see how the data provider derived the properties.

Figure 2-27. The parameter properties for the cmdLookup1 command object

13. Click Cancel when you're done viewing the parameter properties.

The process for configuring the properties for cmdLookup2 is illustrated in Figure 2-28 and is described in the following steps:

1. Add the two bind variables to be used in the Criteria column.

2. check the Output column for the EMAIL and PHONE_NUMBER columns to indicate that these columns should be displayed in the query output.

3. Make sure you uncheck the Output column for the FIRST_NAME and LAST_NAME columns because you want to use these columns in the "where clause" of the SQL statement but you don't want to display their values.

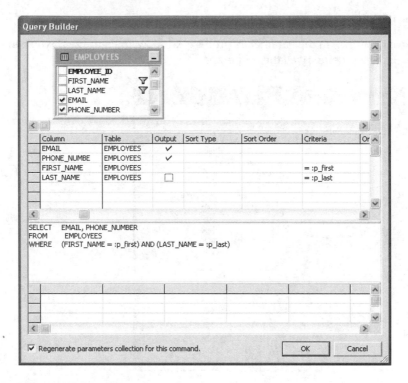

Figure 2-28. *Specifying the cmdLookup2 properties*

At this point, you've completed your visual setup for the sample.

■NOTE Since the CommandText for the two NoBinds command objects involves concatenating values at run time, you do not specify that property at this time.

The Connect Button Code

This code (see Listing 2-40) operates in very much the same manner as the code using the Oracle Data Provider.

Listing 2-40. *The Connect Button Code*

```
private void btnConnect_Click(object sender, System.EventArgs e)
{
  if (oraConn.State != ConnectionState.Open)
  {
    try
    {
      oraConn.Open();
```

```
        MessageBox.Show(oraConn.ConnectionString, "Successful Connection");
      }
      catch (Exception ex)
      {
        MessageBox.Show(ex.Message,"Exception Caught");
      }
    }
}
```

As you can see here, the code only has to perform an Open method call because the ConnectionString property was set at design time using the visual designer.

The Get IDs Button Code

Like the code for the Connect button, this code is the same as the code from the equivalent hand-built sample, except that the creation of the OracleCommand object and the setting of its properties have been removed. Listing 2-41 contains the code for this task.

Listing 2-41. *The Get IDs Button Code*

```
private void btnGetIDs_Click(object sender, System.EventArgs e)
{
  try
  {
    // get a data reader
    OracleDataReader dataReader = cmdGetIDs.ExecuteReader();

    // simply iterate the result set and add
    // the values to the drop down list
    while (dataReader.Read())
    {
      // cbEmpIds is combo box on form
      cbEmpIds.Items.Add(dataReader.GetDecimal(0));
    }
  }
  catch (Exception ex)
  {
    MessageBox.Show(ex.Message,"Exception Caught");
  }
}
```

The Lookup 1 Button Code

The code for the Lookup 1 button is contained in Listing 2-42. As with the other code in this section, this code omits the object creation and parameter setting code.

Listing 2-42. *The Lookup 1 Button Code*

```
private void btnLookup1_Click(object sender, System.EventArgs e)
{
  // cbEmpIds is combo box on form
  object selectedItem = cbEmpIds.SelectedItem;

  if (selectedItem != null)
  {
    // we need to set the parameter value
    cmdLookup1.Parameters[0].Value = Convert.ToDecimal(selectedItem.ToString());

    // get our data reader
    OracleDataReader dataReader = cmdLookup1.ExecuteReader();

    // get the results - our query will only return 1 row
    // since we are using the primary key
    if (dataReader.Read())
    {
      // lblFirstName and lblLastName are labels on the form
      lblFirstName.Text = dataReader.GetString(0);
      lblLastName.Text = dataReader.GetString(1);
    }

    dataReader.Close();
    dataReader.Dispose();
  }
}
```

The Lookup 2 Button Code

As with the Lookup 1 button code, this code omits the object creation and parameter setting code. However, this code uses positional rather than named binding because the BindByName property is not supported by the Microsoft data provider. This is different from the code that uses the Oracle Data Provider. Listing 2-43 contains the code for this button.

Listing 2-43. *The Lookup 2 Button Code*

```
private void btnLookup2_Click(object sender, System.EventArgs e)
{
  // we need to bind in order since the Microsoft provider
  // does not support the BindByName property
  // lblFirstName and lblLastName are labels on the form
  cmdLookup2.Parameters[0].Value = lblFirstName.Text;
  cmdLookup2.Parameters[1].Value = lblLastName.Text;

  // get our data reader
  OracleDataReader dataReader = cmdLookup2.ExecuteReader();
```

```
// get the results - our query will only return 1 row
// since we are using known unique values for the first
// and last names
if (dataReader.Read())
{
  // lblEmailText and lblPhoneText are labels on the form
  lblEmailText.Text = dataReader.GetString(0);
  lblPhoneText.Text = dataReader.GetString(1);
}

dataReader.Close();

dataReader.Dispose();
}
```

The No Binds Button Code

The code for the No Binds button resembles the code from the previous section because we must build the CommandText property within the code itself. The main difference is that you aren't creating the command object and setting the properties. This code is contained in Listing 2-44.

Listing 2-44. *The No Binds Button Code*

```
private void btnNoBinds_Click(object sender, System.EventArgs e)
{
  // this illustrates the "traditional" approach
  // that does not use bind variables

  // cbEmpIds is combo box on the form
  object selectedItem = cbEmpIds.SelectedItem;

  if (selectedItem != null)
  {
    OracleDataReader dataReader;

    // we must build our command text string
    // since we are concatenating values at run time
    cmdNoBinds1.CommandText = "select first_name, last_name from employees
    where employee_id = " + selectedItem.ToString();

    // get our data reader
    dataReader = cmdNoBinds1.ExecuteReader();

    // get the results - our query will only return 1 row
    // since we are using the primary key
    if (dataReader.Read())
    {
```

```
    // lblFirstName and lblLastName are labels on the form
    lblFirstName.Text = dataReader.GetString(0);
    lblLastName.Text = dataReader.GetString(1);
}

dataReader.Close();

// get the data that Lookup 2 performed above
// again, we must build the string here in code
// rather than in the design environment
// lblFirstName and lblLastName are labels on the form
cmdNoBinds2.CommandText = "select email, phone_number from employees
where first_name = '" + lblFirstName.Text + "'
and last_name = '" + lblLastName.Text +"'";

// get our data reader
dataReader = cmdNoBinds2.ExecuteReader();

// get the results - our query will only return 1 row
// since we are using known unique values for the first
// and last names
if (dataReader.Read())
{
    // lblEmailText and lblPhoneText are labels on the form
    lblEmailText.Text = dataReader.GetString(0);
    lblPhoneText.Text = dataReader.GetString(1);
}

dataReader.Close();
dataReader.Dispose();
  }
}
```

As you can see from the sample code in this section, the primary difference is how you create objects and set properties. Of course, in the previous section, you could have elected to create all of your objects at the form level as you did in this section. However, in this section, you had to create the objects at the form level because you used the visual design tools. If you had chosen not to use the visual tools, the code you created here, with the obvious omission of the features provided by the Oracle Data Provider that are not present in the Microsoft provider, would have been remarkably similar. This sample provides the same functionality as the hand-built ODP.NET sample, including the bind variable behavior you explored using SQL*Plus.

Chapter 2 Wrap-Up

Similar to the first chapter, this chapter contains a lot of foundational information. I began the chapter with a look at the template projects that I used to create the sample projects in this chapter. I then showed you how to develop a simple, but complete, data retrieval application before I moved into an investigation of the data provider classes that are most relevant for data retrieval operations. Along the way, I highlighted differences between the Oracle Data Provider with the Microsoft provider and explained which features are not currently available in the Microsoft provider. In particular, I examined the connection, command, parameter, and reader classes in a fair amount of detail. Familiarity with these classes will go a long way as you develop applications—they are used in virtually all applications that work with the Oracle database.

I concluded this chapter with a series of samples designed to highlight key areas of the data provider classes. These samples, although certainly not exhaustive, should provide a strong base from which to further explore data retrieval topics I didn't address here. You will, of course, be using the data retrieval concepts and techniques developed here throughout the remainder of the book. In fact, in the next chapter, you will learn that the data retrieval principles are still relevant.

CHAPTER 3

■ ■ ■

Manipulating Data

If you think of the act of working with data as a coin, then this chapter is the logical "flip side of the coin" from the previous chapter. Although the technical definition of the Data Manipulation Language (DML) statements includes the SELECT statement, in this chapter, I primarily limit myself to discussing INSERT, UPDATE, and DELETE statements. In this chapter, you'll explore how to use the data provider classes to perform these operations.

Oracle Architecture Principles Still Apply

Keep in mind that the principle of coding *with* the Oracle architecture rather than *against* it, as I discussed in Chapter 2, applies to DML as well as it does to data retrieval.

That is to say that just because you're performing a DML operation doesn't mean that you don't have to take into account things such as the Shared Pool and the proper way to use bind variables. Just as when you're using SELECT statements, you can, and absolutely should, reuse SQL statements with a DML statement. In addition, some sort of data retrieval is typically involved in a data manipulation operation. Data you retrieve from the database is often the source of changes posted back to the database after you complete some processing activity.

Furthermore, you must understand several other fundamental tenets of the Oracle database architecture before you start modifying data through your .NET code. Here are the two principle characteristics that, when taken together, can serve to differentiate Oracle from any other database:

The locking mechanism: Oracle's unique approach to locking manifests itself in the following core principles, which I discuss in the next couple of sections.

- Oracle only uses row-level locks and never escalates to the table level.

- Readers of data don't block other users from moving that same data, and vice versa.

Multiversioning and read consistency (MVRC): Oracle provides a consistent view of the data with respect to the point at which a transaction starts. It does this by maintaining enough information internally to rebuild any data block to its state at the start of the transaction.

Perhaps, strictly speaking, this list is actually three characteristics; however, multiversioning and read consistency are so closely coupled that they're usually taken as a single characteristic.

Exploring Oracle's Locking Mechanism

Without locks, the database very quickly becomes unusable and data most certainly becomes corrupt. The primary purpose of locks is to ensure data integrity, which makes sense. If two users are allowed to modify the same data at the same time, it's not difficult to see that this is a data integrity issue. However, if you're accustomed to the locking mechanism in other database systems, then Oracle's implementation of locks may surprise you somewhat.

The first important aspect to consider about Oracle's locking mechanism is that Oracle uses *row-level* locking. For example, even if you are updating every row in a million-row table, Oracle places a row-level lock on each row. You may think that such a locking mechanism involves a large overhead, but this isn't the case. Rather than storing the information about row-level locks in the data dictionary, which I touched on back in Chapter 1, Oracle actually records this information in the data block that holds the row. This is one of the gems of the Oracle design—by placing the lock information on the data block (which Oracle is going to have to visit in any case) and not using a lock manager, Oracle avoids significant amounts of overhead. If you query the v$lock data dictionary view expecting to see the individual locks, you don't see them, which may surprise you. Now you know that the reason for this is that the lock information is on the data block, not in the dictionary or a lock manager. It is vital that you understand that Oracle's natural behavior is to use row-level locks. This is a good thing; it leads to increased performance and scalability.

■**TIP** The v$lock view (as well as others) is documented in the Oracle Server Reference manual.

The second point to consider is an extension of the first. Oracle doesn't escalate locks. If you're approaching Oracle from a SQL Server background, you must understand that the locking mechanism in Oracle is one of the primary differences between the two databases. In Oracle, as opposed to SQL Server, if you're locking every row in a table, Oracle doesn't escalate those locks into a full table lock. By not escalating locks, Oracle allows for increased performance and scalability.

Here's an example. Let's say that two users are working with some data that is in a single table. User A decides to update data that affects about 80 percent of the rows in the table. If Oracle performed lock escalation as SQL Server does, it might look at that 80 percent and decide to just lock the whole table, thus "saving" on the number of locks that it has to use.

However, shortly after User A starts the update, User B decides to update a single row in the same table. The row isn't in the set of rows that User A is updating but remember, in our hypothetical situation, Oracle decided to lock to the whole table. As a result, User B is unable to perform the update and must wait for the table to be unlocked. So, even though User B is working with a row that is not even part of User A's transaction, User B must wait.

This is *not* how Oracle works. By using row-level locks, Oracle allows User B to perform the update without being blocked or having to wait because User A caused a lock escalation. In addition, since Oracle has stored the lock status of a row in the data block rather than in the data dictionary or a lock manager, Oracle is able to avoid contention on a row-lock status table—in fact, no such table exists. Oracle doesn't need to maintain lock information in a table (which could then be a point of contention) since the information is stored in the data block.

Another key component of Oracle's architecture with which you must work in harmony is the way readers and writers of data behave. Readers of data don't block writers of data and writers don't block readers. Again, if you're coming to Oracle from a database such as SQL Server, this may shock you initially. This point is so important, it bears repeating: In Oracle, readers and writers don't block each other by default. However, I do cover how you can force this type of serialization when I discuss the For Update clause in the "Multiversioning and Read Consistency" section.

In SQL Server, if you're reading data, you can rely on the fact that the data you're reading doesn't change while you're reading it. In Oracle, that data can't change as you read it. However, you don't see the changes as you are reading it. This is because the data you're reading is all consistent to a point in time; this is the topic of the next section.

Multiversioning and Read Consistency

In the last section, I talked about how, in Oracle, readers don't block writers, and vice versa. This is accomplished because of multiversioning and read consistency (MVRC). These concepts are fundamental to the way Oracle operates. Taken together, it is these concepts that separate Oracle from virtually every other database product.

It may seem somewhat surprising that multiple versions of a piece of data can exist. How on earth does Oracle keep them straight, and how can you be sure that you're working with the correct version of the data? The simple answer is that you don't need to be concerned, because Oracle ensures that you are *always* working with a consistent version of the data. The multiple versions of data exist in special Oracle structures known as *undo* or *rollback segments*. Let's look at an example of how this works. Please note that I omit some detail here so that I can focus on the concept rather than the internal mechanism through which Oracle accomplishes this feat.

When you make a change to a block of Oracle data, Oracle makes a copy of that block and stores it in the undo (or rollback) segment. The undo segment contains enough information about the block of data to undo (hence the name) the changes made to it and to make it look like it did at the beginning of the transaction. Oracle has a special internal clock known as the System Change Number (SCN). Oracle can compare the current SCN value with the SCN value that existed at the start of a transaction. If you're querying data that is (or was) being updated, Oracle can look through the undo segment(s) to find the proper copy of the data as it existed when your query began. This is another important point to remember. Your session only sees data that was *committed* at the time your transaction began.

Transactions in Oracle occur with respect to a specific SCN. By utilizing the above method of multiversioning, Oracle creates a view of data as it existed when a transaction starts. The concept of *read consistency* means that inside a transaction, Oracle views all data as it existed at the time (SCN) the transaction *started*.

In this way, Oracle works differently than most other databases. You can't approach Oracle assuming that it works like other databases or you'll almost certainly be in for an unwelcome surprise. By understanding the basic operating principles of the Oracle database, and by creating your applications to work in harmony with those principles, you'll avoid most of the pitfalls that befall a project that is either about to become isolated from the database or is always in this state.

Locking and MVRC in Action

Using SQL*Plus, the sample user SCOTT, and a clause that is a part of the SQL SELECT statement, you can investigate how the locks appear in the v$lock view.

■**NOTE** The SCOTT user is a sample user who has been part of the Oracle database for quite some time. By default, the password for this user is TIGER. I created SCOTT as part of the install in the Appendix, but you can also created this user by running the %ORACLE_HOME%\rdbms\admin\scott.sql script. You can also create the tables that comprise the SCOTT schema in another schema by executing the %ORACLE_HOME%\ sqlplus\demo\demobld.sql script provided with the Oracle server software. If you need to have this user or the schema created, simply run the appropriate script or consult with your system administrator.

In Listing 3-1, you create a SQL*Plus session to your standard database TNS alias as the user SCOTT. You then query the EMP table specifying the For Update clause in the SELECT statement. This clause causes a lock to be placed on each row.

Listing 3-1. *Using For Update to Lock Rows*

```
C:\>sqlplus scott@oranet

SQL*Plus: Release 10.1.0.2.0 - Production on Sun May 9 13:53:27 2004

Copyright (c) 1982, 2004, Oracle.  All rights reserved.

Enter password:

Connected to:
Oracle Database 10g Enterprise Edition Release 10.1.0.2.0 - Production
With the Partitioning, OLAP and Data Mining options

SQL> select empno, ename, job, sal from emp for update;

    EMPNO ENAME      JOB              SAL
---------- ---------- ---------- ----------
     7369 SMITH      CLERK            800
     7499 ALLEN      SALESMAN        1600
     7521 WARD       SALESMAN        1250
     7566 JONES      MANAGER         2975
     7654 MARTIN     SALESMAN        1250
     7698 BLAKE      MANAGER         2850
     7782 CLARK      MANAGER         2450
     7788 SCOTT      ANALYST         3000
     7839 KING       PRESIDENT       5000
     7844 TURNER     SALESMAN        1500
     7876 ADAMS      CLERK           1100
```

```
     7900 JAMES      CLERK            950
     7902 FORD       ANALYST         3000
     7934 MILLER     CLERK           1300

14 rows selected.

SQL>
```

Once you lock the rows in the EMP table, start another SQL*Plus session using your administrative user and examine the lock view. Once you create a SQL*Plus session as your administrative user, query the v$session view to determine the SID of the session you created as SCOTT.

■**NOTE** The SID value in v$session isn't the same as a database SID. In this case, it is the Session ID.

You can now use this information to query the v$lock view. Both of these queries are illustrated in Listing 3-2.

Listing 3-2. *Examining Your Locks*

```
C:\>sqlplus oranetadmin@oranet

SQL*Plus: Release 10.1.0.2.0 - Production on Sun May 9 13:55:30 2004

Copyright (c) 1982, 2004, Oracle.  All rights reserved.

Enter password:

Connected to:
Oracle Database 10g Enterprise Edition Release 10.1.0.2.0 - Production
With the Partitioning, OLAP and Data Mining options

SQL> select sid from v$session where username = 'SCOTT';

       SID
----------
       153

1 row selected.

SQL> select sid, type, id1, lmode, request
  2  from v$lock where sid = 153;
```

```
       SID TY        ID1      LMODE     REQUEST
---------- -- ---------- ---------- ----------
       153 TX      262161          6           0
       153 TM       49049          2           0
```

2 rows selected.

SQL>

Interestingly, your query has returned two rows. As I mentioned earlier, individual row locks aren't stored in the data dictionary, so you don't expect to see 14 rows returned—a row for each row in the EMP table. However, you might have expected a single row to be returned. The reason you got two rows back is this: Oracle placed a TM lock on the table in addition to your transaction lock (TX). The *TM lock* is a DML lock that prevents changes to the structure of the table while you're holding the TX lock. The *TX lock* represents the transaction lock placed on your behalf. Of course, on your system, the return values may well be slightly different. As documented in the Oracle Server Reference manual, the lock mode (lmode) of "6" indicates an exclusive lock. Since you specified the For Update clause in the SELECT statement, you've been given an exclusive lock on each row in the EMP table. You can again query the data dictionary to verify that the TM lock is on the EMP table as follows:

```
SQL> select object_name from all_objects where object_id = 49049;

OBJECT_NAME
------------------------------
EMP

1 row selected.

SQL>
```

You can release the locks you've acquired by simply rolling back or committing your transaction in SQL*Plus:

```
SQL> rollback;

Rollback complete.

SQL>
```

You can verify that your locks have been released by executing the query against the v$lock view that you used in Listing 3-2:

```
SQL> select * from v$lock where sid = 153;

no rows selected

SQL>
```

The final consideration you want to look at here is the fact that writers don't block readers, and readers don't block writers as I talked about earlier. Again, let me stress that this is a *very* important distinction from other databases. At the risk of repeating myself, this is very important to understand. Let's use the example from earlier again. If User A is updating 80 percent of the table and User B wants to *query* (rather than update) a single row that happens to be in the set of rows that User A is updating, the row-level locks that Oracle has placed on behalf of User A won't block User B from reading the data. This can be a surprise if you aren't expecting it. Likewise, if User A is querying 80 percent of the table and User B wants to update a single row (or all of them) in User A's row set, User A's action doesn't cause User B to be blocked.

You'll illustrate this principle by using two SQL*Plus sessions. However, you'll use the SCOTT user in both sessions. In the first SQL*Plus session (see Listing 3-3) you're generous and provide a 20-percent pay increase to each employee and verify the increase. You then look at the same table from the second SQL*Plus (see Listing 3-4) session.

Listing 3-3. *Providing a 20-Percent Pay Increase and Verifying the Increase*

```
C:\>sqlplus scott@oranet

SQL*Plus: Release 10.1.0.2.0 - Production on Sun May 9 13:58:49 2004

Copyright (c) 1982, 2004, Oracle.  All rights reserved.

Enter password:

Connected to:
Oracle Database 10g Enterprise Edition Release 10.1.0.2.0 - Production
With the Partitioning, OLAP and Data Mining options

SQL> select ename, sal from emp;

ENAME           SAL
---------- ----------
SMITH           800
ALLEN          1600
WARD           1250
JONES          2975
MARTIN         1250
BLAKE          2850
CLARK          2450
SCOTT          3000
KING           5000
TURNER         1500
ADAMS          1100
JAMES           950
FORD           3000
MILLER         1300
```

```
14 rows selected.

SQL> update emp set sal = sal * 1.2;

14 rows updated.

SQL> select ename, sal from emp;

ENAME           SAL
---------- ----------
SMITH           960
ALLEN          1920
WARD           1500
JONES          3570
MARTIN         1500
BLAKE          3420
CLARK          2940
SCOTT          3600
KING           6000
TURNER         1800
ADAMS          1320
JAMES          1140
FORD           3600
MILLER         1560

14 rows selected.

SQL>
```

In Listing 3-4, you start a second SQL*Plus session as SCOTT and query the EMP table.

Listing 3-4. *Querying the EMP Table from a Second SQL*Plus Session*

```
C:\>sqlplus scott@oranet

SQL*Plus: Release 10.1.0.2.0 - Production on Sun May 9 13:58:49 2004

Copyright (c) 1982, 2004, Oracle.  All rights reserved.

Enter password:

Connected to:
Oracle Database 10g Enterprise Edition Release 10.1.0.2.0 - Production
With the Partitioning, OLAP and Data Mining options

SQL> select ename, sal from emp;
```

```
ENAME            SAL
----------  ----------
SMITH            800
ALLEN           1600
WARD            1250
JONES           2975
MARTIN          1250
BLAKE           2850
CLARK           2450
SCOTT           3000
KING            5000
TURNER          1500
ADAMS           1100
JAMES            950
FORD            3000
MILLER          1300

14 rows selected.

SQL>
```

What has happened here? Have you lost the 20-percent pay increase? No, the answer is that you didn't *commit* the transaction in your first session. Since you didn't commit the transaction, the changes aren't visible to the second session even though you logged in as user SCOTT. In fact, no matter what user you use in your second session, the changes aren't visible in that session. This sample highlights two important characteristics:

- The update in session 1 didn't block session 2 from reading the table.

- The changes made in session 1 aren't visible in session 2 (or any other session).

In this small sample, I illustrated how Oracle didn't block session 2 from reading the EMP table even though you're updating it. As in the earlier example, simply roll back the transaction on the EMP table in order to close the transaction. Of course, if you're feeling especially generous, you could commit the transaction instead of rolling it back.

If you recall, earlier in the chapter I mentioned that you could use the For Update clause to cause a reader of data to wait on a writer of data. When you're using the For Update clause, you can specify an optional parameter. That parameter is the wait/nowait parameter. The default value is wait, which means that the session waits indefinitely to acquire the row locks. If you specify nowait as you do in your sample here, Oracle generates an error indicating that the locks can't be acquired immediately. In Listing 3-5, you start a SQL*Plus session and issue an UPDATE statement, which results in a row-level lock.

Listing 3-5. *Creating a Row-Level Lock*

```
C:\>sqlplus scott/tiger@oranet

SQL*Plus: Release 10.1.0.2.0 - Production on Tue Aug 10 10:59:50 2004
```

```
Copyright (c) 1982, 2004, Oracle.  All rights reserved.


Connected to:
Oracle Database 10g Enterprise Edition Release 10.1.0.2.0 - Production
With the Partitioning, Oracle Label Security, OLAP and Data Mining options

SQL> update emp set sal=10000 where empno=7788;

1 row updated.
```

Now you have a lock on the row for employee number 7788 (empno=7788). In a second SQL*Plus session, you issue a SELECT statement for that employee number and include the For Update nowait clause. Your SELECT statement fails because you're attempting to lock an already locked row. This is illustrated in Listing 3-6.

Listing 3-6. *Attempting to Read the Locked Row Using a For Update nowait Clause*

```
C:\>sqlplus scott/tiger@oranet

SQL*Plus: Release 10.1.0.2.0 - Production on Tue Aug 10 11:02:30 2004

Copyright (c) 1982, 2004, Oracle.  All rights reserved.


Connected to:
Oracle Database 10g Enterprise Edition Release 10.1.0.2.0 - Production
With the Partitioning, Oracle Label Security, OLAP and Data Mining options

SQL> select ename from emp where empno=7788 for update nowait;
select ename from emp where empno=7788 for update nowait
                      *
ERROR at line 1:
ORA-00054: resource busy and acquire with NOWAIT specified
```

As you can see, Oracle immediately returns an error indicating that the row can't be read and locked. Most importantly, no data is returned as it was in the earlier examples that illustrated how writers don't block readers. In this case, you have simulated a writer blocking a reader by asking to lock the row.

If you're willing to wait until the lock on the row is released, you can omit the nowait parameter. In this case, the second session appears to hang until the lock is released on the resource. This method is illustrated here using the second session from Listing 3-9:

```
SQL> select ename from emp where empno=7788 for update;
```

After you submit the statement, the SQL*Plus session appears not to do anything. This is because Oracle is waiting on the lock to be released on the row in session 1 (see Listing 3-3). By rolling back (or committing) the transaction in session 1, you read the data and acquire a lock on the row in session 2. Here's what it looks like when you roll back the transaction:

```
SQL> rollback;

Rollback complete.
```

Once the rollback has completed, the second session immediately retrieves the data and locks the row as illustrated here:

```
ENAME
----------
SCOTT

1 row selected.

SQL> rollback;

Rollback complete.
```

Because you placed a lock on the row, I've elected to roll back the For Update in the second session and thus release the lock.

Using the Data Provider Classes

While examining DML operations, you use the following five data provider classes:

The OracleParameter Class: Used to create and pass parameters to and from the database.

The OracleCommand Class: Used to pass commands to the database and retrieve results.

The OracleCommandBuilder Class: Used to allow the data provider to create SQL statements automatically to be used by the OracleDataAdapter class.

The OracleDataAdapter Class: Used to populate a DataSet and pass updates in the DataSet to the database.

The OracleTransaction Class: Used to explicitly create and control database transactions.

Of these classes, the OracleCommandBuilder, OracleDataAdapter, and OracleTransaction classes are new to your toolkit. I introduced you to the OracleParameter and OracleCommand classes in Chapter 2. Rather than rehash all of the material covered for these two classes, I have you explore only the areas most relevant to DML operations. Your exploration of the data provider classes in this chapter will be somewhat shorter because you only examine the properties and methods that differ from those discussed in Chapter 2.

The OracleParameter Class

These are the two properties of the OracleParameter class that you examine in this section:

- The ArrayBindSize property
- The ArrayBindStatus property

■**NOTE** The Array Bind properties and functionality aren't supported by the current version of the Microsoft data provider.

The ArrayBindSize Property

The `ArrayBindSize` property is a read-write property implemented as an array of integer values. The default value for this property is `null`. You use this property to specify or retrieve the size of individual array elements when you're using array binding. Array binding allows for an `OracleParameter` object to represent an array of values rather than a single value. By using the array binding feature, you make it possible for an application to perform an insert, update, or delete operation on an array of values in a single database round-trip. Array binding allows Oracle to execute the statement many times over in a manner similar to the way a SQL statement that uses bind variables allows Oracle to execute that statement many times. In fact, you use bind variables with array binding.

■**TIP** The array binding feature is for INSERT, UPDATE, and DELETE statements only—it isn't designed to work with SELECT statements.

Before a statement executes, the data provider checks the `ArrayBindSize` property to determine the maximum size of an array element. After a statement executes, this property specifies the actual size of an array element. You work with the `ArrayBindSize` property in more detail later in the chapter.

■**TIP** This property is only meaningful (and is required) when you work with variable-sized elements such as those represented by the OracleDbType.Varchar2 type. This property is ignored when you work with fixed-size elements such as numeric data.

If we use the EMPLOYEES table in the HR user schema as an example, the FIRST_NAME and LAST_NAME columns are both defined as VARCHAR2 columns. Listing 3-7 illustrates the structure of the EMPLOYEES table.

Listing 3-7. *The EMPLOYEES Table*

```
C:\>sqlplus hr/demo@oranet

SQL*Plus: Release 10.1.0.2.0 - Production on Tue May 18 13:45:44 2004

Copyright (c) 1982, 2004, Oracle.  All rights reserved.
```

CHAPTER 3 ■ MANIPULATING DATA

```
Connected to:
Oracle Database 10g Enterprise Edition Release 10.1.0.2.0 - Production
With the Partitioning, OLAP and Data Mining options

SQL> desc employees
 Name                                      Null?    Type
 ----------------------------------------- -------- ------------
 EMPLOYEE_ID                               NOT NULL NUMBER(6)
 FIRST_NAME                                         VARCHAR2(20)
 LAST_NAME                                 NOT NULL VARCHAR2(25)
 EMAIL                                     NOT NULL VARCHAR2(25)
 PHONE_NUMBER                                       VARCHAR2(20)
 HIRE_DATE                                 NOT NULL DATE
 JOB_ID                                    NOT NULL VARCHAR2(10)
 SALARY                                             NUMBER(8,2)
 COMMISSION_PCT                                     NUMBER(2,2)
 MANAGER_ID                                         NUMBER(6)
 DEPARTMENT_ID                                      NUMBER(4)
SQL>
```

As you can see in the output of the SQL*Plus describe (desc) command, the FIRST_NAME column is defined as a VARCHAR2(20) and the LAST_NAME column is defined as a VARCHAR2(25). The following code snippet sets the ArrayBindSize property based on the LAST_NAME and FIRST_NAME columns of the EMPLOYEES table.

```
// create a parameter for the last name
OracleParameter p_last_name = new OracleParameter("p_last_name",
  OracleDbType.Varchar2);

// create a parameter for the first name
OracleParameter p_first_name = new OracleParameter("p_first_name",
  OracleDbType.Varchar2);

// work with 4 elements at a time
p_last_name.ArrayBindSize = new Int32[4];
p_first_name.ArrayBindSize = new Int32[4];

// set the maximum size for each element
for (int i = 0; i < 4; i++)
{
  p_last_name.ArrayBindSize[i] = 25;
  p_first_name.ArrayBindSize[i] = 20;
}
```

The ArrayBindStatus Property

The `ArrayBindStatus` property is a read-write property that you implement as an array of `OracleParameterStatus` values. The following are the three values in the `OracleParameterStatus` you'll use:

Success: Indicates that the value was successfully assigned to the column for input parameters or to the array variable for output parameters.

NullFetched: Indicates that a `null` was fetched from the database.

NullInsert: Indicates that a `null` should be inserted in the database.

Like the `ArrayBindSize` property, you can set the `ArrayBindStatus` property before the statement executes to give the data provider the information relevant to your current operation. You need to set the `ArrayBindStatus` property to `OracleParameterStatus.NullInsert` before the statement executes if you wish to insert a `null` value into the database using the array binding mechanism.

■**NOTE** Don't attempt to insert a `null` value by assigning `null` to an array element. This won't work correctly because it sets the array element to `null` rather than inserting a `null` value. In such cases, use the `NullInsert` enumeration value.

After the statement executes, the `ArrayBindStatus` property is set by the data provider. You can retrieve the value of this property after the statement executes and determine if the operation completed with no errors or if a `null` was fetched from the database.

The following code snippet illustrates how to access this property based on the `FIRST_NAME` column of the EMPLOYEES table.

```
static void Main(string[] args)
{
  // simple counter
  int i = 0;

  // create a parameter for the first name
  OracleParameter p_first_name = new OracleParameter("p_first_name",
    OracleDbType.Varchar2);

  // work with 4 elements at a time
  p_first_name.ArrayBindSize = new Int32[4];

  // set the maximum size for each element
  for (i = 0; i < 4; i++)
  {
    p_first_name.ArrayBindSize[i] = 20;
  }
```

```
// ...perform an array bind operation...
// simulate the results here...
// this will set each element to 'success'
OracleParameterStatus[] testStatus = new OracleParameterStatus[4];

p_first_name.ArrayBindStatus = testStatus;

// display the array bind status for each element
for (i = 0; i < 4; i++)
{
  Console.WriteLine("ArrayBindStatus[{0}] = {1}",
    i.ToString(), p_first_name.ArrayBindStatus[i].ToString());
}
}
```

The OracleCommand Class

The OracleCommand class provides the ArrayBindCount property, which is the only property specifically related to DML operations. Of course, the other properties such as the CommandText property (discussed in Chapter 2) are still relevant when we're discussing DML operations. You use the ArrayBindCount property to inform the data provider of the number of elements in the array associated with the DML operation. The default value of the ArrayBindCount property is 0, indicating that an array operation isn't used.

In order to enable array operations, set the ArrayBindCount property to the number of elements you want to use in the array. This property allows the data provider to correctly interpret the Value property of an OracleParameter object as an array. If this property isn't set, the default value of 0 isn't used by the data provider, and array operations aren't enabled. The following code snippet illustrates how to set this property.

TIP You should set the value of the ArrayBindCount property before you assign the Value property of the OracleParameter object.

```
// instantiate a default command object
OracleCommand cmd = new OracleCommand();

// inform the command object that we will be
// using array binding and will use 4 elements
// in our array
cmd.ArrayBindCount = 4;
```

The OracleDataAdapter Class

The OracleDataAdapter class functions as a broker of sorts between the Oracle database and the DataSet resident in host memory. Although it is possible to use this class for a read-only data retrieval operation, it is primarily suited to operations that involve changing data. The

OracleDataReader class, as discussed in Chapter 2, is better suited to read-only operations. The OracleDataAdapter class provides four constructors that you can use to instantiate a new object. Listing 3-8 illustrates these constructors as well as how to properly use them.

Listing 3-8. *The OracleDataAdapter Class Constructors*

```
// create a "basic" data adapter using all default values
OracleDataAdapter da1 = new OracleDataAdapter();

// we can pass a command object to a constructor and the
// select command text for the command object will serve
// as the basis for the select command text for the data
// adapter
OracleCommand cmd1 = new OracleCommand("select * from emp");
OracleDataAdapter da2 = new OracleDataAdapter(cmd1);

// we can pass the select command text and an oracle connection
OracleConnection conn1 = new OracleConnection();
OracleDataAdapter da3 = new OracleDataAdapter("select * from emp", conn1);

// the final constructor allows the specification of both
// the command text and the command connection string
OracleDataAdapter da4 = new OracleDataAdapter("select * from emp",
  "User Id=scott; Password=tiger; Data Source=oranet");
```

The OracleDataAdapter class provides the following six properties that you'll use frequently when implementing DML operations using the data adapter.

The **DeleteCommand property:** Specifies an OracleCommand object that deletes data from the database.

The **InsertCommand property:** Specifies an OracleCommand object that inserts data in the database.

The **Requery property:** Determines if the statement represented by the SelectCommand property executes when the Fill method is invoked.

The **SafeMapping property:** Maps column names in the result set to .NET data types to preserve data.

The **SelectCommand property:** Specifies an OracleCommand object that selects data from the database.

The **UpdateCommand property:** Specifies an OracleCommand object that updates data in the database.

■**NOTE** The Requery and SafeMapping properties are not available in the current version of the Microsoft data provider.

The Command Properties

Because each of the four Command properties function in a similar manner, I address them as a group rather than individually. Each Command property name is prefaced with a DML operation name making the function of each individual property obvious. What is perhaps not as obvious is that the properties aren't implemented as string properties as you may expect. The properties are implemented as read-write OracleCommand objects. The immediate implication of this is that you don't set the value of the property by assigning a string value to it. For example, the following code illustrates an *incorrect* manner of assigning a value to the SelectCommand property.

```
// this is an *incorrect* manner of assigning
// the SelectCommand property for a data adapter
OracleDataAdapter da1 = new OracleDataAdapter();
da1.SelectCommand = "select * from emp";
```

In order to correctly assign a value to a Command property for a data adapter object, you must instantiate an OracleCommand object, set the CommandText property, and assign the OracleCommand object to the appropriate Command property. One of the immediate benefits of this mechanism is that using bind variables (or parameter objects) is just as simple with the Command properties as it is when you're working with any other class. The following code illustrates a proper method of assigning the SelectCommand property and uses a bind variable.

```
// create a command object to use with the data adapter
OracleCommand cmdTest = new OracleCommand();
cmdTest.CommandText = "select ename from emp where empno = :p1";

// create a parameter object for the command object
// command text placeholder
OracleParameter p1 = new OracleParameter();
p1.Value = 7839;

// add the parameter to the command object
// parameters collection
cmdTest.Parameters.Add(p1);

// create a "default" data adapter and
// assign the select command property
OracleDataAdapter da1 = new OracleDataAdapter();
da1.SelectCommand = cmdTest;
```

The other three Command properties are set in a similar fashion. Make sure when you're setting the property that the CommandText property is specified appropriately. For example, the preceding code could have assigned the command object to the DeleteCommand property rather than the SelectCommand property. This action wouldn't cause a compile-time error; however, semantically it makes no sense to do this.

The Requery Property

The Requery property is a read-write Boolean property that has a default value of True. The purpose of this property is to enhance performance for forward-only fetches. If you set this property to False, then subsequent fetches from the cursor used by the data adapter object don't re-execute the query represented by the SelectCommand property. This property requires the connection object you used to fill the data set to remain available for the duration of the data adapter lifetime. If you wish to fetch groups of records in a forward-only fashion into the data set on the client, setting this property to False avoids the overhead involved in fetching the entire result set multiple times. The following code illustrates how to set this property.

■NOTE The Requery property isn't available in the current Microsoft data provider.

```
// create an OracleDataAdapter
OracleDataAdapter da1 = new OracleDataAdapter();
da1.Requery = false;
```

The SafeMapping Property

In Chapter 2, you explored using the typed data accessors to retrieve data from a result set and map it into a .NET data type. For values in the Oracle database that are too large to fit into a .NET data type, you can use the SafeMapping property. The SafeMapping property is a read-write property you implement as a hashtable that allows you to specify in code how you wish to map Oracle database types (as represented in a result set) into .NET data types. One of the main reasons you may wish to do this is that the Oracle database can hold a numeric value of up to 38 digits. This exceeds the .NET Framework's ability to store numeric values. By using this property, you can store numeric values that are larger than the .NET Framework can cope with. In order to achieve this, you may use this property as a mechanism to override the default type mapping between values. In addition, when you take advantage of this ODP.NET feature, when values are updated in the database from a DataSet, you don't loose any precision when you attempt to store a number that is too large for the .NET Framework to handle. This property is disabled by default. The following code illustrates how you can map a large numeric column in a result set to a .NET string data type.

■NOTE Only the .NET string and byte[] data types are available for SafeMapping, and this property isn't supported by the current version of the Microsoft data provider.

```
// a simple select to illustrate the use of safe mapping
// assume quantum_weight is a number with more than 28 digits
string sql = "select quantum_weight from elements where element_id = :p_id;

// simple connect string to connect to the standard tns alias
string connString = "User Id=physicsuser; Password=sample; Data Source=physics";
```

```
// create a new data adapter using one of the "specialized" constructors
OracleDataAdapter da = new OracleDataAdapter(sql, connString);

// use safe mapping to map the quantum_weight
// column to a .NET string data type
da.SafeMapping.Add("quantum_weight",typeof(string));
```

The OracleDataAdapter Methods

The `OracleDataAdapter` class provides two methods that you must have to operate the data adapter as a broker: `Fill` and `Update`. You call the `Fill` method to populate the `DataSet` with data from the database, and you call the `Update` method when you need to propagate changes in the local `DataSet` back to the database.

■**NOTE** The `DataSet` is a .NET Framework–provided class that represents an in-memory cache of data. If you need a refresher on the `DataSet`, consult the .NET Framework Class Library for full details.

You inherit both of these from the .NET Framework `DbDataAdapter` class. The Oracle Data Provider for .NET provides an additional four overloaded versions of the `Fill` method that you use when working with the `OracleRefCursor` class. I look at the `OracleRefCursor` class in more detail in Chapter 5.

Using the `Fill` method is very simple. You complete most of the work you need to do to utilize the `Fill` method before you actually call the method. In order to call the `Fill` method, typically you instantiate a `DataSet` and pass it as a parameter to the `Fill` method call. Listing 3-9 contains sample code that populates a `DataSet` object using the data adapter `Fill` method.

Listing 3-9. *Using the Fill Method*

```
static void Main(string[] args)
{
  // a simple select to use with the fill method
  string sqlStmt = "select empno, ename, hiredate from emp order by empno";

  // simple connect string to connect to the standard tns alias
  string connString = "User Id=scott; Password=tiger; Data Source=oranet";

  // create a connection to the database as the demo user scott
  OracleConnection oraConn = new OracleConnection(connString);

  // will use later
  OracleDataAdapter da = null;

  try
  {
```

```
    oraConn.Open();
  }
  catch (Exception ex)
  {
    Console.WriteLine("Exception Caught: {0}", ex.Message);
  }

  if (oraConn.State == ConnectionState.Open)
  {
    // create a new data adapter
    da = new OracleDataAdapter(sqlStmt, oraConn);

    // create a "default" data set object
    DataSet ds = new DataSet();

    // Fill the data set object using the simple query
    da.Fill(ds);

    // indicate that the data set was filled successfully
    Console.WriteLine("DataAdapter filled.");

    oraConn.Close();
  }

  da.Dispose();
  oraConn.Dispose();
}
```

As with the `Fill` method, you don't need to expend much effort to use the `Update` method. Changes you wish to propagate back to the database are "captured" in the `DataTable` associated with the `DataSet` object. When you perform the update operation, typically you call the `Update` method to pass the `DataSet` and `DataTable` as parameters. You can see this process in Listing 3-10.

Listing 3-10. *Using the Update Method*

```
static void Main(string[] args)
{
  // a simple select to use with the fill and update methods
  string sqlStmt = "select empno, ename, sal from emp order by empno";

  // simple connect string to connect to the standard tns alias
  string connString = "User Id=scott; Password=tiger; Data Source=oranet";

  // create a connection to the database as the demo user scott
  OracleConnection oraConn = new OracleConnection(connString);
```

```
// will use later
OracleDataAdapter da = null;

try
{
  oraConn.Open();
}
catch (Exception ex)
{
  Console.WriteLine("Exception Caught: {0}", ex.Message);
}

if (oraConn.State == ConnectionState.Open)
{
  // create a new data adapter
  da = new OracleDataAdapter(sqlStmt, oraConn);

  // define our update command to use later
  // notice we use bind variables here
  da.UpdateCommand = new OracleCommand("update emp set sal = :p1 " +
    "where empno = :p2", oraConn);

  // add parameters to collection
  da.UpdateCommand.Parameters.Add(":p1", OracleDbType.Decimal, 0, "SAL");
  da.UpdateCommand.Parameters.Add(":p2", OracleDbType.Decimal, 0, "EMPNO");

  // create a "default" data set object
  DataSet ds = new DataSet();

  // Fill the data set object using the simple query
  da.Fill(ds, "EMP");

  // Retrieve the data table from the result set
  DataTable dt = ds.Tables["EMP"];

  // Retrieve the first row from the data table
  // since our query was ordered by empno, the first
  // row will be for empno 7369 or ename "SMITH"
  DataRow dr = dt.Rows[0];

  // change the sal from 800 to 1200
  dr["SAL"] = 1200;

  // at this point the change is local to the data set/table
  // in order to propagate the change to the database we call
  // the update method
  da.Update(ds, "EMP");
```

```
   // at this point the update has succeeded and is committed
   // in the database

   oraConn.Close();
 }

 da.Dispose();
 oraConn.Dispose();
}
```

The OracleCommandBuilder Class

As you can see in the code from the previous section, you manually defined your update command to be used by the data adapter. For simple, single-table updates, you can use the `OracleCommandBuilder` class to automatically build your DML statements for you. This can remove some of the tedium involved in manually creating statements in simple situations. The `OracleCommandBuilder` class provides two properties that are of interest:

> **The `DataAdapter` property:** Specifies the `OracleDataAdapter` object for which this builder generates statements.

> **The `CaseSensitive` property:** Specifies if quotes should be used to preserve identifier case.

■**NOTE** You implement the `CaseSensitive` property slightly differently in the Microsoft data provider. This single property is implemented as a pair of properties—the `QuotePrefix` and `QuoteSuffix` properties.

The `DataAdapter` property is read-write and is implemented as an instance of an `Oracle-DataAdapter` object. You use this property to simply inform the command builder with which instance of the data adapter class it is associated. It has a default value of `null`. The `CaseSensitive` property is a Boolean property that has a default value of `False`. Like the `DataAdapter` property, this property is a read-write property.

■**TIP** Don't be confused by the `CaseSensitive` property. This property doesn't set whether the database is or is not case-sensitive. It sets whether case for identifiers is preserved or not.

When you create objects in Oracle, such as through SQL*Plus or Oracle Enterprise Manager for example, the object names are secretly folded into uppercase when the object is created. If you don't use quotation marks to preserve the case of the object, Oracle continues to automatically fold references to the object in question into uppercase. I highly recommend not using quotation marks to preserve case. If you choose to do so, all references to the object must use quotation marks in order to be correctly resolved. In Listing 3-11 the implications of using quotation marks are highlighted.

Listing 3-11. *Using Quotation Marks for an Object*

```
C:\>sqlplus oranetuser/demo@oranet

SQL*Plus: Release 10.1.0.2.0 - Production on Wed May 19 16:28:33 2004

Copyright (c) 1982, 2004, Oracle.  All rights reserved.


Connected to:
Oracle Database 10g Enterprise Edition Release 10.1.0.2.0 - Production
With the Partitioning, OLAP and Data Mining options

SQL> create table lowercase
  2  (
  3    c number(4)
  4  );

Table created.

SQL> select table_name from user_tables where table_name = 'LOWERCASE';

TABLE_NAME
-------------------------------
LOWERCASE

1 row selected.

SQL> drop table lowercase;

Table dropped.

SQL> create table "lowercase"
  2  (
  3    c number(4)
  4  );

Table created.

SQL> select table_name from user_tables where table_name = 'LOWERCASE';

no rows selected

SQL> select table_name from user_tables where table_name = 'lowercase';
```

```
TABLE_NAME
------------------------------
lowercase

1 row selected.

SQL> select * from lowercase;
select * from lowercase
              *
ERROR at line 1:
ORA-00942: table or view does not exist


SQL> select * from "lowercase";

no rows selected

SQL>
```

As you can see, when I created the table lowercase, I didn't use quotation marks. When I queried the data dictionary, I specified the table in uppercase. This was necessary because Oracle folded the name lowercase into LOWERCASE when it created the table. Next I dropped the table and re-created it using quotation marks. Now when I query the data dictionary, I receive a message indicating no records were found that matched my criteria. In this case, I had to specify the table name in lowercase since I asked Oracle to preserve the case for me. This doesn't seem overly cumbersome—after all, I asked Oracle to preserve the case. However, when I attempt to query the table (even though it has no rows) I receive a message that indicates that the table doesn't exist. This is because Oracle folded the name lowercase into LOWERCASE since I didn't use quotes. In order to query the table, I must enclose the table name in quotes as illustrated in the final query.

This is where the CaseSensitive property comes into play. By setting the CaseSensitive property to True, the Oracle Data Provider automatically encloses our object names (as well as column names) in quotes. However, my belief is that it is much simpler to work with non-quoted identifiers. In fact, it is possible that not every tool handles the object names correctly if you use quotes. Of course, if you have existing objects that you created using quoted identifiers, this property makes working with those objects in code easier since you don't have to manually create quotes around the object names.

The OracleTransaction Class

When working with data retrieval operations, you weren't concerned about transactions. You simply issued an SQL statement to select the data you desired and allowed Oracle to return a read-consistent view of that data. However, when you're working with data manipulation operations, transactions become much more visible and important.

In simple terms, a *transaction* is a logical grouping of operations that make up a single unit of work. A single operation or multiple operations may be performed within the context of a transaction. For example, a transaction may consist of a single UPDATE statement that updates one row in a table. On the other hand, a transaction may also consist of three INSERT statements, one UPDATE statement, and two DELETE statements. A transaction isn't limited in the number or type of operations you may perform within its context. A classic example of a transaction is the transfer of money from one bank account to another. Both the withdrawal of the money from the first account and the deposit of the money into the second account must succeed for the transaction to succeed. Otherwise the accounts are left in an inconsistent state.

Transactions within the Oracle database are an area that sometimes can be confusing. We have access to two modes of transactions. The default, and most popular, transaction mode is known as the Read Committed mode. The second type of mode is known as the Serializable or Repeatable Read mode. Oracle uses the Read Committed mode by default. You saw an example of this in operation when I demonstrated how separate SQL*Plus sessions can't see data that isn't committed in the other session. This is the essence of the Read Committed mode—only data committed at the time a transaction begins is visible to that transaction.

For transactions operating in the Serializable mode, things are a little different. This is an area where Oracle's architectural differences have a major impact. If you're accustomed to working with a database such as Microsoft SQL Server, you may be familiar with the database placing row-level shared read locks on the data involved in your transaction. This is a way to prevent other sessions from modifying data that read by your session. On the surface, this may seem like a fine idea. However, Oracle takes a different approach. Recall that in Oracle, writers and readers don't block each other. Writers are only blocked by other writers. Oracle places a premium on concurrency and scalability, and implementing locks that block readers of data doesn't fit in with that approach.

So, how does Oracle implement the Serializable mode? This is where Oracle's multiversioning functionality enters the picture. As a result of Oracle's multiversioning and read consistency model, a Serializable mode transaction returns data consistent with respect to the time the transaction began (as with read-committed mode); however, the big difference is that during the time the Serializable transaction is active, it is blind to changes that may occur in the database as a result of other sessions, even if those changes are committed. Using the Serializable mode in other database products is apt to produce data consistent with respect to the time that the transaction *ends*. This is a very non-Oracle thing to do, so to speak.

■**NOTE** You must be aware of the impact that Oracle's architecture has on database operations. It isn't safe to assume that Oracle functions in a manner similar to other databases. It's possible that the same standards-compliant statement may produce different results in different databases using the same data.

As you discovered in Chapter 2, you must explicitly tell the Oracle database to commit or roll back a transaction, which allows you to decide on the duration of your transactions. You have to explicitly commit your transaction in SQL*Plus for it to be visible to your second SQL*Plus session. In contrast to this, an important aspect of transactions in Oracle is that they begin, by default, implicitly. You don't have to issue a begin transaction statement. However, you will come across tools and data access mechanisms that may or may not explicitly begin, commit, or roll back transactions. If you are using the Oracle Data Provider for .NET, you'll find that when you call the ExecuteNonQuery method, transactions are implicitly started and committed automatically when the SQL statement associated with the ExecuteNonQuery method succeeds.

Think back to the classic example of transferring money between bank accounts. You don't want the first transaction (the withdrawal) to be committed if the deposit fails for some reason. However, if you implemented the process as two separate ExecuteNonQuery method calls, this is possible. This is where you'll find the OracleTransaction class helpful. When you use the OracleTransaction class, you have control over the beginning and ending of your transactions and can, therefore, perform multiple operations in the context of a single transaction.

The OracleTransaction class is a simple class. It provides no constructors. In order to create a transaction class object, you call the BeginTransaction method on the OracleConnection object. The OracleTransaction class exposes the following two properties:

The IsolationLevel property: Specifies the isolation level for the transaction.

The Connection property: Specifies the connection for this transaction.

The IsolationLevel property is read-only and is an enumeration defined by the .NET Framework. The property may be set to either of the following values:

IsolationLevel.ReadCommitted: Specifies the Read Committed level discussed earlier.

IsolationLevel.ReadSerializable: Specifies the Serializable level discussed earlier.

The IsolationLevel.ReadCommited is the default level. Because the property is a read-only property, you pass the level you wish to use as a parameter in the call to the BeginTransaction method. Like the IsolationLevel, the Connection property is a read-only property. Since the BeginTransaction method is exposed by the OracleConnection class, you don't need to set the Connection property for a transaction object.

You use the following three methods exposed by the OracleTransaction class when you're working with transactions within the database:

The Commit method: Commits the transaction making any changes permanent.

The Rollback method: Rolls back or cancels the transaction.

The Save method: Creates a savepoint in the transaction.

■**NOTE** The Save method isn't supported in the current version of the Microsoft data provider.

The Commit method is the data provider that is equivalent of typing **commit** in SQL*Plus. It commits the transaction and causes the transaction to enter a completed state; basically it makes any changes in the transaction permanent. The Commit method takes no parameters and returns no value. It is invoked when no errors have occurred and when your transaction is logically complete.

The Rollback method is the logical opposite of the Commit method. You might invoke it when an error has occurred or when a user changes their mind. In an application that allows user input, a user may input an incorrect value. By prompting the user and permitting a roll-back, you can provide them with an opportunity to correct a data entry error before they commit the transaction.

NOTE Once you begin a transaction by calling the `BeginTransaction` method, it must end one way or another. You must either commit or roll back the transaction.

When a rollback operation occurs, you have the option of rolling back every operation that has occurred in the context of your transaction, or you can create markers in your transaction known as *savepoints*. Think of a savepoint as a way of adding labels in your transaction. Then you can roll back a transaction to a specific label or savepoint. Any work you complete prior to a savepoint isn't affected by a rollback to that savepoint. On the other hand, any work you complete after that savepoint is undone.

NOTE Even if you use savepoints, at the end of the transaction, you must still either commit or roll back the transaction as a whole.

The following code snippet demonstrates typical usage of the `OracleTransaction` class.

```
// get a transaction object by beginning a transaction
// assume oraConn is a valid connection
OracleTransaction ot1 = oraConn.BeginTransaction();

try
{
  // ... perform an operation and commit on success rollback on failure ...
  ot1.Commit();
}
catch (OracleException ex)
{
  // operations threw an exception so rollback
  ot1.Rollback();
};
```

Transaction Practices

You can use transactions to group together a logical unit of work. Yet one of the most common practices is to break what should be a single transaction into a group of smaller transactions. Often this is done with the intent of making the load lighter on the database. Generally the transaction involves a large insert, update, or delete process with a commit performed every so often. However, the database is designed to handle large volume transactions and can cope quite well if you configure it properly.

Therein lies the rub. You must coordinate between the developers, designers, and administrators to properly size the structures so the database is properly configured for the load you are going to place on it. If you do this, there is no reason to commit a transaction before its logical conclusion; doing so has the opposite outcome from what you often desire.

When a transaction is active, it takes place inside the database, not in the data provider. The `OracleTransaction` class represents a database operation. Therefore, if a change related to the transaction occurs inside the database, it is unknown to the transaction object in the client code. One way in which such an invisible change can happen is when code performs a Data Definition Language (DDL) operation. A typical application doesn't normally perform DDL operations such as create table, drop table, alter table, and so on. However, you may come across circumstances where this does, in fact, occur. If you do have code that performs a DDL operation, you must be aware that the DDL operation causes an implicit commit to occur in the database. Because this commit happened outside the scope of an `OracleTransaction` object, the object is unaware of the commit. This can lead to difficult-to-discover bugs and synchronization issues between the database and the client code. If you need to perform a DDL operation, perform it outside of an active transaction in .NET code.

One final issue you should be aware of with respect to transaction practices relates to local versus distributed transactions. In Oracle, you can connect two (or more) databases together. When you connect one database to another, objects in the remote database are accessible from the local (or source) database. The method through which this is accomplished is known as a *database link*.

The `OracleTransaction` represents a local transaction not a remote transaction. That is, it deals with transactions in the database defined by the `OracleConnection` object from which it was created. Don't attempt to use the `OracleTransaction` class for transactions that occur in a remote database.

Implementing DML Operations

As a way of bringing together the concepts and various objects discussed in the chapter, in this section, I create a mixture of console and forms-based applications. In these applications, I illustrate how to implement DML operations using the various classes exposed by the data provider. You'll use your standard-privileged user and your standard TNS alias for these samples. These applications illustrate that data manipulation operations are really no more difficult than data retrieval operations, and, in fact, the data retrieval principles and techniques are still valid while you're performing data manipulation.

■**NOTE** The code in these samples doesn't include any exception handling code, which I cover in the next chapter. As a result, all the sample code assumes that form fields are completed properly in order to function correctly.

Using OracleDataAdapter and OracleCommandBuilder

The use of the OracleDataAdapter and OracleCommandBuilder classes in conjunction with a data-bound object such as a Data Grid is one of the most common methods of providing DML operations in an application. In this sample (OraDataAdapter), which you can find in this chapter's folder of the Downloads section of the Apress website (www.apress.com), you create a simple table via SQL*Plus using your standard-privileged user. Then you create a forms-based application that uses a Data Grid along with the OracleDataAdapter and OracleCommandBuilder classes to expose DML functionality. The table that you use is fairly simple and similar to the tables you've used in other examples. Listing 3-12 illustrates the creation of your table in SQL*Plus.

Listing 3-12. *Creating the Sample Table*

```
C:\>sqlplus oranetuser/demo@oranet

SQL*Plus: Release 10.1.0.2.0 - Production on Mon May 24 11:20:17 2004

Copyright (c) 1982, 2004, Oracle.  All rights reserved.


Connected to:
Oracle Database 10g Enterprise Edition Release 10.1.0.2.0 - Production
With the Partitioning, OLAP and Data Mining options
SQL> create table squad
  2  (
  3    player_num number(2) primary key,
  4    last_name  varchar2(32) not null,
  5    first_name varchar2(32) not null,
  6    position   varchar2(32),
  7    club       varchar2(32)
  8  );

Table created.

SQL> create index squad_idx01 on squad (last_name, first_name);

Index created.

SQL> exit
Disconnected from Oracle Database 10g Enterprise Edition Release 10.1.0.2.0 -
Production
With the Partitioning, OLAP and Data Mining options

C:\>
```

For this sample, you create a simple application that allows the end user to view, add, update, and remove players from the squad or team. The application's single form is depicted in Figure 3-1.

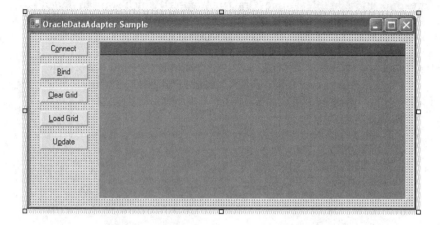

Figure 3-1. *The form used by the OracleDataAdapter and OracleCommandBuilder sample*

The Form-Level Fields

The following four fields are declared at the form-level in this sample:

public OracleConnection oraConn: The connection object.

public OracleDataAdapter oraAdapter: The data adapter object.

public OracleCommandBuilder oraBuilder: The command builder object.

public DataSet dsSquad: The data set object.

These fields are used in various pieces of code throughout the sample.

The Connect Button

The code to create and open your connection to the database is presented in Listing 3-13. This code is the same code that was used in the examples in Chapter 2.

Listing 3-13. *The Connect Button Code*

```
private void btnConnect_Click(object sender, System.EventArgs e)
{
  // create a basic connection string using our
  // standard Oracle user
  string connString = "User Id=oranetuser; Password=demo; Data Source=oranet";

  // only connect if we are not yet connected
  if (oraConn.State != ConnectionState.Open)
```

```
    {
      try
      {
        oraConn.ConnectionString = connString;

        oraConn.Open();

        MessageBox.Show(oraConn.ConnectionString, "Successful Connection");
      }
      catch (Exception ex)
      {
        MessageBox.Show(ex.Message,"Exception Caught");
      }
    }
  }
}
```

The Bind Button

Although the code for the Bind button is reasonably simple, it performs the following four important tasks:

- Creating the OracleCommandBuilder object
- Creating the OracleDataAdapter object
- Creating and filling the DataSet object
- Binding the DataSet to the DataGrid object

The code to accomplish these tasks is contained in Listing 3-14.

Listing 3-14. *The Bind Button Code*

```
private void btnBind_Click(object sender, System.EventArgs e)
{
  if (oraConn.State == ConnectionState.Open)
  {
    // build our 'select' command string
    string strSelect = "select player_num, ";
    strSelect += "last_name, ";
    strSelect += "first_name, ";
    strSelect += "position, ";
    strSelect += "club ";
    strSelect += "from squad ";
    strSelect += "order by player_num";

    // make sure the connection is open
    if (oraConn.State == ConnectionState.Open)
    {
```

```
    // create a new Oracle Data Adapter using our
    // select string and Oracle connection opened by
    // the Connect button
    oraAdapter = new OracleDataAdapter(strSelect, oraConn);

    // create an Oracle command builder for the adapter
    // the command builder will remove the need to manually
    // create the insert, update, and delete statements
    // we must be using a single table for this to work properly
    oraBuilder = new OracleCommandBuilder(oraAdapter);

    // create a new data set object
    dsSquad = new DataSet("dsSquad");

    // fill the data set from our adapter object
    oraAdapter.Fill(dsSquad,"SQUAD");

    // bind to the data grid
    dgSquad.SetDataBinding(dsSquad,"SQUAD");
  }

  // disable the button so we don't 're-bind'
  btnBind.Enabled = false;
 }
}
```

The Clear Grid Button

The Clear Grid button simply clears the `DataSet` and sets the `DataGrid` binding to a `null` value in order to reset or clear the grid. This code is shown in Listing 3-15.

Listing 3-15. *The Clear Grid Button Code*

```
private void btnClear_Click(object sender, System.EventArgs e)
{
  // simple operation to clear the grid
  dsSquad.Clear();
  dgSquad.SetDataBinding(null,null);
}
```

The Load Grid Button

The Load Grid button clears the grid and then loads it. If the button didn't first clear the grid, it would repeatedly add the same content. In order to clear the grid, it simply calls the Clear Grid button `Click` method. This code is contained in Listing 3-16.

Listing 3-16. *The Load Grid Button Code*

```
private void btnLoad_Click(object sender, System.EventArgs e)
{
  // clear the grid first
  btnClear_Click(sender, e);

  // fill the adapter
  oraAdapter.Fill(dsSquad,"SQUAD");

  // bind the data grid to the data set
  dgSquad.SetDataBinding(dsSquad,"SQUAD");
}
```

The Update Button Code

The code behind the Update button is surprisingly short and simple. Because you've used the `OracleCommandBuilder` class, the SQL statements necessary to perform the insert, update, and delete operations are generated for you. This makes the code in Listing 3-17 compact and per-haps even a bit trivial.

Listing 3-17. *The Update Button Code*

```
private void btnUpdate_Click(object sender, System.EventArgs e)
{
  oraAdapter.Update(dsSquad,"SQUAD");
}
```

Using the form is simple. Once the application has started, click the Connect button and then the Bind button. The form is now in a state where you may manipulate data. Of course, you didn't add any data at the time the table is created, so you should add some now. Figure 3-2 illustrates the form at run-time after you've added a few records to the form. The database hasn't been updated at this point.

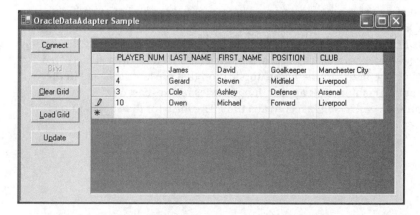

Figure 3-2. *The OracleDataAdapter sample form at run-time*

Once you're satisfied with a few entries, click the Update button to update and commit the data in the database. In order to verify that the data was correctly inserted in the database, click the Clear button and then the Load Grid button. The results of this are illustrated in Figure 3-3 using the sample data created in Figure 3-2.

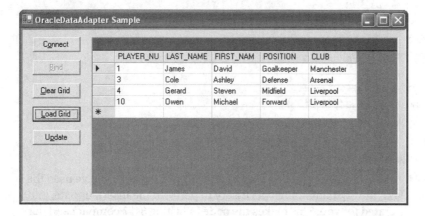

Figure 3-3. *The grid is populated with the data you inserted*

Notice how the data was resorted based on the PLAYER_NUM column as defined in the SQL statement code for the Bind button. This is the reason for including the Order By clause in the statement. The grid control allows full manipulation of the data contained in the table. Simply highlight a row and press Delete to remove it. You must click the Update button for the changes to be committed to the database. You can verify this by make several changes and clicking the Load Grid button without clicking the Update button. The grid will be reset to the way it was before you made the changes.

Performing Manual DML Operations

As you saw in the previous example, the OracleDataAdapter and the OracleCommandBuilder classes provide a simple and easy-to-use method for exposing DML capabilities in an application. However, there may be times when you wish to use a manual method of providing these capabilities. This may happen when you aren't using a data-bound control, for example. In this sample (ManualDML), which is available in this chapter's folder of the Downloads section of the Apress website (www.apress.com), you utilize the same SQUAD table that you created in the previous sample. You create a forms-based application that presents the data in the SQUAD table in a columnar fashion. This application provides record-based DML. By *record-based,* I mean that you work with a single record at a time. The form for the application is presented in Figure 3-4.

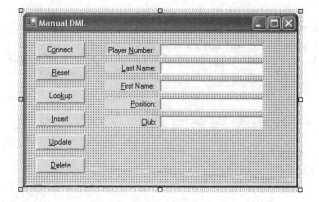

Figure 3-4. *The manual DML form*

The Connect Button Code

Listing 3-18 contains the standard Connect button code you've used in the samples thus far.

Listing 3-18. *The Connect Button Code*

```
private void btnConnect_Click(object sender, System.EventArgs e)
{
  // create a basic connection string using our
  // standard Oracle user
  string connString = "User Id=oranetuser; Password=demo; Data Source=oranet";

  // only connect if we are not yet connected
  // oraConn is a form-level, public field of type
  // OracleConnection
  if (oraConn.State != ConnectionState.Open)
  {
    try
    {
      oraConn.ConnectionString = connString;

      oraConn.Open();

      MessageBox.Show(oraConn.ConnectionString, "Successful Connection");
    }
    catch (Exception ex)
    {
      MessageBox.Show(ex.Message,"Exception Caught");
    }
  }
}
```

The Reset Button Code

The code for the Reset button is very simple and doesn't perform any database operations. As indicated by the name, this button simply resets the form by clearing the text box controls and setting focus on the Player Number text box. This code is presented in Listing 3-19.

Listing 3-19. *The Reset Button Code*

```
private void btnReset_Click(object sender, System.EventArgs e)
{
  // these are the text boxes on the form
  txtPlayerNum.Text = "";
  txtLastName.Text = "";
  txtFirstName.Text = "";
  txtPosition.Text = "";
  txtClub.Text = "";

  txtPlayerNum.Focus();
}
```

The Lookup Button Code

The SQUAD table was defined with a Primary Key column at the time it was created. The Primary Key for the table is the PLAY_NUM column. You take advantage of this fact in the code for the Lookup button in Listing 3-20. This code assumes that a valid number has been entered into the text box on the form. Based on the value in the text box, the code issues a simple SELECT statement against the database and populates the text boxes based on the data returned from the database.

Listing 3-20. *The Lookup Button Code*

```
private void btnLookup_Click(object sender, System.EventArgs e)
{
  // perform this action if we are connected
  if (oraConn.State == ConnectionState.Open)
  {
    // sql statement to look up a player based on
    // the player number
    // we use a bind variable for the player number
    string sqlLookup = "select last_name, ";
    sqlLookup += "first_name, ";
    sqlLookup += "position, ";
    sqlLookup += "club ";
    sqlLookup += "from squad ";
    sqlLookup += "where player_num = :player_num";

    // create our command object and set properties
    OracleCommand cmdLookup = new OracleCommand();
```

```
cmdLookup.CommandText = sqlLookup;
cmdLookup.Connection = oraConn;

// create our parameter object for the player number
// in our sample we are assuming a number is
// entered in the player number text box
OracleParameter pPlayerNum = new OracleParameter();
pPlayerNum.OracleDbType = OracleDbType.Decimal;
pPlayerNum.Value = Convert.ToDecimal(txtPlayerNum.Text);

// add the parameter to the collection
cmdLookup.Parameters.Add(pPlayerNum);

// execute the sql statement and populate the text
// boxes if a record is returned
OracleDataReader dataReader = cmdLookup.ExecuteReader();

if (dataReader.Read())
{
    txtLastName.Text = dataReader.GetString(0);
    txtFirstName.Text = dataReader.GetString(1);
    txtPosition.Text = dataReader.GetString(2);
    txtClub.Text = dataReader.GetString(3);
}
else
{
    MessageBox.Show("No record for Player Number Found" , "No Record Found");
}

// explictly close and dispose our objects
dataReader.Close();
dataReader.Dispose();
pPlayerNum.Dispose();
cmdLookup.Dispose();
    }
}
```

The Insert Button Code

In the code for the Insert button, you're performing your first true DML operation in the sample. Technically, the code in the Lookup button performed a DML operation by issuing a SELECT statement; however, a SELECT statement is somewhat passive in nature. The code in Listing 3-21 is more active in that it actually causes a change in the database to occur by inserting a new record into your table. As you can see in the code, you're putting into practice the material from the previous chapters by using bind variables in your code. Like the other code, this code assumes that the fields in the form are completed properly.

Listing 3-21. *The Insert Button Code*

```
private void btnInsert_Click(object sender, System.EventArgs e)
{
  // perform this action if we are connected
  if (oraConn.State == ConnectionState.Open)
  {
    // sql statement to insert a new record using binds
    string sqlInsert = "insert into squad ";
    sqlInsert += "(player_num, last_name, first_name, position, club) ";
    sqlInsert += "values (:p_num, :p_last, :p_first, :p_pos, :p_club)";

    // create our command object and set properties
    OracleCommand cmdInsert = new OracleCommand();
    cmdInsert.CommandText = sqlInsert;
    cmdInsert.Connection = oraConn;

    // create our parameter object for the player number
    // in our sample we are assuming a number is
    // entered in the player number text box
    OracleParameter pPlayerNum = new OracleParameter();
    pPlayerNum.OracleDbType = OracleDbType.Decimal;
    pPlayerNum.Value = Convert.ToDecimal(txtPlayerNum.Text);

    // create our parameter object for the last name
    // in our sample we are assuming text is
    // entered in the last name text box
    OracleParameter pLastName = new OracleParameter();
    pLastName.Value = txtLastName.Text;

    // create our parameter object for the first name
    // in our sample we are assuming text is
    // entered in the first name text box
    OracleParameter pFirstName = new OracleParameter();
    pFirstName.Value = txtFirstName.Text;

    // create our parameter object for the position
    // in our sample we are assuming text is
    // entered in the position text box
    OracleParameter pPosition = new OracleParameter();
    pPosition.Value = txtPosition.Text;

    // create our parameter object for the club
    // in our sample we are assuming text is
    // entered in the club text box
    OracleParameter pClub = new OracleParameter();
    pClub.Value = txtClub.Text;
```

```
    // add the parameters to the collection
    cmdInsert.Parameters.Add(pPlayerNum);
    cmdInsert.Parameters.Add(pLastName);
    cmdInsert.Parameters.Add(pFirstName);
    cmdInsert.Parameters.Add(pPosition);
    cmdInsert.Parameters.Add(pClub);

    // execute the insert statement
    cmdInsert.ExecuteNonQuery();

    MessageBox.Show("Record Inserted Successfully" , "Record Inserted");

    // reset the form
    btnReset_Click(sender, e);

    // explictly dispose our objects
    pClub.Dispose();
    pPosition.Dispose();
    pFirstName.Dispose();
    pLastName.Dispose();
    pPlayerNum.Dispose();
    cmdInsert.Dispose();
  }
}
```

The Update Button Code

Like the code for the Insert button, the code for the Update button, as presented in Listing 3-22, is active code. Also like the Insert button code, this code assumes the form is properly completed for it to function properly.

An interesting issue raised in this code is related to updating columns where the value hasn't changed. This code simply updates all columns in the SQUAD table based on the values in the form. If only a single column value has changed, it may be overkill to update all of the columns. This is one of the differentiators between the Oracle Data Provider and the Microsoft data provider. The Oracle Data Provider builds statements based on changed columns and therefore, doesn't send extra data across the network needlessly.

On the other hand, especially if you're using the Microsoft data provider, you may find it unwieldy to write code that keeps track of the original value in the fields and then create an UPDATE statement that only updates the columns where the value has changed. This is an area where you must have application-specific knowledge. Also, you must cooperate with your administrator to determine the impact of updating all columns.

Listing 3-22. *The Update Button Code*

```
private void btnUpdate_Click(object sender, System.EventArgs e)
{
  // perform this action if we are connected
  if (oraConn.State == ConnectionState.Open)
```

```
{
    // sql statement to update a record using binds
    string sqlUpdate = "update squad ";
    sqlUpdate += "set last_name = :p_last, ";
    sqlUpdate += "first_name = :p_first, ";
    sqlUpdate += "position = :p_pos, ";
    sqlUpdate += "club = :p_club " ;
    sqlUpdate += "where player_num = :p_num";

    // create our command object and set properties
    OracleCommand cmdUpdate = new OracleCommand();
    cmdUpdate.CommandText = sqlUpdate;
    cmdUpdate.Connection = oraConn;

    // create our parameter object for the player number
    // in our sample we are assuming a number is
    // entered in the player number text box
    OracleParameter pPlayerNum = new OracleParameter();
    pPlayerNum.OracleDbType = OracleDbType.Decimal;
    pPlayerNum.Value = Convert.ToDecimal(txtPlayerNum.Text);

    // create our parameter object for the last name
    // in our sample we are assuming text is
    // entered in the last name text box
    OracleParameter pLastName = new OracleParameter();
    pLastName.Value = txtLastName.Text;

    // create our parameter object for the first name
    // in our sample we are assuming text is
    // entered in the first name text box
    OracleParameter pFirstName = new OracleParameter();
    pFirstName.Value = txtFirstName.Text;

    // create our parameter object for the position
    // in our sample we are assuming text is
    // entered in the position text box
    OracleParameter pPosition = new OracleParameter();
    pPosition.Value = txtPosition.Text;

    // create our parameter object for the club
    // in our sample we are assuming text is
    // entered in the club text box
    OracleParameter pClub = new OracleParameter();
    pClub.Value = txtClub.Text;

    // add the parameters to the collection
    cmdUpdate.Parameters.Add(pLastName);
```

```
    cmdUpdate.Parameters.Add(pFirstName);
    cmdUpdate.Parameters.Add(pPosition);
    cmdUpdate.Parameters.Add(pClub);
    cmdUpdate.Parameters.Add(pPlayerNum);

    // execute the update statement
    cmdUpdate.ExecuteNonQuery();

    MessageBox.Show("Record Updated Successfully" , "Record Updated");

    // reset the form
    btnReset_Click(sender, e);

    // explictly dispose of our objects
    pPlayerNum.Dispose();
    pClub.Dispose();
    pPosition.Dispose();
    pFirstName.Dispose();
    pLastName.Dispose();
    cmdUpdate.Dispose();
  }
}
```

The Delete Button Code

The final piece of code to examine in the ManualDML sample is the code for the Delete button. Deleting a record from the database is a simple operation, and to do this, you use your Primary Key column in your code, as illustrated in Listing 3-23. Using the Primary Key ensures that you only delete a single record from the table at most.

Listing 3-23. *The Delete Button Code*

```
private void btnDelete_Click(object sender, System.EventArgs e)
{
  // perform this action if we are connected
  if (oraConn.State == ConnectionState.Open)
  {
    // sql statement to delete a record using a bind
    string sqlDelete = "delete from squad where player_num = :p_num";

    // create our command object and set properties
    OracleCommand cmdDelete = new OracleCommand();
    cmdDelete.CommandText = sqlDelete;
    cmdDelete.Connection = oraConn;

    // create our parameter object for the player number
    // in our sample we are assuming a number is
    // entered in the player number text box
```

```
OracleParameter pPlayerNum = new OracleParameter();
pPlayerNum.OracleDbType = OracleDbType.Decimal;
pPlayerNum.Value = Convert.ToDecimal(txtPlayerNum.Text);

// add the parameters to the collection
cmdDelete.Parameters.Add(pPlayerNum);

// execute the delete statement
cmdDelete.ExecuteNonQuery();

MessageBox.Show("Record Deleted Successfully" , "Record Deleted");

// reset the form
btnReset_Click(sender, e);

// explictly dispose of our objects
pPlayerNum.Dispose();
cmdDelete.Dispose();
    }
}
```

Figure 3-5 shows the form at run-time after you've added a new record to the table. As with the previous sample, experiment with each of the functionalities to verify that the code functions as you expect it to.

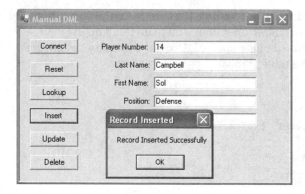

Figure 3-5. *The ManualDML form at run-time*

Using Host Language Array Binding

One possible shortcoming present in the previous examples is that each DML action requires a round-trip to the database. Although this may not be an issue in an application where the user has think time, for applications that are more batch-oriented, reducing the number of round-trips between the database server and the client may have positive performance implications. In addition, fewer round-trips means that less network bandwidth is consumed by the application. Not only does this method allow for fewer round-trips, it allows Oracle to reuse statements; this is similar to what happens when you're using bind variables, as I noted when we discussed the `ArrayBindSize` property earlier in the chapter. The net effect of this is reduced workload on the server, and, of course, reduced workload allows for the higher performance and scalability of an application.

In this section, I address using host language array binding to perform insert, update, and delete operations. (In Chapter 5, you examine another method of performing array operations known as PL/SQL Associative Arrays.) Here, you use a console application to demonstrate the array binding technique. You can find this project (ArrayBinding) in this chapter's folder in the Downloads section of the Apress website (`www.apress.com`).

■NOTE This feature isn't available in the current version of the Microsoft data provider.

First, you create a test table to use for your code, as illustrated in Listing 3-24. This simple table contains three columns and no indexes. You can also create the update and delete functions this code performs in this sample by using simple SQL statements; however, your aim here is to illustrate how to perform the principle DML operations using the array binding technique.

This does raise an interesting issue though. Often, it is easy to think in a more procedural or record-based fashion, especially when you're focused on creating application code. On the other hand, the database is designed to work best with sets of data. As you already saw when I illustrated the effect the `FetchSize` property has on retrieval time, it's possible to work in a single-row fashion across a set of data, it just typically isn't as efficient as working with the same data as a set. My view is that the array binding feature of the data provider is likely to be most useful when you're performing insert operations. Performing DML operations in a single SQL statement, if possible, leads to code that is easier to maintain and consumes fewer resources overall. On the other hand, if you determine that you do need to use the array binding feature in your application, this sample provides you with the necessary knowledge to do so.

Listing 3-24. *Creating the Array Test Table*

```
C:\>sqlplus oranetuser/demo@oranet

SQL*Plus: Release 10.1.0.2.0 - Production on Tue May 25 16:32:29 2004

Copyright (c) 1982, 2004, Oracle.  All rights reserved.


Connected to:
Oracle Database 10g Enterprise Edition Release 10.1.0.2.0 - Production
With the Partitioning, OLAP and Data Mining options

SQL> create table array_test
  2  (
  3    c1 number(4),
```

```
4    c2 varchar2(32),
5    c3 varchar2(32)
6  );
```

Table created.

```
SQL> exit
Disconnected from Oracle Database 10g Enterprise Edition Release 10.1.0.2.0 -
Production
With the Partitioning, OLAP and Data Mining options
```

```
C:\>
```

The code to accomplish the DML tasks consists of the class Main function and three class helper methods. The code for the Main method is presented in Listing 3-25. As you can see, this code creates an Oracle connection and then calls the helper methods.

Listing 3-25. *The Array Binding Main Method*

```
static void Main(string[] args)
{
  // need to call our helper methods
  Class1 theClass = new Class1();

  // our standard connect string
  string connStr = "User Id=oranetuser; Password=demo; Data Source=oranet";

  // create the connection
  OracleConnection oraConn = new OracleConnection(connStr);

  // open the connection to the database
  oraConn.Open();

  // call our helper method to insert using array binding
  theClass.arrayInsert(oraConn);

  // call our helper method to update using array binding
  theClass.arrayUpdate(oraConn);

  // call our helper method to delete using array binding
  theClass.arrayDelete(oraConn);

  // explicitly close the connection
  oraConn.Close();

  // explicitly dispose the connection object
  oraConn.Dispose();
}
```

The arrayInsert Helper Method

The code in Listing 3-26 inserts 1,024 rows into the ARRAY_TEST table. It performs this task by building three arrays—one for each column. After the arrays have been created and populated, the code creates OracleParameter objects for each array. Finally, the code creates an OracleCommand object, sets the important ArrayBindCount property, and executes the statement to insert the rows.

Listing 3-26. *The arrayInsert Helper Method*

```
private void arrayInsert(OracleConnection con)
{
  // used to load array values
  int i;

  // sql statement to insert our array values
  string sqlInsert = "insert into array_test (c1, c2, c3) ";
  sqlInsert += "values (:c1, :c2, :c3)";

  // create and populate array for column 1
  int[] c1_vals = new int[1024];

  for (i = 0; i < 1024; i++)
  {
    c1_vals[i] = i;
  }

  // create and populate array for column 2
  string[] c2_vals = new string[1024];

  for (i = 0; i < 1024; i++)
  {
    c2_vals[i] = "Column 2 Row " + i.ToString();
  }

  // create and populate array for column 3
  string[] c3_vals = new string[1024];

  for (i = 0; i < 1024; i++)
  {
    c3_vals[i] = "Column 3 Row " + i.ToString();
  }

  // create parameter for column 1
  OracleParameter c1 = new OracleParameter();
  c1.OracleDbType = OracleDbType.Decimal;
  c1.Value = c1_vals;
```

```
  // create parameter for column 2
  OracleParameter c2 = new OracleParameter();
  c2.OracleDbType = OracleDbType.Varchar2;
  c2.Value = c2_vals;

  // create parameter for column 3
  OracleParameter c3 = new OracleParameter();
  c3.OracleDbType = OracleDbType.Varchar2;
  c3.Value = c3_vals;

  // create the command object
  OracleCommand cmdInsert = new OracleCommand();
  cmdInsert.Connection = con;
  cmdInsert.CommandText = sqlInsert;
  cmdInsert.ArrayBindCount = c1_vals.Length;

  // add the parameters to the collection
  cmdInsert.Parameters.Add(c1);
  cmdInsert.Parameters.Add(c2);
  cmdInsert.Parameters.Add(c3);

  // insert all 1024 rows in one round-trip
  cmdInsert.ExecuteNonQuery();
}
```

The arrayUpdate Helper Method

Rather than update the entire table, the code in Listing 3-27 updates the "lower" 512 rows of the rows inserted by the arrayInsert helper method. This code follows the same basic pattern established in the arrayInsert helper method. Because the values in the C1 column are sequential, you're able to simply loop through a set of values to build the two arrays the code uses. You're adding 2,000 to the value of C1 for values that are in the inclusive range of 0 to 511. Once this method completes, the C1 values are in groups of 512 to 1,023 and 2,000 to 2,511.

Listing 3-27. *The arrayUpdate Helper Method*

```
private void arrayUpdate(OracleConnection con)
{
  // we will update the "lower" 512 rows in the array_test table

  // used to load array values
  int i;

  // sql statement to update our array values
  string sqlUpdate = "update array_test set c1 = :p1 where c1 = :p2";
```

```
// create and populate array for new column 1 values
int[] c1_new = new int[512];

for (i = 0; i < 512; i++)
{
  c1_new[i] = i + 2000;
}

// create and populate array for existing column 2 values
int[] c1_old = new int[512];

for (i = 0; i < 512; i++)
{
  c1_old[i] = i;
}

// create parameter for new column 1 values
OracleParameter p1 = new OracleParameter();
p1.OracleDbType = OracleDbType.Decimal;
p1.Value = c1_new;

// create parameter for old column 1 values
OracleParameter p2 = new OracleParameter();
p2.OracleDbType = OracleDbType.Decimal;
p2.Value = c1_old;

// create the command object
OracleCommand cmdInsert = new OracleCommand();
cmdInsert.Connection = con;
cmdInsert.CommandText = sqlUpdate;
cmdInsert.ArrayBindCount = c1_new.Length;

// add the parameters to the collection
cmdInsert.Parameters.Add(p1);
cmdInsert.Parameters.Add(p2);

// update 512 rows in one round-trip
cmdInsert.ExecuteNonQuery();
}
```

The arrayDelete Helper Method

The final method you'll use in the sample code is the arrayDelete method. As with the delete methods in the first two samples, the delete method in Listing 3-28 is slightly more simple than the insert and update methods. Although you aren't using a primary key, you know that the values the method deletes are contiguous. Again, this allows you to use a loop to build an array and then process it in the same manner as you did with the other two methods.

Listing 3-28. *The arrayDelete Helper Method*

```
private void arrayDelete(OracleConnection con)
{
  // delete the rows that we did not update

  // used to load array values
  int i;

  // sql statement to delete our array values
  string sqlDelete = "delete from array_test where c1 = :p1";

  // create and populate array for column 1 values
  // that we did not update
  int[] c1_vals = new int[512];

  for (i = 512; i < 1024; i++)
  {
    c1_vals[i - 512] = i;
  }

  // create parameter for column 1 values
  OracleParameter p1 = new OracleParameter();
  p1.OracleDbType = OracleDbType.Decimal;
  p1.Value = c1_vals;

  // create the command object
  OracleCommand cmdInsert = new OracleCommand();
  cmdInsert.Connection = con;
  cmdInsert.CommandText = sqlDelete;
  cmdInsert.ArrayBindCount = c1_vals.Length;

  // add the parameters to the collection
  cmdInsert.Parameters.Add(p1);

  // delete 512 rows in one round-trip
  cmdInsert.ExecuteNonQuery();
}
```

Using the OracleTransaction Class

When you invoke the ExecuteNonQuery method of the OracleCommand class, the action represented by that command is typically committed in the database. For a single, atomic action,
you may well want this. However, if multiple actions compose a logical transaction, this is not
what you want. By using the OracleTransaction class, you'll find that you have a finer degree
of control over when a commit occurs in the local database.

> ■**NOTE** A local database is the database represented by the connection object, not whether that database is on the same host as the application. In contrast, a remote database is represented by a database link object in the local database as discussed earlier in the chapter.

In addition, the `OracleTransaction` class allows you to back out of a transaction if a user decides, for example, not to commit the transaction. In this sample, you create a console application that illustrates wrapping multiple actions into a single transaction as well as backing out of a transaction. You also utilize SQL*Plus at various pause points to examine your table to verify that the code is performing as expected. Listing 3-29 shows you how to create the table you use for this sample as well as how to create a couple of starter rows. You work with a simple bank application called OraTransaction, which you can find in this chapter's folder in the Downloads section of the Apress website (www.apress.com) to illustrate the following:

- Rolling back a transaction

- Committing a transaction

- Performing multiple actions in a single transaction

Listing 3-29. *Creating the Transaction Test Table*

```
C:\>sqlplus oranetuser/demo@oranet

SQL*Plus: Release 10.1.0.2.0 - Production on Wed May 26 10:53:21 2004

Copyright (c) 1982, 2004, Oracle.  All rights reserved.


Connected to:
Oracle Database 10g Enterprise Edition Release 10.1.0.2.0 - Production
With the Partitioning, OLAP and Data Mining options

SQL> create table trans_test
  2  (
  3    acct_id number(2),
  4    balance number(12,2)
  5  );

Table created.

SQL> insert into trans_test (acct_id, balance) values (1, 10000.00);

1 row created.
```

```
SQL> insert into trans_test (acct_id, balance) values (2, 1000.00);

1 row created.

SQL> commit;

Commit complete.

SQL> exit
Disconnected from Oracle Database 10g Enterprise Edition Release 10.1.0.2.0 -
Production
With the Partitioning, OLAP and Data Mining options

C:\>
```

The Main Method Code

The code for the Main method in Listing 3-30 is similar to the code for the previous samples. Again, you call on a few class helper methods to perform the bulk of the work. This code handles a few obligatory tasks, such as creating the connection to the database, and then calls the helper methods.

Listing 3-30. *The Main Method Code*

```
static void Main(string[] args)
{
  // need to call our helper methods
  Class1 theClass = new Class1();

  // our standard connect string
  string connStr = "User Id=oranetuser; Password=demo; Data Source=oranet";

  // create the connection
  OracleConnection oraConn = new OracleConnection(connStr);

  // open the connection to the database
  oraConn.Open();

  // call helper method to illustrate rolling back
  theClass.testRollback(oraConn);

  // call helper method to illustrate committing
  theClass.testCommit(oraConn);

  // call helper method to illustrate multiple actions
  theClass.testMultiple(oraConn);
```

```
  // explicitly close the connection
  oraConn.Close();

  // explicitly dispose of the connection object
  oraConn.Dispose();
}
```

The testRollback Method Code

On the surface, the code in Listing 3-31 appears somewhat busy or slightly complicated. However, you can see that this code follows your basic pattern of building SQL statements, creating parameter objects for the bind variables, and executing the statements. An important distinction between this code and the previous code is that here, you're explicitly starting a transaction within the database. You can see this in the following extract from the sample code:

```
// Explicitly begin a transaction
OracleTransaction trans = con.BeginTransaction();
```

Once you have begun a transaction, the code performs an update of the table; you can examine the results of this action in SQL*Plus as well as from within the sample application. Near the end of the method, you're explicitly rolling back the transaction, thus undoing the update. This is accomplished by the following code extract:

```
trans.Rollback();
```

After you have rolled back the update action, you're prompted to examine the table in SQL*Plus to verify that the change isn't, in fact, made permanent.

■**NOTE** Technically, it's incorrect to state that a change didn't occur as a result of the rollback operation. The operation was actually fully completed in the database; you simply chose not to accept it by rolling back the change.

Listing 3-31. *The testRollback Method Code*

```
private void testRollback(OracleConnection con)
{
  // sql statement to add :amount units to the balance
  // for acct_id :acct_id
  string sqlUpdate = "update trans_test ";
  sqlUpdate += "set balance = balance + :amount ";
  sqlUpdate += "where acct_id = :acct_id";

  // sql statement to verify that our session can "see"
  // the updated data
  string sqlSelect = "select acct_id, balance ";
```

```
sqlSelect += "from trans_test ";
sqlSelect += "where acct_id = :acct_id";

// create parameter for balance
OracleParameter amount = new OracleParameter();
amount.OracleDbType = OracleDbType.Decimal;
amount.Precision = 12;
amount.Scale = 2;
amount.Value = 500;

// create parameter for acct_id
OracleParameter acct_id = new OracleParameter();
acct_id.OracleDbType = OracleDbType.Decimal;
acct_id.Precision = 2;
acct_id.Value = 2;

// create the command object for the update
OracleCommand cmdUpdate = new OracleCommand();
cmdUpdate.Connection = con;
cmdUpdate.CommandText = sqlUpdate;

// add the parameters to the collection
cmdUpdate.Parameters.Add(amount);
cmdUpdate.Parameters.Add(acct_id);

// Explicitly begin a transaction
OracleTransaction trans = con.BeginTransaction();

// update the balance, but will not automatically commit
cmdUpdate.ExecuteNonQuery();

// at this point the update has actually happened
// in the database and will be visible to our session only
// we will illustrate how we can see this from our session
// but not from another session
OracleCommand cmdSelect = new OracleCommand();
cmdSelect.Connection = con;
cmdSelect.CommandText = sqlSelect;

// create parameter for acct_id
// can't reuse the parameter from above
// because it still belongs to the parameter
// collection for the update command object
OracleParameter acct_id2 = new OracleParameter();
acct_id2.OracleDbType = OracleDbType.Decimal;
```

```csharp
acct_id2.Precision = 2;
acct_id2.Value = 2;

// add the parameters to the collection
cmdSelect.Parameters.Add(acct_id2);

// get a data reader from the command object
OracleDataReader reader = cmdSelect.ExecuteReader();

// display the acct_id and balance
// balance should be 1500 for acct_id 2
if (reader.Read())
{
  Console.WriteLine("Update has taken place, but not been committed...");
  Console.WriteLine("Acct ID: " + reader.GetDecimal(0).ToString());
  Console.WriteLine("Balance: " + reader.GetDecimal(1).ToString());
  Console.WriteLine("Examine in SQL*Plus...");
  Console.ReadLine();
}

// at this point we have verified that the update did
// take place, however it has not been committed.
// we will rollback the transaction to prevent it from
// being committed.
trans.Rollback();

// close the reader before reusing
reader.Close();

// get the reader again
reader = cmdSelect.ExecuteReader();

// display the acct_id and balance
// balance should now be 1000 for acct_id 2
// since we rolled back the transaction
if (reader.Read())
{
  Console.WriteLine();
  Console.WriteLine("Update has taken place, and rolled back...");
  Console.WriteLine("Acct ID: " + reader.GetDecimal(0).ToString());
  Console.WriteLine("Balance: " + reader.GetDecimal(1).ToString());
  Console.WriteLine("Examine in SQL*Plus...");
  Console.ReadLine();
}
}
```

The testCommit Method Code

As you saw in the code for the `testRollback` method, wrapping database operations within a transaction provides you with the ability to determine at what point you should issue a commit or rollback command to the database. The code for the `testCommit` method is very similar to that in Listing 3-31. The only material difference between the two methods is this:

```
trans.Commit();
```

Rather than rolling back the update as you did in the previous method, here you're making the change permanent by issuing the commit command to the database. The effects of this is visible when you look at the output of running the application.

The testMultiple Method Code

The `testMultiple` method code in Listing 3-32 illustrates how you can group multiple database operations within a single transaction. If you're not using transactions explicitly in your code, the data provider automatically commits your statements upon successful execution. As you can see in the method code, your second update operation causes the balance to become negative. However, since you're working inside of a single transaction, this fact isn't visible to any other session in the database. Without the presence of the transaction, this fact would be visible to other sessions.

This code performs three distinct operations on your test table within the context of a single transaction. The overall result of the three operations is a positive balance. Because you've already examined the fact that the results of your operations aren't visible to other sessions until the commit command is issued, this code doesn't provide the same pause points as the previous code did.

Listing 3-32. *The testMultiple Method Code*

```
private void testMultiple(OracleConnection con)
{
  // sql statement to add :amount units to the balance
  // for acct_id :acct_id
  // :amount may be a negative number
  string sqlUpdate = "update trans_test ";
  sqlUpdate += "set balance = balance + :amount ";
  sqlUpdate += "where acct_id = :acct_id";

  // sql statement to verify that our session can "see"
  // the updated data
  string sqlSelect = "select acct_id, balance ";
  sqlSelect += "from trans_test ";
  sqlSelect += "where acct_id = :acct_id";

  // create parameter for amount/balance
  OracleParameter amount = new OracleParameter();
  amount.OracleDbType = OracleDbType.Decimal;
  amount.Precision = 12;
```

```
amount.Scale = 2;
amount.Value = -5000;

// create parameter for acct_id
OracleParameter acct_id = new OracleParameter();
acct_id.OracleDbType = OracleDbType.Decimal;
acct_id.Precision = 2;
acct_id.Value = 1;

// create second parameter for acct_id
OracleParameter acct_id2 = new OracleParameter();
acct_id2.OracleDbType = OracleDbType.Decimal;
acct_id2.Precision = 2;
acct_id2.Value = 1;

// create the command object for the update
OracleCommand cmdUpdate = new OracleCommand();
cmdUpdate.Connection = con;
cmdUpdate.CommandText = sqlUpdate;

// add the parameters to the collection
cmdUpdate.Parameters.Add(amount);
cmdUpdate.Parameters.Add(acct_id);

// Explicitly begin a transaction
OracleTransaction trans = con.BeginTransaction();

// update the balance, but will not automatically commit
cmdUpdate.ExecuteNonQuery();

// at this point the update has actually happened
// in the database and will be visible to our session only
OracleCommand cmdSelect = new OracleCommand();
cmdSelect.Connection = con;
cmdSelect.CommandText = sqlSelect;

// add the parameters to the collection
cmdSelect.Parameters.Add(acct_id2);

// get a data reader from the command object
OracleDataReader reader = cmdSelect.ExecuteReader();

// display the acct_id and balance
// balance should be 5000 for acct_id 1
if (reader.Read())
{
  Console.WriteLine();
```

```
    Console.WriteLine("Update has taken place, but not been committed...");
    Console.WriteLine("Acct ID: " + reader.GetDecimal(0).ToString());
    Console.WriteLine("Balance: " + reader.GetDecimal(1).ToString());
}

// execute the update again
// this will cause the balance to become negative
// a business rule would be needed to determine if
// this is acceptable
// the end result of the 3 actions is a positive number
amount.Value = -7000;
cmdUpdate.ExecuteNonQuery();

// close the reader before reusing
reader.Close();

// get the reader again
reader = cmdSelect.ExecuteReader();

// display the acct_id and balance
// balance should be -2000 for acct_id 1
if (reader.Read())
{
  Console.WriteLine();
  Console.WriteLine("Update has taken place, but not been committed...");
  Console.WriteLine("The balance has become negative, but the transaction");
  Console.WriteLine("has not been committed so this may be acceptable");
  Console.WriteLine("Acct ID: " + reader.GetDecimal(0).ToString());
  Console.WriteLine("Balance: " + reader.GetDecimal(1).ToString());
}

// execute the update again
amount.Value = 3000;
cmdUpdate.ExecuteNonQuery();

// we will commit the transaction making it "permanent"
trans.Commit();

// close the reader before reusing
reader.Close();

// get the reader again
reader = cmdSelect.ExecuteReader();

// display the acct_id and balance
// balance should be 1000 for acct_id 1
if (reader.Read())
{
```

```
        Console.WriteLine();
        Console.WriteLine("Update has taken place, and been committed...");
        Console.WriteLine("Acct ID: " + reader.GetDecimal(0).ToString());
        Console.WriteLine("Balance: " + reader.GetDecimal(1).ToString());
    }
}
```

Running the Transaction Sample

Now that you understand the sample code goals and the means by which you accomplish those goals, you'll examine the output of the application. The application provides console output as well as opportunities to verify in SQL*Plus that the code is performing as we have discussed.

Upon start up, the application creates the connection to the database and invokes the first helper method. The initial output from the application should resemble the following:

```
C:\My Projects\ProOraNet\Oracle\C#\Chapter03\OraTransaction\bin\Debug>↵
OraTransaction.exe
Update has taken place, but not been committed...
Acct ID: 2
Balance: 1500
Examine in SQL*Plus...
```

As indicated in the application's output, the update operation has taken place, and the code *in the application* is able to see the transaction as illustrated by the balance increasing from 1,000 to 1,500. Examining the table from within a SQL*Plus session illustrates that the balance for acct_id 2 is still 1,000 *outside of the application*.

```
C:\>sqlplus oranetuser/demo@oranet

SQL*Plus: Release 10.1.0.2.0 - Production on Wed May 26 13:23:16 2004

Copyright (c) 1982, 2004, Oracle.  All rights reserved.


Connected to:
Oracle Database 10g Enterprise Edition Release 10.1.0.2.0 - Production
With the Partitioning, OLAP and Data Mining options

SQL> select acct_id, balance from trans_test order by acct_id;

   ACCT_ID    BALANCE
---------- ----------
         1      10000
         2       1000

2 rows selected.

SQL>
```

Simply pressing the Enter key causes the application to move to the next step in processing. You can see that the balance now reflects the original value as a result of rolling back the
update operation.

```
Update has taken place, and rolled back...
Acct ID: 2
Balance: 1000
Examine in SQL*Plus...
```

By issuing the same SELECT statement in SQL*Plus, you illustrate that the change hasn't
been committed in the database.

```
SQL> select acct_id, balance from trans_test order by acct_id;

   ACCT_ID    BALANCE
---------- ----------
         1      10000
         2       1000

2 rows selected.

SQL>
```

Again, pressing the Enter key causes the application to continue. At this point, the test-
Commit method is invoked. The initial output of the testCommit method is similar to that of the
testRollback method.

```
Update has taken place, but not been committed...
Acct ID: 2
Balance: 1500

Update has taken place, and been committed...
Acct ID: 2
Balance: 1500

Examine in SQL*Plus...
```

As you can see in the output, the change to the table is visible to the sample application
code. However, the change is now also visible to other sessions outside of the sample application since the update operation was committed.

```
SQL> select acct_id, balance from trans_test order by acct_id;

   ACCT_ID    BALANCE
---------- ----------
         1      10000
         2       1500

2 rows selected.

SQL>
```

After you press the Enter key, the application invokes the final test method. The `test-Multiple` method performs the three operations we discussed earlier and writes some informational messages to the console along the way.

```
Update has taken place, but not been committed...
Acct ID: 1
Balance: 5000

Update has taken place, but not been committed...
The balance has become negative, but the transaction
has not been committed so this may be acceptable
Acct ID: 1
Balance: -2000

Update has taken place, and been committed...
Acct ID: 1
Balance: 1000
```

When the application completes, a final check from within SQL*Plus reveals that the balance for `acct_id` 1 has reached its final value of 1,000.

```
SQL> select acct_id, balance from trans_test order by acct_id;

    ACCT_ID    BALANCE
---------- ----------
         1       1000
         2       1500

2 rows selected.

SQL>
```

In this sample, you allowed the balance to become negative (if only for a short period of time). If the table had a constraint on the balance column that specified that the balance couldn't be less than 0, you would have to handle that in your code. This is another example of why cooperation and communication between the developers, administrators, and users is important. Where to place logic to handle business rules is beyond the scope of what I can address in this book, but be aware that the results of those decisions may impact your coding choices or options.

Chapter 3 Wrap-Up

I began this chapter with the simple assertion that the principles and architecture attributes discussed in Chapter 2 are still valid when you perform data retrieval operations. The sample code in this chapter has taken those principles into account as you examined the various data provider classes typically involved in data retrieval. Rather than rehash the material from the previous chapter, you simply examined the new methods and properties as they relate to the data manipulation operations: insert, update, and delete.

Throughout the chapter you worked with various code snippets and short samples. I concluded the chapter with a series of more in-depth samples that illustrated the ways to perform the DML operations using the data provider classes. In particular, I examined how the `Oracle-CommandBuilder` and `OracleDataAdapter` classes allow for easy DML operations when you're working with a single table. For situations where manual DML is required, I illustrated how this is simple to achieve. You also investigated how to use the host language array binding as a method to work with bulk DML. Perhaps one of the more important topics I addressed was that of the `OracleTransaction` class. This class allows you to control when a commit command is issued to the database. In addition, it allows you to undo a transaction by issuing a rollback command. This functionality isn't possible when you aren't using the transaction class.

Now that you've completed this chapter, you have a solid foundation for the remainder of the book. We have addressed the data retrieval and data manipulation topics as well as developed some best practices that you'll continue to incorporate into your code. An area that I haven't really touched on up to this point is error or exception handling. This is the topic of the next chapter.

CHAPTER 4

■ ■ ■

Oracle Exception and Error Classes

In software development, it is a fact of life that at one point or another, an error or exception will occur. The root cause may be a soft error, such as incorrect data input, or it may be a hard error, such as the failure of a physical component. In this chapter, you look at the following three classes you can use to detect and communicate with an error or exception:

The OracleException class: Represents an exception the data provider detects. An exception object contains at least one error object.

The OracleError class: Represents an error that the Oracle software reports.

The OracleErrorCollection class: Represents a collection of OracleError objects and is useful when you're working with array operations.

In this chapter, I focus specifically on database errors and exceptions that the Oracle Data Provider for .NET may detect and report rather than on errors and exceptions in general. I also examine an approach to logging exceptions in order to illustrate how to use these classes.

The OracleException Class

Exception handling is a responsive activity. What I mean by this is that if your exception handler is executing, the event that generated the exception has already occurred and the exception handler is executing in response to that event. Certain types of exceptions may be more easily corrected within code, while others lend themselves to a more general "simply report it" approach. For example, if your code requests a lock on an object, and the lock request fails, your code can decide to wait and retry the lock request after a certain period of time has elapsed if that makes sense in the context of your application. On the other hand, if a user enters an incorrect password, generally it doesn't make sense to wait and retry the connection request again. It is likely that the password is still incorrect.

■**TIP** In order to implement exception handling, your code must catch OracleException objects rather than OracleError objects. It isn't possible to catch OracleError objects directly.

The Oracle Data Provider for .NET informs you that an exception has occurred via the OracleException class. Your code deals with these events through the typical try-catch-finally exception handling mechanism. Rather than catching a general Exception, you're interested in catching an OracleException. If you plan to catch exceptions of type OracleException in addition to exceptions of type Exception, you must place the OracleException higher in the catch block. That is, the OracleException can't follow an Exception in the catch blocks; you must catch it before you attempt to catch an Exception. The following code snippet illustrates this practice:

```
try
{
  // perform an operation that may throw an OracleException or an Exception
}
catch (OracleException ex)
{
  // do something with the OracleException
}
catch (Exception ex)
{
  // do something with the more general exception
}
finally
{
  // perform operation irrespective of whether an exception occurred
}
```

The OracleException class exposes six properties in addition to the base properties present in the .NET Framework Exception class. These are the additional properties exposed by the Oracle Data Provider for .NET:

DataSource: The TNS alias used for the connection.

Errors: A collection of OracleError objects.

Message: The error message(s) in the exception.

Number: Typically the Oracle error number as documented in the "Oracle Database Error Messages" guide in the Oracle supplied documentation. This can also be an internal data provider error, which is, unfortunately, not externally documented.

Procedure: The name of a stored procedure or function if the exception occurs when a stored procedure or function executes.

Source: Specifies the name of the data provider.

The DataSource Property

The DataSource property of the OracleException class corresponds to the Data Source attribute specified in the connection string. As you might expect, this property is a read-only property, and it's returned as a .NET string. If the error occurs during a process, such as logging in to the database, the value of this property is an empty string. For this property to be meaningful, there must be a valid connection.

The Errors Property

The Errors property, a read-only property, exposes a collection of OracleError objects. The collection is a typical .NET collection, and it contains at least one OracleError object. The collection may contain more than one object. I discuss OracleError objects in more detail in the following section. This property is returned as an instance of the OracleErrorCollection class.

The Message Property

The Message property, also read-only, is returned as a .NET string. An interesting aspect of this property is that it represents a concatenation of all the message strings from the OracleError objects in the Errors collection. This is similar to the error stack output you might see generated in SQL*Plus or other development environments or languages. When you're working with this property, use the carriage return as the separator token for the strings. However, the final string in the property isn't terminated with a carriage return. Don't confuse this property with the ToString method; calling the ToString method of an OracleException object returns the Oracle Data Provider for a .NET exception stack.

The Number Property

The read-only Number property is returned as a .NET int data type. This number may be either an Oracle internal error number or a data provider error number. If you have programmed using other Oracle data access technologies before, you may expect this number to be negative. When using ODP.NET, however, it is a positive number. If this number represents an internal Oracle error number, it represents the top-level error number in the error stack.

The Procedure Property

The Procedure property is a .NET string data type. It represents the name of the stored procedure or function that generated the error and the resulting exception, if applicable. This doesn't apply to anonymous PL/SQL blocks—if the error isn't in a stored procedure or function, the value of the property is an empty string. This property is set for procedures and functions whether they're stand-alone or part of a package. This is also a read-only property.

The Source Property

The Source property is returned as a .NET string data type and represents the name of the data provider. Like the other properties, it is read-only. For all of the .NET code in this book, the property has the value "Oracle Data Provider for .NET".

Using the OracleException Class

Now that you basically understand the OracleException class, let's create a small console application that catches a few exceptions and writes the properties of the associated Oracle-Exception object for each exception to the console. You write SQL statements against a very small table, so begin by creating the table as illustrated in Listing 4-1. Don't insert any rows into the test table.

Listing 4-1. *A Small Test Table for the Exception Class Sample*

```
C:\>sqlplus oranetuser@oranet

SQL*Plus: Release 10.1.0.2.0 - Production on Fri Aug 20 11:14:55 2004

Copyright (c) 1982, 2004, Oracle.  All rights reserved.

Enter password:

Connected to:
Oracle Database 10g Enterprise Edition Release 10.1.0.2.0 - Production
With the Partitioning, Oracle Label Security, OLAP and Data Mining options

SQL> create table exception_test
  2  (
  3    c number(4)
  4  );

Table created.

SQL> exit
Disconnected from Oracle Database 10g Enterprise Edition↵
 Release 10.1.0.2.0 - Production
With the Partitioning, Oracle Label Security, OLAP and Data Mining options

C:\>
```

After you create the table to use in your test, create a new console application and add a reference to the Oracle.DataAccess.dll assembly to the project. Listing 4-2 illustrates the core code used in this example. You can access the full code (OraException) in this chapter's folder in the Downloads section of the Apress website (www.apress.com).

Listing 4-2. *The Main Code for the OracleException Sample*

```csharp
using System;
using System.Data;
using Oracle.DataAccess.Client;

namespace OraException
{
  /// <summary>
  /// Summary description for Class1.
  /// </summary>
  class Class1
  {
    /// <summary>
    /// The main entry point for the application.
    /// </summary>
    [STAThread]
    static void Main(string[] args)
    {
      Class1 theClass = new Class1();

      theClass.oraException1();
      theClass.oraException2();
      theClass.oraException3();
    }

    void oraException1()
    {
      // create a connection string with an incorrect password
      // this is so an exception is thrown when the connection
      // is opened
      string c1 = "User Id=oranetuser;Password=badpass;Data Source=oranet";
      OracleConnection oraConn = new OracleConnection(c1);

      try
      {
        // This will throw an exception since we have
        // used an incorrect password
        oraConn.Open();
      }
      catch (OracleException ex)
      {
        // Write the properties to the console
        Console.WriteLine("Caught OracleException #1:");
        Console.WriteLine("  DataSource: " + ex.DataSource);
        Console.WriteLine("  Errors Count: " + ex.Errors.Count.ToString());
        Console.WriteLine("  Message: " + ex.Message);
        Console.WriteLine("  Number: " + ex.Number.ToString());
```

```
      Console.WriteLine("  Procedure: " + ex.Procedure);
      Console.WriteLine("  Source: " + ex.Source);
      Console.WriteLine();
    }
    finally
    {
      if (oraConn.State == ConnectionState.Open)
      {
        oraConn.Close();
      }
    }

    oraConn.Dispose();
}

void oraException2()
{
  // create a connection string using our standard user and
  // standard tns alias
  string c1 = "User Id=oranetuser;Password=demo;Data Source=oranet";
  OracleConnection oraConn = new OracleConnection(c1);

  // This command will attempt to gather statistics on a table
  // that does not exist in our schema.  This will cause an
  // exception to be thrown.
  string l_sql = "begin " +
    "dbms_stats.gather_table_stats(" +
    "ownname=>'ORANETUSER',tabname=>'DOES_NOT_EXIST');" +
    "end;";

  OracleCommand oraCmd = new OracleCommand(l_sql,oraConn);

  try
  {
    oraConn.Open();

    oraCmd.ExecuteNonQuery();
  }
  catch (OracleException ex)
  {
    // Write the properties to the console
    Console.WriteLine("Caught OracleException #2:");
    Console.WriteLine("  DataSource: " + ex.DataSource);
    Console.WriteLine("  Errors Count: " + ex.Errors.Count.ToString());
    Console.WriteLine("  Message: " + ex.Message);
    Console.WriteLine("  Number: " + ex.Number.ToString());
    Console.WriteLine("  Procedure: " + ex.Procedure);
```

```
      Console.WriteLine("  Source: " + ex.Source);
      Console.WriteLine();
    }
    finally
    {
      if (oraConn.State == ConnectionState.Open)
      {
        oraConn.Close();
      }
    }

    oraConn.Dispose();
}

void oraException3()
{
  // create a connection string using our standard user and
  // standard tns alias
  string c1 = "User Id=oranetuser;Password=demo;Data Source=oranet";
  OracleConnection oraConn = new OracleConnection(c1);

  // Attempt to update the exception_test table.
  // This update will 'fail' since there are no values
  // in the table.
  string l_sql = "update exception_test set c=1 where c=0";

  OracleCommand oraCmd = new OracleCommand(l_sql,oraConn);

  try
  {
    oraConn.Open();

    oraCmd.ExecuteNonQuery();
  }
  catch (OracleException ex)
  {
    // Write the properties to the console
    Console.WriteLine("Caught OracleException #3:");
    Console.WriteLine("  DataSource: " + ex.DataSource);
    Console.WriteLine("  Errors Count: " + ex.Errors.Count.ToString());
    Console.WriteLine("  Message: " + ex.Message);
    Console.WriteLine("  Number: " + ex.Number.ToString());
    Console.WriteLine("  Procedure: " + ex.Procedure);
    Console.WriteLine("  Source: " + ex.Source);
    Console.WriteLine();
  }
  finally
```

```
    {
      if (oraConn.State == ConnectionState.Open)
      {
        oraConn.Close();
      }
    }

    oraConn.Dispose();
  }
 }
}
```

As you can see in Listing 4-2, the sample code is composed of the obligatory Main method and three helpers. The oraException1 helper method attempts to connect to the database with an incorrect password. The oraException2 helper method makes a call to an Oracle PL/SQL routine that attempts to generate statistics on a nonexistent table. Finally, the oraException3 helper method attempts to update the test table. Listing 4-3 represents the output of the sample program.

Listing 4-3. *The Output of the OracleException Sample*

```
C:\My Projects\ProOraNet\Oracle\C#\Chapter04\OraException\bin\Debug>⏎
OraException.exe
Caught OracleException #1:
  DataSource:
  Errors Count: 1
  Message: ORA-1017: invalid username/password; logon denied
  Number: 1017
  Procedure:
  Source: Oracle Data Provider for .NET

Caught OracleException #2:
  DataSource: oranet
  Errors Count: 1
  Message: ORA-20000: Unable to analyze TABLE "ORANETUSER".⏎
 "DOES_NOT_EXIST", insufficient privileges
or does not exist
ORA-06512: at "SYS.DBMS_STATS", line 11558
ORA-06512: at "SYS.DBMS_STATS", line 11587
ORA-06512: at line 1
  Number: 20000
  Procedure:
  Source: Oracle Data Provider for .NET

C:\My Projects\ProOraNet\Oracle\C#\Chapter04\OraException\bin\Debug>
```

As illustrated in Listing 4-3, using the OracleException class is a straightforward process, and the data provider populates the properties for the OracleException object with relevant information. The Procedure property isn't populated because we didn't invoke code in a stored procedure or function. You may be wondering what happened to the output from the third helper method. Well, there is no output from that method because an exception wasn't thrown. I included this method to illustrate that an operation that affects no rows in the database is *not* considered an error or an exception. As a result, you can't write code in an exception handler to be invoked when no rows are affected by the database operation.

Two points of interest about the output of the oraException2 method—the Message property illustrates the concatenation of underlying messages and the Number property represents the top-level error number. You can see in the output of the Message property that four individual message strings are concatenated to produce this output. In this sample, the Number property is assigned the top-level error number of 20000 rather than one of the three 6512 values that appear in the Message property.

The OracleError Class

As I discussed earlier in the chapter, your code must catch an OracleException object rather than an OracleError object. The OracleError class doesn't inherit from the System.Exception class or a child of that class; rather, it inherits directly from the Object class. However, this doesn't mean that the OracleError object is inaccessible from your code. Whenever you catch an exception, you can gain access to the underlying OracleError objects via the OracleError-Collection class. In this section, I discuss the OracleError class and I discuss the OracleError-Collection class in the following section.

The OracleError Class Properties

Like the OracleException class, the OracleError class exposes six properties you will find useful. These six properties are as follows:

ArrayBindIndex: Specifies which row in an array operation triggered an exception.

DataSource: The TNS alias used for the connection.

Message: The error message(s) that are in the exception.

Number: Typically the Oracle error number as documented in the "Oracle Database Error Messages" guide in the Oracle-supplied documentation. This can also be an internal data provider error, which is unfortunately, not externally documented.

Procedure: The name of a stored procedure or function if the exception occurs when a stored procedure or function executes.

Source: Specifies the name of the data provider.

Of these six properties, the DataSource, Procedure, and Source properties function in the same manner as their counterparts in the OracleException class. The Message and Number properties function in a very similar manner to their OracleException class counterparts with the following differences:

- The Message property doesn't represent a concatenation of messages; it is specific to the current instance of the OracleError class.

- The Number property represents the error number for the current instance of the OracleError class rather than a top-level error number in an exception.

The ArrayBindIndex property is a property that doesn't exist in the OracleException class. This property is a read-only property that returns the zero-based index of a row in an array. The property is returned as a .NET int data type. You use this property when you're using array binding in bulk operations. For example, if you submit an array with 16 rows to the server for processing and the 9th row in the array causes an error to occur, the return value of this property is 8 for the OracleError object associated with that row. It is possible to have multiple rows in the array produce errors. In this case, each row that causes an error has a separate OracleError object associated with it.

Using the OracleError Class

Since the OracleError class is, in many ways, similar to the OracleException class, you modify the sample code here that you used in the preceding section, which illustrated how to use the OracleError class. In order to keep the sample small, you use the oraException2 helper method you used when working with the OracleException class. Rather than write the properties of the OracleException class to the console, you get an OracleError object from the OracleException class and display the values of the properties for this object. Listing 4-4 contains the modified code from the OraError project in the code download (visit this chapter's folder in the Downloads section of the Apress website) to achieve this.

Listing 4-4. *The Main Code for the OracleError Sample*

```
using System;
using System.Data;
using Oracle.DataAccess.Client;

[ code snipped ]

static void Main(string[] args)
{
  // create a connection string using our standard user and
  // standard tns alias
  string c1 = "User Id=oranetuser;Password=demo;Data Source=oranet";
  OracleConnection oraConn = new OracleConnection(c1);

  // This command will attempt to gather statistics on a table
  // that does not exist in our schema. This will cause an
```

```
  // exception to be thrown.
  string l_sql = "begin " +
    "dbms_stats.gather_table_stats(" +
    "ownname=>'ORANETUSER',tabname=>'DOES_NOT_EXIST');" +
    "end;";

OracleCommand oraCmd = new OracleCommand(l_sql,oraConn);

try
{
  oraConn.Open();

  oraCmd.ExecuteNonQuery();
}
catch (OracleException ex)
{
  // Now that we have an OracleException, we can
  // get the error object.
  OracleError theError = ex.Errors[0];

  // Write the properties to the console as we did
  // with the OracleException.  The values here will
  // be remarkably similar to those in the OracleException
  // sample code.
  Console.WriteLine("OracleError properties:");
  Console.WriteLine("  ArrayBindIndex: " +
    theError.ArrayBindIndex.ToString());
  Console.WriteLine("  DataSource: " + theError.DataSource);
  Console.WriteLine("  Message: " + theError.Message);
  Console.WriteLine("  Number: " + theError.Number.ToString());
  Console.WriteLine("  Procedure: " + theError.Procedure);
  Console.WriteLine("  Source: " + theError.Source);
  Console.WriteLine();
}
finally
{
  if (oraConn.State == ConnectionState.Open)
  {
    oraConn.Close();
  }
}

oraConn.Dispose();
}
```

After running the sample code in Listing 4-4, you receive output such as that in Listing 4-5. With the exception of the inclusion of the ArrayBindIndex property and the exclusion of the Errors.Count property, this output is identical to the output from Listing 4-3.

Listing 4-5. *The Output of the OracleError Sample*

```
C:\My Projects\ProOraNet\Oracle\C#\Chapter04\OraError\bin\Debug>OraError
OracleError properties:
  ArrayBindIndex: 0
  DataSource: oranet
  Message: ORA-20000: Unable to analyze TABLE "ORANETUSER".↵
 "DOES_NOT_EXIST", insufficient privileges
or does not exist
ORA-06512: at "SYS.DBMS_STATS", line 11558
ORA-06512: at "SYS.DBMS_STATS", line 11587
ORA-06512: at line 1

  Number: 20000
  Procedure:
  Source: Oracle Data Provider for .NET

C:\My Projects\ProOraNet\Oracle\C#\Chapter04\OraError\bin\Debug>
```

The reason for the similarity between the output of the OracleException example and the OracleError example is that there is only a single OracleError object in the Errors collection. The procedure property output is empty because a stored procedure (or function) isn't used in this sample. (I cover stored procedures and functions in Chapter 5.) When you examine the output of the samples, you may wonder why there is only a single OracleError object in the Errors collection. After all, there appear to be three occurrences of the ORA-06512 error. This is because the database engine returns the error as a single error with everything all rolled up. When there is more than a single OracleError object, you can use the Errors.Count property in conjunction with the OracleErrorsCollection class and iterate through the OracleError objects.

The OracleErrorCollection Class

The OracleErrorCollection class inherits from the standard ArrayList class. This class doesn't expose any additional properties or methods above and beyond those that are present in the ArrayList class, though it does overload the Equals method in order to compare objects.

■**CAUTION** If you're using an unpatched 9i client (i.e., version 9.2.0.1.0), it's possible that only a single error object exists in the collection. When you're using a patched 9i client or the 10g client, this appears to be resolved.

You look at a brief sample that illustrates how to use the OracleErrorCollection class to round out your examination of the error and exception classes. The code in Listing 4-6 is a simple variation of the core code you've been using throughout the samples in this chapter. This sample is the OraErrorCollection project available in the code download.

Listing 4-6. *Accessing the OracleErrorCollection*

```
static void Main(string[] args)
{
  // create a connection string using our standard user and
  // standard tns alias
  string c1 = "User Id=oranetuser;Password=demo;Data Source=oranet";
  OracleConnection oraConn = new OracleConnection(c1);

  // This command will attempt to insert values that are too
  // large based on the table definition. The first two values
  // should not be in error and the last two should fail.
  // Even though the first two values are not in error, the
  // entire insert operation will fail.
  string l_sql = "insert into exception_test(c) values (:c)";

  // our test array to use for the insert operation
  int[] testArray - new int[4]{9998,9999,10000,10001};

  // create a command object and set the values
  // the ArrayBindCount is a necessary property
  OracleCommand oraCmd = new OracleCommand();

  oraCmd.Connection = oraConn;
  oraCmd.CommandText = l_sql;
  oraCmd.ArrayBindCount = testArray.Length;

  // create a parameter object to hold our array
  // and add it to our command object's Parameters
  // collection
  OracleParameter p1 = new OracleParameter("c", OracleDbType.Int32);
  p1.Direction = ParameterDirection.Input;
  p1.Value = testArray;

  oraCmd.Parameters.Add(p1);

  try
  {
    oraConn.Open();

    // This should throw an exception
    oraCmd.ExecuteNonQuery();
  }
  catch (OracleException ex)
  {
    Console.WriteLine("Caught OracleException:");
    Console.WriteLine("  DataSource: " + ex.DataSource);
    Console.WriteLine("  Errors Count: " + ex.Errors.Count.ToString());
```

```
      Console.WriteLine("  Message: " + ex.Message);
      Console.WriteLine("  Number: " + ex.Number.ToString());
      Console.WriteLine("  Procedure: " + ex.Procedure);
      Console.WriteLine("  Source: " + ex.Source);
      Console.WriteLine();

      // iterate through the error collection and
      // display properties for each error object
      // to the console.
      for (int i=0; i<ex.Errors.Count; i++)
      {
        Console.WriteLine("ErrorCollection[{0}]:", i);
        Console.WriteLine("  ArrayBindIndex: " +
          ex.Errors[i].ArrayBindIndex.ToString());
        Console.WriteLine("  DataSource: " + ex.Errors[i].DataSource);
        Console.WriteLine("  Message: " + ex.Errors[i].Message);
        Console.WriteLine("  Number: " + ex.Errors[i].Number.ToString());
        Console.WriteLine("  Procedure: " + ex.Errors[i].Procedure);
        Console.WriteLine("  Source: " + ex.Errors[i].Source);
        Console.WriteLine();
      }
    }
    finally
    {
      if (oraConn.State == ConnectionState.Open)
      {
        oraConn.Close();
      }
    }

    // explicitly dispose of our objects
    p1.Dispose();
    oraCmd.Dispose();
    oraConn.Dispose();
}
```

The output of the code in Listing 4-6 follows the same pattern as in the previous samples. The primary difference in the code here is that you're using the OracleErrorCollection class through the Errors property of the OracleException object. By simply getting the Count property, you loop through the collection and display the property values to the console. Listing 4-7 illustrates the results of running the sample code.

Listing 4-7. *Output of the OracleErrorCollection Sample Code*

```
C:\My Projects\ProOraNet\Oracle\C#\Chapter04\OraErrorCollection\bin\Debug>↵
OraErrorCollection.exe
Caught OracleException:
```

```
  DataSource: oranet
  Errors Count: 3
  Message: ORA-24381: error(s) in array DML

ORA-01438: value larger than specified precision allows for this column

ORA-01438: value larger than specified precision allows for this column
  Number: 24381
  Procedure:
  Source: Oracle Data Provider for .NET

ErrorCollection[0]:
  ArrayBindIndex: 0
  DataSource: oranet
  Message: ORA-24381: error(s) in array DML

  Number: 24381
  Procedure:
  Source: Oracle Data Provider for .NET

ErrorCollection[1]:
  ArrayBindIndex: 2
  DataSource: oranet
  Message: ORA 01438: value larger than specified precision↩
 allows for this column

  Number: 1438
  Procedure:
  Source: Oracle Data Provider for .NET

ErrorCollection[2]:
  ArrayBindIndex: 3
  DataSource: oranet
  Message: ORA-01438: value larger than specified precision↩
 allows for this column

  Number: 1438
  Procedure:
  Source: Oracle Data Provider for .NET

C:\My Projects\ProOraNet\Oracle\C#\Chapter04\OraErrorCollection\bin\Debug>
```

When you examine the output of the sample code, you can see how the OracleException object has concatenated the messages from the underlying Error objects and that the Error Count property is 3 rather than 1 as it has been in our other samples. On some clients prior to 10g, the second value that should have caused an error may have an ArrayBindIndex value of 0 and no Message property value.

> **■CAUTION** If all the elements in the array "error out," then a `NullReferenceException` run-time exception may occur in the data provider. Thoroughly test the usage of array binding and the `OracleError-Collection` class.

An Exception Logging Approach

I'm going to begin this section with what may seem like a strange statement: The notion of common sense doesn't belong in software development. Let's explore this notion briefly to illustrate why I am making this statement. If you say to someone, "Absence makes the heart grow fonder." their response might be, "Well, of course! Everyone knows that—that's common sense!" Now, here is the problem with common sense: two (or more) notions can be in conflict or opposition with one another. If you say to another individual, "Out of sight, out of mind." that individual's response might be the same as the first person's response. Common sense allows these two oppositional notions to exist without concern. They both seem to make common sense after all.

Rather than rely on the notion of common sense in software development, I prefer to rely on *context sense* instead. Context sense simply means taking a pragmatic approach. Try asking yourself, "Does what this piece of code is doing make sense in the context of the application?" or "Does what this functionality provides make sense in the context of the business need?" for example. Common sense may say, "You must trap all potential errors." Context sense may say, "Judiciously applying exception trapping makes the most sense in this application." For example, would you place the following in a try-catch-finally block?

```
i++;
```

I suspect not—at least not as a stand-alone block of code. However, you may come across situations where this makes sense. You need to know the context in order to make a reasonable decision.

The approach you're going to work through here may (or may not) make sense in your environment or specific application. This is a *logging* approach and not a *handling* approach. Exception handling is one of the areas where you must apply context sense. For instance, would you handle an invalid login attempt by looping until a valid login is entered? Probably not. You'd loop a finite number of times and then quit. What if the application is a batch application? Would you prompt for user input? Is there any point in continuously looping when a batch application submits the same login credentials each time? Of course not. Is there any value in prompting for user input in an application that has no "live" user at the time it is run?

You need a small table to implement this sample, so let's begin by creating the table (see Listing 4-8).

Listing 4-8. *Creating the Exception Logging Table*

```
C:\>sqlplus oranetuser@oranet

SQL*Plus: Release 10.1.0.2.0 - Production on Fri Aug 20 13:13:53 2004

Copyright (c) 1982, 2004, Oracle.  All rights reserved.
```

```
Enter password:

Connected to:
Oracle Database 10g Enterprise Edition Release 10.1.0.2.0 - Production
With the Partitioning, Oracle Label Security, OLAP and Data Mining options

SQL> create table app_exceptions
  2  (
  3    exception_date    date,
  4    username          varchar2(30),
  5    exception_message varchar2(512)
  6  );

Table created.

SQL> exit
Disconnected from Oracle Database 10g Enterprise Edition⤸
 Release 10.1.0.2.0 - Production
With the Partitioning, Oracle Label Security, OLAP and Data Mining options

C:\>
```

Your approach here is to log errors that occur outside of a valid database connection as Application Events accessible via the Event Viewer. For errors that occur in the context of a valid database connection, simply insert the current date, user name, and exception message into your table. In both cases, you also write the exception information to the console window to serve as visible notification that an exception or error occurred. Listing 4-9 contains the full code you use to accomplish this. You can find this project (ExceptionApproach) in this chapter's folder in the Downloads section of the Apress website (www.apress.com).

Listing 4-9. *The Complete Code for the Exception Approach Sample*

```
using System;
using System.Data;
using System.Diagnostics;
using Oracle.DataAccess.Client;

namespace ExceptionApproach
{
  /// <summary>
  /// Summary description for Class1.
  /// </summary>
  class Class1
  {
    /// <summary>
    /// The main entry point for the application.
    /// </summary>
    [STAThread]
```

```
static void Main(string[] args)
{
  Class1 theClass = new Class1();

  // Create a connection string using our standard user with
  // an incorrect password. This will throw an error.
  string c1 = "User Id=oranetuser;Password=badpass;Data Source=oranet";
  OracleConnection conn_1 = new OracleConnection(c1);

  // create a connection string using our standard user and
  // standard tns alias
  string c2 = "User Id=oranetuser;Password=demo;Data Source=oranet";
  OracleConnection conn_2 = new OracleConnection(c2);

  string exceptionInfo = "";

  // try to open a connection with an incorrect password
  // this will fail, so log to the Application log
  try
  {
    conn_1.Open();
  }
  catch (OracleException ex)
  {
    exceptionInfo = "Caught OracleException: " + ex.Message + "\r\n";
    exceptionInfo += "Location: Main method, conn_1.open event\r\n";

    theClass.writeAppLog(exceptionInfo);

    Console.WriteLine(exceptionInfo);
  }
  finally
  {
    if (conn_1.State == ConnectionState.Open)
    {
      conn_1.Close();
    }
  }

  conn_1.Dispose();

  // Try to open a connection with the correct connect
  // information. This should not fail.
  try
  {
    conn_2.Open();
  }
  catch (OracleException ex)
```

```
    {
      exceptionInfo = "Caught OracleException: " + ex.Message + "\r\n";
      exceptionInfo += "Location: Main method, conn_2.open event\r\n";

      theClass.writeAppLog(exceptionInfo);

      Console.WriteLine(exceptionInfo);
    }

    // execute our test if we have an open connection
    if (conn_2.State == ConnectionState.Open)
    {
      // The column c is defined as number(4), so this
      // will be an error. Insert this into our table
      // rather than into the Application log.
      string l_sql = "insert into exception_test(c) values (10001)";
      OracleCommand oraCmd = new OracleCommand(l_sql,conn_2);

      try
      {
        oraCmd.ExecuteNonQuery();
      }
      catch (OracleException ex)
      {
        exceptionInfo = "Caught OracleException: " + ex.Message + "\r\n";
        exceptionInfo += "Location: Main method, insert into↵
        exception_test event\r\n";
        exceptionInfo += "Connect: " + conn_2.ConnectionString;

        theClass.writeAppTable(exceptionInfo, conn_2);

        Console.WriteLine(exceptionInfo);
      }
    }

    if (conn_2.State == ConnectionState.Open)
    {
      conn_2.Close();
    }

    conn_2.Dispose();
}

void writeAppLog(string p_message)
{
  // Open the Application log on the local machine
  EventLog appLog = new EventLog("Application");
```

```
  // create our event source if it does not exist
  if (!EventLog.SourceExists("ExceptionApproach"))
  {
    EventLog.CreateEventSource("ExceptionApproach", "Application");
  }

  // set the source as our source
  appLog.Source = "ExceptionApproach";

  // write entry to application log
  appLog.WriteEntry(p_message, EventLogEntryType.Error);

  // explicitly close and dispose of the appLog
  appLog.Close();
  appLog.Dispose();
}

void writeAppTable(string p_message, OracleConnection p_conn)
{
  // This is the sql that we will use to insert a
  // row into the app_exceptions table.
  // We use a bind variable for the message column.
  // sysdate and user functions supplied by the database
  // They get the current date/time and username respectively.
  string l_sql = "insert into app_exceptions " +
    "(exception_date, username, exception_message) " +
    "values (sysdate, user, :1)";

  // bind the message passed as a parameter
  // we defined the column in the table as varchar2(512)
  // so ensure we use a message that is no greater than
  // 512 bytes in length
  OracleParameter oraParam = new OracleParameter();
  oraParam.OracleDbType = OracleDbType.Varchar2;
  oraParam.Direction = ParameterDirection.Input;

  if (p_message.Length < 513)
  {
    oraParam.Value = p_message;
  }
  else
  {
    oraParam.Value = p_message.Substring(1,512);
  }

  // Create the command object, add the bind parameter
  // and insert.
```

```
    OracleCommand oraCmd = new OracleCommand(l_sql,p_conn);

    oraCmd.Parameters.Add(oraParam);

    oraCmd.ExecuteNonQuery();

    // explicitly dispose of our objects
    oraParam.Dispose();
    oraCmd.Dispose();
    }
  }
}
```

To illustrate the approach clearly in this sample, you explicitly call the Application log helper or the Table log helper methods. You could enhance this simply by checking for a valid connection to the database and then calling the appropriate logging method based on the outcome of that check. Of course, you can extend this approach and customize it in many ways. It is only a starting point, and certainly not appropriate for all circumstances. Use context sense when you're deciding whether the approach is worthwhile for a specific implementation. Figure 4-1 illustrates the Event Viewer log after you run the sample code (ExceptionApproach), which is available in this chapter's folder of the Downloads section of the Apress website (www.apress.com).

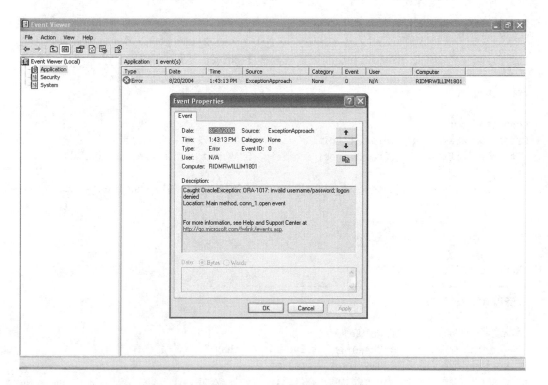

Figure 4-1. *The entry in the Application log after running the sample*

In Figure 4-1, you can clearly see information that would be useful during a debugging or support exercise. The date, time, program (the source property), and client computer are all visible in the event log. Opening the event in the Event Viewer reveals the informational message I inserted into the log. This message identifies what the exception or error is and the location within the program that generated the exception or error. Here you can see the equivalent information I wrote to the console window:

```
C:\My Projects\ProOraNet\Oracle\C#\Chapter04\ExceptionApproach\bin\Debug>↵
ExceptionApproach.exe
Caught OracleException: ORA-1017: invalid username/password; logon denied
Location: Main method, conn_1.open event
```

The second exception that occurs in the sample happens in the context of an open database connection. I elected to write the exception information to a table in the database, and in Listing 4-10, you can see that the information was, in fact, inserted into the exception logging table. Since this took place in the context of an open database connection, you can see the connect string that was used. In Chapter 7, I discuss using what is known as *operating system (O/S) authentication* to connect to the database. Using O/S authentication, you can also easily insert the operating system user ID into the logging information.

Listing 4-10. *The Entry in Our Exception Logging Table*

```
C:\>sqlplus oranetuser@oranet

SQL*Plus: Release 10.1.0.2.0 - Production on Fri Aug 20 14:00:37 2004

Copyright (c) 1982, 2004, Oracle.  All rights reserved.

Enter password:

Connected to:
Oracle Database 10g Enterprise Edition Release 10.1.0.2.0 - Production
With the Partitioning, Oracle Label Security, OLAP and Data Mining options

SQL> select   to_char(exception_date,'DD-MON-YYYY HH24:MI:SS') exception_date,
  2           username,
  3           exception_message
  4  from      app_exceptions;

EXCEPTION_DATE       USERNAME
-------------------- ------------------------------
EXCEPTION_MESSAGE
-----------------------------------------------------
20-AUG-2004 14:17:32 ORANETUSER
Caught OracleException: ORA-01438: value larger than↵
 specified precision allows for this column
Location: Main method, insert into exception_test event
Connect: User Id=oranetuser;Data Source=oranet
```

```
1 row selected.

SQL> exit
Disconnected from Oracle Database 10g Enterprise Edition⏎
 Release 10.1.0.2.0 - Production
With the Partitioning, Oracle Label Security, OLAP and Data Mining options

C:\>
```

You can see from the results of querying your application's exception logging table that the date, user, error message, and information message (including the target table and event) are all inserted into the logging table. In Listing 4-11, you can see the information written to the console window for this exception.

Listing 4-11. *The Second Exception Information as Displayed in the Console Window*

```
Caught OracleException: ORA-01438: value larger than specified precision allows
for this column
Location: Main method, insert into exception_test event
Connect: User Id=oranetuser;Data Source=oranet

C:\My Projects\ProOraNet\Oracle\C#\Chapter04\ExceptionApproach\bin\Debug>
```

Chapter 4 Wrap-Up

In this chapter, I showed you the primary classes you use to detect and report exceptions and errors. In working through a set of samples, you explored the various properties and methods that are available when you're working with these classes. Exception handling is a highly application-dependent activity, and it requires that you know the context of the application as well as its business purpose. For this reason, no clear-cut rule defines exactly when and how an application should respond to errors or exceptions.

However, an application shouldn't "silently discard" errors by catching and ignoring them. The practice that I apply involves implementing error handling in the client. That is, my preference is to allow errors or exceptions to propagate out of the database and be trapped and handled in the client application. The client application is where the context sense is maintained and is, therefore, the best place to handle exceptions and errors. Rounding out the chapter, I examined why this context sense is important and created a sample application that illustrates one method of approach for dealing with exceptions and errors.

CHAPTER 5

■■■

Using PL/SQL from .NET

In a sense, this chapter represents a slight shift in focus from the previous chapters; here, you step out of the .NET environment, to a degree, and delve more deeply into the database itself. The capabilities afforded by Oracle PL/SQL are often overlooked, especially when you're using a development environment outside of the database. This chapter isn't about becoming a PL/SQL expert or dissecting advanced PL/SQL techniques; it gives you enough information to enable you to start using PL/SQL with your .NET programs. The primary focus isn't on *creating* PL/SQL, but on *using* it. It isn't possible to provide a comprehensive examination of everything PL/SQL has to offer in a single chapter—entire books are devoted to that subject. Therefore, your goal in this chapter is to understand how to effectively use PL/SQL to perform common tasks from a .NET program. Specifically, you examine the following topics:

Why use PL/SQL?: You aren't required to use PL/SQL per se, though there are benefits to using it. In this section, you learn why you may find using PL/SQL beneficial.

PL/SQL Packages: Packages and package bodies are an important aspect of PL/SQL. You get to explore how to use packages and package bodies when creating stored PL/SQL code.

Anonymous PL/SQL Blocks: It's possible to use PL/SQL code that isn't stored in the database. Using anonymous blocks is the mechanism used to accomplish this.

Parameters and Return Values: As with plain SQL statements, you can pass parameters to as well as receive return values from PL/SQL. You'll work through a sample using the `OracleParameter` class that illustrates how to do this.

The `Ref Cursor` PL/SQL Data Type: You use a `Ref Cursor` to pass a pointer to a result set on the server to a client. In this section, you develop a familiarity with what `Ref Cursors` are and how to declare them.

Returning Result Sets from PL/SQL: In this section, I use the `Ref Cursor` PL/SQL data type and the `OracleRefCursor` data provider class to illustrate how to pass a pointer that points to a server-based result set to a .NET client program.

Using PL/SQL Associative Arrays: PL/SQL Associative Arrays are arrays PL/SQL can use. In this section, you create a sample application that uses PL/SQL Associative Arrays rather than the host language arrays you used in Chapter 3.

> **■NOTE** A number of PL/SQL components are part of a database installation and are available for general use. These components are published in the "PL/SQL Packages and Types" reference manual included in the Oracle documentation set. In addition, the "PL/SQL User's Guide and Reference" is valuable. If you need to brush up on your PL/SQL skills, I recommend consulting these guides. In addition, *Mastering Oracle PL/SQL: Practical Solutions* (Apress, 2004) is an excellent resource.

Why Use PL/SQL?

This question may immediately come to mind. After all, it's certainly possible to write entire programs or systems without ever writing or calling a single line of PL/SQL code. However, as is often said, just because you *can* do it that way doesn't mean that you *should* do it that way.

PL/SQL is tightly integrated with both the Oracle database and the SQL language. For example, Oracle column types are, in general, PL/SQL data types and vice versa. This means you can work with a single variable that is of the correct data type for both the table and the language. In fact, the PL/SQL language has constructs that enable this seamlessly.

> **■NOTE** Consult the PL/SQL manuals for information on the %type and %ROWtype attributes, which automatically allow declaration of a PL/SQL variable with the correct data type based on the table structure. When you use this method of declaring variables and the underlying length or type of the column changes, this change is transparent to your PL/SQL code and requires no (or at least reduced) code rework.

To declare a variable of the same type and length as a table column, declare the variable of type `tablename.column` and append %type. For example, say you have a table named EMPLOYEES and that table has a column called LAST_NAME that holds an employee's last name. To declare the variable `l_emp_last_name` of this type, you simply declare it as `l_emp_last_name` EMPLOYEES.LAST_NAME%type. In PL/SQL, the variable type follows the variable name rather than preceding it. If you increase the length of the LAST_NAME column from 30 to 48 characters, this change can be transparent to your PL/SQL code that uses this table. In this case, the `l_emp_last_name` variable automatically increases in length to 48. You'll see an example of this as you work through the code in this chapter.

You can use PL/SQL as a security tool as well. It's possible to create a PL/SQL procedure that returns data from a database table to which the user has no direct access. Because the user has no access to the table directly, they aren't able to browse the table using an external tool. Of course, the user needs the appropriate permissions to execute the PL/SQL procedure for this scenario to work correctly, but this is easily accomplished by the administrator of the database.

As you saw when we discussed the FetchSize property in Chapter 2, working with data in sets rather than as individual rows has some performance benefits. PL/SQL offers an alternative way to work with data in batches rather than as discrete rows known as *associative arrays*. Using this functionality, you can perform array-based operations with PL/SQL instead of host language array operations. You learn more about this later in the chapter.

Although there are many reasons to use PL/SQL, as a .NET programmer, you may find that it feels somewhat unnatural to move code out of the .NET environment and into the database. However, PL/SQL was created for the purpose of working with data in an Oracle database, and it does a very good job. Recent releases of the database include enhancements to the PL/SQL compiler and optimizer, which make it even more appealing from a pure performance perspective. The following sections illustrate how using PL/SQL from the .NET environment is made simple by the data provider.

■TIP When working with PL/SQL procedures, functions, packages, and so forth, you should coordinate appropriate object permissions with your administrator. Although this applies in general, of course, it is particularly important when you're working with PL/SQL code. Database roles, by default, are not active when a stored procedure is executing; this can be very confusing for you to troubleshoot if the object privileges are granted to a database role rather than directly to a user. This is fully documented in the "PL/SQL User's Guide and Reference" in the supplied documentation.

PL/SQL Packages

A *package* is a construct that PL/SQL inherited from Ada—the language upon which PL/SQL is based. In a nutshell, a PL/SQL package is a mechanism for storing or bundling related items together as a single logical entity. A package is composed of two distinct pieces:

The package specification: Defines what is contained in the package and is akin to a header file in a language such as C++. Items defined in the specification are *public*. That is, code outside of the specification and body can see these items. The *specification* is the published interface to a package.

The package body: Contains the code for the procedures and functions defined in the specification. The body may also contain code not declared in the specification; in this case, this code is *private*. Other code in the same body can see and invoke this code, but code outside of the body can't.

These two pieces are stored as separate objects in the data dictionary, and they are visible in the user_source view among others. The specification is stored as the PACKAGE type, and the body is stored as the PACKAGE BODY type. You see an example of this shortly.

It's possible to have a specification with no body. It isn't possible, however, to have a body with no specification. For example, you can use a specification with no body to declare a set of public constants; because a set of constants doesn't need an implementation, a body isn't necessary.

Creating a Package Specification and Body

Here is the syntax for creating a package specification:

```
create [or replace] package <package name> {is | as}
<package specification contents>
end [<package name>];
```

When you create a package specification, the optional or replace clause indicates to Oracle that it should replace an existing package specification if one exists. This is a shorthand method that avoids having to first drop a package specification when you're recreating it. You must specify one of the is or as clauses, but not both. I tend to use the as clause when I'm creating package specifications and bodies and the is clause when I'm creating the procedures and functions that reside in the body. I do this solely because it makes the text flow better when I'm reading it (you'll see an example of this when you create a package body). The package specification is terminated with the end keyword, and optionally, the package specification name may follow it.

When you're creating the package body, the syntax is virtually identical to that of the package specification. The only difference in the syntax between the two is the addition of the body keyword to the create clause. Here is the syntax for creating a package body:

```
create [or replace] package body <package name> {is | as}
<package body contents>
end [<package name>];
```

Of course, an empty specification and body aren't of much use. Therefore, I'll briefly examine the syntax you'd use to create a procedure or function within the package body. As you may imagine, the syntax to accomplish this is fairly similar to that of the specification and body:

```
procedure <procedure name> ([<procedure parameters>]) [is | as]
  <variable declarations>
begin
  <procedure body>
[exception]
  <exception block if exception keyword used>
end [procedure name];
```

In order to create a function, you use a similar syntax:

```
function <function name> ([<function parameters>]) return <return type> [is | as]
  <variable declarations>
begin
  <function body>
[exception]
  <exception block if exception keywork used>
end [function name];
```

You may notice that the exception block is an optional component of a procedure or function. The PL/SQL code you develop in this book doesn't make use of this block. Instead you'll let any exceptions raised inside a PL/SQL block of code propagate back to your .NET programs. For additional information on this block, see the Oracle-supplied documentation or *Mastering Oracle PL/SQL: Practical Solutions,* which I mentioned previously.

Now that you've seen the syntax you need to create a package specification, a package body, and a procedure or function, you can create a simple specification and body. In addition, you can query the data dictionary view user_source to see some information related to the specification and body. This simple package contains a public variable and a procedure that displays the value of that variable in the SQL*Plus command window. Listing 5-1 contains the code to create the package specification.

Listing 5-1. *Creating a Simple Package Specification*

```
C:\>sqlplus oranetuser@oranet

SQL*Plus: Release 10.1.0.2.0 - Production on Tue Aug 24 21:12:25 2004

Copyright (c) 1982, 2004, Oracle.  All rights reserved.

Enter password:

Connected to:
Oracle Database 10g Enterprise Edition Release 10.1.0.2.0 - Production
With the Partitioning, Oracle Label Security, OLAP and Data Mining options

SQL>  create or replace package simple_pkg as
  2     l_hello_text varchar2(40) := 'Hello from a simple PL/SQL package!';
  3     procedure display_message;
  4   end simple_pkg;
  5   /

Package created.
```

As you can see in Listing 5-1, this code creates a simple package specification that contains one variable and declares one procedure that will be in the package body. The code in Listing 5-2 is used to create the package body.

Listing 5-2. *Creating the Package Body*

```
SQL> create or replace package body simple_pkg as
  2     procedure display_message is
  3     begin
  4       dbms_output.put_line(l_hello_text);
  5     end display_message;
  6   end simple_pkg;
  7   /

Package body created.
```

As you can see, Listing 5-2 ends with the package body being successfully created. This procedure does nothing more than invoke an Oracle-supplied PL/SQL procedure called put_line, which resides in the dbms_output package. The *l_hello_text* variable is passed as a parameter to this procedure. This package is fully documented in the "PL/SQL Packages and Types" manual in the Oracle documentation set.

Now that you've created the specification and body, you can invoke the procedure from your SQL*Plus session, as illustrated in Listing 5-3. Here is the syntax you use to call a packaged procedure: *<owner>.<package>.<procedure or function name>*. The *<owner>* is optional if the user making the call owns the package, as is the case in Listing 5-3.

Listing 5-3: *Invoking the Simple Procedure*

```
SQL> set serveroutput on size 1000000 format word_wrapped
SQL> begin
  2     simple_pkg.display_message;
  3  end;
  4  /
Hello from a simple PL/SQL package!

PL/SQL procedure successfully completed.
```

In Listing 5-3, you first enable output in your SQL*Plus session so that you can see the output of the procedure. If you execute the procedure and only see the PL/SQL procedure successfully completed. text, it is likely that serveroutput hasn't been enabled in SQL*Plus. After enabling output, invoke your procedure and see the results of displaying the value of the *l_hello_text* variable.

Querying the user_source View

The user_source data dictionary view contains the definition of the package specification and body for the simple_pkg you just created. The structure of this view is presented in Listing 5-4.

Listing 5-4. *The user_source View Structure*

```
SQL> desc user_source
 Name            Null?    Type
 -------------------- ---------------
 NAME                     VARCHAR2(30)
 TYPE                     VARCHAR2(12)
 LINE                     NUMBER
 TEXT                     VARCHAR2(4000)
```

You may recall that I mentioned earlier that the package specification is stored as type PACKAGE in the data dictionary. Listing 5-5 is where you can clearly see this. If you issue a query similar to that in Listing 5-5, you'll display the code that makes up the package specification.

Listing 5-5. *Displaying the Package Specification as Stored in the user_source View*

```
SQL> select   text
  2  from      user_source
  3  where     name = 'SIMPLE_PKG'
  4  and       type = 'PACKAGE'
  5  order by line;

TEXT
--------------------------------------------------------------------
package simple_pkg as
  l_hello_text varchar2(40) := 'Hello from a simple PL/SQL package!';
  procedure display_message;
end simple_pkg;

4 rows selected.
```

In order to see the contents of the package body, you simply need to change the type to PACKAGE BODY as illustrated in Listing 5-6.

Listing 5-6. *Displaying the Package Body as Stored in the user_source View*

```
SQL> select    text
  2  from       user_source
  3  where      name = 'SIMPLE_PKG'
  4  and        type = 'PACKAGE BODY'
  5  order by line;

TEXT
----------------------------------------
package body simple_pkg as
  procedure display_message is
  begin
    dbms_output.put_line(l_hello_text);
  end display_message;
end simple_pkg;

6 rows selected.
```

Procedure and Function Overloading

Like other languages, PL/SQL allows for procedure and function overloading. If you aren't familiar with this concept, it basically means that a package may contain multiple versions of a procedure or a function. The different versions are distinguished by the signature. This means that each version of a procedure or function must have a distinct set of parameter types.

In order to take advantage of overloading, you must use packages. You can't use overloading for stand-alone procedures or functions. The following code snippet illustrates basic overloading.

```
create package overloadtest as
  procedure tproc;
  procedure tproc(p_in_value varchar2);
end;
```

As you can see, two procedures are declared in the specification, and both are named tproc. Of course, both versions of the procedure need to be implemented in the package body. When the PL/SQL run-time engine encounters a call to tproc with no parameters, the first version of the procedure is invoked. If the PL/SQL run-time engine encounters a call to tproc with a varchar2 parameter, the second version of the procedure is invoked. You'll see overloading in action in the complete samples later in the chapter.

Anonymous PL/SQL Blocks

In Listing 5-3, you invoked your simple package procedure by wrapping the call with the begin and end keywords. In doing this, you created what is known as an *anonymous PL/SQL block*. This block is so named because it isn't a named block as your specification, body, and procedure are. Typically, an anonymous block is constructed and executed a single time. Good coding practices dictate that if a block is called multiple times, generally, it's converted to a packaged procedure or function where feasible. If, for example, you're creating an application that executes an anonymous block against a database that the user chooses at run-time, it may not be feasible to convert that block to a stored procedure or function. In addition, as is the case here, you generally use anonymous blocks to invoke stored code in the database. However, this isn't a requirement, as you'll see shortly.

Here's how to construct an anonymous block:

```
[declare]
  <variable declarations>
begin
  <block body>
end;
```

The declare keyword is optional, but you must specify it if you're going to use variable declarations. If the block uses no variables (as was the case in Listing 5-3) this keyword is omitted. You can see an anonymous block by implementing the simple_pkg as an anonymous block. Listing 5-7 illustrates this process and its output.

Listing 5-7. *Implementing the simple_pkg as an Anonymous Block*

```
SQL> set serveroutput on size 1000000 format word_wrapped
SQL> declare
  2    l_hello_text varchar2(48) := 'Hello from a simple PL/SQL⤶
anonymous block!';
  3  begin
  4    dbms_output.put_line(l_hello_text);
  5  end;
  6  /
Hello from a simple PL/SQL anonymous block!

PL/SQL procedure successfully completed.
```

Although anonymous blocks are probably most frequently used to invoke other procedures or functions, you can also use them to batch SQL statements as a single group. You can see this in Listing 5-8.

Listing 5-8. *Using an Anonymous Block to Batch Statements*

```
SQL> create table anon_test
  2  (
  3    name_id number(4) primary key,
  4    name varchar2(32)
  5  );
```

```
Table created.

SQL> begin
  2     insert into anon_test (name_id, name) values (1, 'John');
  3     insert into anon_test (name_id, name) values (2, 'Paul');
  4     insert into anon_test (name_id, name) values (3, 'George');
  5     insert into anon_test (name_id, name) values (4, 'Ringo');
  6  end;
  7  /

PL/SQL procedure successfully completed.

SQL> commit;

Commit complete.

SQL> select    name_id,
  2            name
  3  from      anon_test
  4  order by name_id;

  NAME_ID NAME
---------- ------------
        1 John
        2 Paul
        3 George
        4 Ringo

4 rows selected.
```

Here is a question that comes up frequently: "What would happen if one of the batched statements violated the primary key?" As you discovered in Chapter 3, Oracle transactions either successfully complete or fail as a whole. Therefore, if one of the batched statements violates the primary key constraint, the entire anonymous block is rolled back. You can see this in Listing 5-9.

Listing 5-9. *A Single Statement Causes the Entire Block to Be Rolled Back*

```
  1  begin
  2     insert into anon_test (name_id, name) values (5, 'Micky');
  3     insert into anon_test (name_id, name) values (6, 'Michael');
  4     insert into anon_test (name_id, name) values (7, 'Peter');
  5     insert into anon_test (name_id, name) values (1, 'David');
  6* end;
SQL> /
begin
*
ERROR at line 1:
```

```
ORA-00001: unique constraint (ORANETUSER.SYS_C006173) violated
ORA-06512: at line 5

SQL> select   name_id,
  2           name
  3  from      anon_test
  4  order by name_id;

  NAME_ID NAME
---------- --------------------------------
        1 John
        2 Paul
        3 George
        4 Ringo

4 rows selected.

SQL>
```

Even though only one of the name_id values in the anonymous block violated the primary key (the statement on line 5 in the anonymous block), the entire block is rolled back.

Parameters and Return Values

Back in Chapter 2, I discussed the OracleParameter class and the Direction property exposed by that class. You can use this class to pass parameters to and from your PL/SQL code. When you're working with PL/SQL, your parameters may be input only parameters, input/output parameters, output only parameters, or return values from stored functions. Of course, it's also possible to have a procedure that takes no parameters.

The different modes or directions that a parameter may take are consistent with parameters in other programming languages. You use an input parameter to pass a value to a procedure or function, and such a parameter is read-only within the body of the procedure or function. In contrast, you use an output parameter to return a value to the calling program. When you're using an output parameter, the PL/SQL code changes the value of the variable representing the parameter. The input/output parameter is a hybrid of the input and output parameters. You can use it to pass a value to a procedure; the procedure may then modify it to return a value to the calling program. The return value of a function is assigned to a parameter that you declare using the ParameterDirection.ReturnValue enumeration.

In order to demonstrate using PL/SQL code and the different parameter directions from .NET, I'll show you how to create a table, LEAGUE_RESULTS, using a standard user. You'll use this table for the remaining sample code in this chapter. Listing 5-10 illustrates how to create the table using SQL*Plus.

Listing 5-10. *Creating the Sample Table*

```
C:\>sqlplus oranetuser@oranet

SQL*Plus: Release 10.1.0.2.0 - Production on Wed Jun 2 11:13:50 2004
```

```
Copyright (c) 1982, 2004, Oracle.  All rights reserved.

Enter password:

Connected to:
Oracle Database 10g Enterprise Edition Release 10.1.0.2.0 - Production
With the Partitioning, OLAP and Data Mining options

SQL> create table league_results
  2  (
  3     position      number(2) primary key,
  4     team          varchar2(32),
  5     played        number(2),
  6     wins          number(2),
  7     draws         number(2),
  8     losses        number(2),
  9     goals_for     number(3),
 10     goals_against number(3)
 11  );

Table created.
```

In order to illustrate how to use the different parameter directions and return a value from a function, I'll show you how to create a PL/SQL package, called league_test, which contains the following three procedures and one function:

Insert_row: Allows you to populate the sample table using input parameters.

Retrieve_row: Retrieves data from the table using output parameters.

Calculate_points: Accepts an input/output parameter to identify a particular team in your table, and then modifies the value of this parameter to reflect the number of points that the specified team has accumulated.

get_team: Retrieve a value from the table using a function.

Listing 5-11 shows the package specification where you declare the procedures and function and the package body that contains them. I created this code in the same SQL*Plus session as the table in Listing 5-10.

Listing 5-11. *The league_test PL/SQL Package and Package Body*

```
SQL> create or replace package league_test as
  2     procedure insert_row(p_position in number,
  3        p_team in varchar2,
  4        p_played in number,
  5        p_wins in number,
  6        p_draws in number,
  7        p_losses in number,
```

```
 8      p_goals_for in number,
 9      p_goals_against in number);
10
11    procedure retrieve_row(p_position in number,
12      p_team out varchar2,
13      p_played out number,
14      p_wins out number,
15      p_draws out number,
16      p_losses out number,
17      p_goals_for out number,
18      p_goals_against out number);
19
20    procedure calculate_points(p_inout in out number);
21
22    function get_team(p_position in number) return varchar2;
23  end league_test;
24  /

Package created.

SQL> create or replace package body league_test as
 2    procedure insert_row(p_position in number,
 3      p_team in varchar2,
 4      p_played in number,
 5      p_wins in number,
 6      p_draws in number,
 7      p_losses in number,
 8      p_goals_for in number,
 9      p_goals_against in number) is
10    begin
11      -- insert a row into the table
12      insert into league_results (position,
13        team,
14        played,
15        wins,
16        draws,
17        losses,
18        goals_for,
19        goals_against)
20      values (p_position,
21        p_team,
22        p_played,
23        p_wins,
24        p_draws,
25        p_losses,
26        p_goals_for,
27        p_goals_against);
28    end insert_row;
```

```
29
30    procedure retrieve_row(p_position in number,
31      p_team out varchar2,
32      p_played out number,
33      p_wins out number,
34      p_draws out number,
35      p_losses out number,
36      p_goals_for out number,
37      p_goals_against out number) is
38    begin
39      -- this returns the columns for a given position in the table
40      select    team,
41                played,
42                wins,
43                draws,
44                losses,
45                goals_for,
46                goals_against
47      into      p_team,
48                p_played,
49                p_wins,
50                p_draws,
51                p_losses,
52                p_goals_for,
53                p_goals_against
54      from      league_results
55      where     position = p_position;
56    end retrieve_row;
57
58    procedure calculate_points(p_inout in out number) is
59    begin
60      -- this returns the number of points for a given position
61      -- in the table
62      -- points are calculated as:
63      --   3 points for a win
64      --   1 point for a draw
65      --   0 points for a loss
66      select    (wins * 3) + (draws)
67      into      p_inout
68      from      league_results
69      where     position = p_inout;
70    end calculate_points;
71
72    function get_team(p_position in number) return varchar2 is
73      l_team league_results.team%type;
74    begin
75      -- simply get the team for a given position
76      select    team
```

```
77      into     l_team
78      from     league_results
79      where    position = p_position;
80
81      return l_team;
82    end get_team;
83  end league_test;
84  /
```

Package body created.

At this point, you're ready to create your .NET code that instantiates the Main class and invokes a series of methods to utilize the procedures and the function that you created. You'll create a console application to accomplish this, and, as with your other code, you'll use some helper methods to separate and modularize the code. This sample (Parameters) is available in this chapter's folder in the Downloads section of the Apress website (www.apress.com).

The Main procedure for your sample is presented in Listing 5-12. This procedure simply creates a connection to the database and calls your helper methods.

Listing 5-12. *The Main Procedure*

```
static void Main(string[] args)
{
  // for using our helpers
  Class1 theClass = new Class1();

  // create our standard connection
  string connStr = "User Id=oranetuser; Password=demo; Data Source=oranet";
  OracleConnection oraConn = new OracleConnection(connStr);

  oraConn.Open();

  // call the helper methods
  Console.WriteLine("Executing input parameter sample...");
  theClass.load_table(oraConn);

  Console.WriteLine("Executing ouput parameter sample...");
  theClass.retrieve_row(oraConn, 4);

  Console.WriteLine("Executing input/output parameter sample...");
  theClass.calculate_points(oraConn, 4);

  Console.WriteLine("Executing return value parameter sample...");
  theClass.get_team(oraConn, 4);

  oraConn.Close();

  oraConn.Dispose();
}
```

The load_table Method

In this sample, the code for the load_table method is very simple. It serves as a wrapper for calling the do_insert method. The code in Listing 5-13 loads the sample table with the results of the 2003–2004 English Premier League season final standings. As you can see in Listing 5-13, this code performs a series of single row inserts. You learn how to perform array operations using PL/SQL a little later in the chapter.

Listing 5-13. *The load_table Code*

```
private void load_table(OracleConnection con)
{
  insert_row(con, 1, "Arsenal", 38, 26, 12, 0, 73, 26);
  insert_row(con, 2, "Chelsea", 38, 24, 7, 7, 67, 30);
  insert_row(con, 3, "Manchester United", 38, 23, 6, 9, 64, 35);
  insert_row(con, 4, "Liverpool", 38, 16, 12, 10, 55, 37);
  insert_row(con, 5, "Newcastle United", 38, 13, 17, 8, 52, 40);
  insert_row(con, 6, "Aston Villa", 38, 15, 11, 12, 48, 44);
  insert_row(con, 7, "Charlton Athletic", 38, 14, 11, 13, 51, 51);
  insert_row(con, 8, "Bolton Wanderers", 38, 14, 11, 12, 48, 56);
  insert_row(con, 9, "Fulham", 38, 14, 10, 14, 52, 46);
  insert_row(con, 10, "Birmingham City", 38, 12, 14, 12, 43, 48);
  insert_row(con, 11, "Middlesbrough", 38, 13, 9, 16, 44, 52);
  insert_row(con, 12, "Southampton", 38, 12, 11, 15, 44, 45);
  insert_row(con, 13, "Portsmouth", 38, 12, 9, 17, 47, 54);
  insert_row(con, 14, "Tottenham Hotspur", 38, 13, 6, 19, 47, 57);
  insert_row(con, 15, "Blackburn Rovers", 38, 12, 8, 18, 51, 59);
  insert_row(con, 16, "Manchester City", 38, 9, 14, 15, 55, 54);
  insert_row(con, 17, "Everton", 38, 9, 12, 17, 45, 57);
  insert_row(con, 18, "Leicester City", 38, 6, 15, 17, 48, 65);
  insert_row(con, 19, "Leeds United", 38, 8, 9, 21, 40, 79);
  insert_row(con, 20, "Wolverhampton Wanderers", 38, 7, 12, 19, 38, 77);

  Console.WriteLine("Table successfully loaded.");
  Console.WriteLine();
}
```

The insert_row Code

The code for the insert_row helper method is where you really start to see how to utilize PL/SQL code from your .NET code. You create an input parameter object for each parameter and assign attributes and values as you've done in previous samples. The important differences between the code in Listing 5-14 and previous code is that you're specifying your package and stored procedure name (league_test.insert_row) instead of literal SQL text for the CommandText property, and you're specifying CommandType.StoredProcedure instead of CommandType.Text. You may also notice that my coding preference is to name my .NET methods the same as the PL/SQL procedure or function they'll invoke. This standard or coding preference isn't a requirement. Other than these two primary differences, this code is similar to what you used up to now.

Listing 5-14. *The insert_row Code*

```
private void insert_row(OracleConnection con,
  decimal position,
  string team,
  decimal played,
  decimal wins,
  decimal draws,
  decimal losses,
  decimal goals_for,
  decimal goals_against)
{
  // create parameter objects for each parameter
  OracleParameter p_position = new OracleParameter();
  OracleParameter p_team = new OracleParameter();
  OracleParameter p_played = new OracleParameter();
  OracleParameter p_wins = new OracleParameter();
  OracleParameter p_draws = new OracleParameter();
  OracleParameter p_losses = new OracleParameter();
  OracleParameter p_goals_for = new OracleParameter();
  OracleParameter p_goals_against = new OracleParameter();

  // set non-default attribute values
  p_position.OracleDbType = OracleDbType.Decimal;
  p_played.OracleDbType = OracleDbType.Decimal;
  p_wins.OracleDbType = OracleDbType.Decimal;
  p_draws.OracleDbType = OracleDbType.Decimal;
  p_losses.OracleDbType = OracleDbType.Decimal;
  p_goals_for.OracleDbType = OracleDbType.Decimal;
  p_goals_against.OracleDbType = OracleDbType.Decimal;

  // assign values
  p_position.Value = position;
  p_team.Value = team;
  p_played.Value = played;
  p_wins.Value = wins;
  p_draws.Value = draws;
  p_losses.Value = losses;
  p_goals_for.Value = goals_for;
  p_goals_against.Value = goals_against;

  // create the command object and set attributes
  OracleCommand cmd = new OracleCommand("league_test.insert_row", con);
  cmd.CommandType = CommandType.StoredProcedure;

  // add parameters to collection
  cmd.Parameters.Add(p_position);
  cmd.Parameters.Add(p_team);
```

```
cmd.Parameters.Add(p_played);
cmd.Parameters.Add(p_wins);
cmd.Parameters.Add(p_draws);
cmd.Parameters.Add(p_losses);
cmd.Parameters.Add(p_goals_for);
cmd.Parameters.Add(p_goals_against);

// execute the command
cmd.ExecuteNonQuery();
}
```

The retrieve_row Code

In contrast to the insert_row code, which uses input parameters exclusively, the retrieve_row code in Listing 5-15 uses output parameters for the majority of its functionality. However, the code is again similar in nature. You're creating parameters, setting attributes, executing a call to a stored procedure, and displaying the results to the console window. The comments embedded in the code indicate what task each particular section of the code is performing.

Listing 5-15. *The retrieve_row Code*

```
private void retrieve_row(OracleConnection con, decimal position)
{
  // this retrieves a row and displays to the console
  // it uses the position column to determine which row
  // to retrieve and display

  // create parameter objects for each parameter
  OracleParameter p_position = new OracleParameter();
  OracleParameter p_team = new OracleParameter();
  OracleParameter p_played = new OracleParameter();
  OracleParameter p_wins = new OracleParameter();
  OracleParameter p_draws = new OracleParameter();
  OracleParameter p_losses = new OracleParameter();
  OracleParameter p_goals_for = new OracleParameter();
  OracleParameter p_goals_against = new OracleParameter();

  // set non-default attribute values
  p_position.OracleDbType = OracleDbType.Decimal;
  p_played.OracleDbType = OracleDbType.Decimal;
  p_wins.OracleDbType = OracleDbType.Decimal;
  p_draws.OracleDbType = OracleDbType.Decimal;
  p_losses.OracleDbType = OracleDbType.Decimal;
  p_goals_for.OracleDbType = OracleDbType.Decimal;
  p_goals_against.OracleDbType = OracleDbType.Decimal;

  p_team.Direction = ParameterDirection.Output;
  p_played.Direction = ParameterDirection.Output;
```

```
    p_wins.Direction = ParameterDirection.Output;
    p_draws.Direction = ParameterDirection.Output;
    p_losses.Direction = ParameterDirection.Output;
    p_goals_for.Direction = ParameterDirection.Output;
    p_goals_against.Direction = ParameterDirection.Output;

    p_team.Size = 32;

    // assign values for input parameter
    p_position.Value = position;

    // create the command object and set attributes
    OracleCommand cmd = new OracleCommand("league_test.retrieve_row", con);
    cmd.CommandType = CommandType.StoredProcedure;

    // add parameters to collection
    cmd.Parameters.Add(p_position);
    cmd.Parameters.Add(p_team);
    cmd.Parameters.Add(p_played);
    cmd.Parameters.Add(p_wins);
    cmd.Parameters.Add(p_draws);
    cmd.Parameters.Add(p_losses);
    cmd.Parameters.Add(p_goals_for);
    cmd.Parameters.Add(p_goals_against);

    // execute the command
    cmd.ExecuteNonQuery();

    // output the row to the console window
    Console.WriteLine("     Position: " + position.ToString());
    Console.WriteLine("         Team: " + p_team.Value);
    Console.WriteLine("       Played: " + p_played.Value.ToString());
    Console.WriteLine("         Wins: " + p_wins.Value.ToString());
    Console.WriteLine("        Draws: " + p_draws.Value.ToString());
    Console.WriteLine("       Losses: " + p_losses.Value.ToString());
    Console.WriteLine("    Goals For: " + p_goals_for.Value.ToString());
    Console.WriteLine("Goals Against: " + p_goals_against.Value.ToString());
    Console.WriteLine();
}
```

The calculate_points Code

The code for the calculate_points method uses an input/output parameter to pass a position
value to the database. The database uses that same parameter to return the total points
achieved for that team. Input/output parameters are analogous to a pointer in that they allow
the method to change the value of the parameter. Although I am illustrating how to use an

input/output parameter with a numeric value in Listing 5-16, you can also use them for text transformation. For example, you can pass a text value to a procedure, and the procedure can transform the text in some manner, such as by performing encryption or creating a checksum value. A numeric accumulator is also something that you can easily implement using an input/output parameter.

Listing 5-16. *The calculate_points Code*

```
private void calculate_points(OracleConnection con, decimal inout)
{
  // this gets the total points for a team in position inout
  // and returns the value using the inout parameter

  // create parameter object and set attributes
  OracleParameter p_inout = new OracleParameter();
  p_inout.OracleDbType = OracleDbType.Decimal;
  p_inout.Direction = ParameterDirection.InputOutput;
  p_inout.Value = inout;

  // create the command object and set attributes
  OracleCommand cmd = new OracleCommand("league_test.calculate_points", con);
  cmd.CommandType = CommandType.StoredProcedure;

  // add parameter to the collection
  cmd.Parameters.Add(p_inout);

  // execute the command
  cmd.ExecuteNonQuery();

  // output the result to the console window
  Console.WriteLine("Total Points for position {0}: {1}",
    inout.ToString(), p_inout.Value.ToString());

  Console.WriteLine();
}
```

The get_team Code

The code in Listing 5-17 utilizes the get_team function and illustrates how to use a return value from a function. Using a return value from a function is not especially different from using an output parameter in a procedure. In many cases, it's a matter of semantics or established coding standards. Both accomplish the same task. Because you're retrieving a single value and are using a single input parameter, the code is shorter than that in the previous examples.

Listing 5-17. *The get_team Code*

```
private void get_team(OracleConnection con, decimal position)
{
    // gets the name of the team in position

    // create parameter objects and set attributes
    OracleParameter p_position = new OracleParameter();
    p_position.OracleDbType = OracleDbType.Decimal;
    p_position.Value = position;

    OracleParameter p_retval = new OracleParameter();
    p_retval.Direction = ParameterDirection.ReturnValue;
    p_retval.Size = 32;

    // create the command object and set attributes
    OracleCommand cmd = new OracleCommand("league_test.get_team", con);
    cmd.CommandType = CommandType.StoredProcedure;

    // add parameters to the collection
    cmd.Parameters.Add(p_retval);
    cmd.Parameters.Add(p_position);

    // execute the command
    cmd.ExecuteNonQuery();

    // output the result to the console window
    Console.WriteLine("Team in position {0}: {1}",
        position.ToString(), p_retval.Value.ToString());
}
```

Running the Parameters Sample Application

The sample application doesn't provide any user interactivity, but you can clearly see the results of running the application in a console window. Listing 5-18 illustrates the results of running the application.

Listing 5-18. *The Sample Application Output*

```
C:\My Projects\ProOraNet\Oracle\C#\Chapter05\Parameters\bin\Debug>↵
Parameters.exe
Executing input parameter sample...
Table successfully loaded.

Executing ouput parameter sample...
    Position: 4
        Team: Liverpool
```

```
       Played: 38
         Wins: 16
        Draws: 12
       Losses: 10
    Goals For: 55
Goals Against: 37

Executing input/output parameter sample...
Total Points for position 4: 60

Executing return value parameter sample...
Team in position 4: Liverpool

C:\My Projects\ProOraNet\Oracle\C#\Chapter05\Parameters\bin\Debug>
```

In the output in Listing 5-19, you can clearly see the results of your procedures and function that return values from the database. However, you don't see the full results of the input parameter code that loads the table. In this listing, I've slightly reformatted the output to prevent line wrapping.

Listing 5-19. *The league_results Table*

```
SQL> select * from league_results order by position;

POS TEAM                  PLAYED  WINS DRAWS LOSSES  FOR  AGAINST
---- --                 -------- ------- ----- ------ ----- ---------
   1 Arsenal                 38    26    12      0    73       26
   2 Chelsea                 38    24     7      7    67       30
   3 Manchester United       38    23     6      9    64       35
   4 Liverpool               38    16    12     10    55       37
   5 Newcastle United        38    13    17      8    52       40
   6 Aston Villa             38    15    11     12    48       44
   7 Charlton Athletic       38    14    11     13    51       51
   8 Bolton Wanderers        38    14    11     12    48       56
   9 Fulham                  38    14    10     14    52       46
  10 Birmingham City         38    12    14     12    43       48
  11 Middlesbrough           38    13     9     16    44       52
  12 Southampton             38    12    11     15    44       45
  13 Portsmouth              38    12     9     17    47       54
  14 Tottenham Hotspur       38    13     6     19    47       57
  15 Blackburn Rovers        38    12     8     18    51       59
  16 Manchester City         38     9    14     15    55       54
  17 Everton                 38     9    12     17    45       57
  18 Leicester City          38     6    15     17    48       65
  19 Leeds United            38     8     9     21    40       79
  20 Wolverhampton Wanderers 38     7    12     19    38       77

20 rows selected.
SQL>
```

The Ref Cursor PL/SQL Data Type

One of the primary purposes of the Ref Cursor data type is that it allows PL/SQL to return a result set to a program written in another language. You can also use Ref Cursors within PL/SQL; however, in this section, you'll examine them from the perspective of returning results to an external program. By *external*, I mean a program you wrote in a language other than PL/SQL—one that doesn't reside in the database.

Although I typically refer to "returning a result set," a key attribute of using a Ref Cursor is that the result set actually remains on the server. What is returned to the client is a pointer to the result set on the server. This has an important ramification; when you're using Ref Cursors, the cursor is only valid for an open database connection—if the connection is closed, the Ref Cursor is no longer valid. This makes sense because the Ref Cursor is a pointer to a result set on the server; with no underlying connection, the pointer is invalid. Once you close a Ref Cursor, the resources held on the server are also released.

■**NOTE** The OracleRefCursor class is used with Ref Cursors in the Oracle data provider. You can access the Ref Cursors via the OracleDataReader class in the Microsoft data provider.

Declaring a Ref Cursor Variable in PL/SQL

Before you can return a Ref Cursor to a calling program, you must declare a variable of the appropriate type. Unfortunately, you can't directly declare a variable to be a Ref Cursor. Instead, you must create a user-defined type and declare your variable to be of that type. Although this sounds confusing, it's really quite simple. The following code snippet illustrates this process:

```
-- create the type
type ref_cursor is ref cursor;
-- create the variable of type ref_cursor
l_cursor ref_cursor;
```

A Ref Cursor can be of two types:

Weakly typed: No return type is specified when the type is defined.

Strongly typed: A return type is specified when the type is defined.

The preceding code creates a weakly typed cursor type since no return type was defined. In order to create a strongly typed cursor type, you'll need to use code similar to the following:

```
-- create the type
type ref_cursor is ref cursor return league_results%rowtype;
-- create the variable of type ref_cursor
l_cursor ref_cursor;
```

In this code, a strongly typed cursor type is created. This Ref Cursor can only return a result set that has the structure of the LEAGUE_RESULTS table. The primary advantage of a weakly typed cursor is that you can use it to return any type of result set since no return type was defined. On the other hand, the PL/SQL compiler can check that a strongly typed cursor is associated only with queries that return the correct columns and column types.

NOTE If you know the type that a cursor needs to return, use a strongly typed cursor. If you don't, use a weakly typed cursor. For example, if the cursor returns data from a table whose structure you know at design time, you can use a strongly typed cursor. If the cursor returns data from a table that a user chooses dynamically at run-time, use a weakly typed cursor.

Returning Result Sets from PL/SQL

Earlier in the chapter, you returned values from the database using PL/SQL output, input/output, and function return value parameters. This approach works well when you're dealing with single row or single value results. However, when you're returning multiple rows, a better approach is to return a set of data rather than using individual parameters and values.

As you've just seen, the Ref Cursor is designed for this purpose. Recall the sample code from Chapter 2 where I illustrated the results of single-row fetching versus multiple-row fetching. This is the same principle you employ when you're using PL/SQL to return results from the database. Generally, you can return (or fetch) data in sets more successfully than implementing the same activity using single-row operations. This doesn't mean, however, that the techniques you utilized in the previous section no longer apply when you're returning sets of data. The techniques that you used to return values as parameters are still valid when you're returning sets of data—you still return the data as an output parameter or as a function return value. In this case, the output parameter or return value is a Ref Cursor rather than a scalar value.

You acquire the OracleRefCursor object as an output parameter or a function return value of type OracleDbType.RefCursor. There are no constructors for the OracleRefCursor class. Once you've acquired a PL/SQL Ref Cursor as an OracleRefCursor, you can populate an Oracle-DataReader or a DataSet object in your code. Although you can update data in a DataSet, a Ref Cursor itself isn't updateable. Therefore, if you choose to implement the capability to update data you retrieve via a Ref Cursor, you must provide a custom SQL statement for the Oracle-DataAdapter object. I address returning data rather than updating data from a Ref Cursor in this section.

Because you've already seen how to fill a DataGrid using a DataSet in Chapter 2, here, you'll create a console application that displays, as a comma-separated list, the contents of the LEAGUE_RESULTS table that you created and populated in the previous section.

Once you've acquired the Ref Cursor and populated an OracleDataReader, you'll see that it is no different working with the data than what you do if you use a SQL statement in your .NET code. However, because the code that returns your set of data resides in the database, it receives all the benefits that I mentioned earlier in the chapter, that is, it is compiled and available for the database server to reuse it.

To return the Ref Cursor from the database, you create a new package and package body as illustrated in Listing 5-20. You can also return a Ref Cursor using an anonymous block. The technique is the same as I illustrate here. The only difference is that the code resides in an anonymous block instead of a package. Here, you're using a get_table procedure and get_table function to illustrate the two different means of returning your cursor. The get_table routine is overloaded, and when the package code executes, the PL/SQL run-time determines (based on the different signatures of the two routines) the appropriate routine to invoke. I discussed overloading earlier in the chapter.

Listing 5-20. *Creating the league_rc PL/SQL Code*

```
C:\>sqlplus oranetuser@oranet

SQL*Plus: Release 10.1.0.2.0 - Production on Wed Aug 25 11:50:46 2004

Copyright (c) 1982, 2004, Oracle.  All rights reserved.

Enter password:

Connected to:
Oracle Database 10g Enterprise Edition Release 10.1.0.2.0 - Production
With the Partitioning, Oracle Label Security, OLAP and Data Mining options

SQL> create or replace package league_rc as
  2    type ref_cursor is ref cursor return league_results%rowtype;
  3
  4    function get_table return ref_cursor;
  5    procedure get_table (p_cursor out ref_cursor);
  6  end league_rc;
  7  /

Package created.

SQL> create or replace package body league_rc as
  2    function get_table return ref_cursor is
  3      l_cursor ref_cursor;
  4    begin
  5      open l_cursor for
  6      select    position,
  7                team,
  8                played,
  9                wins,
 10                draws,
 11                losses,
 12                goals_for,
 13                goals_against
 14      from      league_results
```

```
15      order by position;
16
17      return l_cursor;
18    end get_table;
19
20    procedure get_table (p_cursor out ref_cursor) is
21    begin
22      open p_cursor for
23      select   position,
24               team,
25               played,
26               wins,
27               draws,
28               losses,
29               goals_for,
30               goals_against
31      from     league_results
32      order by position;
33    end get_table;
34  end league_rc;
35  /
```

Package body created.

In the PL/SQL code, you can see that you're declaring Ref_Cursor as a strongly typed Ref
Cursor type. This is how you return the cursor to your .NET client code. In each routine, the
cursor opens using a basic SELECT statement that retrieves and orders all of the rows in the
LEAGUE_RESULTS table. This is an area where PL/SQL excels. Due to the tight integration of
SQL and PL/SQL, you're able to embed SQL statements in your PL/SQL code with no modifi-
cations.

The Main method for your console application, which is the RefCursor solution in this
chapter's folder in the Downloads section of the Apress website (www.apress.com), is presented
in Listing 5-21. As you can see, it is similar to the previous code you've examined.

Listing 5-21. *The Main Method Code*

```
static void Main(string[] args)
{
  // for using our helpers
  Class1 theClass = new Class1();

  // create our standard connection
  string connStr = "User Id=oranetuser; Password=demo; Data Source=oranet";
  OracleConnection oraConn = new OracleConnection(connStr);

  oraConn.Open();

  // call the helper methods
```

```
    Console.WriteLine("Invoking ref cursor function...");
    theClass.call_function(oraConn);

    Console.WriteLine("Invoking ref cursor procedure...");
    theClass.call_procedure(oraConn);

    oraConn.Close();

    oraConn.Dispose();
}
```

The call_function Code

The call_function helper method in Listing 5-22 invokes the get_table function rather than the procedure in your PL/SQL package. Because you've declared the parameter direction to be a return value (ParameterDirection.ReturnValue) for your parameter, the code the data provider sent to the database causes the PL/SQL engine to invoke your function rather than your procedure. (Refer to the discussion of the Direction property in Chapter 2 if you need a refresher on this property.)

As I indicate with the code comments, it's important to assign the OracleDbType property correctly. By moving the code that deals with the data directly into the database, you simplify the .NET code you need.

Listing 5-22. *The call_function Code*

```
private void call_function(OracleConnection con)
{
  // create the command object and set attributes
  OracleCommand cmd = new OracleCommand("league_rc.get_table", con);
  cmd.CommandType = CommandType.StoredProcedure;

  // create parameter object for the cursor
  OracleParameter p_refcursor = new OracleParameter();

  // this is vital to set when using ref cursors
  p_refcursor.OracleDbType = OracleDbType.RefCursor;
  p_refcursor.Direction = ParameterDirection.ReturnValue;

  cmd.Parameters.Add(p_refcursor);

  OracleDataReader reader = cmd.ExecuteReader();

  while (reader.Read())
  {
    Console.Write(reader.GetDecimal(0).ToString() + ",");
    Console.Write(reader.GetString(1) + ",");
    Console.Write(reader.GetDecimal(2).ToString() + ",");
    Console.Write(reader.GetDecimal(3).ToString() + ",");
```

```
      Console.Write(reader.GetDecimal(4).ToString() + ",");
      Console.Write(reader.GetDecimal(5).ToString() + ",");
      Console.Write(reader.GetDecimal(6).ToString() + ",");
      Console.WriteLine(reader.GetDecimal(7).ToString());
    }

    Console.WriteLine();

    reader.Close();
    reader.Dispose();
    p_refcursor.Dispose();
    cmd.Dispose();
}
```

The call_procedure Code

The call_procedure code, as presented in Listing 5-23, is very similar to the code for the call_function method. You shouldn't be surprised by this. Because you elected to use an over-loaded PL/SQL routine in the database, the primary difference between the two methods is that the parameter direction is specified differently. In order to correctly invoke your proce-dure in the database, you must declare the parameter direction to be an output parameter rather than a return value as you did in the call_function code. As with the function call code, you must correctly assign the OracleDbType as a RefCursor.

Listing 5-23. *The call_procedure Code*

```
private void call_procedure(OracleConnection con)
{
  // create the command object and set attributes
  OracleCommand cmd = new OracleCommand("league_rc.get_table", con);
  cmd.CommandType = CommandType.StoredProcedure;

  // create parameter object for the cursor
  OracleParameter p_refcursor = new OracleParameter();

  // this is vital to set when using ref cursors
  p_refcursor.OracleDbType = OracleDbType.RefCursor;
  p_refcursor.Direction = ParameterDirection.Output;

  cmd.Parameters.Add(p_refcursor);

  OracleDataReader reader = cmd.ExecuteReader();

  while (reader.Read())
  {
    Console.Write(reader.GetDecimal(0).ToString() + ",");
    Console.Write(reader.GetString(1) + ",");
    Console.Write(reader.GetDecimal(2).ToString() + ",");
```

```
        Console.Write(reader.GetDecimal(3).ToString() + ",");
        Console.Write(reader.GetDecimal(4).ToString() + ",");
        Console.Write(reader.GetDecimal(5).ToString() + ",");
        Console.Write(reader.GetDecimal(6).ToString() + ",");
        Console.WriteLine(reader.GetDecimal(7).ToString());
    }

    Console.WriteLine();

    reader.Close();
    reader.Dispose();
    p_refcursor.Dispose();
    cmd.Dispose();
}
```

Running the RefCursor Sample Application

When you run the sample application, it creates two sets of output to the console window.
The output is the same for each method, as illustrated in Listing 5-24. As with the parameters
sample from the previous section, whether you choose to use a procedure or a function often
comes down to semantics. As you discovered in the call_procedure and call_function code,
using either mechanism is very similar.

Listing 5-24. *The RefCursor Application Output*

```
C:\My Projects\ProOraNet\Oracle\C#\Chapter05\RefCursor\bin\Debug>RefCursor.exe
Invoking ref cursor function...
1,Arsenal,38,26,12,0,73,26
2,Chelsea,38,24,7,7,67,30
3,Manchester United,38,23,6,9,64,35
4,Liverpool,38,16,12,10,55,37
5,Newcastle United,38,13,17,8,52,40
6,Aston Villa,38,15,11,12,48,44
7,Charlton Athletic,38,14,11,13,51,51
8,Bolton Wanderers,38,14,11,12,48,56
9,Fulham,38,14,10,14,52,46
10,Birmingham City,38,12,14,12,43,48
11,Middlesbrough,38,13,9,16,44,52
12,Southampton,38,12,11,15,44,45
13,Portsmouth,38,12,9,17,47,54
14,Tottenham Hotspur,38,13,6,19,47,57
15,Blackburn Rovers,38,12,8,18,51,59
16,Manchester City,38,9,14,15,55,54
17,Everton,38,9,12,17,45,57
18,Leicester City,38,6,15,17,48,65
19,Leeds United,38,8,9,21,40,79
20,Wolverhampton Wanderers,38,7,12,19,38,77
```

```
Invoking ref cursor procedure...
1,Arsenal,38,26,12,0,73,26
2,Chelsea,38,24,7,7,67,30
3,Manchester United,38,23,6,9,64,35
[duplicate output snipped]
20,Wolverhampton Wanderers,38,7,12,19,38,77

C:\My Projects\ProOraNet\Oracle\C#\Chapter05\RefCursor\bin\Debug>
```

Performing Bulk Operations

Earlier in the chapter, you used a routine in a PL/SQL package to insert rows into the LEAGUE_RESULTS table. That procedure inserted a single row at a time and was called repeatedly for each row that you inserted. As you saw in Chapters 2 and 3, performing operations in bulk can be a more efficient manner. The Oracle Data Provider for .NET allows you to use array binding to accomplish this when you're using arrays in .NET code. You can also use PL/SQL arrays, which are known as PL/SQL Associative Arrays. On major advantage of using these arrays, is that you can pass arrays to and from your PL/SQL code stored in the database, which means you can retrieve data in arrays, which you weren't able to do when using host language arrays.

■**NOTE** The PL/SQL Associative Array feature isn't available in the current version of the Microsoft data provider.

PL/SQL Associative Arrays

A PL/SQL Associative Array is also known as a *PL/SQL Index-By Table*. The reason for this is that when you create a type to represent the array, you use the keywords table and index by. The syntax to declare such a type looks like this:

```
type <type name> is table of <data type> index by binary_integer
```

This creates an in-memory structure that is a set of key and value pairs. Specifying the index by binary_integer clause means that the key is an integer value. The value associated with each integer key is of type <data type>, which you specified when you created the type. For instance, to create an associative array that has integer key values and varchar2 data values with a maximum length of 32, you use a statement such as the following:

■**NOTE** In version 9i and later, you can also specify varchar2 as the index by instead of binary_integer. This is documented in the PL/SQL User's Guide and Reference shipped with the Oracle documentation.

```
type t_assoc_array is table of varchar2(32) index by binary_integer;
```

Rather than specifying specific data types, you can also use the %type keyword we've discussed previously. This is illustrated by the following:

```
type t_assoc_array is table of league_results.team%type index by binary_integer;
```

The type created in here is of the same data type as the team column in the LEAGUE_RESULTS table.

You can access individual key/value pairs in the array by using a subscript operator and specifying the index value. For example, using the t_assoc_array type and an anonymous block, you can create a variable of this type and access individual elements as illustrated in Listing 5-25.

▪NOTE Two dashes (--) are used to indicate a single line comment in PL/SQL. You can also use the C language convention of /* and */ for multiline comments.

Listing 5-25. *Creating an Associative Array Variable and Accessing Elements*

```
SQL> declare
  2     -- create the type
  3     type t_assoc_array is table of varchar2(32) index by binary_integer;
  4     -- create a variable of that type
  5     l_assoc_variable t_assoc_array;
  6     -- another variable to assign the value
  7     l_temp varchar2(32);
  8  begin
  9     -- add an element to the array
 10     l_assoc_variable(1) := 'An associative array value';
 11     -- get the element from the array
 12     l_temp := l_assoc_variable(1);
 13     -- display the value
 14     dbms_output.put_line(l_temp);
 15  end;
 16  /
An associative array value

PL/SQL procedure successfully completed.
```

In order to determine the index value for the first or last element in an associative array, you can use the first and last properties. These supply the equivalent of the lower and upper bounds of a .NET array. Listing 5-26 illustrates accessing these properties.

Listing 5-26. *Accessing the first and last Properties of an Associative Array*

```
SQL> declare
  2     -- create the type
  3     type t_assoc_array is table of varchar2(32) index by binary_integer;
```

```
 4      -- create a variable of that type
 5      l_assoc_variable t_assoc_array;
 6   begin
 7      -- add some elements to the array
 8      l_assoc_variable(1) := 'Element 1';
 9      l_assoc_variable(2) := 'Element 2';
10      l_assoc_variable(3) := 'Element 3';
11      l_assoc_variable(4) := 'Element 4';
12      -- display the lower bound
13      dbms_output.put_line(l_assoc_variable.first);
14      -- display the upper bound
15      dbms_output.put_line(l_assoc_variable.last);
16   end;
17   /
1
4
```

```
PL/SQL procedure successfully completed.
```

Using Bulk Binding

Using the first and last properties of an associative array does allow you to iterate over the array using a for loop. However, this isn't a very efficient method of performing this activity. Fortunately, PL/SQL allows you to perform operations on the array in bulk. Using bulk bind-ing, you can populate an entire array in a single operation. You can also access all elements in an array in a single operation. To perform this operation when you're using an UPDATE, INSERT, or DELETE statement, you use the forall keyword. To perform this when doing a SELECT, spec-ify the bulk collect keywords. Remember that these bulk operations take place on a PL/SQL Associative Array and not inside a plain SQL statement. You must use an anonymous block, a procedure, or a function to accomplish this task.

In order to use bulk binding, you must, of course, first create an associative array. The general syntax for using bulk binding with an UPDATE, INSERT, or DELETE statement is as follows:

```
forall <indexer> in <array.first>..<array.last>
  <update, insert, or delete statement> <array(<indexer>)>;
```

If you use the t_assoc_array and the l_assoc_variable from the previous section, an insert operation using bulk binding into a table named t would resemble the following code snippet:

```
forall x in l_assoc_variable.first..l_assoc_variable.last
  insert into t values (l_assoc_variable(x));
```

Using bulk binding with a select operation works in a similar manner. Again if you use the same associative array and variable, a bulk select would be similar to the following:

```
select    column
bulk collect into l_assoc_variable
from      t
order by t;
```

The Associative Array Bulk Sample Application

When you're working with PL/SQL arrays, you perform the same basic operations that you did when you were using host language arrays. Your sample console application (Associative in this chapter's folder of the Downloads section of the Apress website) ties together the concepts of PL/SQL Associative Arrays and bulk binding. This sample follows the pattern that you've developed of creating parameter objects, setting attribute values, adding the parameters to the command object parameter collection, and finally executing the code associated with the command object. In contrast to the code in Chapter 3, this code invokes stored procedures in the database to insert and select the sample data rather than utilize SQL statements embedded in the .NET code.

Listing 5-27 illustrates how to create the package and package body that contain the following two stored procedures that you use in this sample:

bulk_insert: This procedure performs a bulk insert (using an associative array) of data in the LEAGUE_RESULTS table.

bulk_select: This procedure performs a bulk select (using an associative array) of data from the LEAGUE_RESULTS table.

In the package declaration, you create a type for each column in the database table. This serves as your array inside of the PL/SQL code. You marshal data between the database and your .NET code using `OracleParameter` objects and these PL/SQL arrays. The PL/SQL procedures themselves are quite simple. They simply insert all of the values in the passed-in array into the LEAGUE_RESULTS table, or they return all of the data in the table to your client code.

Listing 5-27. *Creating the PL/SQL Package and Package Body*

```
C:\>sqlplus oranetuser@oranet

SQL*Plus: Release 10.1.0.2.0 - Production on Wed Aug 25 12:57:04 2004

Copyright (c) 1982, 2004, Oracle.  All rights reserved.

Enter password:

Connected to:
Oracle Database 10g Enterprise Edition Release 10.1.0.2.0 - Production
With the Partitioning, Oracle Label Security, OLAP and Data Mining options

SQL> create or replace package league_associative as
  2     -- create a type for each column
  3     type t_position is table of league_results.position%type
  4       index by binary_integer;
  5     type t_team is table of league_results.team%type
  6       index by binary_integer;
  7     type t_played is table of league_results.played%type
  8       index by binary_integer;
  9     type t_wins is table of league_results.wins%type
```

```
10        index by binary_integer;
11     type t_draws is table of league_results.draws%type
12        index by binary_integer;
13     type t_losses is table of league_results.losses%type
14        index by binary_integer;
15     type t_goals_for is table of league_results.goals_for%type
16        index by binary_integer;
17     type t_goals_against is table of league_results.goals_against%type
18        index by binary_integer;
19
20     -- the procedures that will perform our work
21     procedure bulk_insert (p_position in t_position,
22                            p_team in t_team,
23                            p_played in t_played,
24                            p_wins in t_wins,
25                            p_draws in t_draws,
26                            p_losses in t_losses,
27                            p_goals_for in t_goals_for,
28                            p_goals_against in t_goals_against);
29
30     procedure bulk_select (p_position out t_position,
31                            p_team out t_team,
32                            p_played out t_played,
33                            p_wins out t_wins,
34                            p_draws out t_draws,
35                            p_losses out t_losses,
36                            p_goals_for out t_goals_for,
37                            p_goals_against out t_goals_against);
38  end league_associative;
39  /

Package created.

SQL>
SQL> create or replace package body league_associative as
 2     procedure bulk_insert (p_position in t_position,
 3                            p_team in t_team,
 4                            p_played in t_played,
 5                            p_wins in t_wins,
 6                            p_draws in t_draws,
 7                            p_losses in t_losses,
 8                            p_goals_for in t_goals_for,
 9                            p_goals_against in t_goals_against) is
10     begin
11       forall i in p_position.first..p_position.last
12       insert into league_results (position,
13                                    team,
14                                    played,
```

```
15                                 wins,
16                                 draws,
17                                 losses,
18                                 goals_for,
19                                 goals_against)
20                         values (p_position(i),
21                                 p_team(i),
22                                 p_played(i),
23                                 p_wins(i),
24                                 p_draws(i),
25                                 p_losses(i),
26                                 p_goals_for(i),
27                                 p_goals_against(i));
28     end bulk_insert;
29
30     procedure bulk_select (p_position out t_position,
31                            p_team out t_team,
32                            p_played out t_played,
33                            p_wins out t_wins,
34                            p_draws out t_draws,
35                            p_losses out t_losses,
36                            p_goals_for out t_goals_for,
37                            p_goals_against out t_goals_against) is
38     begin
39       select    position,
40                 team,
41                 played,
42                 wins,
43                 draws,
44                 losses,
45                 goals_for,
46                 goals_against
47         bulk collect into p_position,
48                           p_team,
49                           p_played,
50                           p_wins,
51                           p_draws,
52                           p_losses,
53                           p_goals_for,
54                           p_goals_against
55         from      league_results
56         order by position;
57     end bulk_select;
58   end league_associative;
59   /
```

Package body created.

SQL>

Now that you have successfully created your PL/SQL code, you can create the familiar looking Main method as illustrated in Listing 5-28. Here, you'll use an addition to the source code file that you haven't seen before; you include using Oracle.DataAccess.Types; at the top of the source code file. Although I've included this namespace in the template applications in the code download, this is the first time you've expressly needed to use it. You need to determine what type of value your parameter represents in the code that displays the data in the console window, and including the Types enumeration in your source file makes this easier.

Listing 5-28. *The Main Method Code*

```
static void Main(string[] args)
{
  // for using our helpers
  Class1 theClass = new Class1();

  // create our standard connection
  string connStr = "User Id=oranetuser; Password=demo; Data Source=oranet";
  OracleConnection oraConn = new OracleConnection(connStr);

  oraConn.Open();

  // call the helper methods
  Console.WriteLine("Truncating table...");
  theClass.truncate_table(oraConn);
  Console.WriteLine("Completed truncating table...");
  Console.WriteLine();

  Console.WriteLine("Executing associative insert...");
  theClass.associative_insert(oraConn);
  Console.WriteLine("Completed associative insert...");
  Console.WriteLine();

  Console.WriteLine("Executing associative select...");
  theClass.associative_select(oraConn);
  Console.WriteLine("Completed associative select...");

  oraConn.Close();

  oraConn.Dispose();
}
```

The truncate_table Helper Method Code

Because you'll load the exact same data that already resides in the LEAGUE_RESULTS table shortly, you need to remove the existing data first. The truncate_table helper method in Listing 5-29 accomplishes this task. If you didn't remove the data, you'd get a constraint violation for the primary key column position.

Listing 5-29. *The truncate_table Method Code*

```
private void truncate_table(OracleConnection con)
{
  // a very simple helper method to truncate the
  // league_results table
  // since we will be inserting data that would
  // violate the primary key otherwise

  // create the command object and set attributes
  OracleCommand cmd = new OracleCommand("truncate table league_results", con);

  cmd.ExecuteNonQuery();
}
```

The associative_insert Method Code

The associative_insert method in Listing 5-30 is responsible for setting up all the parameter objects and invoking the PL/SQL procedure that you created earlier. Because you aren't using default values for most of the attributes in this code, the code may seem more verbose than the code you've seen up to now. However, the code repeats the same basic pattern that the other code you've created follows.

 In the same way that you must set the OracleDbType correctly for code that uses a Ref Cursor, you must set the CollectionType property to PLSQLAssociativeArray for your code to function properly. Once you've set the attributes for your objects, assign values to the parameter objects. You're using the same data that you used earlier to populate the LEAGUE_RESULTS table. However, in this code, you're populating the table in a single database call and round-trip.

Listing 5-30. *The associative_insert Method Code*

```
private void associative_insert(OracleConnection con)
{
  // create the command object and set attributes
  OracleCommand cmd = new OracleCommand("league_associative.bulk_insert", con);
  cmd.CommandType = CommandType.StoredProcedure;

  // create parameter objects for each parameter
  OracleParameter p_position = new OracleParameter();
  OracleParameter p_team = new OracleParameter();
  OracleParameter p_played = new OracleParameter();
  OracleParameter p_wins = new OracleParameter();
  OracleParameter p_draws = new OracleParameter();
  OracleParameter p_losses = new OracleParameter();
  OracleParameter p_goals_for = new OracleParameter();
  OracleParameter p_goals_against = new OracleParameter();

  // set parameter type for each parameter
  p_position.OracleDbType = OracleDbType.Decimal;
```

```
p_team.OracleDbType = OracleDbType.Varchar2;
p_played.OracleDbType = OracleDbType.Decimal;
p_wins.OracleDbType = OracleDbType.Decimal;
p_draws.OracleDbType = OracleDbType.Decimal;
p_losses.OracleDbType = OracleDbType.Decimal;
p_goals_for.OracleDbType = OracleDbType.Decimal;
p_goals_against.OracleDbType = OracleDbType.Decimal;

// set the collection type for each parameter
p_position.CollectionType = OracleCollectionType.PLSQLAssociativeArray;
p_team.CollectionType = OracleCollectionType.PLSQLAssociativeArray;
p_played.CollectionType = OracleCollectionType.PLSQLAssociativeArray;
p_wins.CollectionType = OracleCollectionType.PLSQLAssociativeArray;
p_draws.CollectionType = OracleCollectionType.PLSQLAssociativeArray;
p_losses.CollectionType = OracleCollectionType.PLSQLAssociativeArray;
p_goals_for.CollectionType = OracleCollectionType.PLSQLAssociativeArray;
p_goals_against.CollectionType = OracleCollectionType.PLSQLAssociativeArray;

// set the parameter values
p_position.Value = new decimal[20]{1, 2, 3, 4, 5, 6, 7, 8, 9, 10,
                                   11, 12, 13, 14, 15, 16, 17, 18, 19, 20};

p_team.Value = new string[20]{"Arsenal", "Chelsea",
                              "Manchester United", "Liverpool",
                              "Newcastle United", "Aston Villa",
                              "Charlton Athletic", "Bolton Wanderers",
                              "Fulham", "Birmingham City",
                              "Middlesbrough", "Southampton",
                              "Portsmouth", "Tottenham Hotspur",
                              "Blackburn Rovers", "Manchester City",
                              "Everton", "Leicester City",
                              "Leeds United", "Wolverhampton Wanderers"};

p_played.Value = new decimal[20]{38, 38, 38, 38, 38, 38, 38, 38, 38, 38,
                                 38, 38, 38, 38, 38, 38, 38, 38, 38, 38};

p_wins.Value = new decimal[20]{26, 24, 23, 16, 13, 15, 14, 14, 14, 12, 13,
                               12, 12, 13, 12, 9, 9, 6, 8, 7};

p_draws.Value = new decimal[20]{12, 7, 6, 12, 17, 11, 11, 11, 10, 14, 9,
                                11, 9, 6, 8, 14, 12, 15, 9, 12};

p_losses.Value = new decimal[20]{0, 7, 9, 10, 8, 12, 13, 12, 14, 12,
                                 16, 15, 17, 19, 18, 15, 17, 17, 21, 19};

p_goals_for.Value = new decimal[20]{73, 67, 64, 55, 52, 48, 51, 48, 52, 43,
                                    44, 44, 47, 47, 51, 55, 45, 48, 40, 38};
```

```
    p_goals_against.Value = new decimal[20]{26, 30, 35, 37, 40, 44, 51, 56, 46, 48,
                                            52, 45, 54, 57, 59, 54, 57, 65, 79,
                                            77};

    // set the size for each array
    p_position.Size = 20;
    p_team.Size = 20;
    p_played.Size = 20;
    p_wins.Size = 20;
    p_draws.Size = 20;
    p_losses.Size = 20;
    p_goals_for.Size = 20;
    p_goals_against.Size = 20;

    // set array bind size for the team column since it
    // is a variable size type (varchar2)
    p_team.ArrayBindSize = new int[20]{32, 32, 32, 32, 32, 32, 32, 32, 32, 32,
                                       32, 32, 32, 32, 32, 32, 32, 32, 32, 32};

    // add the parameters to the command object
    cmd.Parameters.Add(p_position);
    cmd.Parameters.Add(p_team);
    cmd.Parameters.Add(p_played);
    cmd.Parameters.Add(p_wins);
    cmd.Parameters.Add(p_draws);
    cmd.Parameters.Add(p_losses);
    cmd.Parameters.Add(p_goals_for);
    cmd.Parameters.Add(p_goals_against);

    // execute the insert
    cmd.ExecuteNonQuery();
}
```

The associative_select Method Code

Once you've inserted the data into the table, select it back out and display it to the console window. The associative_select method code performs these tasks for you. The code in Listing 5-31 is shorter than the code for the associative_insert method since you aren't required to establish parameter values. The important distinctions between this code and the code for the associative_insert method are that you declare the parameters as output parameters and that you assign the array values initially as null.

After performing the requisite setting of attribute values and so forth, you invoke the stored procedure that returns a PL/SQL Associative Array to your .NET code. The .NET code involved in this operation isn't materially different from the code that employed host language array binding.

In the loop that displays the parameter values to the console, you can see the reason for including using Oracle.DataAccess.Types; at the beginning of the source file. Your code needs to determine what type of value a parameter object represents so that it may be output to the console window correctly. By including the namespace, your code is slightly more compact. The loop determines the number of iterations your code must make to retrieve the size attribute from the p_position parameter. All the parameters have the same number of elements. Once the number of overall iterations is determined, you iterate the parameter collection to display the parameter values for each row returned.

Listing 5-31. *The associative_select Method Code*

```
private void associative_select(OracleConnection con)
{
  // create the command object and set attributes
  OracleCommand cmd = new OracleCommand("league_associative.bulk_select", con);
  cmd.CommandType = CommandType.StoredProcedure;

  // create parameter objects for each parameter
  OracleParameter p_position = new OracleParameter();
  OracleParameter p_team = new OracleParameter();
  OracleParameter p_played = new OracleParameter();
  OracleParameter p_wins = new OracleParameter();
  OracleParameter p_draws = new OracleParameter();
  OracleParameter p_losses = new OracleParameter();
  OracleParameter p_goals_for = new OracleParameter();
  OracleParameter p_goals_against = new OracleParameter();

  // set parameter type for each parameter
  p_position.OracleDbType = OracleDbType.Decimal;
  p_team.OracleDbType = OracleDbType.Varchar2;
  p_played.OracleDbType = OracleDbType.Decimal;
  p_wins.OracleDbType = OracleDbType.Decimal;
  p_draws.OracleDbType = OracleDbType.Decimal;
  p_losses.OracleDbType = OracleDbType.Decimal;
  p_goals_for.OracleDbType = OracleDbType.Decimal;
  p_goals_against.OracleDbType = OracleDbType.Decimal;

  // set the collection type for each parameter
  p_position.CollectionType = OracleCollectionType.PLSQLAssociativeArray;
  p_team.CollectionType = OracleCollectionType.PLSQLAssociativeArray;
  p_played.CollectionType = OracleCollectionType.PLSQLAssociativeArray;
  p_wins.CollectionType = OracleCollectionType.PLSQLAssociativeArray;
  p_draws.CollectionType = OracleCollectionType.PLSQLAssociativeArray;
  p_losses.CollectionType = OracleCollectionType.PLSQLAssociativeArray;
  p_goals_for.CollectionType = OracleCollectionType.PLSQLAssociativeArray;
  p_goals_against.CollectionType = OracleCollectionType.PLSQLAssociativeArray;

  // set the direct for each parameter
  p_position.Direction = ParameterDirection.Output;
```

```
    p_team.Direction = ParameterDirection.Output;
    p_played.Direction = ParameterDirection.Output;
    p_wins.Direction = ParameterDirection.Output;
    p_draws.Direction = ParameterDirection.Output;
    p_losses.Direction = ParameterDirection.Output;
    p_goals_for.Direction = ParameterDirection.Output;
    p_goals_against.Direction = ParameterDirection.Output;

    // set the parameter values to null initially
    p_position.Value = null;
    p_team.Value = null;
    p_played.Value = null;
    p_wins.Value = null;
    p_draws.Value = null;
    p_losses.Value = null;
    p_goals_for.Value = null;
    p_goals_against.Value = null;

    // set the size for each array
    p_position.Size = 20;
    p_team.Size = 20;
    p_played.Size = 20;
    p_wins.Size = 20;
    p_draws.Size = 20;
    p_losses.Size = 20;
    p_goals_for.Size = 20;
    p_goals_against.Size = 20;

    // set array bind size for the team column since it
    // is a variable size type (varchar2)
    p_team.ArrayBindSize = new int[20]{32, 32, 32, 32, 32, 32, 32, 32, 32, 32,
                                32, 32, 32, 32, 32, 32, 32, 32, 32, 32};

    // add the parameters to the command object
    cmd.Parameters.Add(p_position);
    cmd.Parameters.Add(p_team);
    cmd.Parameters.Add(p_played);
    cmd.Parameters.Add(p_wins);
    cmd.Parameters.Add(p_draws);
    cmd.Parameters.Add(p_losses);
    cmd.Parameters.Add(p_goals_for);
    cmd.Parameters.Add(p_goals_against);

    // execute the insert
    cmd.ExecuteNonQuery();

    // display as comma separated list
    // field_count is used to determine when
```

```
   // we have completed a "line"
   int field_count = 1;
   for (int i = 0; i < p_position.Size; i++)
   {
     foreach (OracleParameter p in cmd.Parameters)
     {
       if (p.Value is OracleDecimal[])
       {
         Console.Write((p.Value as OracleDecimal[])[i]);
       }
       if (p.Value is OracleString[])
       {
         Console.Write((p.Value as OracleString[])[i]);
       }

       if (field_count < 8)
       {
         Console.Write(",");
       }
       else
       {
         field_count = 0;
       }

       field_count++;
     }
     Console.WriteLine();
   }
}
```

Running the Associative Sample

Like the previous samples, the Associative sample doesn't require any user input. You place a few lines of code to indicate where you are in the execution of the code. You can see these informational messages in the output of the sample in Listing 5-32. The program output is the same as the output from the Ref Cursor sample as you might expect—after all, you used the same data for both samples.

Listing 5-32. *The Associative Sample Output*

```
C:\My Projects\ProOraNet\Oracle\C#\Chapter05\Associative\bin\Debug>⏎
Associative.exe
Truncating table...
Completed truncating table...

Executing associative insert...
Completed associative insert...
```

```
Executing associative select...
1,Arsenal,38,26,12,0,73,26
2,Chelsea,38,24,7,7,67,30
3,Manchester United,38,23,6,9,64,35
4,Liverpool,38,16,12,10,55,37
5,Newcastle United,38,13,17,8,52,40
6,Aston Villa,38,15,11,12,48,44
7,Charlton Athletic,38,14,11,13,51,51
8,Bolton Wanderers,38,14,11,12,48,56
9,Fulham,38,14,10,14,52,46
10,Birmingham City,38,12,14,12,43,48
11,Middlesbrough,38,13,9,16,44,52
12,Southampton,38,12,11,15,44,45
13,Portsmouth,38,12,9,17,47,54
14,Tottenham Hotspur,38,13,6,19,47,57
15,Blackburn Rovers,38,12,8,18,51,59
16,Manchester City,38,9,14,15,55,54
17,Everton,38,9,12,17,45,57
18,Leicester City,38,6,15,17,48,65
19,Leeds United,38,8,9,21,40,79
20,Wolverhampton Wanderers,38,7,12,19,38,77
Completed associative select...

C:\My Projects\ProOraNet\Oracle\C#\Chapter05\Associative\bin\Debug>
```

Chapter 5 Wrap-Up

As I indicated at the beginning of the chapter, this chapter isn't about becoming a PL/SQL expert. However, I designed it to illustrate a topic that is sometimes (or often?) overlooked, yet one that provides a programming technique that is no more difficult than embedding SQL directly into your client code. I showed you some areas that you'll most often encounter when you use PL/SQL in conjunction with .NET code. Specifically I addressed the following:

Reasons for using PL/SQL: Even though you aren't required to use PL/SQL, it has its benefits. We examined these.

Using PL/SQL packages: Packages and package bodies are an important aspect of PL/SQL. You saw how to use these when you're creating stored PL/SQL code.

Working with anonymous PL/SQL blocks: You learned how to use anonymous blocks to invoke code stored in the database and to batch SQL statements.

Applying parameters and return values: You learned to pass parameters to and receive return values from PL/SQL. You built a sample using the OracleParameter class that illustrates how to do this.

Employing the Ref Cursor PL/SQL data type: You learned that using this data type is a way to pass a pointer to a result set on the server to a client. In this section, you became familiar with and learned to understand Ref Cursors and how you declare them.

Returning result sets from PL/SQL: You learned how to apply your newfound knowledge of the Ref Cursor PL/SQL data type and the `OracleRefCursor` data provider class to pass a pointer to a server-based result set to a .NET client program.

Using PL/SQL Associative Arrays: You saw how to create a sample application that uses PL/SQL Associative Arrays rather than using host language arrays. You also became familiar with performing bulk binding operations.

As you saw in Chapter 4, pragmatism and context sense are important aspects of a development effort. Using PL/SQL appropriately can serve to separate the logic and processes that deal directly with the data in a database from the logic and processes that deal with client-side issues. In addition to this separation of duties, the PL/SQL compiler compiles and optimizes code stored in PL/SQL packages once rather than possibly submitting and optimizing it multiple times, as may happen with embedded code that resides in the client. As you'll see in Chapter 6, sometimes using a supplied PL/SQL package is the easiest way to accomplish a task.

CHAPTER 6

■ ■ ■

Working with Large Objects

One of the features of the Oracle database is its ability to easily work with data types that are designed to hold nontraditional data. Typically, two classes of data fall under the umbrella of large objects: semistructured and unstructured data. The data types that you've seen up to this point have all been what are classified as structured data types. These are the types that are most familiar to those working with Oracle. Using these data types, you're able to take a concept, such as an employee, and break it down into a set of attributes such as name, position, department, supervisor, and so forth. Each of these attributes is typically represented by a column in a simple or basic table.

When working with data that is either semistructured or unstructured, it isn't generally possible (or makes no sense) to break the data down into smaller structured components. One method of determining if the data in question falls into either category of semistructured or unstructured data is to answer the question, "Can the database make sense out of the data as it is?" Although this is something of a rhetorical question, it provides a way to classify the data. When you're working with the attributes of an employee, for example, a database can make sense of a department number for an employee in that it relates to a department number in a department table. However, if the database contains an image that represents a retinal scan for that employee, can the database relate the stream of binary data that makes up the image to anything else? Here's another way of looking at the question: Would you create a separate column for each byte that makes up the image and store that image as a series of columns that each hold a byte? Or, would you create a single column to hold the data as a distinct and complete data type? Of course, when you're working with traditional, relational data types, you also run the risk of over-normalizing and breaking the data down into pieces that are too small. The point is, when you're working with large object data, the data typically isn't broken down into smaller components.

One of the benefits of the large object data types is that they can store, not surprisingly, very large amounts of data. In fact, you can store data well into the gigabytes in size using the 10g release and up to 4 gigabytes in previous releases. In this chapter, you'll focus on data that is stored in, but not interpreted by, the database. The data in this chapter is meaningful outside of the database itself, thus illustrating the semistructured or unstructured nature of large object data.

Overview of Oracle Large Objects

The following four types of large objects are available for use with the Oracle database:

BFILE: A file that resides outside of the database and is accessed in a binary, read-only manner by the database.

CLOB: A character (i.e., non-binary) large object that resides inside the database.

NCLOB: A character large object that resides inside the database and is stored in the national character set of the database.

BLOB: A binary large object that is stored inside the database in contrast to the BFILE type.

■**NOTE** The large object support in the data provider requires an application to maintain the database connection throughout the lifetime of the large object itself. If the database connection is closed or disconnected, any large objects created on that connection should be disposed within the application because the state of the objects is now suspect.

The BFILE Large Object Type

The BFILE large object type is distinct from the other three types in that it isn't actually stored in the database. The BFILE, or binary file, type is stored as an operating system file that is external to the database. The database stores a pointer to the BFILE object in a column defined as a BFILE data type. As its name suggests, the database accesses the BFILE as a binary file. This doesn't mean that the BFILE must actually be a binary file; for example, you can use a text file as a BFILE. It just means that the file is accessed as a binary file.

Some important ramifications result from the BFILE object being external to the database: the BFILE object is a read-only object, the BFILE object doesn't participate in transactions, and the BFILE must be accessible to the Oracle server process. This last point is often overlooked and can cause confusion. The BFILE must be located on a filesystem that the Oracle server process can see. When you're using attached drives on a Windows server, those drives aren't visible to a server process. Because the BFILE object is read-only, it's suited for binary data that isn't manipulated by an application. A prime example of this type of file is a multimedia streaming presentation. In addition, a BFILE object is also frequently used to load data into another large object type where it can then be manipulated if necessary.

■**NOTE** Oracle doesn't verify that a BFILE actually exists when you create the BFILE in the database. Instead, it checks for the existence of the BFILE when you access it. Therefore, it's possible to create a BFILE in the database that doesn't yet exist.

The CLOB Large Object Type

You use the CLOB large object type to store text (or string) data, typically using the database's character set as the encoding character set. The CLOB data type is an internal data type, meaning the data is stored in the database rather than on the filesystem as is the case with a BFILE. The CLOB data is stored in the database in a fixed-width format. If the database character set is a multibyte character set (a requirement for a varying-width character set), then CLOB data is stored internally in a format known as UCS-2.

The UCS-2 format is a 16-bit, fixed-width format. If the database character set is a single-byte character set (i.e., non-varying width) then the data is stored using that fixed-width character set. Typically, you'll use the CLOB data type when the length of the stored data exceeds 4,000 bytes—the limit of the varchar2 data type. The CLOB data type is a read-write data type that may also participate in database transactions.

■**NOTE** Although the MS Help file that ships with the Oracle Data Provider indicates that the data provider uses the client character set, this seems to be incorrect. The data provider works with the data using the UCS-2 character set irrespective of client character set.

The NCLOB Large Object Type

Like the CLOB data type, you use the NCLOB data type to store string or character-based data. However, unlike the CLOB data type, you can store the NCLOB data type in a variable-width format if the national character set of the database is variable width. It's possible to store data that can be stored in a CLOB in an NCLOB, though doing so *may* waste space in the database if the national character set is a fixed-width character set. The storage used for an NCLOB is possibly double that of a CLOB based on the underlying character sets. If this is the situation, you can effectively store half the amount of data in an NCLOB as you could in a CLOB. The idea is to only store data that requires an NCLOB in an NCLOB.

The BLOB Large Object Type

While the BFILE date type represents binary data stored outside of the database itself, you use the BLOB data type to store any data as binary data inside the database. Because the data is stored inside the database, BLOB data is read-write and may participate in database transactions. Of course, it's possible to store textual data in a BLOB column; however, it's processed as binary data by the database. As long as the application working with the data is written in a manner that takes this into account, it works. However, it may be more appropriate to use the CLOB or NCLOB data types when you're working with text data.

One advantage that the BLOB data type possesses over the BFILE data type is that it's stored in the database, which makes it easy to back up or move the BLOB data. Another benefit is that it's possible to work with the BLOB data in chunks rather than as a single unit. Of course, this is application dependent, and it may not make sense to work the data in a manner other than as a single entity. When you're working with a BFILE object, Oracle isn't aware of what happens to the object, so you must ensure that the database and the actual object are synchronized manually. For example, if you move the object to a different operating system directory, you must also update the database to indicate this.

■**TIP** In order to work with the large objects easily in a .NET project, you should include the `Oracle.Data-Access.Types` namespace for the Oracle Data Provider for .NET in your project. The template projects in the code download (you can access these from the Downloads section of the Apress website) include this namespace.

■**NOTE** If you're using the Microsoft data provider, the large object types are represented by the `OracleLob` class and the `OracleBFile` class in the `System.Data.OracleClient` namespace.

Working with BFILE Objects

Because a `BFILE` object resides outside the database, you must have some way to inform the database of the file's physical operating system location. The manner in which you do this is via the `DIRECTORY` database object. A `DIRECTORY` object, which was introduced with Oracle9i, replaces the older method of using the `utl_file_dir` initialization file parameter, which has deprecated. Using the `DIRECTORY` object is a much more flexible method of working with directories; you should use it instead of the deprecated initialization file parameter. A `DIRECTORY` object is an alias that is limited to 30 bytes in length. Unlike most schema objects, the `DIRECTORY` object isn't owned by the user that creates it—once it's created, it's placed in a single namespace that is common to the entire database and it's owned by the SYS user. As a result, all `DIRECTORY` objects must have a unique name.

When you create a `DIRECTORY` object, the physical operating system path the object represents doesn't need to include the trailing delimiter—either a \ or a / depending on your operating system. For example, on Windows, a valid specification would be `C:\Temp` or `C:\Temp\`. Similarly, on UNIX, a path to the `tmp` directory could be specified as `/tmp` or `/tmp/`. The syntax for creating the object requires the path to be enclosed in single tick quotes. This has the side effect of making the path name case-sensitive. On an operating system that doesn't employ case-sensitive path names, this isn't an issue. However, if the database you're using resides on such an operating system, you must be sure to specify the path name correctly. You'll see how to create a directory object in more detail later in the chapter when you work through the sample code.

The OracleBFile Class

A `BFILE` object is represented in .NET code as an `OracleBFile` object. Using an instance of the `OracleBFile` class, you can retrieve the pointer to the `BFILE` data in the database from your .NET code. Once you have a "pointer" to the `BFILE` data, you can perform various non-write operations on the file represented by the pointer. The `OracleBFile` class provides 12 properties and 21 methods for your use. I'll demonstrate how to use the most common properties and methods in the sample code later in this chapter. Before you create the sample, you'll take a look at the properties and methods exposed by the `OracleBFile` class. The `OracleBFile` class is in the `Oracle.DataAccess.Types` namespace whereas most of the other classes you've been using are located in the `Oracle.DataAccess.Client` namespace.

The CanRead Property

The `CanRead` property is a read-only, Boolean property that indicates whether the stream for the object can be read. The following code snippet illustrates how to use this simple property.

```
// assumes we have a valid connection
// and bfile object (bfile)
if (bfile.CanRead)
{
  // perform a read operation
}
```

TIP This property is always `True` if the connection associated with the `OracleBFile` object is open and the object hasn't been disposed of.

The CanSeek Property

The `CanSeek` property is a read-only, Boolean property that indicates if it is possible to perform forward and backward seek operations on the underlying stream for the `LOB` object. Like the `CanRead` property, using this property is simple, as demonstrated here:

```
// assumes we have a valid connection
// and bfile object (bfile)
if (bfile.CanSeek)
{
  // perform a seek operation
}
```

TIP This property is always `True` if the connection associated with the `OracleBFile` object is open and the object hasn't been disposed of.

The CanWrite Property

The `CanWrite` property is a Boolean property implemented for its compatibility with the other `LOB` object types. This property is always `False` for an instance of the `OracleBFile` class.

The Connection Property

The Connection property is a read-only property that returns a reference to the OracleConnection object associated with the OracleBFile object. In order to set the Connection property for the object, you use one of the constructors for the OracleBFile class. The following code illustrates getting a reference to the Connection object:

```
// get a reference to the connection
// used by the bfile object
OracleConnection bfileConn = bfile.Connection;
```

The DirectoryName Property

The DirectoryName property is a read-write property that takes or returns a string object as its value. This property coincides with the directory you create using the CREATE DIRECTORY command in the database. This code shows you that the property may be read or written. It's limited to 30 bytes in length.

```
// get the directory name
string bfileDir = bfile.DirectoryName;
```

```
// set the directory name
bfile.DirectoryName = "C_TEMP";
```

■**NOTE** If you attempt to use a directory specified by the deprecated utl_file_dir initialization parameter, you receive an ORA-22285 error indicating that a valid DIRECTORY object doesn't exist.

The FileExists Property

You use the Boolean, read-only FileExists property to determine if the BFILE represented by the OracleBFile object does, in fact, exist. Like with the other properties, the use of the FileExists property is straightforward:

```
// determine if file exists
if (bfile.FileExists)
{
  // perform an operation on the file
}
```

The FileName Property

The FileName property is a read-write string property. You use it in conjunction with the DirectoryName property to identify the physical file at the operating system level. This property is limited to 255 bytes in length. Here is an example of how to use this property:

```
// get the file name
string bfileName = bfile.FileName;

// set the file name
bfile.FileName = "bfile_test.txt";
```

The IsEmpty Property

The Boolean IsEmpty property is a read-only property that indicates whether the file represented by the OracleBFile object contains data. Typically code takes action as long as the file
isn't empty, as is illustrated here:

```
// take action if the file is
// not empty
if (!bfile.IsEmpty)
{
  // perform an action
}
```

> **NOTE** The IsEmpty property isn't implemented by the Microsoft data provider. The Microsoft data
> provider exposes the IsNull property instead.

The IsOpen Property

Typically you use this property to ensure that the BFILE is in an open state before you perform
an action such as a read from the file. Use this property to indicate if the file has been opened
by your code, not if another process has the file open. The following code illustrates using the
Boolean IsOpen property:

```
// take action if the file is open
if (bfile.IsOpen)
{
  // perform an action that requires the file to be open
}
```

> **NOTE** This property isn't exposed by the current version of the Microsoft data provider.

The Length Property

The Length property is a read-only property that returns an Int64 value. This property specifies the length, in bytes, of the file. How to retrieve the value of this property is illustrated here:

```
// get file length in bytes
Int64 bfileLen = bfile.Length;
```

The Position Property

Like the Length property, the Position property is an Int64 value property. Unlike the Length property, the Position property may be set as well as read. Use this property to adjust the position of the read pointer in the underlying stream object. The value for this property may be 0 up to the range permitted by the Int64 data type. The following code illustrates how to use this property:

```
// get the position property
Int64 bfilePos = bfile.Position;

// set the position property
bfile.Position = 16;
```

> **NOTE** This property is related to the stream operations (such as the Read method) that may be performed on the BFILE. It is possible to set this property to a value beyond the end of the file. If you do so, a stream operation such as Read doesn't throw an exception. Instead it simply returns 0 as the number of bytes read and the buffer passed to it isn't populated.

The Value Property

The read-only Value property permits the OracleBFile object to return its contents as a byte array. You can use the Length property combined with the Value property to create a byte array of the appropriate size, as illustrated in the following code; however, this isn't necessary.

```
// create an appropriate size array
// and get the data using the value
// property
byte[] bfileByte = new byte[bfileLen];
bfileByte = bfile.Value;

// can also just declare a byte[]
byte[] bfileBuffer = bfile.Value;
```

The data provider allocates the byte array based on the length and returns a correctly sized byte array to the calling application. Declaring a variable of type byte[] is sufficient as illustrated in the second section of the preceding code snippet.

> **NOTE** This property isn't affected by the Position property and the Position property isn't affected by this property.

The Close Method

The Close method doesn't close the BFILE object on the server; instead, it closes the underlying stream for the OracleBFile object in your .NET code. Any resources associated with the underlying stream object are released when the stream is closed. As illustrated in the following code, the Close method doesn't return a value.

```
// close the underlying stream object
bfile.Close();
```

Once a stream has been closed, you must reopen the BFILE object to acquire a new stream. The Close method severs the connection between the OracleBFile object in your .NET code and the BFILE object on the server. In some ways (though not all), invoking this method is similar to setting the OracleBFile object equal to null, because disposing of the object and setting it equal to a new BFILE are the only meaningful options available once you've invoked this method.

The CloseFile Method

You use the CloseFile method to close the BFILE object on the server, as illustrated here:

```
// close the bfile object
bfile.CloseFile();
```

This method has no return value and doesn't throw an exception if it's invoked on a BFILE object that's already closed. Unlike the Close method, this method doesn't close the OracleBFile object. For example, after invoking this method, you can still retrieve the value of the IsOpen property. If you do, it's False, but you can still access it. After you invoke the Close property, you won't even be able to access the IsOpen property.

The OpenFile Method

The OpenFile method returns no value, but you can use the IsOpen property after invoking this method to determine if the BFILE was successfully opened. Most of the active operations (such as read) require the BFILE to be in an open state in order to function properly. You must correctly set the DirectoryName and FileName properties prior to invoking this method. How to set these properties and invoke the OpenFile method is depicted in the following code:

```
// set the directory object name
bfile.DirectoryName = "C_TEMP";

// set the file name propety
bfile.FileName = "bfile_test.txt";

// open the bfile
bfile.OpenFile();

// make sure the file opened successfully
if (bfile.IsOpen)
{
  // perform processing on open file
}
```

The Read Method

Once you've successfully opened the BFILE, you can use the Read method to read data from the physical file. The Read method returns an int value, indicating the number of bytes that were read from the file. This method takes three parameters: a byte array to store the results of the read operation, an int that indicates an offset in the byte array where the results of the read should be placed, and an int that specifies the number of bytes to read from the BFILE. Using this method, you can read through the BFILE in chunks. The following code illustrates one method of reading the first 16 bytes of the underlying file.

```
// read the first 16 bytes of the file
byte[] bfileBuffer = new byte[16];
int bytesRead = bfile.Read(bfileBuffer, 0, 16);
```

■**NOTE** You can use the ReadByte method, which is inherited from the Stream object, to read through the stream a byte at a time.

The Search Method

The Search method exposes the functionality to search for a *binary* pattern in the BFILE object. The method returns an Int64, which represents the one-based position of the search pattern's occurrence. The method takes three parameters: a byte array, which specifies the pattern; an Int64, which specifies the offset to begin the search; and an Int64, which represents the *n*th occurrence of the pattern. The third parameter allows you to search for the first occurrence, or the second occurrence, or the third occurrence, and so on, up to the *n*th occurrence. The value of this parameter can be as large as the value that can be expressed by an Int64 of the pattern in the file. The search pattern itself is limited to 16,383 bytes in length. The following code searches for the first occurrence of the binary pattern 84 beginning at the start of the file. This method returns 0 if the pattern isn't found in the file.

■**NOTE** This method isn't available in the current version of the Microsoft data provider.

```
// search for a pattern
byte[] pattern = new byte[1]{84};
Int64 patternOffset = bfile.Search(pattern, 0, 1);
```

■**CAUTION** The documentation may incorrectly indicate that this method returns an int rather than an Int64 depending on the version of the documentation you have. There are some differences in the documentation that ships with the data provider and the documentation that is integrated with the Visual Studio Help system.

The Seek Method

The Seek method takes two parameters and returns an Int64 value. The following two parameters are accepted by the Seek method: an Int64 that indicates the offset at which the seek operation will begin, and a value of the System.IO.SeekOrigin enumeration. Typically you use this method to position the read pointer to either the beginning or the end of the underlying stream object. The return value of this method indicates the position of the read pointer in bytes within the BFILE. The following code illustrates how to move the read pointer to the end of the file and then reposition it to the beginning of the file.

```
// position the read pointer at the end of the file
// position will equal bfile.Length
Int64 position = bfile.Seek(0, SeekOrigin.End);

// position the read pointer at the start of the file
position = bfile.Seek(0, SeekOrigin.Begin);
```

NOTE While looking at the OracleBFile methods, I touched on the most commonly used methods. For a complete list of all the methods available, consult the Oracle Data Provider for .NET documentation.

The BFile Sample

To illustrate how to use a BFILE, you'll create a sample application that performs the following activities:

Create a BFILE entry in a table: You'll use the built-in BFILENAME function in the database to create an entry that points to the BFILE outside the database.

Retrieve the BFILE entry from the database: You'll use the GetOracleBFile method provided by the data reader object to retrieve the entry created earlier.

Display the property values: You'll display the properties and related values of the BFILE object to the console window.

Display the BFILE content: You'll display the content of the BFILE itself to the console window.

In order to create a DIRECTORY object as in Listing 6-1, the user that creates the object must have either the CREATE ANY DIRECTORY system privilege or must be assigned a database role that has the privilege. Because the standard user that you've been using doesn't have this privilege, you're using the administrative-privileged user to perform this activity. You're also granting the ability to read from and write to this directory to the standard-privileged user.

Listing 6-1. *Creating the Directory Object*

```
C:\Temp>sqlplus oranetadmin/demo@oranet

SQL*Plus: Release 10.1.0.2.0 - Production on Mon Jun 7 13:54:36 2004

Copyright (c) 1982, 2004, Oracle.  All rights reserved.


Connected to:
Oracle Database 10g Enterprise Edition Release 10.1.0.2.0 - Production
With the Partitioning, OLAP and Data Mining options

SQL> create directory c_temp as 'C:\Temp';

Directory created.

SQL> grant read, write on directory c_temp to oranetuser;

Grant succeeded.

SQL> exit
Disconnected from Oracle Database 10g Enterprise Edition↵
 Release 10.1.0.2.0 - Production
With the Partitioning, OLAP and Data Mining options

C:\Temp>
```

■**TIP** Oracle doesn't verify that the operating system directory specified in the CREATE DIRECTORY statement is valid at the time the DIRECTORY object is created. You should ensure that the directory is valid to avoid possible difficulty in tracking down a bug later.

Now that you've created the DIRECTORY object, you'll create a table to test the BFILE functionality. Listing 6-2 shows the table being created using the standard privileged user. Because the DIRECTORY object resides in a namespace that is available to this user, you don't need to (nor can you) qualify the DIRECTORY object with an owning user.

Listing 6-2. *Creating the BFILE Test Table*

```
C:\>sqlplus oranetuser/demo@oranet

SQL*Plus: Release 10.1.0.2.0 - Production on Mon Jun 7 14:11:20 2004

Copyright (c) 1982, 2004, Oracle.  All rights reserved.
```

```
Connected to:
Oracle Database 10g Enterprise Edition Release 10.1.0.2.0 - Production
With the Partitioning, OLAP and Data Mining options

SQL> create table bfile_test
  2  (
  3    file_loc bfile
  4  );

Table created.

SQL> exit
Disconnected from Oracle Database 10g Enterprise Edition⤶
 Release 10.1.0.2.0 - Production
With the Partitioning, OLAP and Data Mining options

C:\>
```

The final piece you need to put in place before you create the sample application is a text file to use as the test BFILE object. Because I've created my directory object to point to C:\Temp, I've created a simple text file in that directory. The contents of the file are presented in Listing 6-3.

Listing 6-3. *The Test Text File Contents*

```
C:\Temp>type bfile_test.txt
This is a simple text file that is used to test the
BFILE functionality.

The actual contents of this file are not important.

This is the last line in the file.

C:\Temp>
```

The Main Method

The Main method code from the BFileTest project in this chapter's folder in the Downloads section of the Apress website (www.apress.com) is presented in Listing 6-4. This method gets the ball rolling by instantiating the class and then invoking the methods to perform the tasks I outlined earlier. As you can see, this code uses the Oracle.DataAccess.Types namespace in addition to the Oracle.DataAccess.Client namespace. I've included both of these name-spaces in the template projects in the code download.

Listing 6-4. *The Main Method Code*

```
using System;
using System.Text;
```

```
using Oracle.DataAccess.Client;
using Oracle.DataAccess.Types;

[ visual studio generated code snipped ]

static void Main(string[] args)
{
  // used for accessing the helper methods
  Class1 theClass = new Class1();

  // create our standard connection
  string connStr = "User Id=oranetuser; Password=demo; Data Source=oranet";
  OracleConnection oraConn = new OracleConnection(connStr);

  oraConn.Open();

  // insert a row into the test table
  theClass.insert_row(oraConn);

  // get the bfile from the database
  // table and display properties / content
  theClass.get_bfile(oraConn);
}
```

The insert_row Method Code

The insert_row method, in Listing 6-5, is responsible for inserting a single row into your test table. This method performs the first task you established for the sample. The main point of interest in this code is the BFILENAME function in the SQL statement. This function is a built-in function in the database. It takes two parameters: a directory name and a file name. The function takes the two parameters and returns the BFILE, which is stored in the table column. This function is a convenient way to initialize a BFILE column in a table.

Listing 6-5. *The insert_row Method Code*

```
private void insert_row(OracleConnection con)
{
  // this helper inserts a row into the test
  // table (bfile_test)
  // the lob locator points to 'c:\temp\bfile_test.txt'

  // the sql statement to insert a test row
  string sqlText = "insert into bfile_test (file_loc) ";
  sqlText += "values (BFILENAME(:p_dir, :p_file))";

  // the command object associated with the sql statement
  OracleCommand cmd = new OracleCommand(sqlText, con);
```

```
  // the parameter objects
  OracleParameter p_dir = new OracleParameter();
  p_dir.Size = 6;
  p_dir.Value = "C_TEMP";

  OracleParameter p_file = new OracleParameter();
  p_file.Size = 14;
  p_file.Value = "BFILE_TEST.TXT";

  // add the parameters to the collection
  cmd.Parameters.Add(p_dir);
  cmd.Parameters.Add(p_file);

  // execute the command
  cmd.ExecuteNonQuery();
}
```

The get_bfile Method Code

The get_bfile method performs the bulk of the work in this simple application (see Listing 6-6). This method performs the remaining three tasks you established for the sample. Specifically, this method

Retrieves the BFILE from the database: The BFILE locator is retrieved from the BFILE_TEST table using the GetOracleBFile method.

Displays the property values: The sample code writes the value of each property to the console window.

Displays the content of the BFILE: The sample code writes the content of the BFILE to the console window.

Listing 6-6. *The get_bfile Method Code*

```
private void get_bfile(OracleConnection con)
{
  // this helper gets the bfile from the database
  // table, displays the property values, and
  // writes the content of the file to the console
  string sqlText = "select file_loc from bfile_test";

  // the command object
  OracleCommand cmd = new OracleCommand(sqlText, con);

  // get a data reader for the command object
  OracleDataReader dataReader = cmd.ExecuteReader();

  OracleBFile bfile = null;
```

```
  if (dataReader.Read())
  {
    // use the typed accessor to get the bfile
    bfile = dataReader.GetOracleBFile(0);
  }

  // open the file
  bfile.OpenFile();

  // display the property values
  Console.WriteLine("Retrieved bfile from database...");
  Console.WriteLine("  CanRead = " + bfile.CanRead.ToString());
  Console.WriteLine("  CanSeek = " + bfile.CanSeek.ToString());
  Console.WriteLine("  CanWrite = " + bfile.CanWrite.ToString());
  Console.WriteLine("  Connection = " + bfile.Connection.ConnectionString);
  Console.WriteLine("  DirectoryName = " + bfile.DirectoryName.ToString());
  Console.WriteLine("  FileExists = " + bfile.FileExists.ToString());
  Console.WriteLine("  FileName = " + bfile.FileName.ToString());
  Console.WriteLine("  IsEmpty = " + bfile.IsEmpty.ToString());
  Console.WriteLine("  IsOpen = " + bfile.IsOpen.ToString());
  Console.WriteLine("  Length = " + bfile.Length.ToString());
  Console.WriteLine("  Position = " + bfile.Position.ToString());
  Console.WriteLine("  Value = " + bfile.Value.ToString());

  // convert the byte array to a string
  // to pass to the WriteLine method
  // since WriteLine does not take a byte array as a parameter
  UTF7Encoding utf = new UTF7Encoding();
  Console.WriteLine("  Value = \n" + utf.GetString(bfile.Value));
}
```

Running the BFile Test Application

The BFile Test application doesn't require any user input; it simply connects to the database
and performs the activities outlined earlier in "The BFILE Sample" section. I've presented the
results of running the application in Listing 6-7.

Listing 6-7. *The Output of the BFile Test Application*

```
C:\My Projects\ProOraNet\Oracle\C#\Chapter06\BFileTest\bin\Debug>BFileTest.exe
Retrieved bfile from database...
  CanRead = True
  CanSeek = True
  CanWrite = False
  Connection = User Id=oranetuser; Data Source=oranet
  DirectoryName = C_TEMP
  FileExists = True
  FileName = BFILE_TEST.TXT
```

```
IsEmpty = False
IsOpen = True
Length = 168
Position = 0
Value = System.Byte[]
Value =
This is a simple text file that is used to test the
BFILE functionality.

The actual contents of this file are not important.

This is the last line in the file.

C:\My Projects\ProOraNet\Oracle\C#\Chapter06\BFileTest\bin\Debug>
```

As you can see in the output of the application, the property values are what you'd expect to see, given the material I've covered thus far. The Value property of the BFILE is displayed twice: once to illustrate that it is a byte array, and then to display the byte array as a string.

Working with CLOB and NCLOB Objects

In contrast to a BFILE, a CLOB and an NCLOB reside inside the database. Therefore, they are treated much more like traditional columns in a table. They may participate in transactions and are read-write. Also, they are recoverable as part of a database restore or a flashback operation. In short, they reside inside the database, support read consistency, and receive the same benefits as other internal data types.

Both the CLOB and NCLOB data types are used to store large amounts of character data. In the 10g release, a LOB column data type can reach into the terabyte range. In earlier versions, they could each hold just a tick under 4 gigabytes of data—$((2^{32})-1)$ to be precise. The difference between the two types is that the CLOB data type stores data using the standard database character set whereas the NCLOB data type stores data using the national database character set. Both of these character sets are defined when the database is created. The standard character set is the character set that is used by default and nothing needs to be done to use this character set—it just happens. The national character set is typically used to store Unicode data when the standard character set doesn't support storing Unicode data.

One issue that isn't a concern when you're using the BFILE data type is storage. The file is outside the database; therefore, the database doesn't have any storage to allocate for the file. However, with LOB data, which is stored in the database, you should discuss the issue of storage with the administrator of the system to ensure that it is properly addressed. In short, there are two methods for storing LOB data: in-line or out-of-line.

For LOB data that is less than 4,096 bytes (4K) in size, I generally recommend in-line storage. For LOBs of this size, it may make more sense to use a varchar2 since that data type can hold up to 4,000 characters (using a single-byte character set). In-line storage means that the data is stored along with the other table columns in the row that holds the LOB data. For LOB data that exceeds 4K in size, you must use out-of-line storage. This means that a locator is stored in the row along with the other table columns that points to the real data. The actual LOB data is stored outside of the table row, thus the name. The in-line storage can be more efficient since Oracle may only have to go to a single location to get all of the data for a row. However, with large LOBs, in-line storage may not be as efficient, depending on how the data is distributed across the data blocks that compose a table. This could lead to a situation known as *row-chaining*—when the data is too large to fit in a single row, Oracle must store the data across multiple rows in the data block(s). With out-of-line storage, Oracle must get the locator and non-LOB data from a location and then retrieve the LOB data from the out-of-line storage location.

The OracleClob Class

When you're using the Oracle Data Provider for .NET, both the CLOB and NCLOB data types are represented by the OracleClob class. This class is in the Oracle.DataAccess.Types namespace rather than the Oracle.DataAccess.Client namespace.

■**NOTE** The Microsoft data provider utilizes the OracleLob class, which is located in the System.Data.Oracle-Client namespace, to provide LOB functionality.

Because the LOB classes all share common functionality, many of the properties and methods that I covered for the OracleBFile class apply to the OracleClob class. Rather than cover ground that I've already covered, I limit our exploration of the OracleClob class to the properties and methods that you haven't yet seen.

■**NOTE** Since an NCLOB is really a CLOB that just happens to use the national character set, I refer to the CLOB data type for both NCLOB and CLOB data types. I've highlighted any differences between the two types as necessary.

The IsInChunkWriteMode Property

The IsInChunkWriteMode is a read-only, Boolean property that indicates whether the CLOB has been opened with index updates deferred. This is a performance benefit when multiple (or chunk) updates occur on the LOB. You can update the indexes in a single operation once all the updates are complete instead of with each update. When you're using a BFILE, you have to open the file to read it. However, a CLOB resides inside the database and you don't need to do anything special to a CLOB (such as opening it) to read it. You open a CLOB when a write operation to the CLOB needs to occur. The following code highlights how to use this property. See "The BeginChunkWrite Method" section later in this chapter for more information.

```
// determine if the clob is in an open state
bool clobOpen = clob.IsInChunkWriteMode;
```

The IsNClob Property

As its name suggests, you use the IsNClob property to determine if the CLOB is an NCLOB object. You might be surprised that this Boolean property is read-only because the column definition in the database table determines if the data type is a CLOB or an NCLOB. The following simple code fragment accesses this property.

```
// determine if the clob is an nclob
bool isNClob = clob.IsNClob;
```

■**TIP** If you're creating a CLOB in your .NET code using the OracleClob class in the data provider, you can create an NCLOB by passing True for the Boolean bNCLOB parameter in the constructor.

The IsTemporary Property

If code creates a LOB but doesn't insert it into a table, that LOB is temporary. Once the LOB is inserted into the table, it becomes permanent. The IsTemporary property is a read-only, Boolean property that allows you to determine if the LOB you're using is temporary. You can use this property as illustrated here:

```
// determine if the clob is a temporary clob
bool isTemp = clob.IsTemporary;
```

The OptimumChunkSize Property

The OptimumChunkSize property returns an int value that represents the size, in bytes, that the data provider uses as the minimum size for sending or receiving data during read and write operations. This property is a read-only property. The following code illustrates retrieving the value for this property.

```
// determine the chunk size
int chunkSize = clob.OptimumChunkSize;
```

The Value Property

The Value property for a CLOB functions in the same manner as the Value property for the OracleBFile class. However, since a CLOB represents character data, the Value property returns a string object for a CLOB. If a string object is returned, no conversion from a byte array is required, as illustrated here:

■**NOTE** The default is to return data as a string. However, you can still return data into a character or byte array if you want to.

```
// get the value
// no conversion is necessary
string clobValue = clob.Value;
```

■TIP This property can return a value of up to 2GB in size. For CLOBs larger than this, you can use the Read method to access the data beyond the 2GB boundary.

The Append Method

The Append method is an overloaded method that allows data to be appended to a CLOB object. Using the Append method, you can append to a CLOB from another CLOB, to a CLOB from a byte array, and to a CLOB from a char array. When you're using the array overloads, you may specify the offset into the source array as well as the number of characters to append. When using the byte array overloaded method, you must specify an even number for both the offset and the number of bytes to append. This is because characters are represented as pairs of bytes. The following code illustrates how to use each of the overloaded Append methods.

■CAUTION The documentation that ships with some versions of the Oracle Data Provider incorrectly indicates that the byte array overloaded method returns an int rather than a void.

```
// the append method overloads
OracleClob sourceClob = new OracleClob(con);
OracleClob destClob = new OracleClob(con);
destClob.Append(sourceClob);

byte[] sourceByte = new byte[4]{1, 2, 3, 4};
destClob.Append(sourceByte, 0, 4);

char[] sourceChar = new char[3]{'A', 'B', 'C'};
destClob.Append(sourceChar, 0, 3);
```

The BeginChunkWrite Method

The BeginChunkWrite method is a mechanism through which you may open a CLOB with index updates deferred. You can use the IsInChunkWriteMode property, discussed earlier, to determine if this is how the CLOB was opened. As I discussed earlier, you don't need to open a CLOB for a read operation, and because the CLOB resides in the database, an OpenFile method, such as the one that exists for the OracleBFile class, isn't necessary. This method, which returns no value, exists for performance reasons. When you open a CLOB using this method, any domain or function-based indexes that exist on the CLOB aren't updated until the EndChunkWrite method is called. The following code illustrates how to open a CLOB using this method.

```
// open the clob deferring domain and
// function-based index updates
clob.BeginChunkWrite();
```

The EndChunkWrite Method

In order to close a CLOB opened using the BeginChunkWrite method, you should call the End-ChunkWrite method. Like the BeginChunkWrite method, this method has no return value. You may use the IsInChunkWriteMode property to determine if the CLOB is opened or closed. This method causes any deferred index updates to complete when it is invoked. The following code invokes this method.

```
// close the clob and update domain
// and function-based indexes (if any)
clob.EndChunkWrite();
```

The Erase Method

The Erase method is an overloaded method you can use to delete content from a CLOB. The parameterless overloaded method simply deletes all content from the CLOB. An overloaded version of the method that allows you to specify the offset and number of characters to erase is also available. Both of these methods return an Int64 value that indicates the actual number of characters erased as illustrated in the following code:

```
// erase first two characters
Int64 charsErased = destClob.Erase(0,2);

// erase all remaining characters
charsErased = destClob.Erase();
```

The SetLength Method

You may use this method to adjust the length of the CLOB to a *lower* value. You can't use the method to expand the CLOB. The method takes a single parameter that specifies the new length for the CLOB. If you specify 0 as the new length, this effectively truncates the CLOB. The following code snippet illustrates how to trim a CLOB as well as how to truncate it.

■NOTE This method overrides Stream.Length and sets the length of the CLOB in *characters*. The length property returns the length of the CLOB in *bytes*.

```
// trim the clob to 4 chars
clob.SetLength(4);

// truncate the clob
clob.SetLength(0);
```

The Write Method

There are two overloaded versions of the Write method. You may pass either a byte array or a char array as the first parameter. The second parameter is the offset parameter. The offset parameter specifies the offset into the array, not the offset into the CLOB. You use the Position property to determine where the write occurs in the CLOB. The third parameter is the count parameter. This parameter specifies the amount to write in bytes or characters. When you're using a byte array, the count parameter must be an even number. How to use both overloaded methods is presented in the following code:

```
// write the byte array to clob
clob.Write(sourceByte, 0, 4);

// write char array to clob
clob.Write(sourceChar, 0, 3);
```

The Data Reader Typed Accessors

The OracleDataReader class provides two typed accessors to retrieve a CLOB into an OracleClob .NET data type. The GetOracleClob method returns CLOB data into an OracleClob variable. This method doesn't place a lock on the row containing the CLOB. If, for example, you know that you want to update the CLOB data, you may use the GetOracleClobForUpdate method to place a lock on the row that contains the CLOB column. If the row containing the CLOB data is already locked, the GetOracleClobForUpdate method waits indefinitely for the lock to be released. If you don't want to wait, or you only want to wait for a specified number of seconds, you may use an overloaded version of this method. The overloaded version allows you to specify that you don't wish to wait or the number of seconds you are willing to wait. You'll see an example of this method in the sample application.

■**NOTE** In order to use the "willing to wait *x* seconds" option, you must be using an Oracle9i or higher database. For versions prior to 9i, this feature is ignored and an indefinite wait ensues.

The CLOB Sample

In order to illustrate how to work with CLOB data, I use some of the material from earlier in the chapter: the DIRECTORY object and a BFILE that you created. Here you'll load a file into the database as a CLOB, display the properties of the CLOB, and lastly, perform some manipulation of the CLOB. You'll see how to do the following:

Load a CLOB: You'll use an anonymous PL/SQL block, which we discussed in Chapter 5, to load a CLOB into the database.

Display the properties: You'll access the properties of the CLOB that we've discussed earlier and write their values to the console window.

Manipulate the CLOB: You retrieve the CLOB from the database and read, search, and write to it.

Before you can begin, you need to create a table to hold your data. The table that you'll use is a simple table with two columns. I present the table creation process in Listing 6-8. The clob_id column makes it easy to identify a row and it serves as the primary key for the table as well. The clob_id column is also required for updating the CLOB.

> **CAUTION** The Oracle Data Provider for .NET documentation suggests you can use a unique index in place of a primary key. However, there appear to be some issues with this at this time. If possible, use a primary key as I do in Listing 6-8.

Listing 6-8. *Creating the clob_test Table*

```
C:\>sqlplus oranetuser/demo@oranet

SQL*Plus: Release 10.1.0.2.0 - Production on Tue Jun 8 22:24:25 2004

Copyright (c) 1982, 2004, Oracle.  All rights reserved.


Connected to:
Oracle Database 10g Enterprise Edition Release 10.1.0.2.0 - Production
With the Partitioning, OLAP and Data Mining options

SQL> create table clob_test
  2  (
  3    clob_id   number primary key,
  4    clob_data clob
  5  );

Table created.

SQL> exit
Disconnected from Oracle Database 10g Enterprise Edition↵
 Release 10.1.0.2.0 - Production
With the Partitioning, OLAP and Data Mining options

C:\>
```

Next you create a text file that you use to populate the clob_data column in the table. You could easily use SQL*Plus to insert a small bit of data into the table, but a far more likely scenario for loading a CLOB column is via an external text document. Recall that earlier you created a DIRECTORY object that represents the C:\Temp operating system directory. Listing 6-9 illustrates how to create a text file you can use as the source for loading into the CLOB column. As you can see, it is simply a listing of the files in the \bin directory for my ORACLE_HOME.

Listing 6-9. *Creating the Text File to Load into the Table*

```
C:\>dir c:\oracle\10.1\database\bin > c:\temp\orabin.txt

C:\>dir c:\temp\orabin.txt
 Volume in drive C has no label.
 Volume Serial Number is 4847-2DDB

 Directory of c:\temp

06/08/2004  10:32 PM                21,440 orabin.txt
               1 File(s)            21,440 bytes
               0 Dir(s)   50,566,971,392 bytes free

C:\>
```

You use an anonymous block to submit a set of SQL and PL/SQL statements to the database to load the text file into the clob_data column. An *anonymous block* is a method of submitting PL/SQL code to the database from outside the database itself. As its name implies, an anonymous block doesn't have a name associated with it like a stored procedure does. Also unlike a stored procedure, an anonymous block isn't persisted in the database; it's submitted to the database, processed, and then forgotten. An anonymous block contains any valid PL/SQL code and can call other PL/SQL procedures or functions. This is a handy feature that you'll use to invoke procedures in the DBMS_LOB package, which is an Oracle-supplied package. You've already seen the built-in BFILENAME function, which you'll employ in your anonymous block.

The Main Method

Listing 6-10 contains the code for the Main method of the ClobTest application. The code establishes a connection to the database and calls three helper methods to perform the activities I just outlined.

Listing 6-10. *The Main Method Code*

```
static void Main(string[] args)
{
  // used for accessing the helper methods
  Class1 theClass = new Class1();

  // create our standard connection
  string connStr = "User Id=oranetuser; Password=demo; Data Source=oranet";
  OracleConnection oraConn = new OracleConnection(connStr);

  oraConn.Open();

  theClass.load_file(oraConn);
```

```
theClass.display_properties(oraConn);

theClass.manipulate_clob(oraConn);
}
```

The load_file Method

You use the anonymous block we discussed at the beginning of this section in the load_file method, which is presented in Listing 6-11. The code for this method first truncates the test table to ensure that you're starting with a clean slate. It then builds the anonymous block and submits it to the database. The anonymous block code uses the DIRECTORY object that you created earlier to create a BFILE that represents the orabin.txt file. The code then calls three procedures in the DBMS_LOB-supplied PL/SQL package to actually load the text file into the CLOB.

Listing 6-11. *The load_file Method Code*

```
private void load_file(OracleConnection con)
{
  Console.WriteLine("Truncating table and loading file...");
  // ensure the table is empty
  string sql = "truncate table clob_test";

  OracleCommand cmd = new OracleCommand(sql, con);

  cmd.ExecuteNonQuery();

  // build the anonymous block and execute it
  sql = "declare";
  sql += "  /* local variables to hold the lob locators */";
  sql += "  l_clob  clob;";
  sql += "  l_bfile bfile;";
  sql += "begin";
  sql += "  /* this is a method to get the lob locator */";
  sql += "  /* for the lob column in the table */";
  sql += "  /* by inserting an empty_clob and returning */";
  sql += "  /* into the local clob variable, we easily */";
  sql += "  /* acquire the lob locator */";
  sql += "  insert into clob_test (clob_id, clob_data)";
  sql += "  values (1, empty_clob())";
  sql += "  returning clob_data into l_clob;";
  sql += "  /* this is the file we will load */";
  sql += "  l_bfile := bfilename('C_TEMP', 'ORABIN.TXT');";
  sql += "  /* the file must be opened prior to loading */";
  sql += "  dbms_lob.fileopen(l_bfile);";
  sql += "  /* this procedure performs the actual data load */";
  sql += "  /* it does not perform character set conversion */";
  sql += "  /* if character set conversion is required, */";
```

```
sql += "   /* the loadclobfromfile procedure may be used */";
sql += "   /* however, if you do not need character set */";
sql += "   /* conversion, this procedure is much simpler */";
sql += "   dbms_lob.loadfromfile(l_clob, l_bfile,
  dbms_lob.getlength(l_bfile));";
sql += "   /* close the bfile after loading it */";
sql += "   dbms_lob.fileclose(l_bfile);";
sql += "   /* commit the transaction */";
sql += "   commit;";
sql += "end;";

cmd.CommandText = sql;

cmd.ExecuteNonQuery();

Console.WriteLine("Table successfully loaded...");
Console.WriteLine();
}
```

The display_properties Method

The code for the display_properties method is fairly compact. As its name implies, the method code in Listing 6-12 displays the values for each of the main properties after you acquire the CLOB from the database. The code employs a typed accessor to retrieve the CLOB from the data reader object.

Listing 6-12. *The display_properties Code*

```
private void display_properties(OracleConnection con)
{
  Console.WriteLine("Retrieving clob and displaying properties...");

  // this method simply displays the properties
  // and the values for the clob
  string sql = "select clob_data from clob_test where clob_id = 1";

  OracleCommand cmd = new OracleCommand(sql, con);

  OracleDataReader dataReader = cmd.ExecuteReader();

  // read the 1 row result
  dataReader.Read();

  // use typed accessor that does not lock row
  OracleClob clob = dataReader.GetOracleClob(0);

  // display each property value
  Console.WriteLine("  CanRead = " + clob.CanRead.ToString());
```

```
Console.WriteLine("  CanSeek = " + clob.CanSeek.ToString());
Console.WriteLine("  CanWrite = " + clob.CanWrite.ToString());
Console.WriteLine("  Connection = " + clob.Connection.ConnectionString);
Console.WriteLine("  IsEmpty = " + clob.IsEmpty.ToString());
Console.WriteLine("  IsInChunkWriteMode = " +
  clob.IsInChunkWriteMode.ToString());
Console.WriteLine("  IsNCLOB = " + clob.IsNClob.ToString());
Console.WriteLine("  IsTemporary = " + clob.IsTemporary.ToString());
Console.WriteLine("  Length = " + clob.Length.ToString());
Console.WriteLine("  OptimumChunkSize = " + clob.OptimumChunkSize.ToString());
Console.WriteLine("  Position = " + clob.Position.ToString());
Console.WriteLine("  Value = " + clob.Value);

Console.WriteLine("Completed displaying properties...");
Console.WriteLine();
}
```

The manipulate_clob Method

In the manipulate_clob method, you exercise some of the OracleClob class methods as well as the type accessor that places a lock on the row in the table. You wrap the actions in a transaction since you'll update the CLOB. In particular, you utilize the search, read, and write methods as well as the position property. Because the text file loaded into the CLOB column contains a directory listing of the \bin directory, the Oracle Data Provider for .NET file is included in the listing. The code searches for and manipulates this entry. The code that accomplishes these tasks is in Listing 6-13.

Listing 6-13. *The manipulate_clob Method Code*

```
private void manipulate_clob(OracleConnection con)
{
  // this method performs some clob manipulation
  // using some of the clob methods we have discussed
  Console.WriteLine("Beginning clob manipulation...");

  string sql = "select clob_id, clob_data from clob_test where clob_id = 1";

  OracleCommand cmd = new OracleCommand(sql, con);

  // begin a transaction since we will be updating
  OracleTransaction trans = con.BeginTransaction();

  OracleDataReader dataReader = cmd.ExecuteReader();

  // read the single row result
  dataReader.Read();
```

```
        // use typed accessor that locks the row
        OracleClob clob = dataReader.GetOracleClobForUpdate(1);

        // we are done with the reader now, so we can close it
        dataReader.Close();

        // search for the string "Oracle.DataAccess.dll"
        // in the clob
        char[] charArray = "Oracle.DataAccess.dll".ToCharArray();
        Int64 stringPos = clob.Search(charArray, 0, 1);
        Console.WriteLine("  Found 'Oracle.DataAccess.dll' in position: "
          + stringPos.ToString());

        // set the position to the beginning of the
        // search string
        clob.Position = (stringPos - 1) * 2;

        // read the string and display it
        char[] charBuffer = new char[21];
        clob.Read(charBuffer, 0, 21);
        Console.Write("  Current value: ");
        Console.WriteLine(charBuffer);

        // set the position to the beginning of the
        // search string
        clob.Position = (stringPos - 1) * 2;

        // change the string to uppercase
        charArray = "ORACLE.DATAACCESS.DLL".ToCharArray();
        clob.Write(charArray, 0, charArray.Length);

        // reposition to the beginning of the search string
        clob.Position = (stringPos - 1) * 2;

        // read the string and display it
        clob.Read(charBuffer, 0, 21);
        Console.Write("  New value: ");
        Console.WriteLine(charBuffer);

        // commit the trans making the changes permanent
        trans.Commit();

        Console.WriteLine("Completed clob manipulation...");
}
```

Running the ClobTest Sample

Because the output of the sample program is rather lengthy, I've redirected it into a text file to make it easier to examine. I've presented relevant portions here; however, I've cut some pieces of output so that this would work for this book's page format and so you'd have an easier time viewing it. Listing 6-14 contains the slightly edited output of the application.

Listing 6-14. *The ClobTest Sample Output*

```
Truncating table and loading file...
Table successfully loaded...

Retrieving clob and displaying properties...
  CanRead = True
  CanSeek = True
  CanWrite = True
  Connection = User Id=oranetuser; Data Source=oranet
  IsEmpty = False
  IsInChunkWriteMode = False
  IsNCLOB = False
  IsTemporary = False
  Length = 42880
  OptimumChunkSize = 16264
  Position = 0
  Value =  Volume in drive C has no label.
 Volume Serial Number is 4847-2DDB

 Directory of c:\oracle\10.1\database\bin

05/13/2004  01:54 PM    <DIR>          .
05/13/2004  01:54 PM    <DIR>          ..
11/24/2003  04:15 PM           260,531 adinit.dat
01/12/2004  12:03 PM           257,024 agent.exe
01/12/2004  12:03 PM           254,464 agntsvc.exe
03/08/2004  03:13 PM            28,944 agtctl.exe
03/08/2004  03:20 PM            16,384 asmtool.exe
03/08/2004  03:20 PM            24,576 asmtoolg.exe
03/06/2004  01:19 AM           108,920 cemutls.exe
03/06/2004  01:23 AM           205,088 clscfg.exe

[ snipped output ]

03/08/2004  03:11 PM            45,328 WRAP.EXE
02/03/2004  10:09 PM           811,480 xml.exe
02/03/2004  10:00 PM           983,948 xmlcg.exe
02/03/2004  10:00 PM           713,436 xsl.exe
12/18/2003  03:38 PM             1,052 xsql.bat
12/18/2003  03:38 PM               578 xsqlproxy.bat
```

```
02/03/2004  10:00 PM           628,944 xvm.exe
07/16/1998  04:36 PM           104,448 zip.exe
             408 File(s)    126,434,621 bytes
               2 Dir(s)  50,567,090,176 bytes free

Completed displaying properties...

Beginning clob manipulation...
  Found 'Oracle.DataAccess.dll' in position: 7493
  Current value: Oracle.DataAccess.dll
  New value: ORACLE.DATAACCESS.DLL
Completed clob manipulation...
```

Because the Value property represents the entire file, the output of that property is a single value in the CLOB column; I've edited it for brevity. In the output, you can see the property values. In particular, the Write property has a value of True rather than False as was the case for the BFILE sample. The output indicates the location in the CLOB where the Oracle.Data-Access.dll string was found and then displays the old and new string values at that location in the CLOB.

Working with BLOB Objects

BLOB objects are to binary data what CLOB objects are to character data. In fact, all of the properties and methods associated with a CLOB object (with the exception of the IsNClob property) are relevant to BLOB objects. You can use BLOB objects as a way to store binary data directly in the database. They function in the same manner as the CLOB objects you've just seen. It's important to note that although you typically use BLOB columns in a table to store data where the native data format is binary, such as for an image, you can store any data in binary form in a BLOB column. For example, you can store the same file that you loaded into the CLOB column in the previous section into a BLOB column. Of course, in this case, because the file is stored as a binary representation, you need to perform some translation in order to make it meaningful. In addition to a BLOB object that functions in a similar manner to a CLOB object, you may use the DBMS_LOB PL/SQL package to load a BLOB object into a BLOB table column.

■**NOTE** Like the CLOB object support, the BLOB support in the Microsoft data provider uses the OracleLob class, which is located in the System.Data.OracleClient namespace.

The BLOB Sample

In order to understand how to work with BLOB data, in this section, you create a windows-based application that loads an image file into a table and then displays the image in a form. This is a common use for a BLOB column. Of course, you can load other file types such as a

PDF document, a word processing document, a spreadsheet document, and so on. You use the same methodology to load the image file that you used in the CLOB sample.

In general, BLOB data is data that is meaningful to an external application such as a word processor, an image viewer, and so on. In this situation, you typically modify the data outside of the database and then replace the entire BLOB with the new version. It is possible to use the methods of the OracleBlob class to perform in-place editing of BLOB data; however, to do so, you need specific knowledge of the format of the data being stored in the BLOB column.

To begin the BLOB sample, you'll create a table similar to the one you created for the CLOB sample. The only difference in the code in Listing 6-15 is the LOB column data type. Of course, here you're using a BLOB rather than a CLOB.

Listing 6-15. *Creating the BLOB Sample Table*

```
C:\>sqlplus oranetuser/demo@oranet

SQL*Plus: Release 10.1.0.2.0 - Production on Wed Jun 9 16:09:44 2004

Copyright (c) 1982, 2004, Oracle.  All rights reserved.


Connected to:
Oracle Database 10g Enterprise Edition Release 10.1.0.2.0 - Production
With the Partitioning, OLAP and Data Mining options

SQL> create table blob_test
  2  (
  3    blob_id   number primary key,
  4    blob_data blob
  5  );

Table created.

SQL> exit
Disconnected from Oracle Database 10g Enterprise Edition⤶
 Release 10.1.0.2.0 - Production
With the Partitioning, OLAP and Data Mining options

C:\>
```

In order to create an image file for you to load into the BLOB column, I took a screen shot of the Apress website (see Figure 6-1), which displays some information about this book. Of course, you can use any image file (or other file type, for that matter) that you desire. The concepts that you put into practice here apply to BLOB files in general.

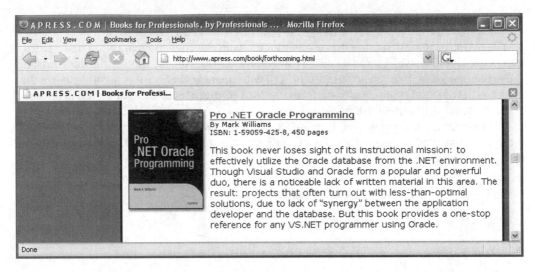

Figure 6-1. *The image file that you load into the database*

The BLOB Test Form

The design time representation of the form the sample uses appears in Figure 6-2. The form has three button controls and a picture box control. You'll examine the code behind each of the button controls shortly. However, as you can infer from their respective text labels, the buttons load the image file from the operating system directory into the database, display the image in the database in the picture box control, and clear the picture box control.

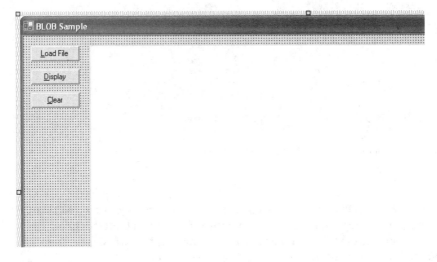

Figure 6-2. *The design time view of the test form*

The Load File Button Code

The code in Listing 6-16 is very similar to the code you used to load the text file into the CLOB in the previous section. Since you're using a windows-based application, the calls to display text to the console window have been replaced with calls to display message boxes instead. The anonymous block is virtually identical; the only difference is the substitution of BLOB objects for CLOB objects. Rather than creating a form-level field to hold the OracleConnection, this code creates a connection within the handler for each button click event.

Listing 6-16. *The Load File Button Code*

```
private void btnLoad_Click(object sender, System.EventArgs e)
{
  // create our standard connection
  string connStr = "User Id=oranetuser; Password=demo; Data Source=oranet";
  OracleConnection con = new OracleConnection(connStr);

  con.Open();

  MessageBox.Show("Truncating table...", "BLOB Sample");

  // ensure the table is empty
  string sql = "truncate table blob_test";

  OracleCommand cmd = new OracleCommand(sql, con);

  cmd.ExecuteNonQuery();

  MessageBox.Show("Table truncated.", "BLOB Sample");

  MessageBox.Show("Loading table...", "BLOB Sample");

  // build the anonymous block and execute it
  sql = "declare";
  sql += "   /* local variables to hold the lob locators */";
  sql += "   l_blob  blob;";
  sql += "   l_bfile bfile;";
  sql += "begin";
  sql += "   /* this is a method to get the lob locator */";
  sql += "   /* for the lob column in the table */";
  sql += "   /* by inserting an empty_clob and returning */";
  sql += "   /* into the local clob variable, we easily */";
  sql += "   /* acquire the lob locator */";
  sql += "   insert into blob_test (blob_id, blob_data)";
  sql += "   values (1, empty_blob())";
  sql += "   returning blob_data into l_blob;";
```

```
sql += "   /* this is the file we will load */";
sql += "   l_bfile := bfilename('C_TEMP', 'APRESS_WEBSITE.TIF');";
sql += "   /* the file must be opened prior to loading */";
sql += "   dbms_lob.fileopen(l_bfile);";
sql += "   /* this procedure performs the actual data load */";
sql += "   dbms_lob.loadfromfile(l_blob, l_bfile,
  dbms_lob.getlength(l_bfile));";
sql += "   /* close the bfile after loading it */";
sql += "   dbms_lob.fileclose(l_bfile);";
sql += "   /* commit the transaction */";
sql += "   commit;";
sql += "end;";

cmd.CommandText = sql;

cmd.ExecuteNonQuery();

MessageBox.Show("Table loaded.", "BLOB Sample");
}
```

The Display Button Code

The code for the Display button in Listing 6-17 is, perhaps, surprisingly compact. This code employs the same technique to retrieve the BLOB data from the table that you used when working with CLOB data. Because you aren't updating the BLOB, you don't need a transaction and you can use the typed accessor that doesn't place a lock on the row in the table. The only trick in this code is that you create a MemoryStream from the Value property of the BLOB. By doing this, you can easily create a bitmap and then assign this bitmap to the Image property of the picture box control. Displaying the image is almost trivial using this mechanism. However, you may need to size the picture box control and form if you use an image other than the one included in the code download.

▪ NOTE I've included the System.IO namespace to make accessing the MemoryStream easier.

Listing 6-17. *The Display Button Code*

```
private void btnDisplay_Click(object sender, System.EventArgs e)
{
  // create our standard connection
  string connStr = "User Id=oranetuser; Password=demo; Data Source=oranet";
  OracleConnection con = new OracleConnection(connStr);

  con.Open();
```

```
    string sql = "select blob_data from blob_test where blob_id = 1";

    OracleCommand cmd = new OracleCommand(sql, con);

    OracleDataReader dataReader = cmd.ExecuteReader();

    // read the single row result
    dataReader.Read();

    // use typed accessor to retrieve the blob
    OracleBlob blob = dataReader.GetOracleBlob(0);

    // we are done with the reader now, so we can close it
    dataReader.Close();

    // create a memory stream from the blob
    MemoryStream ms = new MemoryStream(blob.Value);

    // set the image property equal to a bitmap
    // created from the memory stream
    pictureBox1.Image = new Bitmap(ms);
}
```

The Clear Button Code

Listing 6-18 contains the code for the Clear button. This code does nothing more than set the Image property to null on the picture box control. The code is included to allow you to test the loading of the image from the database. By using the Clear button, you ensure that the image really is being loaded from the database.

Listing 6-18. *The Clear Button Code*

```
private void btnClear_Click(object sender, System.EventArgs e)
{
    // simply set the image property to null
    // to 'clear' the picture box control
    pictureBox1.Image = null;
}
```

Running the BLOB Test Sample

After you compile the application, running the application produces the form as illustrated in Figure 6-3. The initial state of the form is simply a blank picture box control.

Figure 6-3. *The BLOB test sample form at run-time*

Clicking the Load File button produces a series of message boxes that indicate the progress as the table in the database is truncated and the image file is loaded using the DIRECTORY object and a BFILE. After the image file has been successfully loaded, the form resembles Figure 6-4.

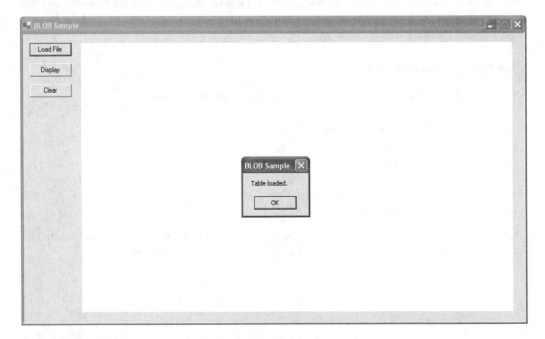

Figure 6-4. *The BLOB test sample form after loading the image*

Once the image has been successfully loaded into the table, clicking the Display button causes the application to read the image from the table and load it into the picture box control. The form now resembles Figure 6-5.

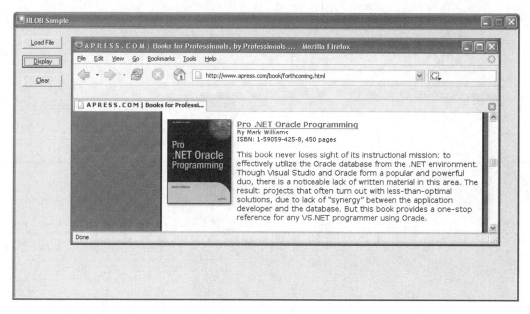

Figure 6-5. *The image is displayed in the picture box control*

Chapter 6 Wrap-Up

Although large object columns aren't as numerous in a typical application as traditional data types are, they offer you a flexible way to use the database for what it does best: managing and processing data. By using a combination of the data provider classes and supplied PL/SQL packages, you'll find that working with large objects is as easy as working with traditional data types. In some respects, using large objects is even easier because of functions such as BFILE-NAME and procedures such as LOADFROMFILE. These functions and procedures greatly simplify the process of loading an external file into the database. Of course, with the exception of the BFILE type, large objects are just another column in the database. They are participants in transactions and therefore, you can commit them or rolled them back as necessary. In addition, they can be flashed back, backed up, and restored.

If you're used to working with traditional data types, you've employed techniques to split a large piece of character data across multiple columns of varchar2 data type or multiple rows. The techniques involved in working with CLOB objects that you've explored in this chapter offer a compelling alternative. When you're working with binary data in the database, the choice is clear: you use a BLOB. If you need to access a file located outside of the database, you have the option of using a BFILE. The ability to use large objects is a powerful tool to add to your development toolkit.

CHAPTER 7

■■■

Advanced Connections and Authentication

In this chapter, you'll revisit the topic of connections, which I first addressed in Chapter 1, as well as look at some additional authentication methods above and beyond the basic user-name/password method that you've used up to this point. You'll examine the difference between privileged and non-privileged connections and learn how to connect to the database using a privileged connection.

A topic you may find confusing is how to use operating system authentication with the Oracle database. In this chapter, you work through the process of configuring the system to allow for Windows operating system authentication and create an operating system–authenticated connection. One of the underutilized features of the Oracle database is its ability to implement password expiration, password lockout and password changing. I'll address these topics and round out the chapter by examining connection pooling and multiplexing.

By this point, you're very familiar with the username/password method of authenticating to the database using the Connection object because that is the method all of the sample code has used thus far. One clear characteristic of this connection method is that the user must provide a username and password. In turn, the password is (ideally) maintained—that is, the password is changed on a regular basis. Sometimes some users see this maintenance as a chore or optional task. As a result, the administrator can implement password rules to enforce things such as required password changes. However, when you use operating system authentication, this activity becomes unnecessary in the database. When you use operating system authentication, you no longer need to maintain passwords in the database. In fact, you can't maintain them in the database because no password information is stored there.

Another type of connection that you haven't yet seen is what is known as a *privileged connection*. Of course, all connections have privileges of some sort. When I'm discussing privileged connections I mean a connection that has one of two system privileges:

The SYSDBA privilege: This is the highest administrative privilege an account can have. This privilege allows the user to perform all activities on a database.

The SYSOPER privilege: This privilege has slightly fewer abilities than the SYSDBA privilege. For example, a user connected with this privilege can't create a new database and may only perform certain types of database recovery operations.

In practice, typical .NET applications don't need to connect to a database with the SYSDBA or SYSOPER privileges. However, you may encounter times when you're creating an application that does need to connect with one of these privileges. For instance, an application that starts up or shuts down a database needs to use the SYSOPER privilege. Such an application can use the SYSDBA privilege, but that is an over-privileging if the application doesn't need to perform activities other than start up or shut down. If you're creating an application that creates an Oracle database from within the application, then you need to connect with the SYSDBA privilege because the SYSOPER privilege doesn't allow for this capability.

You'll also take a look at the ability to connect to the default database. I find this most useful in situations where I don't know the connection information for a database in advance. Another situation where this may come in handy is when databases are in different environments, such as a Sandbox, a Development, and a Test environment. When you allow the application to connect to the default database, you aren't required to configure the networking components as you did in Chapter 1 when you created your standard configuration. Of course, whether or not you want this is a question you and your database administrator need to discuss. I believe this is convenient or a shortcut that you should use where appropriate in your environment.

The Default Database Connection

You can connect to a database without specifying the database in the connection string. When you connect in this manner, the database is known as a default database. The default database is determined by the value of the ORACLE_SID environment variable. The concept of the default database connection is only relevant on a server. As a result, the code you write in this section must run on the same machine as the default Oracle database. Recall that you may assign the value for the ORACLE_SID variable in several places:

The Registry: You can set the ORACLE_SID under the Oracle Home registry hive. On my system, the ORACLE_SID for my 10g installation is set under the `HKLM\SOFTWARE\ORACLE\ KEY_OraDatabase101` key.

The Environment Variables dialog: You can set the ORACLE_SID in the System Variables section.

The Environment Variables dialog: You can set the ORACLE_SID in the User Variables section.

In a Command Prompt window: Using the `set` command, you can set the ORACLE_SID value. For example, `set ORACLE_SID=LT10G`.

The locations where you may specify the value are listed in hierarchical order from lowest precedence to highest. For example, if the value is set in the registry and also in the User Variables section of the Environment Variables dialog, the value specified in the User Variables section takes precedence over the value specified in the registry.

If you need to set values for the Oracle environment variables, I strongly recommend that you set them in the registry and then override them in a command prompt window if you need to. If you choose to set them using the Environment Variables dialog, be aware that it may cause unexpected behavior in the Oracle utilities that can be hard to debug. When multiple versions of the Oracle software are installed on a system, Oracle determines the environment or profile for each version based on the entries specified under the registry hive for each version of the software. This effectively segregates the environment configuration for each version into distinct profiles. When you specify a configuration variable using the Environment Variables dialog, that value overrides any entries in the registry for all versions of the software installed.

As a practical example, let's look at my system; I have Oracle versions 8i, 9i, and 10g installed. Under the registry keys for each of these versions, I've specified the ORACLE_SID for the corresponding version of the database: LT8I for the 8i database, LT9I for the 9i database, and LT10G for the 10g database. If I start the 9i version of SQL*Plus, Oracle uses the LT9I value for the ORACLE_SID because it's specified under the 9i home registry hive. If I specify the ORACLE_SID using the Environment Variables dialog as LT10G, when I start the 9i version of SQL*Plus, the ORACLE_SID is no longer LT9I; it is LT10G. This means that LT10G has become my default database for my 9i software. You'll probably find this confusing, if you are unaware of what has transpired.

If you need to examine the registry to determine the current value for the ORACLE_SID key, the key is located in the HKLM\SOFTWARE\ORACLE\KEY_HomeName hive for 10g and the HKLM\SOFTWARE\ORACLE\HOME*N* hive for previous releases. Refer to Chapter 1 if you need a refresher on the Oracle server architecture.

■**TIP** Because the ORACLE_SID value is stored in the registry, you can't issue an echo %ORACLE_SID% command in a command prompt window to determine the value.

In order to illustrate how to connect to the default database on an Oracle host machine, I take the "HelloOracle" example I used in Chapter 1 and, with a very slight modification, enable it to connect to the default database. By doing so, I create a new Visual Studio solution named DefaultConnection.

■**NOTE** Be sure to add a reference to the Oracle.DataAccess.dll assembly to the project and include the using Oracle.DataAccess.Client; directive at the top of the source file if you're creating a new solution.

Listing 7-1 contains the modified Main method from the HelloOracle example. You can find this sample (DefaultConnection) in this chapter's folder in the Downloads section of the Apress website (www.apress.com).

Listing 7-1. *The Modified Main Method from the HelloOracle Sample*

```
static void Main(string[] args)
{
  // Use the default database by omitting the Data Source connect
  // string attribute.
  String connString = "User Id=oranetuser;Password=demo";
  OracleConnection oraConn = new OracleConnection(connString);

  try
  {
    oraConn.Open();

    Console.WriteLine("\nHello, Default Oracle Database Here!\n");
    Console.WriteLine("Connection String: ");
    Console.WriteLine(oraConn.ConnectionString.ToString() + "\n");
    Console.WriteLine("Current Connection State: ");
    Console.WriteLine(oraConn.State.ToString() + "\n");
    Console.WriteLine("Oracle Database Server Version: ");
    Console.WriteLine(oraConn.ServerVersion.ToString());
  }
  catch (Exception ex)
  {
    Console.WriteLine("Error occured: " + ex.Message);
  }
  finally
  {
    if (oraConn.State == System.Data.ConnectionState.Open)
    {
      oraConn.Close();
    }
  }
}
```

To take advantage of connecting to the default database, the only change you need to make to the source code is in the definition of the connection string. By omitting the Data Source attribute from the connection string, you indicate to the Oracle Data Provider for .NET that you want to connect to the default database. Listing 7-2 contains the output that results from running this example.

Listing 7-2. *The Output of the DefaultConnection Sample*

```
C:\My Projects\ProOraNet\Oracle\C#\Chapter07\DefaultConnection\bin\Debug>↵
DefaultConnection.exe

Hello, Default Oracle Database Here!

Connection String:
User Id=oranetuser;
```

```
Current Connection State:
Open

Oracle Database Server Version:
10g

C:\My Projects\ProOraNet\Oracle\C#\Chapter07\DefaultConnection\bin\Debug>
```

Notice in the output that the connection string that displays no longer contains the Data Source attribute. If you have more than one database on the machine you're using, it's easy to illustrate how you can set the ORACLE_SID environment variable in a command prompt window to override the value set in the registry. This also illustrates that you are, in fact, connecting to the default database as specified by the value of this variable. Listing 7-3 contains the output of the DefaultConnection sample after you change the value of the ORACLE_SID environment variable in the command prompt window.

Listing 7-3. *The Output of the DefaultConnection Example After Changing the ORACLE_SID*

```
C:\My Projects\ProOraNet\Oracle\C#\Chapter07\DefaultConnection\bin\Debug>⏎
set ORACLE_SID=LT8I

C:\My Projects\ProOraNet\Oracle\C#\Chapter07\DefaultConnection\bin\Debug>⏎
DefaultConnection.exe

Hello, Default Oracle Database Here!

Connection String:
User Id=oranetuser;

Current Connection State:
Open

Oracle Database Server Version:
8.1.7.4.1

C:\My Projects\ProOraNet\Oracle\C#\Chapter07\DefaultConnection\bin\Debug>
```

In Listing 7-3, you see that I've overridden the value of the ORACLE_SID as specified in my registry (LT10G) with the value LT8I. The database specified by LT8I is, as I am sure you have guessed, an Oracle8i database that you can see in the Oracle Database Server Version informational output.

At this point, you may be asking yourself what would happen if the value for the ORACLE_SID was missing from the registry and wasn't specified elsewhere. In order to demonstrate what happens in this case, I've temporarily removed the ORACLE_SID key from my registry. Listing 7-4 illustrates what occurs when this is the case. In this listing, I also explicitly undefine the ORACLE_SID value in the command prompt window.

■**CAUTION** If you remove the registry key or set it to no value, be sure you undo this operation immediately after testing.

Listing 7-4. *The Output of the DefaultConnection Sample with No ORACLE_SID Value Set*

```
C:\My Projects\ProOraNet\Chapter07\DefaultConnection\bin\Debug>set ORACLE_SID=

C:\My Projects\ProOraNet\Chapter07\DefaultConnection\bin\Debug>⤸
DefaultConnection.exe
Error occured: ORA-12560: TNS:protocol adapter error

C:\My Projects\ProOraNet\Chapter07\DefaultConnection\bin\Debug>
```

As you can see in Listing 7-4, the Oracle client software immediately returns an error when it is unable to determine a value for the ORACLE_SID variable. To round out your exploration of connecting to the default database, I'll illustrate that the value specified for the ORACLE_SID must be a valid SID. This value can't be a TNS alias.

Listing 7-5 contains the results of running the sample code with a TNS alias specified in place of a valid SID. The error generated in this case is the same as when no value is present.

Listing 7-5. *The Output of the DefaultConnection Sample with an Invalid ORACLE_SID*

```
C:\My Projects\ProOraNet\Chapter07\DefaultConnection\bin\Debug>⤸

set ORACLE_SID=ORANET

C:\My Projects\ProOraNet\Chapter07\DefaultConnection\bin\Debug>⤸
DefaultConnection.exe
Error occured: ORA-12560: TNS:protocol adapter error

C:\My Projects\ProOraNet\Chapter07\DefaultConnection\bin\Debug>
```

Using tnsnames-less Connections

As the number of database installations increases and as systems become more diverse, maintaining a tnsnames.ora file for every database can become cumbersome. Oracle has several solutions to address these concerns including integrating with Microsoft Active Directory and its own Oracle Internet Directory product. However, a more simple, do-it-yourself solution that may be practical involves creating *tnsnames-less connections*.

What this means is that you connect to a database via the Oracle networking architecture but without using a TNS alias specified in a tnsnames.ora file. This is somewhat similar to the way a JDBC Thin driver connection string in Java works. Rather than placing the connection information into a file, you'll embed it into the connection string itself. Using the standard tnsnames method, you've been specifying a connection string such as

```
User Id=oranetuser; Password=demo; Data Source=oranet;
```

where `oranet` is a `tnsnames` alias. You can take the information that the `oranet` alias is used to represent from the tnsnames file and substitute it into the `Data Source` attribute of the connection string. This results in a more busy connection string for the `Connection` object, but I provide some abstraction for this in the sample code. If you use this technique, the connection string above would become

```
"User Id=oranetuser; Password=demo; Data Source=(DESCRIPTION = (ADDRESS_LIST =↵
 (ADDRESS = (PROTOCOL = tcp)(HOST = ridmrwillim1801)(PORT = 1521))↵
 (CONNECT_DATA = (SERVICE_NAME = LT10G.SAND)));"
```

In order to implement this connection technique, you need to know the host, the port, and the service name of the database to which you wish to connect. If you aren't using the service name to connect to a database, you could use the `SID` method instead. However, Oracle recommends the `service name` method for databases version 8i or later. The `service name` method supports Real Application Clusters and Grid systems whereas the `SID` method is directed toward single instance/host systems.

An end user can dynamically supply the `host`, `port`, and `service name` parameters at runtime, or you may specify them in an application-specific configuration file that you create. However, if you store the information in a configuration file, you are basically duplicating the creation of an entry in a `tnsnames.ora` file. As a result, I typically use dynamic values at runtime. How you get the values at run-time is up to you. An end user can dynamically supply them in an interactive application, or they you can read them from a database table—in a noninteractive, system-level application, for example. You'll implement this connection technique by creating a Windows Forms–based application, and you'll supply the required values interactively at run-time.

You can temporarily disable the `tnsnames.ora` file by renaming it to ensure that you're using your tnsnames-less connection. A new feature in the Oracle9i networking components (which carries on into 10g as well) is that the command line utilities tell you which file they used to carry out the request. One of these commands is the tnsping utility. If you've ever used the ping utility, this utility will be very familiar. Instead of pinging any network address, with the tnsping utility, you ping an Oracle listener service. The utility allows you to verify a pathway between Point A and Point B. Listing 7-6 illustrates the simple usage of the tnsping utility. Here, I simply ping the `oranet` TNS alias that you've been using as your standard.

Listing 7-6. *Using the tnsping Utility*

```
C:\>tnsping oranet

TNS Ping Utility for 32-bit Windows: Version 10.1.0.2.0 -↵
 Production on 12-JUL-2004 13:23:55

Copyright (c) 1997, 2003, Oracle.  All rights reserved.

Used parameter files:
c:\oracle\10.1\database\network\admin\sqlnet.ora
```

```
Used TNSNAMES adapter to resolve the alias
Attempting to contact (DESCRIPTION = (ADDRESS_LIST = (ADDRESS = (PROTOCOL = TCP)
(HOST = ridmrwillim1801)(PORT = 1521))) (CONNECT_DATA =↵
 (SERVICE_NAME = LT10G.SAND)))
OK (20 msec)
```

```
C:\>
```

As you might recall from Chapter 1, the sqlnet.ora file is an optional file, but if it exists, it influences the Oracle networking environment. In Listing 7-6, you can see that the Oracle networking client has determined that my machine does have a sqlnet.ora file, and it reads it to extract configuration information. The Used TNSNAMES adapter to resolve the alias informational message indicates that my sqlnet.ora file contains a directive to use the tnsnames.ora file to resolve names.

Listing 7-7 shows what happens when the tnsnames.ora file is renamed, thus preventing the Oracle networking client from using it to resolve names. The sqlnet.ora file has been left intact.

Listing 7-7. *The Results of a tnsping After Renaming the tnsnames.ora File*

```
C:\oracle\10.1\database\network\admin>rename tnsnames.ora tnsnames.ora.bak

C:\oracle\10.1\database\network\admin>tnsping oranet

TNS Ping Utility for 32-bit Windows: Version 10.1.0.2.0 -↵
 Production on 12-JUL-2004 13:25:57

Copyright (c) 1997, 2003, Oracle.  All rights reserved.

Used parameter files:
c:\oracle\10.1\database\network\admin\sqlnet.ora

TNS-03505: Failed to resolve name

C:\oracle\10.1\database\network\admin>
```

Like the previous tnsping, this attempt reads the sqlnet.ora file to retrieve configuration information. However, the tnsnames.ora file no longer exists, so the networking client is unable to resolve the TNS alias oranet. Ordinarily you don't want this to happen. However, for this sample, you want to ensure that the Oracle networking client isn't able to resolve names. To create your tnsnames-less sample, you need to create a new Visual C# Windows application. I have called my Visual Studio solution DynamicConnection, as illustrated in Figure 7-1.

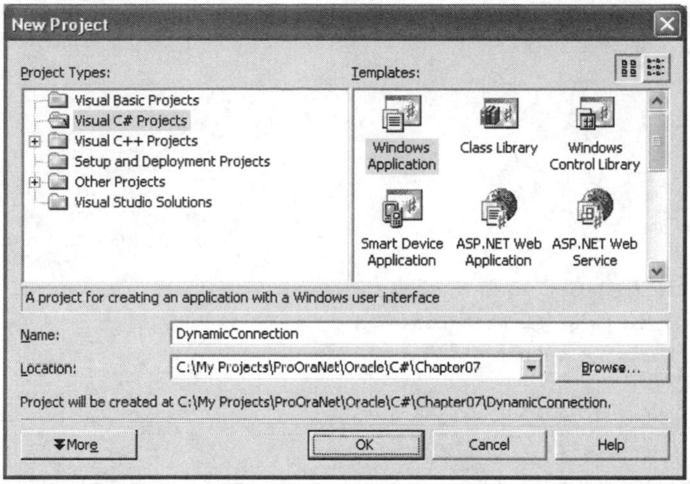

Figure 7-1. *The New Project dialog for the tnsnames-less sample*

Once you've created the project and generated the skeleton code, create the labels, text boxes, and buttons, as illustrated in Figure 7-2. (I've included relevant sections of the code here—for all the details, refer to the code in this chapter's folder on the Apress website.) Of course, you should add a reference to the Oracle Data Provider for .NET assembly to the project and include the relevant using directive in the source code for the form.

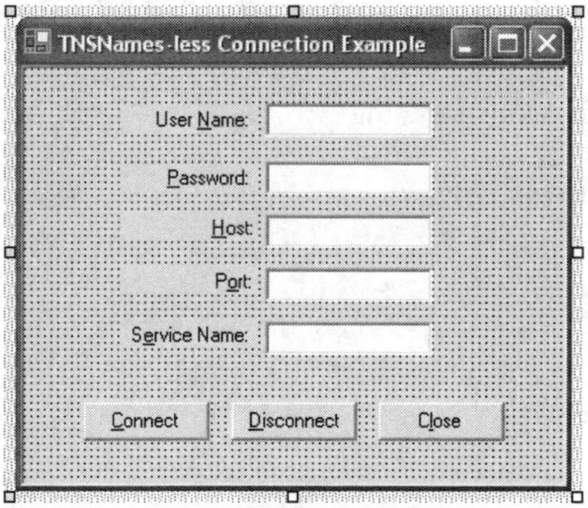

Figure 7-2. *The main form used in the tnsnames-less sample*

For this simple example, you create a single private method that takes the values it needs to generate a TNS connection string as parameters. You call this method by simply passing the values entered on the form. Listing 7-8 contains the private method and the code in the Connect button click event.

Listing 7-8. *The Main Code to Create a tnsnames-less Connection*

```
private void doDynamicConnection(
  string p_user,
  string p_password,
  string p_host,
  string p_port,
  string p_service_name)
{
  // build a tns connection string based on the inputs
  string l_data_source = "(DESCRIPTION=(ADDRESS_LIST=" +
    "(ADDRESS=(PROTOCOL=tcp)(HOST=" + p_host + ")" +
    "(PORT=" + p_port + ")))" +
    "(CONNECT_DATA=(SERVICE_NAME=" + p_service_name + ")))";

  // create the .NET provider connect string
  string l_connect_string = "User Id=" + p_user + ";" +
    "Password=" + p_password + ";" +
    "Data Source=" + l_data_source;

  // attempt to connect to the database
  OracleConnection oraConn = new OracleConnection(l_connect_string);

  try
  {
    oraConn.Open();

    // dislay a simple message box with our data source string
    MessageBox.Show(
      "Connected to data source: \n" + oraConn.DataSource,
      "Dynamic Connection Sample");
  }
  catch (Exception ex)
  {
    MessageBox.Show(ex.Message,"Error Occured");
  }
  finally
  {
    if (oraConn.State == System.Data.ConnectionState.Open)
    {
      oraConn.Close();
    }
  }
}

private void btnConnect_Click(object sender, System.EventArgs e)
{
  doDynamicConnection(
```

```
    txtUserName.Text,
    txtPassword.Text,
    txtHost.Text,
    txtPort.Text,
    txtServiceName.Text);
}
```

Although the code to create the Data Source may seem busy, basically, it dynamically creates the text that appears in a tnsnames.ora file based on the input values. Simply substituting this dynamically generated text in place of the TNS alias in the Data Source attribute of the connection string allows you to connect to a database based on values supplied at run-time. In Figure 7-3, I've completed the form with the same values I used to create the standard TNS alias.

Figure 7-3. *The Dynamic Connection Sample form*

After you complete the form with the appropriate values, click the Connect button. A message box that displays the generated connection string appears. A simple dialog displays if an exception is trapped during the connection attempt. Figure 7-4 shows the dialog that displays given the input values supplied in Figure 7-2.

Dynamic Connection Sample

Connected to data source:
(DESCRIPTION=(ADDRESS_LIST=(ADDRESS=(PROTOCOL=tcp)(HOST=ridmrwillim1801)(PORT=1521)))(CONNECT_DATA=(SERVICE_NAME=lt9i.sand)))

OK

Figure 7-4. *The run-time results of the Dynamic Connection Sample*

The ability to create database connections dynamically at run-time is a powerful capability. You'll find this technique especially useful in situations such as in a system where maintaining a tnsnames.ora file isn't feasible or desirable. One example of such a system is a central repository that connects to various target databases. By creating a database table that contains all the information you need to connect to the target databases, you can easily create a database-driven solution that connects dynamically at run-time to subscribed databases. If you move the functionality demonstrated in the `private` method in your sample form into a library, multiple applications can take advantage of this technique.

Privileged and Non-Privileged Connections

The terms *privileged* and *non-privileged*, when used in conjunction with a connection, don't refer to any specific privileges a user account may or may not have been granted in a database. This is because the privileged and non-privileged refer to *system-level* privileges and not *database-level* privileges. This is most evident by the fact that these privileges allow you to make a connection even if the database itself is not started or opened. Two system-level privileges may be granted: SYSDBA or SYSOPER. Any connection that doesn't utilize either of these privileges is said to be non-privileged. Even though these are system-level privileges, they are, from time to time, referred to as *connection types* or *connection privileges*. This is because when you connect using one of these system-level privileges in a utility such as SQL*Plus, the clause as SYSDBA or as SYSOPER is specified along with the connection string.

The SYSDBA and SYSOPER Privileges

There are a few differences between these two privileges. The SYSDBA privilege is the highest privilege an account may have. An account that has this SYSDBA privilege can perform *any* operation, and for this reason, you should connect to the database using this privilege sparingly and only when you need it. For example, you'll need this privilege when you create a new database or perform certain types of database recovery operations.

The SYSOPER privilege is very similar to the SYSDBA privilege. The only system-level functions the SYSDBA privilege provides that the SYSOPER privilege doesn't are those that let the user create a database and change the character set of a database. As a result, you should take the same care when you grant this privilege that you do with the SYSDBA privilege.

However, one subtle difference between these two is important. When you make a connection using either of these system-level privileges, the connection doesn't utilize the schema normally associated with the account making the connection. For connections you establish using the SYSDBA privilege, the schema used is the SYS schema. Connections that you establish using the SYSOPER privilege, on the other hand, use the PUBLIC schema. This effectively prevents connections that use SYSOPER from being able to view or manipulate data in private schemas.

If you have tried to connect as the user SYS, you may have received the error depicted in Listing 7-9.

Listing 7-9. *Attempting to Connect as SYS in SQL*Plus*

```
C:\>sqlplus /nolog

SQL*Plus: Release 10.1.0.2.0 - Production on Mon Jul 12 13:31:35 2004

Copyright (c) 1982, 2004, Oracle.  All rights reserved.

SQL> connect sys
```

```
Enter password:
ERROR:
ORA-28009: connection to sys should be as sysdba or sysoper
```

```
SQL>
```

The default configuration of Oracle, as installed in the Appendix, is configured so that SYS must explicitly connect as either SYSDBA or SYSOPER. In order to connect as SYSDBA, simply specify as SYSDBA in the connection string.

■**CAUTION** Exercise proper care when you're connecting as SYSDBA. This is a fully privileged connection and should never be used for a normal connection. In addition, make sure you coordinate with your DBA if you're creating an application that makes such connections to the database—any administrator would want to know about an application that makes connections of this type.

Because the SYSDBA and SYSOPER privileges are so powerful, you'll grant them to your administrative user for the samples in this section, and then you'll revoke them when you have completed the samples. Let's begin by connecting as SYS using the SYSDBA privilege. This is one of the few times that you use the SYS user. In this case, it is necessary to connect as SYS in order to grant the SYSDBA privilege. Listing 7-10 demonstrates the process of connecting as SYS and granting the SYSDBA and the SYSOPER privileges. Notice that you're using the default database connection as discussed in the last section.

Listing 7-10. *Connecting as SYS and Granting the SYSDBA and SYSOPER Privileges*

```
C:\>sqlplus /nolog

SQL*Plus: Release 10.1.0.2.0 - Production on Mon Jul 12 13:33:12 2004

Copyright (c) 1982, 2004, Oracle.  All rights reserved.

SQL> connect sys as sysdba
Enter password:
Connected.
SQL> grant sysdba to oranetadmin;

Grant succeeded.

SQL> grant sysoper to oranetadmin;

Grant succeeded.

SQL> exit
Disconnected from Oracle Database 10g Enterprise Edition⏎
```

```
 Release 10.1.0.2.0 - Production
With the Partitioning, OLAP and Data Mining options

C:\>
```

Now that your administrative user has the SYSDBA and the SYSOPER privileges, you can connect with each privilege. When you connect as a privileged connection, as with the SYS user, you must use the as clause to specify which privilege you wish to use for your connection. If you omit the clause, you'll simply connect with your normal, non-privileged account. Listing 7-11 demonstrates these concepts.

■**NOTE** You must install and configure the database and networking components in the same fashion as the setup in the Appendix for this to work properly. This doesn't mean that you must follow the installation steps in the Appendix, only that your configuration must match it. This installation is a preconfigured installation type and it results in an installation configuration that is common.

Listing 7-11. *Connecting with the SYSDBA and SYSOPER Privileges*

```
C:\>sqlplus /nolog

SQL*Plus: Release 10.1.0.2.0 - Production on Mon Jul 12 13:35:02 2004

Copyright (c) 1982, 2004, Oracle.  All rights reserved.

SQL> connect oranetadmin
Enter password:
Connected.
SQL> /* format username column as alphanumeric with width of 16 */
SQL> /* format database column as alphanumeric with width of 24 */
SQL> COL USERNAME FORMAT A16
SQL> COL DATABASE FORMAT A24
SQL> SELECT   A.USERNAME,
  2           B.GLOBAL_NAME DATABASE
  3   FROM    USER_USERS  A,
  4           GLOBAL_NAME B;

USERNAME         DATABASE
---------------- ------------------------
ORANETADMIN      LT10G.SAND

1 row selected.

SQL> connect oranetadmin as sysdba
Enter password:
Connected.
```

```
SQL> SELECT    A.USERNAME,
  2            B.GLOBAL_NAME DATABASE
  3   FROM     USER_USERS  A,
  4            GLOBAL_NAME B;

USERNAME         DATABASE
---------------- ------------------------
SYS              LT10G.SAND

1 row selected.

SQL> connect oranetadmin as sysoper
Enter password:
Connected.
SQL> SELECT    A.USERNAME,
  2            B.GLOBAL_NAME DATABASE
  3   FROM     USER_USERS  A,
  4            GLOBAL_NAME B;

no rows selected

SQL> exit
Disconnected from Oracle Database 10g Enterprise Edition↵
 Release 10.1.0.2.0 - Production
With the Partitioning, OLAP and Data Mining options

C:\>
```

As illustrated in Listing 7-11, when you connect with no system-level privilege specified, you connect to your normal schema of ORANETADMIN. However, when you connect with SYS-DBA or SYSOPER, things begin to get interesting. When you connect with the SYSDBA privilege, your query to determine who you are returns SYS as the username. When you connect with the SYSOPER privilege, your query returns no rows. This is because you're connected to the special schema PUBLIC and not to a real user. To further illustrate this, you'll connect with no system-level privileges, create a table, insert a record, and attempt to query the table. Listing 7-12 contains the code to illustrate this.

Listing 7-12. *Schema Object Visibility When Connecting with System-Level Privileges*

```
C:\>sqlplus /nolog

SQL*Plus: Release 10.1.0.2.0 - Production on Mon Jul 12 13:38:09 2004

Copyright (c) 1982, 2004, Oracle.  All rights reserved.

SQL> connect oranetadmin
Enter password:
Connected.
```

```
SQL> create table t
  2  (
  3    c varchar2(32)
  4  );

Table created.

SQL> insert into t values ('Can you see me?');

1 row created.

SQL> commit;

Commit complete.

SQL> select c from t;

C
--------------------------------
Can you see me?

1 row selected.

SQL> connect oranetadmin as sysdba
Enter password:
Connected.
SQL> select c from t;
select c from t
        *
ERROR at line 1:
ORA-00942: table or view does not exist


SQL> select c from oranetadmin.t;

C
--------------------------------
Can you see me?

1 row selected.

SQL> connect oranetadmin as sysoper
Enter password:
Connected.
SQL> select c from t;
select c from t
        *
```

```
ERROR at line 1:
ORA-00942: table or view does not exist


SQL> select c from oranetadmin.t;
select c from oranetadmin.t
                            *
ERROR at line 1:
ORA-00942: table or view does not exist


SQL> exit
Disconnected from Oracle Database 10g Enterprise Edition↵
 Release 10.1.0.2.0 - Production
With the Partitioning, OLAP and Data Mining options

C:\>
```

As Listing 7-12 illustrates, all goes as expected when you connect with no system-level privileges. You operate as yourself in this connection. When you connect with the SYSDBA privilege, you get an error when you query your table. This is because you're now connected with the SYS schema. However, by specifying the table owner, you are able to successfully query your table. When connected with the SYSOPER privilege, you simply aren't able to see the table at all.

■NOTE If you execute the grant select on t to public command, you can query your table while you're connected with the SYSOPER privilege.

Connecting as a Privileged User

Now that you understand the SYSDBA and SYSOPER privileges, you can examine how to connect from a .NET application using either of these privileges. Under normal circumstances, your applications don't need to connect with either of these system privileges, but if your application needs to shut down or start up a database, for example, it needs to connect with either of these privileges.

Continuing with the trend of keeping things as simple as possible to focus on the topic at hand, you'll create a console application that simply connects as a privileged user, issues the simple "Who am I?" query to verify that you have connected as a privileged user, displays the results, and exits. Listing 7-13 contains the major points in the code for the PrivilegedConnection sample (which you can find in this chapter's folder in the Downloads section of the Apress website). To connect with either privilege, your code needs to include a new attribute in the connection string. The attribute is the DBA Privilege attribute, and it must be assigned either SYSDBA or SYSOPER to be valid.

Listing 7-13. *The SYSDBA and SYSOPER Privilege Test Code*

```
static void Main(string[] args)
{
  Class1 theClass = new Class1();

  // our "basic" connection string
  string conn_1 = "User Id=oranetadmin;" +
    "Password=demo;" +
    "Data Source=oranet";

  // our "sysdba" connection string
  string conn_2 = "User Id=oranetadmin;" +
    "Password=demo;" +
    "Data Source=oranet;" +
    "DBA Privilege=SYSDBA";

  // our "sysoper" connection string
  string conn_3 = "User Id=oranetadmin;" +
    "Password=demo;" +
    "Data Source=oranet;" +
    "DBA Privilege=SYSOPER";

  // our "who am i?" query
  string l_sql = "select a.username, " +
    "b.global_name database " +
    "from user_users a, " +
    "global_name b";

  theClass.privilegeTest(conn_1, l_sql);
  theClass.privilegeTest(conn_2, l_sql);
  theClass.privilegeTest(conn_3, l_sql);
}

void privilegeTest(string p_connect, string p_sql)
{
  // a simple little helper method
  // gets a connection, executes the sql statement,
  // and prints the results (if any) to the console
  OracleCommand oraCmd;
  OracleDataReader oraReader;

  OracleConnection oraConn = new OracleConnection(p_connect);

  try
  {
```

```
    oraConn.Open();

    oraCmd = new OracleCommand(p_sql,oraConn);

    oraReader = oraCmd.ExecuteReader();

    while (oraReader.Read())
    {
      Console.WriteLine("User: ");
      Console.WriteLine("   " + oraReader.GetString(0));
      Console.WriteLine("Database: ");
      Console.WriteLine("   " + oraReader.GetString(1) + "\n");
    }
  }
  catch (Exception ex)
  {
    Console.WriteLine("Error occured: " + ex.Message);
  }
  finally
  {
    if (oraConn.State == System.Data.ConnectionState.Open)
    {
      oraConn.Close();
    }
  }
}
```

After you create the project and successfully compile the code, a sample test should yield results similar to those in Listing 7-14.

Listing 7-14. *The Output from the Privilege Test*

```
C:\My Projects\ProOraNet\Oracle\C#\Chapter07\PrivilegedConnection\bin\Debug>↵
PrivilegedConnection.exe
User:
  ORANETADMIN
Database:
  LT10G.SAND

User:
  SYS
Database:
  LT10G.SAND


C:\My Projects\ProOraNet\Oracle\C#\Chapter07\PrivilegedConnection\bin\Debug>
```

Recall that when you connect with the SYSOPER privilege, you connect to the special PUBLIC schema. Because you connect to the PUBLIC schema, your "Who am I?" query returns no rows, and, therefore, there is output. Now that you've completed your exploration of the SYSDBA and SYSOPER privileges, you'll revoke them from our administrative user. Listing 7-15 illustrates this process.

Listing 7-15. *Revoking the SYSDBA and SYSOPER Privileges*

```
C:\>sqlplus /nolog

SQL*Plus: Release 10.1.0.2.0 - Production on Mon Jul 12 13:43:24 2004

Copyright (c) 1982, 2004, Oracle.  All rights reserved.

SQL> connect sys as sysdba
Enter password:
Connected.
SQL> revoke sysdba from oranetadmin;

Revoke succeeded.

SQL> revoke sysoper from oranetadmin;

Revoke succeeded.

SQL> exit
Disconnected from Oracle Database 10g Enterprise Edition⤶
 Release 10.1.0.2.0 - Production
With the Partitioning, OLAP and Data Mining options

C:\>
```

Connecting via Operating System Authentication

Connecting to a database via operating system authentication involves Oracle authenticating the user account using Windows authentication. Operating system authentication isn't limited to the Windows platform; however, Windows is the only platform I investigated in this section. When you connect via operating system authentication, you don't need the user ID and password. The convention you use to indicate that operating system authentication should be employed is a single forward slash (/) symbol. Rather than specifying a username in the connection string, such as User Id=oranetuser, specify the user ID as User Id=/.

If you aren't working in a stand-alone environment as I am, you may need to coordinate efforts between your database administrator and your operating system administrator in order to enable operating system authentication. There are two classes of operating system authentication you can use: enterprise users and external users. To employ the enterprise users method of authentication, you must have a directory server. Therefore, you need to create an external user authentication scheme.

In this section, you configure operating system authentication using the external user scheme and ensure that everything is working properly by using SQL*Plus as your litmus test. Once you verify that your configuration is working correctly, use your "Who am I?" console application to illustrate connecting via operating system authentication in a .NET application.

Configuring Oracle for Operating System Authentication

In order to properly connect via operating system authentication, you must ensure that Oracle is configured to allow such connections. By default, the sqlnet.ora file contains the entry that enables operating system authentication. As we discussed in Chapter 1, the SQLNET.AUTHENTICATION_SERVICES = (NTS) entry allows for authentication by the operating system. Listing 7-16 is a representative sqlnet.ora file.

Listing 7-16. *An sqlnet.ora File*

```
C:\oracle\10.1\database\network\admin>type sqlnet.ora
# SQLNET.ORA Network Configuration File:⤶
 C:\oracle\10.1\database\network\admin\sqlnet.ora
# Generated by Oracle configuration tools.

SQLNET.AUTHENTICATION_SERVICES= (NTS)

NAMES.DIRECTORY_PATH= (TNSNAMES)

C:\oracle\10.1\database\network\admin>
```

If your sqlnet.ora file doesn't contain the entry for SQLNET.AUTHENTICATION_SERVICES, you must add it to the file. Although the sqlnet.ora file influences the behavior of the Oracle networking components, some parameters influence the behavior of the database itself. These parameters reside in what is known as the init file or the spfile. The spfile exists for Oracle9i and Oracle10g databases, whereas you must use the init file in earlier versions. It's still possible to use an init file in 9i and 10g if you manually configure your database and installation process, but the preconfigured install types and the Oracle tools such as the Database Creation Assistant create an spfile.

You won't make modifications to these parameters here; however, you do need to know the value of one of them, os_authent_prefix, to properly configure your authentication example. Oracle uses this parameter when it is authenticating external users. As the name of the parameter implies, the value of this parameter is prefixed to the operating system username. Listing 7-17 illustrates one method of determining the value of this parameter.

Listing 7-17. *Determining the Value of the os_authent_prefix Parameter*

```
C:\>sqlplus oranetadmin

SQL*Plus: Release 10.1.0.2.0 - Production on Mon Jul 12 13:46:03 2004

Copyright (c) 1982, 2004, Oracle.  All rights reserved.
```

```
Enter password:

Connected to:
Oracle Database 10g Enterprise Edition Release 10.1.0.2.0 - Production
With the Partitioning, OLAP and Data Mining options

SQL> show parameter os_authent_prefix

NAME                         TYPE         VALUE
---------------------------- ------------ ----------------------------
os_authent_prefix            string       OPS$
SQL> exit
Disconnected from Oracle Database 10g Enterprise Edition↵
 Release 10.1.0.2.0 - Production
With the Partitioning, OLAP and Data Mining options

C:\>
```

You can see that, on my system, the value of this parameter is OPS$. The value may be different on your system or it may not be specified at all. If the value isn't specified, it doesn't mean that operating system authentication won't work or isn't available, it just means that no value will be prefixed to an operating system username. The Windows username that I use on my system is willim18, and my host name is ridmrwillim1801. Therefore, when I authenticate using operating system authentication to my database, I authenticate as OPS$RIDMRWILLIM1801\WILLIM18.

Because I authenticate as OPS$RIDMRWILLIM1801\WILLIM18, I need to create that user in the Oracle database. Listing 7-18 illustrates the process of creating a user for operating system authentication.

Listing 7-18. *Creating a User for Operating System Authentication*

```
C:\>sqlplus oranetadmin

SQL*Plus: Release 10.1.0.2.0 - Production on Mon Jul 12 13:47:28 2004

Copyright (c) 1982, 2004, Oracle.  All rights reserved.

Enter password:

Connected to:
Oracle Database 10g Enterprise Edition Release 10.1.0.2.0 - Production
With the Partitioning, OLAP and Data Mining options

SQL> create user "OPS$RIDMRWILLIM1801\WILLIM18" identified externally
  2   default tablespace users
  3   temporary tablespace temp
  4   quota unlimited on users;
```

```
User created.

SQL> grant connect to "OPS$RIDMRWILLIM1801\WILLIM18";

Grant succeeded.

SQL> exit
Disconnected from Oracle Database 10g Enterprise Edition⤶
 Release 10.1.0.2.0 - Production
With the Partitioning, OLAP and Data Mining options

C:\>
```

As you can see, I used the administrative user to log in to SQL*Plus and manually create a new user.

■**TIP** If you are part of a Windows domain, when you create the new user, you should include the domain name in the username. For example, if I was in a domain called Liverpool, my user would be OPS$LIVERPOOL\WILLIM18.

Testing Operating System Authentication

Now that you've successfully created your user to be authenticated by the operating system, you can test this in SQL*Plus quite easily. You only need to specify a forward slash (/) for your connection string. Then execute your "Who am I?" script to verify that you have connected as expected. Listing 7-19 illustrates this process.

Listing 7-19. *Testing Operating System Authentication*

```
C:\>sqlplus /nolog

SQL*Plus: Release 10.1.0.2.0 - Production on Mon Jul 12 13:49:15 2004

Copyright (c) 1982, 2004, Oracle.  All rights reserved.

SQL> connect /
Connected.
SQL> COL USERNAME FORMAT A32
SQL> COL DATABASE FORMAT A24
SQL> SELECT    A.USERNAME,
  2            B.GLOBAL_NAME DATABASE
  3  FROM      USER_USERS   A,
  4            GLOBAL_NAME B;

USERNAME                            DATABASE
```

```
--------------------------------- ------------------------
OPS$RIDMRWILLIM1801\WILLIM18     LT10G.SAND

1 row selected.

SQL> exit
Disconnected from Oracle Database 10g Enterprise Edition↵
 Release 10.1.0.2.0 - Production
With the Partitioning, OLAP and Data Mining options

C:\>
```

By specifying only a / for your connection string, you've successfully connected to your default database using operating system authentication. If you wish to connect to a database using its TNS alias and operating system authentication, you simply supply the TNS alias as part of the connection string as we discussed earlier. Of course, when you connect to a TNS alias, your account must be set up properly in the destination database as it was in Listing 7-19. The sample .NET code you develop in the following section (see Listing 7-20) illustrates both methods of connecting.

Operating System Authentication in .NET

Implementing operating system authentication in .NET code is trivial. Most of the work is in the setup and verification to make sure that the authentication is working as you expect it to. Because you've already set up and verified that your External User account is working as expected, in this section, you implement your "Who am I?" sample query using operating system authentication to the default database as well as your standard TNS alias. Listing 7-20 contains the core code you need to implement your sample. Of course, a reference to the Oracle.DataAccess.dll assembly and a using Oracle.DataAccess.Client; are included in the OSAuthenticatedConnection project (which you can access from this chapter's folder in the Downloads section of the Apress website).

Listing 7-20. *The Core Code for Testing Operating System Authentication*

```
static void Main(string[] args)
{
  Class1 theClass = new Class1();

  // our "default" database connection string
  string conn_1 = "User Id=/";

  // our "tns alias" database connection string
  string conn_2 = "User Id=/;" +
    "Data Source=oranet";

  // our "who am i?" query
  string l_sql = "select a.username, " +
    "b.global_name database " +
```

```
      "from user_users a, " +
      "global_name b";

  Console.WriteLine("Using the default database...");
  theClass.authenticationTest(conn_1, l_sql);

  Console.WriteLine("Using the tns alias...");
  theClass.authenticationTest(conn_2, l_sql);
}

void authenticationTest(string p_connect, string p_sql)
{
  // a simple little helper method
  // gets a connection, executes the sql statement,
  // and prints the results to the console
  OracleCommand oraCmd;
  OracleDataReader oraReader;

  OracleConnection oraConn = new OracleConnection(p_connect);

  try
  {
    oraConn.Open();

    oraCmd = new OracleCommand(p_sql,oraConn);

    oraReader = oraCmd.ExecuteReader();

    while (oraReader.Read())
    {
      Console.WriteLine("User: ");
      Console.WriteLine("   " + oraReader.GetString(0));
      Console.WriteLine("Database: ");
      Console.WriteLine("   " + oraReader.GetString(1) + "\n");
    }
  }
  catch (Exception ex)
  {
    Console.WriteLine("Error occured: " + ex.Message);
  }
  finally
  {
    if (oraConn.State == System.Data.ConnectionState.Open)
    {
      oraConn.Close();
    }
  }
}
```

Running the sample code should produce results that are appropriate for your system and resemble those in Listing 7-21.

Listing 7-21. *The Output of the Operating System Authentication Test*

```
C:\My Projects\ProOraNet\Oracle\C#\Chapter07\OSAuthenticatedConnection\bin\Debug>⤶
OSAuthenticatedConnection.exe
Using the default database...
User:
  OPS$RIDMRWILLIM1801\WILLIM18
Database:
  LT10G.SAND

Using the tns alias...
User:
  OPS$RIDMRWILLIM1801\WILLIM18
Database:
  LT10G.SAND


C:\My Projects\ProOraNet\Oracle\C#\Chapter07\OSAuthenticatedConnection\bin\Debug>
```

As expected, the results of your "Who am I?" query display the same data when connecting via operating system authentication to both the default database and that same database specified as a TNS alias. Using operating system authentication is a viable method for not having to maintain a password for a database user as we discussed earlier. However, if you wish to have a finer grained control over the password, then Oracle can accommodate that as well when you're using database authentication.

Password Management

The topic of password management can be rather broad. I will, therefore, limit the discussion to three areas:

Changing a Database Password: You'll look at changing a password via SQL*Plus as well as in .NET code.

Dealing with Expired Database Passwords: Passwords can expire and thus need to be changed.

Locking Out a Database Password: Accounts can be locked if password rules created by the database administrator are violated.

These are the most common areas for dealing with password management. One common misconception regarding Oracle passwords is that what is stored in the database isn't the actual password. Passwords in Oracle are really one-way hash values that result from an internal algorithm that incorporates the password as defined by the user. It is, therefore, not possible to reverse-engineer an Oracle password—no password is stored in the database, only the result of the one-way hash algorithm.

Changing a Database Password

A database user can change their own password. If the database user has the appropriate database privilege (`alter user`), they may change the password for other users as well.

■NOTE The `alter user` privilege allows for more than just changing another user's password. You can find the complete list of attributes that can be changed by `alter user` under the `alter user` SQL statement reference in the "Database SQL Reference" in the documentation set.

The command you use to change a password is simply `alter user <username>` identified by `<password>`. Listing 7-22 illustrates how to do this via SQL*Plus.

Listing 7-22. *Changing a Password in SQL*Plus*

```
C:\>sqlplus oranetuser@oranet

SQL*Plus: Release 10.1.0.2.0 - Production on Mon Jul 12 13:53:30 2004

Copyright (c) 1982, 2004, Oracle.  All rights reserved.

Enter password:

Connected to:
Oracle Database 10g Enterprise Edition Release 10.1.0.2.0 - Production
With the Partitioning, OLAP and Data Mining options

SQL> alter user oranetuser identified by newpass;

User altered.

SQL> exit
Disconnected from Oracle Database 10g Enterprise Edition↵
 Release 10.1.0.2.0 - Production
With the Partitioning, OLAP and Data Mining options

C:\>
```

The database user, oranetuser, now has the password newpass. You may wish to change the password back to what it was before by simply executing the command and specifying the old password. Listing 7-23 contains the core code for a Windows Forms application named PasswordChange that allows you to change the password back (or to any other value) if you wish. This sample doesn't allow you to change the password for any user in the database—only for the oranetuser user.

Listing 7-23. *Simple Code to Change a Password*

```
private void btnChangePassword_Click(object sender, System.EventArgs e)
{
  if (txtNewPassword.Text != txtConfirmPassword.Text)
  {
    MessageBox.Show("New passwords do not match.", "Password Mismatch");

    return;
  }

  string l_connect = "User Id=" + txtUserName.Text + ";" +
    "Password=" + txtCurrentPassword.Text + ";" +
    "Data Source=" + txtTNSAlias.Text;

  string l_sql = "alter user " + txtUserName.Text + " " +
    "identified by " + txtNewPassword.Text;

  OracleCommand cmd;
  OracleConnection oraConn = new OracleConnection(l_connect);

  try
  {
    oraConn.Open();

    cmd = new OracleCommand(l_sql,oraConn);

    cmd.ExecuteNonQuery();

    MessageBox.Show("Password changed successfully.", "Password Changed");
  }
  catch (Exception ex)
  {
    MessageBox.Show(ex.Message, "Error Occured");
  }
  finally
  {
    if (oraConn.State == System.Data.ConnectionState.Open)
    {
      oraConn.Close();
    }
  }
}
```

Figure 7-5 shows the simple form you'd use to capture the relevant information you need to change the database password.

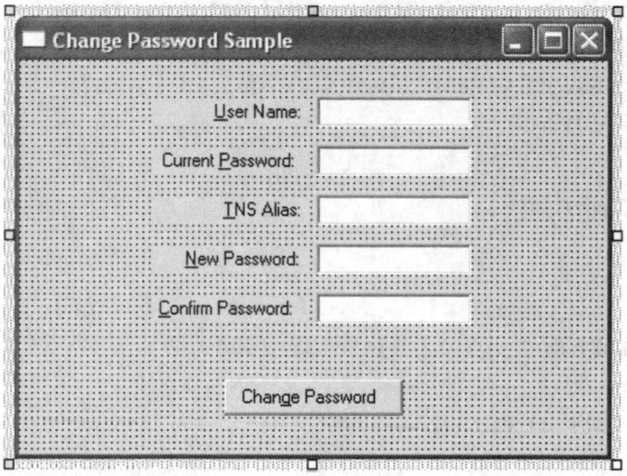

Figure 7-5. *The design-time representation of the form*

Figure 7-6 shows the form at run-time. Because you changed the password for the oranet-user in SQL*Plus earlier, I changed it back to the value of demo, as it was previously.

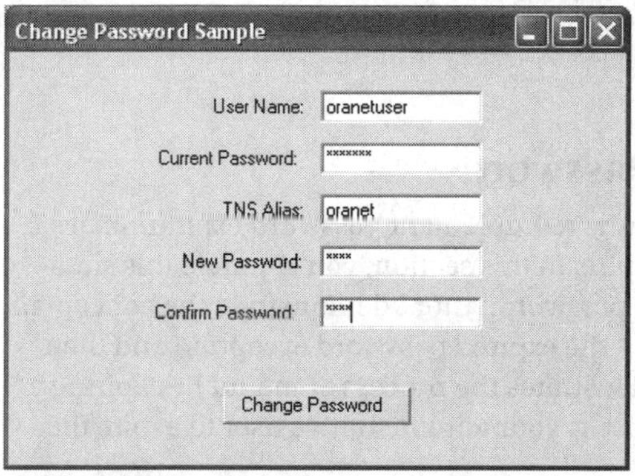

Figure 7-6. *The run-time representation of the form*

Figure 7-7 shows the confirmation message that states that the password was changed successfully.

Figure 7-7. *The confirmation dialog*

To verify that the password for oranetuser was successfully changed from newpass to demo, create a SQL*Plus session and specify the new password. Listing 7-24 illustrates this process (in order to make it explicit that the password was successfully changed, I specify the password as part of the connection string in SQL*Plus).

Listing 7-24. *Verifying That the Password Was Changed*

```
C:\>sqlplus /nolog

SQL*Plus: Release 10.1.0.2.0 - Production on Mon Jul 12 13:56:07 2004

Copyright (c) 1982, 2004, Oracle.  All rights reserved.

SQL> connect oranetuser/demo@oranet
Connected.
SQL> exit
Disconnected from Oracle Database 10g Enterprise Edition↵
 Release 10.1.0.2.0 - Production
With the Partitioning, OLAP and Data Mining options

C:\>
```

Dealing with Expired Database Passwords

If the database administrator for your system elects to implement password expiration, it's possible that the password for your user may expire. In this section, you simulate this situation by using SQL*Plus and manually expiring a password. After I demonstrate the concept in SQL*Plus, you implement the .NET code to catch the expired password exception and then allow the password to be changed. Listing 7-25 illustrates the process of manually expiring a password from SQL*Plus. Notice that you connect as your administrative user to expire the password for your typical-privileged user.

Listing 7-25. *Manually Expiring a Password*

```
C:\>sqlplus oranetadmin@oranet

SQL*Plus: Release 10.1.0.2.0 - Production on Mon Jul 12 14:01:20 2004

Copyright (c) 1982, 2004, Oracle.  All rights reserved.

Enter password:

Connected to:
Oracle Database 10g Enterprise Edition Release 10.1.0.2.0 - Production
With the Partitioning, OLAP and Data Mining options

SQL> alter user oranetuser password expire;
```

```
User altered.

SQL> exit
Disconnected from Oracle Database 10g Enterprise Edition↵
 Release 10.1.0.2.0 - Production
With the Partitioning, OLAP and Data Mining options

C:\>
```

The password for oranetuser has expired. When the user attempts their next connection, Oracle detects that the password has expired and triggers a prompt for a new password. Listing 7-26 illustrates this process.

Listing 7-26. *Detection and Change of the Expired Password*

```
C:\>sqlplus oranetuser@oranet

SQL*Plus: Release 10.1.0.2.0 - Production on Mon Jul 12 14:02:38 2004

Copyright (c) 1982, 2004, Oracle.  All rights reserved.

Enter password:
ERROR:
ORA-28001: the password has expired


Changing password for oranetuser
New password:
Retype new password:
Password changed

Connected to:
Oracle Database 10g Enterprise Edition Release 10.1.0.2.0 - Production
With the Partitioning, OLAP and Data Mining options

SQL> exit
Disconnected from Oracle Database 10g Enterprise Edition↵
 Release 10.1.0.2.0 - Production
With the Partitioning, OLAP and Data Mining options

C:\>
```

▨**NOTE** The password that is initially entered must be the correct expired password. If an invalid password is entered, you receive the standard "invalid username or password" error message instead of being prompted for a new password.

To demonstrate how to trap and process the expired password in .NET, I clone the simple Windows Form application used to change the password. The form itself doesn't change. I simply change the code inside the button click event. Listing 7-27 represents the code that detects the expired password condition and connects with a new password. The new project is called PasswordExpiration (see this chapter's folder on the Downloads section of the Apress website).

Listing 7-27. *Changing an Expired Password*

```
private void btnChangePassword_Click(object sender, System.EventArgs e)
{
  // display a simple message if the "new" and
  // the "confirm" passwords do not match
  if (txtNewPassword.Text != txtConfirmPassword.Text)
  {
    MessageBox.Show("New passwords do not match.", "Password Mismatch");

    return;
  }

  // build a connect string based on the user input
  string l_connect = "User Id=" + txtUserName.Text + ";" +
    "Password=" + txtCurrentPassword.Text + ";" +
    "Data Source=" + txtTNSAlias.Text;

  OracleConnection oraConn = new OracleConnection(l_connect);

  try
  {
    // attempt to open a connection
    // this should fail since we have expired the password
    oraConn.Open();
  }
  catch (OracleException ex)
  {
    // trap the "password is expired" error code
    if (ex.Number == 28001)
    {
      // dislay a simple marker to indicate we trapped the error
      MessageBox.Show("Trapped Expired Password", "Expired Password");

      // this method changes the expired password
      oraConn.OpenWithNewPassword(txtNewPassword.Text);
```

```
    // display a simple marker to indicate password changed
    MessageBox.Show("Changed Expired Password", "Expired Password");
  }
  else
  {
    MessageBox.Show(ex.Message, "Error Occured");
  }
}
finally
{
  if (oraConn.State == System.Data.ConnectionState.Open)
  {
    oraConn.Close();
  }
}
}
```

In Figure 7-8, you can see the form at run-time.

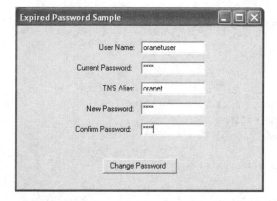

Figure 7-8. *The Expired Password Sample form*

By completing the text field in the form and clicking the Change Password button, you should see the dialog depicted in Figure 7-9.

Figure 7-9. *The Expired Password detected dialog*

After dismissing the dialog that informs you that the expired password condition was detected, you should see the dialog depicted in Figure 7-10.

Figure 7-10. *The Expired Password changed dialog*

To verify that the expired password was correctly changed, use SQL*Plus as illustrated in Listing 7-28.

Listing 7-28. *Verifying That the Expired Password Was Changed*

```
C:\>sqlplus oranetuser@oranet

SQL*Plus: Release 10.1.0.2.0 - Production on Mon Jul 12 14:05:11 2004

Copyright (c) 1982, 2004, Oracle.  All rights reserved.

Enter password:

Connected to:
Oracle Database 10g Enterprise Edition Release 10.1.0.2.0 - Production
With the Partitioning, OLAP and Data Mining options

SQL> exit
Disconnected from Oracle Database 10g Enterprise Edition↵
 Release 10.1.0.2.0 - Production
With the Partitioning, OLAP and Data Mining options

C:\>
```

The sample code, as presented here, doesn't verify that the new password you entered was different from the old one. You should coordinate any password rules such as no password reuse with your database administrator if you're using the password expiration feature. Oracle has the ability to enforce a variety of password rules; however, this is a subject outside the scope of this book because the creation of the password rules in the database relates to your database administrator more than it does to us as developers. The definition of those rules, on the other hand, is something that application developers and corporate security departments are frequently involved in creating. If your database administrator has implemented password rules, it's possible that, in addition to password expiration, you may encounter a user account that has been locked.

Locking Out a Database Account

In addition to an expired password, it's possible that an account can become locked out as a result of database password rules that may be implemented. For example, if the database administrator implements rules that dictate an account becoming locked after three unsuccessful login attempts, and a user inputs an incorrect password three times in succession, the account is then locked out. Unlike the case of an expired password, no method allows a simultaneous change of the password value as well as the password or account state. Once an account is locked, it must be explicitly unlocked. Typically, the database administrator (or similar privileged user) performs the unlocking. This is primarily due to the fact that if an account becomes locked, the database administrator is likely to know why. If an application simply allowed a user to get into a locked account state and then unlock the account, there is little point in implementing the rules that allow the lock to occur in the first place.

In this section, once again you use SQL*Plus to manually place your account into the desired state; then you implement the functionality in .NET code to detect the situation and notify the user. Here, you only detect the locked state and alert the user that the account is locked. If you wish to implement the ability to unlock an account in your application, I suggest you discuss this with your database administrator prior to doing so. Listing 7-29 illustrates how to lock an account using your administrative user in SQL*Plus.

NOTE The act of locking or unlocking an account doesn't affect the password per se. I included it in this section because, from a user perspective, a locked account may be interpreted as a password issue.

Listing 7-29. *Using SQL*Plus to Lock an Account*

```
C:\>sqlplus oranetadmin@oranet

SQL*Plus: Release 10.1.0.2.0 - Production on Mon Jul 12 14:06:29 2004

Copyright (c) 1982, 2004, Oracle.  All rights reserved.

Enter password:

Connected to:
Oracle Database 10g Enterprise Edition Release 10.1.0.2.0 - Production
With the Partitioning, OLAP and Data Mining options

SQL> alter user oranetuser account lock;

User altered.

SQL> exit
Disconnected from Oracle Database 10g Enterprise Edition↵
 Release 10.1.0.2.0 - Production
With the Partitioning, OLAP and Data Mining options

C:\>
```

At this point, your oranetuser account is locked. Any attempt to connect to the database generates a trappable error as illustrated in Listing 7-30.

Listing 7-30. *Attempting to Connect to a Locked Account*

```
C:\>sqlplus /nolog

SQL*Plus: Release 10.1.0.2.0 - Production on Mon Jul 12 14:07:30 2004

Copyright (c) 1982, 2004, Oracle.  All rights reserved.

SQL> connect oranetuser@oranet
Enter password:
ERROR:
ORA-28000: the account is locked


SQL> exit

C:\>
```

As you can see in Listing 7-30, Oracle generates an ORA-28000 error message when it detects an attempt to connect with a locked account. Your test code from the PasswordLocked project in Listing 7-31 (see this chapter's folder in the Downloads section of the Apress website for the complete sample code) takes advantage of this fact to trap the condition and display a simple dialog that indicates that the condition has been trapped.

Listing 7-31. *The Account Locked Test Code*

```
private void btnConnect_Click(object sender, System.EventArgs e)
{
  // build a connect string based on the user input
  string l_connect = "User Id=" + txtUserName.Text + ";" +
    "Password=" + txtCurrentPassword.Text + ";" +
    "Data Source=" + txtTNSAlias.Text;

  OracleConnection oraConn = new OracleConnection(l_connect);

  try
  {
    // attempt to open a connection
    // this should fail since we have locked the account
    oraConn.Open();
  }
  catch (OracleException ex)
  {
    // trap the "account is locked" error code
    if (ex.Number == 28000)
```

```
      {
        // display a simple marker to indicate we trapped the error
        MessageBox.Show("Trapped Locked Account", "Locked Account");
      }
      else
      {
        MessageBox.Show(ex.Message, "Error Occured");
      }
    }
    finally
    {
      if (oraConn.State -- System.Data.ConnectionState.Open)
      {
        oraConn.Close();
      }
    }
  }
}
```

Figure 7-11 shows the design time representation of the form. This is the same form I used in the previous samples except I've removed the New Password and Confirm Password labels and text boxes.

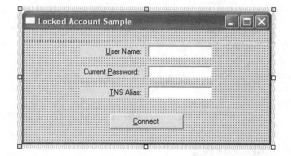

Figure 7-11. *The design time representation of the locked account form*

When you run the sample code and attempt to log in to the database as the oranetuser account as depicted in Figure 7-12, you should receive an error dialog.

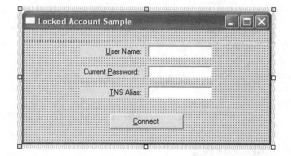

Figure 7-12. *The locked account test form at run-time*

When you click the Connect button, you're presented with the dialog in Figure 7-13.

Figure 7-13. *The dialog indicating you trapped the locked account condition*

Finally, to wrap-up your exploration of locked accounts, you'll unlock the oranetuser account in SQL*Plus using your administrative user. This is illustrated in Listing 7-32.

Listing 7-32. *Unlocking an Account*

```
C:\>sqlplus oranetadmin@oranet

SQL*Plus: Release 10.1.0.2.0 - Production on Mon Jul 12 14:09:09 2004

Copyright (c) 1982, 2004, Oracle.  All rights reserved.

Enter password:

Connected to:
Oracle Database 10g Enterprise Edition Release 10.1.0.2.0 - Production
With the Partitioning, OLAP and Data Mining options

SQL> alter user oranetuser account unlock;

User altered.

SQL> exit
Disconnected from Oracle Database 10g Enterprise Edition⤶
 Release 10.1.0.2.0 - Production
With the Partitioning, OLAP and Data Mining options

C:\>
```

Connection Pooling and Multiplexing

One of the design features of the .NET Framework is increased scalability and more prudent resource usage. One way this design feature is exposed by the Oracle Data Provider for .NET is through the connection pooling mechanism.

■**NOTE** The connection pooling mechanism isn't limited to the Oracle Data Provider for .NET. Other data providers can also expose the connection pooling feature.

The term *multiplexing* can be confused with the term *connection pooling*, though they represent distinct approaches to limiting resource usage. In a multiplexing configuration, a single connection to the resource (a database, in your case) is shared by multiple clients of the resource. The Oracle Data Provider for .NET doesn't expose a multiplexing method. An application (such as a middle-tier application) is responsible for creating the connection and brokering its usage among its clients. However, the database itself supports a multiplexing scheme through the shared server (formerly known as multi-threaded server) connection type. We examined shared server and dedicated server modes in Chapter 1.

On the other hand, since the connection pooling functionality is directly exposed by the data provider, and because it is trivial to implement, you use it as your resource saving method. In fact, you have to explicitly *not* use the connection pooling feature, because it is enabled by default.

In order to see how the connection pooling feature works, you'll create two applications. The first is a simple console application called NoConnectionPooling that explicitly disables connection pooling. The other, called ConnectionPooling, uses the default value of having connection pooling enabled. You'll then run these applications and examine the connections to your database in SQL*Plus. You incorporate a small pause function in your code that gives you time to examine the connections in SQL*Plus. In order to examine the effect of the connection pooling attribute, you have to do a bit of bouncing around between SQL*Plus and your application.

In order to verify that the connection pooling attribute has been disabled and to see the effects of this in SQL*Plus, create a new console application like the one in Listing 7-33.

Listing 7-33. *A Console Application That Disables Connection Pooling*

```
static void Main(string[] args)
{
  // create a connection string to our standard database
  // the pooling=false attribute disables connection pooling
  string l_connect = "User Id=oranetuser;" +
    "Password=demo;" +
    "Data Source=oranet;" +
    "pooling=false";

  OracleConnection conn_1 = new OracleConnection(l_connect);
  conn_1.Open();

  // pause so we can monitor connection in
  // SQL*Plus
  Console.WriteLine("Connection 1 created... Examine in SQL*Plus");
  Console.ReadLine();

  conn_1.Dispose();

  // pause so we can monitor connection in
  // SQL*Plus
  Console.WriteLine("Connection 1 disposed... Examine in SQL*Plus ");
  Console.ReadLine();
```

```
OracleConnection conn_2 = new OracleConnection(l_connect);
conn_2.Open();

// pause so we can monitor connection in
// SQL*Plus
Console.WriteLine("Connection 2 created... Examine in SQL*Plus ");
Console.ReadLine();

conn_2.Dispose();

// pause so we can monitor connection in
// SQL*Plus
Console.WriteLine("Connection 2 disposed... Examine in SQL*Plus ");
Console.ReadLine();
}
```

Here, you repeatedly execute a query in SQL*Plus to monitor your connections. After each Examine in SQL*Plus message, you toggle over to the window where you're running SQL*Plus and execute the query. The query simply displays your user name, the program that is executing, and the time the user logged in to the database. The time that the user logged in to the database is important, because it is this that verifies that you are or aren't using connection pooling. If connection pooling isn't being used, the time that the user logged in to the database varies with the iterations of your query. If connection pooling is being used, the time the user logged in to the database remains constant because the single connection is being reused.

The steps you use to verify if connection pooling is or isn't being used are as follows:

1. Once you have created and compiled your console application, open a command prompt window, change to the directory that contains the executable for your test, and execute the binary, as shown here:

```
C:\My Projects\ProOraNet\Oracle\C#\Chapter07\NoConnectionPooling\bin\Debug> ↵
NoConnectionPooling.exe
Connection 1 created... Examine in SQL*Plus
```

2. Start an SQL*Plus session as illustrated here:

```
C:\>sqlplus oranetadmin@oranet

SQL*Plus: Release 10.1.0.2.0 - Production on Mon Jul 12 18:18:56 2004

Copyright (c) 1982, 2004, Oracle.  All rights reserved.

Enter password:

Connected to:
Oracle Database 10g Enterprise Edition Release 10.1.0.2.0 - Production
With the Partitioning, OLAP and Data Mining options

SQL> COL PROGRAM FORMAT A24
SQL> SELECT    USERNAME,
```

```
  2              PROGRAM,
  3              TO_CHAR(LOGON_TIME,'HH24:MI:SS') LOGON_TIME
  4    FROM      V$SESSION
  5    WHERE     USERNAME = 'ORANETUSER';

USERNAME                        PROGRAM                  LOGON_TI
------------------------------  -----------------------  --------
ORANETUSER                      NoConnectionPooling.exe  18:18:56

1 row selected.
```

3. Press the Enter key to un-pause the application as illustrated in the following code:

```
C:\My Projects\ProOraNet\Oracle\C#\Chapter07\NoConnectionPooling\bin\Debug>⏎
NoConnectionPooling.exe
Connection 1 created... Examine in SQL*Plus

Connection 1 disposed... Examine in SQL*Plus
```

4. Toggle over to the SQL*Plus session and re-execute the query by entering a single forward slash (/) character and pressing Enter. The following code illustrates this:

```
SQL> /

no rows selected
```

Your query has returned no rows because the connection was disposed and you don't have connection pooling enabled.

5. Return to the application window and press the Enter key to un-pause the application as illustrated here:

```
C:\My Projects\ProOraNet\Oracle\C#\Chapter07\NoConnectionPooling\bin\Debug>⏎
NoConnectionPooling.exe
Connection 1 created... Examine in SQL*Plus

Connection 1 disposed... Examine in SQL*Plus

Connection 2 created... Examine in SQL*Plus
```

6. Return to the SQL*Plus session and re-execute the query as you did in step 4. The following code illustrates this:

```
SQL> /

USERNAME                        PROGRAM                  LOGON_TI
------------------------------  -----------------------  --------
ORANETUSER                      NoConnectionPooling.exe  18:28:58

1 row selected.
```

You can see that you've established a new connection and that this connection has a different logon time from the previous connection.

7. Return to the application window and press Enter to un-pause the application as illustrated here:

```
C:\My Projects\ProOraNet\Oracle\C#\Chapter07\NoConnectionPooling\bin\Debug>↵
NoConnectionPooling.exe
Connection 1 created... Examine in SQL*Plus

Connection 1 disposed... Examine in SQL*Plus

Connection 2 created... Examine in SQL*Plus

Connection 2 disposed... Examine in SQL*Plus
```

8. Return to SQL*Plus and re-execute the query. The following code contains the results:

```
SQL> /

no rows selected
```

Once again, your query doesn't return results because you disposed of your second connection.

9. Return to the application window and press Enter to un-pause the application. The application terminates at this point.

In order to demonstrate connection pooling, you'll use virtually the same code as you did in Listing 7-33. The only difference between this code and the following code to demonstrate connection pooling is that you remove the pooling=false attribute from the connection string. Since pooling is True by default, this enables your application to take advantage of connection pooling. Listing 7-34 contains the code you used in your connection pooling test application.

Listing 7-34. *A Console Application That Uses Connection Pooling*

```
static void Main(string[] args)
{
  // create a connection string to our standard database
  // the pooling attribute defaults to "true" so we
  // do not need to include it to enable pooling
  string l_connect = "User Id=oranetuser;" +
    "Password=demo;" +
    "Data Source=oranet";

  OracleConnection conn_1 = new OracleConnection(l_connect);
  conn_1.Open();

  // pause so we can monitor connection in
  // SQL*Plus
  Console.WriteLine("Connection 1 created... Examine in SQL*Plus");
  Console.ReadLine();
```

```
conn_1.Dispose();

// pause so we can monitor connection in
// SQL*Plus
Console.WriteLine("Connection 1 disposed... Examine in SQL*Plus ");
Console.ReadLine();

OracleConnection conn_2 = new OracleConnection(l_connect);
conn_2.Open();

// pause so we can monitor connection in
// SQL*Plus
Console.WriteLine("Connection 2 created... Examine in SQL*Plus ");
Console.ReadLine();

conn_2.Dispose();

// pause so we can monitor connection in
// SQL*Plus
Console.WriteLine("Connection 2 disposed... Examine in SQL*Plus ");
Console.ReadLine();
}
```

You perform the same steps as you did with the no connection pooling example. However, the results of your connection monitoring query are slightly different.

1. Once you've created and compiled your console application, open a command prompt window, change to the directory that contains the executable for your test, and execute the binary. The following code illustrates this process:

```
C:\My Projects\ProOraNet\Oracle\C#\Chapter07\NoConnectionPooling\bin\Debug>↵
ConnectionPooling.exe
Connection 1 created... Hit enter key
```

2. Start an SQL*Plus session as illustrated here:

```
C:\>sqlplus oranetadmin@oranet

SQL*Plus: Release 10.1.0.2.0 - Production on Tue Jul 13 19:03:47 2004

Copyright (c) 1982, 2004, Oracle.  All rights reserved.

Enter password:

Connected to:
Oracle Database 10g Enterprise Edition Release 10.1.0.2.0 - Production
With the Partitioning, OLAP and Data Mining options
```

```
SQL> COL PROGRAM FORMAT A24
SQL> SELECT    USERNAME,
  2            PROGRAM,
  3            TO_CHAR(LOGON_TIME,'HH24:MI:SS') LOGON_TIME
  4  FROM      V$SESSION
  5  WHERE     USERNAME = 'ORANETUSER';

USERNAME                          PROGRAM                  LOGON_TI
------------------------------    ----------------------   --------
ORANETUSER                        ConnectionPooling.exe    19:03:47

1 row selected.
```

3. Press the Enter key to un-pause the application as illustrated in the following code:

```
C:\My Projects\ProOraNet\Oracle\C#\Chapter07\NoConnectionPooling\bin\Debug>⏎
ConnectionPooling.exe
Connection 1 created... Examine in SQL*Plus

Connection 1 disposed... Examine in SQL*Plus
```

4. Toggle over to the SQL*Plus session and re-execute the query by entering a single forward slash (/) and pressing Enter as illustrated here:

```
SQL> /

USERNAME                          PROGRAM                  LOGON_TI
------------------------------    ----------------------   --------
ORANETUSER                        ConnectionPooling.exe    19:03:47

1 row selected.
```

Your query has returned a row even though the connection was disposed of. This is the effect of connection pooling. Rather than terminate your connection, you've returned it to the pool.

5. Return to the application window and press the Enter key to un-pause the application as illustrated here:

```
C:\My Projects\ProOraNet\Oracle\C#\Chapter07\NoConnectionPooling\bin\Debug>⏎
ConnectionPooling.exe
Connection 1 created... Examine in SQL*Plus

Connection 1 disposed... Examine in SQL*Plus

Connection 2 created... Examine in SQL*Plus
```

6. Return to the SQL*Plus session and re-execute the query:

```
SQL> /

USERNAME                      PROGRAM                  LOGON_TI
----------------------------- ------------------------ --------
ORANETUSER                    ConnectionPooling.exe    19:03:47

1 row selected.
```

Even though your application created a new connection, you can see that you haven't created a new database connection. The logon time remains constant—the same as it was for the first connection.

7. Return to the application window and press Enter to un-pause the application:

```
C:\My Projects\ProOraNet\Oracle\C#\Chapter07\NoConnectionPooling\bin\Debug>↩
ConnectionPooling.exe
Connection 1 created... Examine in SQL*Plus

Connection 1 disposed... Examine in SQL*Plus

Connection 2 created... Examine in SQL*Plus

Connection 2 disposed... Examine in SQL*Plus
```

8. Return to SQL*Plus and re-execute the query. Here are the results:

```
SQL> /

USERNAME                      PROGRAM                  LOGON_TI
----------------------------- ------------------------ --------
ORANETUSER                    ConnectionPooling.exe    19:03:47

1 row selected.
```

Once again, your query has returned the same result even though you disposed of your second connection.

9. Return to the application window and press Enter to un-pause the application.

The application terminates. If you executed your query at this point, it wouldn't return a row because the application terminated.

In the second application, you can clearly see the impact of the `pooling` attribute. By allowing connection pooling to take place, you were able to save resources because you didn't need to establish a second connection. You could reuse the existing connection, and thus bypass the overhead associated with starting up a new connection to the database. As an application developer, you have a great deal of control over the connection pooling environment. The complete set of attributes is available in the Oracle Data Provider for .NET documentation set. Connection pooling has a positive impact on web-based applications because they frequently follow a pattern of receiving the request, getting data from the database, and returning results. By maintaining a pool of readily available connections, a web-based application can reduce its service cycle time.

By storing the connection pooling attributes in the application's `web.config` (or `app.config`) file and reading them at application run-time, you can allow an application administrator to tune the connection pool without rewriting or recompiling the application. An example of this may look like the following:

```
<appSettings>
  <add key="Connection Pooling" value="false"/>
</appSettings>
```

If you used the `ConfigurationSettings.AppSettings.GetValues("Connection Pooling")` method to retrieve the value of the `"Connection Pooling"` key, the application would turn connection pooling on or off in a dynamic run-time fashion.

Chapter 7 Wrap-Up

You began this chapter by looking at the default database connection and how to implement the ability to connect to the default database in your code. We discussed how this ability can be a benefit when you don't know the TNS alias for a database in advance. After discussing a default database connection, we examined how to create a tnsnames-less connection. This type of connection affords you a great deal of flexibility, especially in a table-driven sort of application.

We then examined the difference between system-level privileged and non-privileged connections in a fair amount of detail. You created code to connect as a system-level privileged user and, using SQL*Plus, you learned how these types of connections work with the database. In addition to privileged and non-privileged connections, you tackled the sometimes-confusing topic of operating system authentication. You saw how to connect to the default database and a database via the TNS alias using operating system authentication. After looking at the methods to employ authentication by the operating system, you examined a few areas that are common in environments where password rules and account lockout are in effect. And finally, you finished the chapter by taking in a fairly lengthy set of examples that illustrate how to use connection pooling. All in all, we covered a lot of ground in this chapter.

Performing Common Tasks with Oracle Features

Although you have, of course, been focusing on using the Oracle database from within a .NET application throughout the book, in this chapter, you're going to explicitly examine how to perform some common tasks using the Oracle database and a .NET application. You're going to shift your focus to a more task-oriented viewpoint rather than a data provider class or .NET class viewpoint. You might be used to performing these tasks in other databases and may not know the appropriate manner in which to accomplish these tasks in Oracle, or the appropriate manner in which to perform these tasks may be somewhat different in Oracle. The following tasks are the ones you examine and implement in this chapter:

Using anonymous database access in a web application: It isn't feasible to require users to enter a username and password to access public pages. You'll implement a solution that allows users to view pages built from data in the database but doesn't require them to enter a username or password.

Creating paged results in a web application: You can save space on a web page and let the user determine how much data they wish to peruse by allowing them to page through a multirow result set.

Using the Sequence object: This object is analogous to an `identity` column in a SQL Server database; however, you implement the `sequence` object differently. You'll examine how to use the object correctly.

Creating a Top-N query: An application frequently requires the ability to display the top n rows of a result set. You'll create a sample that displays the top three salaries by department.

Using Anonymous Database Access in a Web Application

The time when web-based applications were new has passed. They are now accepted as a normal (or even expected) application type. In many cases, web-based applications are the de facto standard, replacing the so-called legacy, thick application. One of the design goals of the .NET Framework and Visual Studio .NET is to make developing a web-based application as simple and straightforward as developing a traditional application. This goal has been largely achieved.

One topic that frequently arises is how to allow anonymous access to the through a web application. Of course, the connection to the database does actually use a valid user. The term *anonymous* here means a connection that doesn't require the end user to enter any credentials into a web form and pass those credentials to the database in order to create a connection. Instead, operating system authentication (a topic I discussed in the previous chapter) is used to provide anonymous access to the end user.

Fortunately, during the .NET Framework installation (as well as Visual Studio .NET) the installer creates a special local operating system user, the ASPNET user. The ASPNET user caters to just this scenario.

The ASPNET User

The purpose of the ASPNET user is to allow anonymous access to the .NET application provided by the web server. As I just mentioned, the term anonymous indicates that the end user doesn't provide any authentication credentials to the application.

■**NOTE** The ASPNET user doesn't replace the user that IIS uses for anonymous access. These two users are separate and not related.

The ASPNET user is an authenticated user from the perspective of the operating system. The ASPNET user has a password that is created during the installation process. However, you don't know this password nor should you change it. As you can see in Figure 8-1, when you create the user during the installation of the .NET Framework or Visual Studio .NET, the user's password never expires and nor can the user change it.

Figure 8-1. *The ASPNET user properties*

Because the web server uses the ASPNET user to service requests for .NET web applications, this user needs to have appropriate permissions for resources they must access. Clearly your applications need the Oracle client software, and, therefore, the ASPNET user must have appropriate access to the operating system directories where the software is installed. As you just saw, the ASPNET user is considered an authenticated user. Therefore, you can grant appropriate permissions on the Oracle software directories to either the Authenticated Users group or to the ASPNET user directly. The ASPNET user needs to have the read and execute and read rights at a minimum on the Oracle software directories.

TIP In the interests of security, I don't recommend granting the ASPNET user full access to the Oracle software directories.

The ASPNET user needs to have these rights on the directory that serves as the ORACLE_HOME directory and all directories below that one. On my system, I've chosen to apply the permissions to the Authenticated Users group rather than directly to the ASPNET user. This allows any authenticated (i.e., safe) user to read and execute the Oracle software and doesn't allow guest users this ability. In addition, I've also granted the List Folder Contents privilege. You can see these permissions in Figure 8-2.

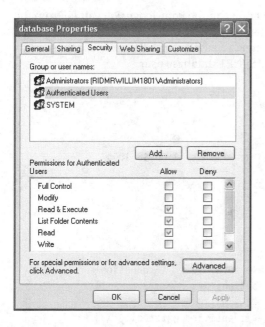

Figure 8-2. *Permissions for the Oracle software directories*

■TIP Setting these permissions appropriately goes a long way toward preventing errors that come from accessing the Oracle software at application run-time. The most common error you encounter when permissions aren't correctly set is "unable to load OraOps10.dll" (or OraOps9.dll). If you do encounter this error and permissions are correctly set, you should also ensure that the ORACLE_HOME\bin directory is in the system path.

Enabling Anonymous Access

Because the .NET environment uses the ASPNET user to provide access to resources, you can create an operating system–authenticated user in the database using the ASPNET user. In this manner, the ASPNET user can't create a session in the database and the end user of the application isn't required to provide any authorization credentials.

■CAUTION Of course, you should only provide this sort of access on data that is open to the public, because then any user running the application can see or modify the data if the application supports it.

To illustrate how to accomplish this task, you draw on the knowledge you gained from the previous chapter and create an operating system–authenticated account for the ASPNET user. You provide this account with only the ability to create a session with the database for security reasons. Listing 8-1 illustrates how to create the ASPNET database user.

Listing 8-1. *Creating the ASPNET Database User*

```
C:\>sqlplus oranetadmin@oranet

SQL*Plus: Release 10.1.0.2.0 - Production on Wed Jul 14 12:06:58 2004

Copyright (c) 1982, 2004, Oracle.  All rights reserved.

Enter password:

Connected to:
Oracle Database 10g Enterprise Edition Release 10.1.0.2.0 - Production
With the Partitioning, OLAP and Data Mining options

SQL> create user "OPS$RIDMRWILLIM1801\ASPNET" identified externally
  2  default tablespace users
  3  temporary tablespace temp;

User created.
```

```
SQL> grant create session to "OPS$RIDMRWILLIM1801\ASPNET";

Grant succeeded.

SQL> exit
Disconnected from Oracle Database 10g Enterprise Edition↵
 Release 10.1.0.2.0 - Production
With the Partitioning, OLAP and Data Mining options

C:\>
```

In this sample, you display the data in the LEAGUE_RESULTS table, which the oranetuser account owns. Because you're granting only the minimum privilege to create a session in the database to the ASPNET database user, you explicitly grant permission to the ASPNET user to select data from LEAGUE_RESULTS table. This process is illustrated in Listing 8-2.

Listing 8-2. *Granting Permission on the LEAGUE_RESULTS Table*

```
C:\>sqlplus oranetuser@oranet

SQL*Plus: Release 10.1.0.2.0 - Production on Wed Jul 14 12:09:30 2004

Copyright (c) 1982, 2004, Oracle.  All rights reserved.

Enter password:

Connected to:
Oracle Database 10g Enterprise Edition Release 10.1.0.2.0 - Production
With the Partitioning, OLAP and Data Mining options

SQL> grant select on league_results to "OPS$RIDMRWILLIM1801\ASPNET";

Grant succeeded.

SQL> exit
Disconnected from Oracle Database 10g Enterprise Edition↵
 Release 10.1.0.2.0 - Production
With the Partitioning, OLAP and Data Mining options

C:\>
```

Now the ASPNET user has the ability to create a session in the database and to select data from the LEAGUE_RESULTS table that the oranetuser user owns. The ASPNET user can't modify data or create objects in the database. Since you don't know what the password is for the ASPNET operating system user, you can't log in as that user and create an ad-hoc session with the database. Only the .NET environment should be able to use the ASPNET user.

In order to illustrate the use of anonymous access in a web application, create a simple ASP.NET web application as illustrated in Figure 8-3. Then use a simple web form with a data grid to display the results of a query against the LEAGUE_RESULTS table. The web form to accomplish this is presented in Figure 8-4.

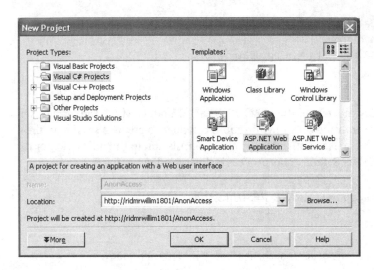

Figure 8-3. *Creating the anonymous access web application project*

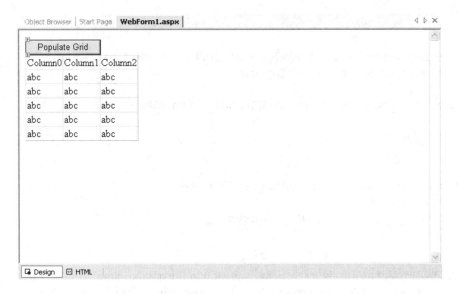

Figure 8-4. *The design-time view of the web form*

Another feature that you use from the previous chapter is the ability to connect to the default database. By using an operating system–authenticated user and the default database, your connection string is a simple forward slash (/) character. The code that achieves your desired results is completely contained in the click event for the button. This code, from the AnonAccess project, which you can access in this chapter's folder in the Downloads section of the Apress website (www.apress.com), is presented in Listing 8-3.

Listing 8-3. *The Code to Populate the Data Grid*

```
private void btnPopulate_Click(object sender, System.EventArgs e)
{
  // create connection using the aspnet o/s account
  // and the default database
  string connStr = "User Id=/";
  OracleConnection oraConn = new OracleConnection(connStr);
  oraConn.Open();

  // the query to retrieve the data from the
  // league_results table owned by oranetuser
  string sql = "select * from oranetuser.league_results order by position";

  // create a data adapter
  OracleDataAdapter da = new OracleDataAdapter(sql, oraConn);

  // create a data set object
  DataSet ds = new DataSet();

  // fill the data set
  da.Fill(ds);

  // bind and fill the data grid
  dgLeagueResults.DataSource = ds;
  dgLeagueResults.DataBind();
}
```

As you can see in Listing 8-3, this code isn't substantially different from the code that you've been developing throughout the book. You rely on the default properties of the data grid to format and present the data that you see in Figure 8-5.

■**NOTE** If you have problems running the samples in debug mode within Visual Studio, please consult the Microsoft Knowledge Base at http://support.microsoft.com for details on what you need to debug locally and remotely.

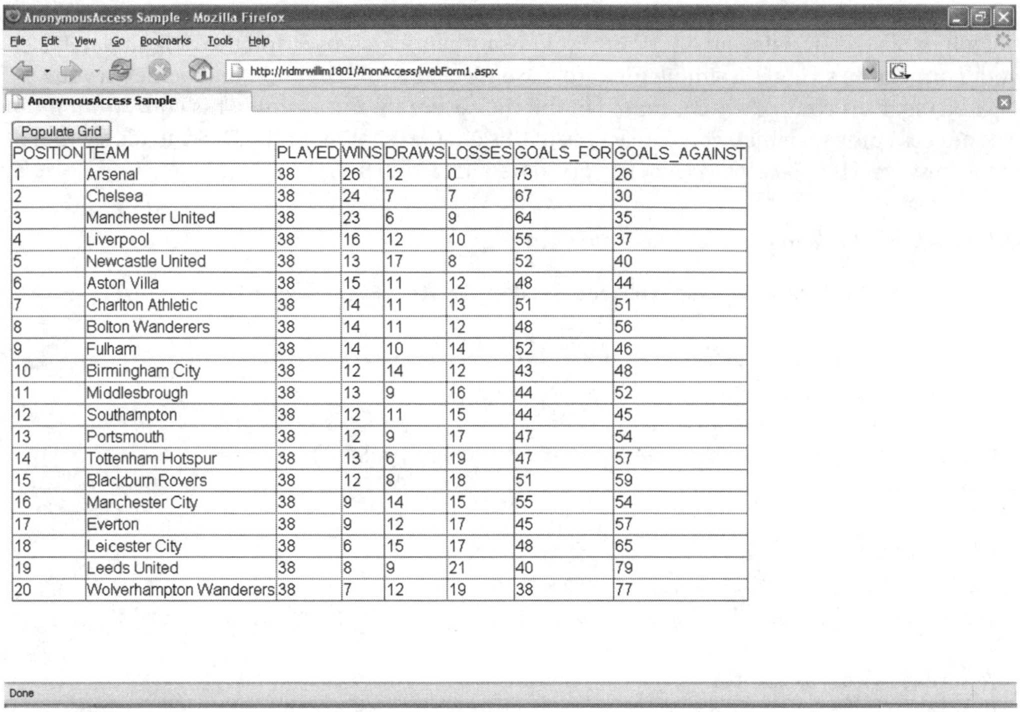

POSITION	TEAM	PLAYED	WINS	DRAWS	LOSSES	GOALS_FOR	GOALS_AGAINST
1	Arsenal	38	26	12	0	73	26
2	Chelsea	38	24	7	7	67	30
3	Manchester United	38	23	6	9	64	35
4	Liverpool	38	16	12	10	55	37
5	Newcastle United	38	13	17	8	52	40
6	Aston Villa	38	15	11	12	48	44
7	Charlton Athletic	38	14	11	13	51	51
8	Bolton Wanderers	38	14	11	12	48	56
9	Fulham	38	14	10	14	52	46
10	Birmingham City	38	12	14	12	43	48
11	Middlesbrough	38	13	9	16	44	52
12	Southampton	38	12	11	15	44	45
13	Portsmouth	38	12	9	17	47	54
14	Tottenham Hotspur	38	13	6	19	47	57
15	Blackburn Rovers	38	12	8	18	51	59
16	Manchester City	38	9	14	15	55	54
17	Everton	38	9	12	17	45	57
18	Leicester City	38	6	15	17	48	65
19	Leeds United	38	8	9	21	40	79
20	Wolverhampton Wanderers	38	7	12	19	38	77

Figure 8-5. *The run-time view of the web form*

Creating Paged Results in a Web Application

A common feature to implement in a web application is the ability to page through the results returned from the database. One way to accomplish this goal is to retrieve the entire result set from the database and implement paging using the cached data. For a small set of data, this is acceptable. However, for larger sets of data, you may be concerned with memory consumption. Therefore, I illustrate how to retrieve the data in pages from the database itself.

Rather than retrieve an entire table or set of data, you need to retrieve ranges of data from the database. To do so, you need to use a form similar to that in the previous example, and you'll use the LEAGUE_RESULTS table again as well. Begin by creating an ASP.NET web application as illustrated in Figure 8-6.

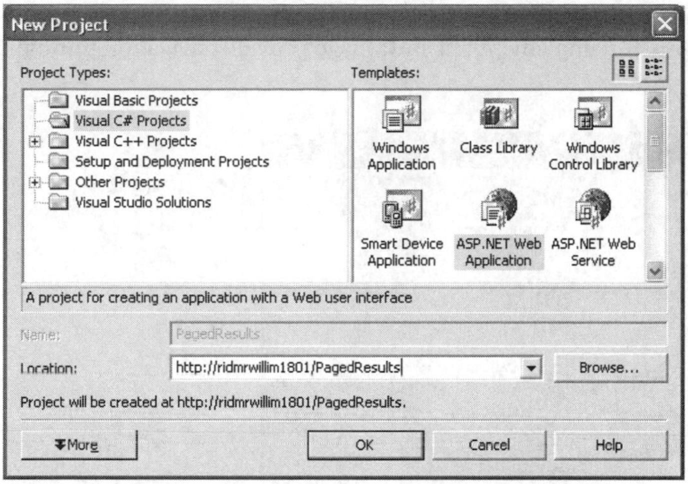

Figure 8-6. *Creating the paged results sample*

Once you've created the project, create a simple form similar to that in Figure 8-7. The < Previous and Next > controls are LinkButton controls. They are contained within an HTML table in order to facilitate layout and alignment at run-time. As with the previous sample, you accept the default values for the data grid except for the paging properties.

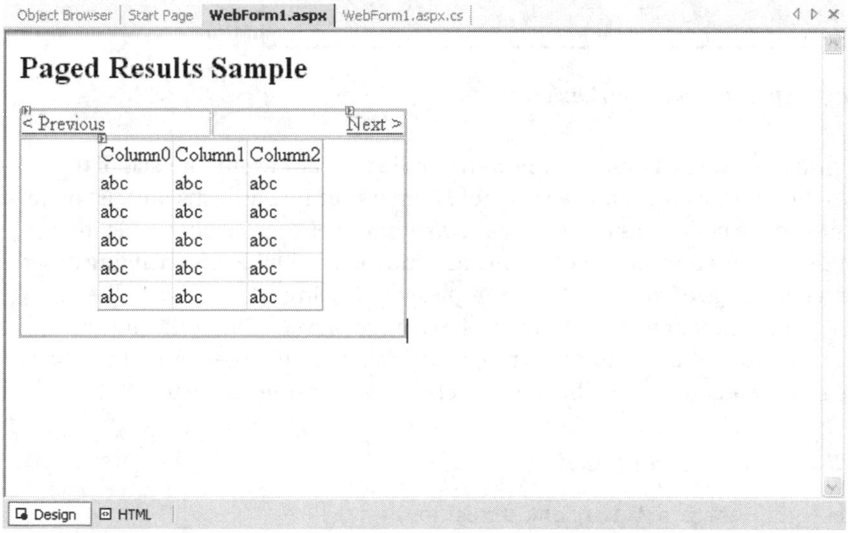

Figure 8-7. *The paged results web form*

In order to allow paging to function properly, set the paging properties of the data grid control as illustrated in Figure 8-8. You implement link buttons to provide navigation through the result set.

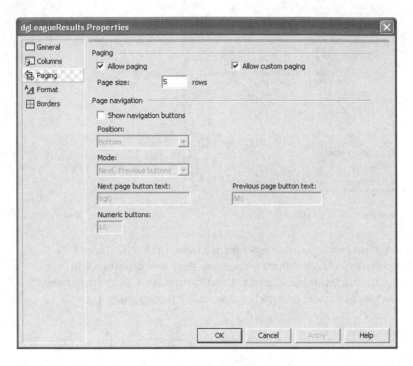

Figure 8-8. *The paging properties of the data grid*

In the code, you use a single helper routine and handle the click event for each of the buttons as well as the page load event. The `fill_grid` helper routine performs the vast majority of the work done in the code. This routine takes two parameters: an `int` that indicates the starting row for this fill operation, and another `int` that indicates whether you're filling based on the next or previous range of rows. For this example, you're using a 1 to indicate the next range of rows; any other number indicates the previous range of rows. The code for the `fill_grid` routine located in the PagedResults project (which you can access from this chapter's folder in the Downloads section of the Apress website) is presented in Listing 8-4.

Listing 8-4. *The fill_grid Helper Routine Code*

```
private void fill_grid(int start_row, int direction)
{
  // set the noninclusive value for the end row
  // in our range
  int end_row = start_row + dgLeagueResults.PageSize;

  // create connection using the aspnet o/s account
  // and the default database
```

```
string connStr = "User Id=/";
OracleConnection oraConn = new OracleConnection(connStr);
oraConn.Open();

// the query to retrieve the paged data from the
// league_results table owned by oranetuser
string sql = "select * ";
sql += "from (select rownum rec_num, a.* ";
sql += "from (select * from oranetuser.league_results order by position) a ";
sql += "where rownum < :end_row) ";
sql += "where rec_num >= :start_row";

// create a data adapter
OracleDataAdapter da = new OracleDataAdapter(sql, oraConn);

// Oracle parameter objects for the
// end and start row parameters
OracleParameter p_end_row = new OracleParameter();
p_end_row.OracleDbType = OracleDbType.Decimal;
p_end_row.Value = end_row;

OracleParameter p_start_row = new OracleParameter();
p_start_row.OracleDbType = OracleDbType.Decimal;
p_start_row.Value = start_row;

// add the parameters to the collection
da.SelectCommand.Parameters.Add(p_end_row);
da.SelectCommand.Parameters.Add(p_start_row);

// create a data set object
DataSet ds = new DataSet();

// fill the data set
da.Fill(ds);

// used to determine if the query returned
// any rows from the database
int t = ds.Tables[0].Rows.Count;

// direction 1 == next
if (direction == 1)
{
  if (t > 0)
  {
    // bind and fill the data grid
    dgLeagueResults.DataSource = ds;
    dgLeagueResults.DataBind();
```

```
      if (btnPrevious.Enabled == false)
      {
        btnPrevious.Enabled = true;
      }
    }
    else
    {
      btnNext.Enabled = false;
    }
  }
  else
  {
    if (t > 0)
    {
      // bind and fill the data grid
      dgLeagueResults.DataSource = ds;
      dgLeagueResults.DataBind();

      if (btnNext.Enabled == false)
      {
        btnNext.Enabled = true;
      }
    }
    else
    {
      btnPrevious.Enabled = false;
    }
  }
}
```

At first glance, this code may appear somewhat complicated. However, it's really just a continuation of code that you've already seen. You're using the same data provider objects, classes, and techniques that you've used in previous chapters. This illustrates the building block nature of .NET applications and how easy it is to develop them using the data provider classes and objects. Although you're performing new or different tasks, you're using the same basic foundation you developed in the early chapters.

Let's begin by calculating the end row in the range that you need to retrieve from the database. Do this by adding the value of the data grid pagesize property (which defines the number of rows per page) to the passed-in start row value, which results in the row number that represents the end of the current page of data. Next, create a connection to the database, define the SQL query to retrieve the data, set up parameter objects, and so forth. (We'll look at the query in more detail shortly.) Once you've created and filled the data set, perform a simple check to determine if any rows returned from the database.

Then perform the appropriate range fill (next or previous), bind the data set to the data grid, and perform a fill operation. The SQL statement performs all the work to create the range of rows. Once you've performed the fill operation, set the enabled property of each LinkButton control appropriately. Because the fill operation can retrieve the exact number of rows in a range so that we arrive at the beginning or end of the data in the table, you don't know that you've reached the boundary of the table until the subsequent range request. Figure 8-9 illustrates the initial appearance of the web form. Notice that the Previous button is disabled since you're at the beginning of the data when the form initially loads.

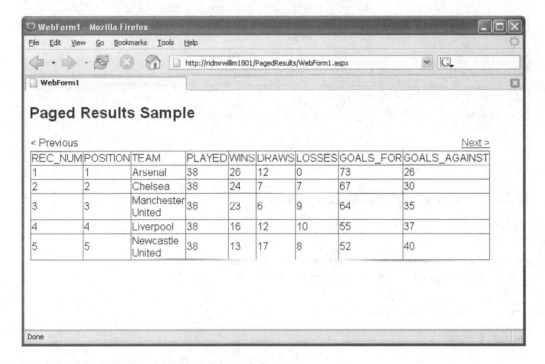

Figure 8-9. *The initial appearance of the web form*

By clicking the Next label, you navigate to the end of the data. Once there, if you click the Next button again, your web form should resemble the one in Figure 8-10. The Next button has been appropriately disabled, indicating that you've reached the end of the data.

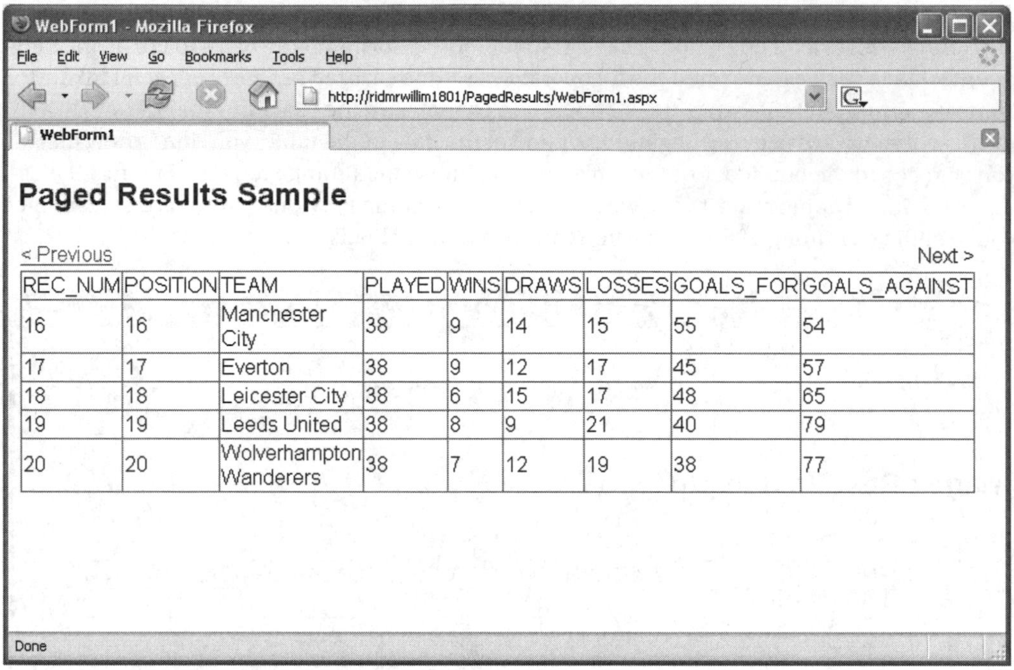

Figure 8-10. *The web form after the last range of data has been retrieved*

Let me explain the query that retrieves the range of rows from the database. I present the query text in Listing 8-5 to make it easier to see what it is doing.

Listing 8-5. *The Paged Results Query*

```
select   *
from     (
         select   rownum rec_num,
                  a.*
         from     (
                  select * from oranetuser.league_results order by position
                  ) a
         where    rownum < :end_row
         )
where    rec_num >= :start_row
```

In order to decipher what this query is doing, work from the inside to the outside. Three queries make up the overall query to retrieve the range of rows. The innermost query simply retrieves all rows from the LEAGUE_RESULTS table. The important characteristic of this query is that the rows are ordered by the position column. Without the order by clause, there is no guarantee that the rows will be returned in any particular order. You need this clause to ensure that data is returned in an ordered manner. You can't rely on an index or the order in which data is inserted into a table to determine the order in which data is returned in a query.

Once you've retrieved the rows from the table in an ordered manner, the middle query simply selects the rownum and the data from the innermost query where the rownum is less than the upper bound for the range of rows. The rownum is a pseudocolumn that Oracle creates on the fly. Oracle assigns this pseudocolumn to a row as the row is retrieved from the database. The rownum is aliased within the SQL statement to rec_num for presentation in the data grid.

The outermost query takes the results of the middle query and simply trims off the head rows (the rows in the result set that appear before your desired start row) to create the final set of rows that represent the range specified.

Now that you understand what the fill_grid routine does, you can examine the code that executes when the page is initially loaded. This code is presented in Listing 8-6.

Listing 8-6. *The Page_Load Method Code*

```
private void Page_Load(object sender, System.EventArgs e)
{
  if (!IsPostBack)
  {
    // fill grid starting with row 1
    // and in the "next" direction
    fill_grid(1,1);

    // since we just loaded the grid
    // there are no previous rows
    btnPrevious.Enabled = false;
  }
}
```

This code is straightforward and serves to initialize the data grid with the first range of rows from the table. Because this is the first range of rows, the Previous button is disabled.

The code that executes when the user clicks the Next button is presented in Listing 8-7.

Listing 8-7. *The btnNext_Click Method*

```
private void btnNext_Click(object sender, System.EventArgs e)
{
  // get the number of rows in the grid
  int numItems = dgLeagueResults.Items.Count;
  int rec_num = 0;

  if (numItems > 0)
  {
    // get the record number for the last row in the grid
    rec_num = Convert.ToInt32(dgLeagueResults.Items[numItems - 1].Cells[0].Text);
  }

  if (rec_num > 0)
  {
```

```
    // fill the grid with the next range
    fill_grid(rec_num + 1,1);
  }
}
```

This code retrieves the number of rows that are currently in the data grid. If at least 1 row is in the data grid, the value of the first column in the last row is retrieved. This is the rec_num column, which is just an alias for the rownum that was generated when the data was retrieved from the database. This value is then incremented by 1 and passed to the fill_grid routine so that the next range of rows can be retrieved and filled into the data grid.

In Listing 8-8, you can see the counterpart to the btnNext_Click code in the btnPrevious_Click code.

Listing 8-8. *The btnPrevious_Click Code*

```
private void btnPrevious_Click(object sender, System.EventArgs e)
{
  // get the number of rows in the grid
  int numItems = dgLeagueResults.Items.Count;
  int rec_num = 0;

  if (numItems > 0)
  {
    // get the record number for the last row in the grid
    rec_num = Convert.ToInt32(dgLeagueResults.Items[numItems - 1].Cells[0].Text);
  }

  if (rec_num > 0)
  {
    // fill the grid with the previous range
    // if the number of rows in the grid
    // is not a multiple of the page size,
    // adjust the starting point
    if ((rec_num % dgLeagueResults.PageSize) == 0)
    {
      fill_grid(rec_num - (dgLeagueResults.PageSize * 2) + 1,0);
    }
    else
    {
      rec_num = rec_num - (rec_num % dgLeagueResults.PageSize);
      fill_grid(rec_num - dgLeagueResults.PageSize + 1,0);
    }
  }
}
```

The code behind the Previous button begins in the same manner as the code behind the Next button. However, when you're moving backward, you'll encounter a concern that you didn't need to address when you moved forward through the row ranges: If the data that is in a range isn't an even multiple of the pagesize of the data grid, it's possible that the data grid will have fewer rows of data than the pagesize property.

To take this into account, first check to see if the number of rows in the grid is a multiple of the page size. If it is, simply set the new start row so that the end row for that range is one less than the head row for the current range. If, on the other hand, the number of rows in the grid doesn't align nicely with the page size, you must adjust the current rec_num down to the beginning of the range. If you don't, the stepping backward operation produces a jagged path that doesn't correctly align the rows with the page size of the data grid.

Using a Sequence Object to Generate a Primary Key Value

The Microsoft SQL Server database has a column property known as an identity property, which is used to create an integer value for a column. Other databases have similar mechanisms to perform this task, and these values are typically used to populate an artificial primary key for a table by generating a unique integer value. By *artificial primary key,* I mean that you aren't using a column that is part of the natural data. For instance, if a first name column and a last name column compose a table, creating a primary key from these two columns isn't feasible because a duplicate value is highly likely. By prepending a unique numeric column to the table, you can guarantee uniqueness.

Tables in Oracle, unlike in Microsoft SQL Server, don't have a property like the identity property. In order to implement the functionality represented by an identity column in SQL Server, in Oracle, you use a sequence.

The main difference between an identity and a sequence is that a sequence is a separate, independent object in the database, whereas the identity is associated with a particular table and column. The sequence stands alone, and there is no formal relationship between a sequence and any other database object.

We, as .NET developers, don't normally create a sequence (or other objects, for that matter) in a *production* database—that is a task that the production database administrator normally undertakes. Nonetheless, it's important to know about the properties of a sequence, how to create them (in a developmental database, for example), and how to use them from your .NET code. In many cases, the default properties of a sequence are sufficient or appropriate. When you're creating a sequence, the only required property you must specify is the name of the sequence. In addition to the name, you may specify the following seven properties:

The INCREMENT BY property: Determines the amount by which a sequence advances.

The START WITH property: Determines the initial value of the sequence.

The MAXVALUE/NOMAXVALUE property: Determines the maximum value (if any) that the sequence may have.

The MINVALUE/NOMINVALUE property: Determines the minimum value (if any) that the sequence may have.

The CYCLE/NOCYCLE property: Determines if values can be reused. That is, this property determines if the sequence wraps to the beginning if it reaches a maximum or minimum value.

The CACHE/NOCACHE property: Determines how many values from the sequence are held in memory to allow the client (including the database itself) faster access.

The ORDER/NOORDER property: Determines if values are guaranteed to be generated in order for a database that is part of a Grid or Real Application Clusters environment.

The INCREMENT BY Property

The INCREMENT BY property may be any integer value (other than 0) that is less than or equal to 28 digits in length. This property specifies the stepping value you use to generate successive values in the sequence. By specifying a negative integer for this property, you can create a descending (rather than ascending) sequence. The default value for this property is 1, which would cause the sequence to generate values such as 1, 2, 3, 4, and so on.

The START WITH Property

The START WITH property may be any integer value (including 0) that is less than or equal to 28 digits in length. You can use this property to override the starting point of a sequence. In an ascending sequence, the default value for this property is the MINVALUE of the sequence. In a descending sequence, the default value is the MAXVALUE of the sequence. For example, if you're creating a new sequence that provides values for a table that already has some data in it, you might use this property to specify a starting point that is greater than any of the existing data in the table.

The MAXVALUE/NOMAXVALUE Property

You use the MAXVALUE/NOMAXVALUE property to specify the maximum value the sequence may create. By specifying NOMAXVALUE (which is the default), the sequence may generate a value up to 10^{27} for an ascending sequence or –1 for a descending sequence. You may also specify a specific value that is less than or equal to 28 digits in length. If you do, it must be equal to or greater than the START WITH property and greater than the MINVALUE property.

The MINVALUE/NOMINVALUE Property

The MINVALUE/NOMINVALUE property works in the same fashion as the MAXVALUE/NOMAXVALUE property. NOMINVALUE is the default and takes a value of 1 for an ascending sequence and -10^{26} for a descending sequence. If you specify a value for this property, it must be less than or equal to 28 digits in length. It must also be less than or equal to the START WITH value and less than the MAXVALUE property.

The CYCLE/NOCYCLE Property

Once a sequence reaches the MAXVALUE for an ascending sequence or the MINVALUE for a descending sequence, it may either stop generating values or wrap around to the beginning of the sequence. The default is NOCYCLE, which causes the sequence to stop. The value that it's wrapped to is either the MINVALUE for an ascending sequence or the MAXVALUE for a descending sequence.

The CACHE/NOCACHE Property

You use the CACHE/NOCACHE property to specify how many values from the sequence should be stored in memory, thus allowing faster access. If you specify CACHE, it must be an integer value with less than or equal to 28 digits in length and it can have a minimum value of 2. If you specify NOCACHE, then no values are cached in memory. The default is to cache 20 values from the sequence.

■**NOTE** Sometimes a developer may implement a practice to set the CACHE property to 0 in the hopes that a gap-free sequence will be guaranteed. This simply isn't possible, so avoid this practice.

The ORDER/NOORDER Property

The ORDER/NOORDER property is only meaningful for databases that are running in a Grid or Real Application Clusters configuration. This property determines whether values are generated in the order they are requested. A sequence always generates unique values; therefore, this property doesn't allow duplicate values to be generated. When a database is running in a non-RAC configuration, values are always generated in order. NOORDER is the default value.

Creating Sequences

As I mentioned earlier, a developer doesn't typically create a sequence in a production database. However, creating a sequence in a development or test database is an activity that you may, on occasion, perform. In order to illustrate the properties of the sequence, you'll create a few sequence objects. In Listing 8-9, you're creating a sequence that uses all default values. This sequence has the following characteristics:

- Is ascending

- Increments by 1

- Starts with 1

- Has no maximum value

- Has a minimum value of 1

- Does not cycle values

- Caches 20 values in memory

- Is NORDER

Listing 8-9. *Creating a sequence with Default Values*

```
C:\>sqlplus oranetuser/demo@oranet

SQL*Plus: Release 10.1.0.2.0 - Production on Wed Jun 30 13:01:58 2004

Copyright (c) 1982, 2004, Oracle.  All rights reserved.


Connected to:
Oracle Database 10g Enterprise Edition Release 10.1.0.2.0 - Production
With the Partitioning, OLAP and Data Mining options

SQL> create sequence seq_test;

Sequence created.
```

You can confirm the properties by querying the user_sequences view. The structure of the view, as well as the results of querying the data for the sequence you just created, are in Listing 8-10.

Listing 8-10. *Viewing the Information About Our Test sequence*

```
SQL> desc user_sequences
 Name                                          Null?    Type
 --------------------------------------------- -------- ------------
 SEQUENCE_NAME                                 NOT NULL VARCHAR2(30)
 MIN_VALUE                                              NUMBER
 MAX_VALUE                                              NUMBER
 INCREMENT_BY                                  NOT NULL NUMBER
 CYCLE_FLAG                                             VARCHAR2(1)
 ORDER_FLAG                                             VARCHAR2(1)
 CACHE_SIZE                                    NOT NULL NUMBER
 LAST_NUMBER                                   NOT NULL NUMBER

SQL> select * from user_sequences where sequence_name='SEQ_TEST';

SEQUENCE_NAME    MIN_VALUE  MAX_VALUE INCREMENT_BY C O CACHE_SIZE LAST_NUMBER
---------------- ---------- ---------- ------------ - - ---------- -----------
SEQ_TEST                 1 1.0000E+27            1 N N         20           1

1 row selected.
```

Here you can see that the sequence has a MINVALUE of 1, has a MAXVALUE of 10^{27}, has an INCREMENT BY of 1, is NOCYCLE, is NOORDER, has a CACHE of 20, and has a LAST_NUMBER of 1. The LAST_NUMBER column indicates the last value in the sequence that has been written to disk. Because you haven't used any values from your sequence, the LAST_NUMBER column is 1.

In Listing 8-11, you're creating a sequence and explicitly specifying each property. This sequence counts down from 10,000 to 0 and then stops. It decrements by 1 for each value it generates. You also cache 10 values in memory.

Listing 8-11. *Creating a sequence with Properties Specified*

```
SQL> drop sequence seq_test;

Sequence dropped.

SQL> create sequence seq_test
  2  increment by -1
  3  start with 10000
  4  maxvalue 10000
  5  minvalue 0
  6  nocycle
  7  cache 10
  8  noorder;

Sequence created.

SQL> select * from user_sequences where sequence_name='SEQ_TEST';
```

SEQUENCE_NAME	MIN_VALUE	MAX_VALUE	INCREMENT_BY	C	O	CACHE_SIZE	LAST_NUMBER
SEQ_TEST	0	10000	-1	N	N	10	10000

```
1 row selected.
```

Once you've created a sequence, you must have some mechanism for generating and accessing values. Because a sequence is an independent database object that isn't tied to a table, the following two pseudocolumns are available for use with a sequence object:

The CURRVAL pseudocolumn: Returns the current value generated by the sequence.

The NEXTVAL pseudocolumn: Generates and retrieves the next value in the sequence.

It is important to note that the CURRVAL pseudocolumn returns the current value that *has been generated* by the sequence. If no value has been generated, such as is the case immediately after the sequence is created, an error is returned.

You can see how these pseudocolumns work in Listing 8-12. Initially the CURRVAL pseudocolumn causes an error because the sequence hasn't generated a value. Once the sequence does generate a value, you can query the current value from the database. You can also see how the sequence is decrementing from 10,000 by 1 when the value is generated.

Listing 8-12. *Using the sequence Pseudocolumns*

```
SQL> select seq_test.currval from dual;
select seq_test.currval from dual
       *
ERROR at line 1:
ORA-08002: sequence SEQ_TEST.CURRVAL is not yet defined in this session


SQL> select seq_test.nextval from dual;

   NEXTVAL
----------
     10000

1 row selected.

SQL> select seq_test.currval from dual;

   CURRVAL
----------
     10000

1 row selected.

SQL> select seq_test.nextval from dual;

   NEXTVAL
----------
      9999

1 row selected.
```

Using Sequences

One question that occasionally arises is, "Why use a sequence at all?" It's possible to imple-ment the functionality provided by a sequence in a do-it-yourself manner. However, in addition to not reinventing the wheel, using the database and the sequence object helps you avoid disk I/O and transaction locking. Reducing disk I/O and locking in an application is an easy way to allow the application to perform better and be more scalable. In a typical do-it-yourself scenario, you place a lock on a table, generate or retrieve a value, and update the table to reflect the new value. In a single user system, this may be acceptable. In a multiuser system, this approach causes other users (and possibly even you) to serialize while you are locking the table and creating a value. The sequence object isn't subject to the serialization and transaction locking that this approach requires. By reducing the amount of serialization that occurs in an application or system, you make that application or system more scalable.

Now that you've seen how to create a sequence, it's time to see how to use the sequence in code. Using a sequence is straightforward. You simply use the NEXTVAL pseudocolumn to insert a value into a primary key field. Before I demonstrate this, I address a few points that are often confusing about the sequence object.

First, it's simply not possible to guarantee a gap-free sequence. One of the most popular things to attempt to do when you're using a sequence is to try and make the sequence gap free. This is usually attempted by specifying NOCACHE for the sequence. It isn't possible because you can lose values in many ways when you are using a sequence. If you generate a value as part of a transaction and that transaction rolls back, then that value is no longer available; it doesn't get returned to the sequence object or cache. If you shut a database down, then the values cached in memory are flushed and not used.

This need for a gap-free sequence is almost always said to be a business requirement. When I'm presented with such a request, I usually respond with a question or two. For instance, what happens if I have to void a check that has been written? The number associated with that check is lost in the sense that it can't be reused. Also, do I create a new account to ensure that all the check numbers are gap free? Of course not. I simply indicate that the number isn't valid and continue. The same should hold for a sequence. If you lose a value from a sequence, you should simply use the next value and continue.

Second, you can't make the value of a sequence the default value for a column in a table; this is an illegal database operation. As we have discussed, just because you can do this sort of thing in other databases doesn't mean that it's correct to do it in Oracle (even if you can do it). The sequence isn't an object you can tie to another object in this manner.

It is possible to use a sequence in a trigger to populate a table column. You'll see this illustrated in the sample code. In the sample, you'll create a trigger on a table that provides a value from the sequence if the client code doesn't provide one. By using a trigger, you're forcing the primary key to be correctly populated irrespective of the client. This means that if you perform an insert using SQL*Plus instead of the .NET client you'll develop, the primary key column is still correctly populated. Your client code uses the same sequence as the trigger to ensure that the values are unique.

TIP When you're using a sequence to populate a column, *always* use the sequence to generate a value. Don't manually insert a value because it's likely to cause a collision between the value you insert manually and one generated by the sequence. The use of a trigger, as I'll illustrate, guarantees that the column is populated by the sequence.

The Sequence Sample Code

To learn how to use a sequence, you'll create a sequence, a table, and a trigger on the table. To do so, you insert a few rows into the table. For half of the rows, you rely on the trigger to provide a value from the sequence. For the other half, you provide the SQL to use the NEXTVAL pseudocolumn in your code. Therefore, the trigger on the table checks if a value was supplied for the primary key column (env_id, in this case) and if none was, it gets the NEXTVAL from your sequence.

Listing 8-13 contains the statements you use to create the sequence, the table, and the trigger.

Listing 8-13. *Creating the Database Objects for the Sequence Sample*

```
C:\>sqlplus oranetuser/demo@oranet

SQL*Plus: Release 10.1.0.2.0 - Production on Wed Jun 30 14:20:00 2004

Copyright (c) 1982, 2004, Oracle.  All rights reserved.


Connected to:
Oracle Database 10g Enterprise Edition Release 10.1.0.2.0 - Production
With the Partitioning, OLAP and Data Mining options

SQL> create sequence env_seq;

Sequence created.

SQL> create table environment
  2  (
  3    env_id number primary key,
  4    env_desc varchar2(32)
  5  );

Table created.

SQL> create trigger env_trig
  2  before insert on environment
  3  for each row
  4  begin
  5    if (:new.env_id is null) then
  6      select env_seq.nextval into :new.env_id from dual;
  7    end if;
  8  end;
  9  /

Trigger created.
```

The Main Method Code

The code for the Main method from the Sequence sample project (in this chapter's folder in the Downloads section of the Apress website) in Listing 8-14 follows the template you've been using throughout the book.

Listing 8-14. *The Main Method Code*

```
static void Main(string[] args)
{
  // used for accessing the helper methods
  Class1 theClass = new Class1();

  // create our standard connection
  string connStr = "User Id=oranetuser; Password=demo; Data Source=oranet";
  OracleConnection oraConn = new OracleConnection(connStr);

  oraConn.Open();

  theClass.insert_trigger(oraConn);

  theClass.insert_notrigger(oraConn);
}
```

The insert_trigger Code

The code for the insert_trigger method, in Listing 8-15, creates an SQL statement that does *not* provide a value for the primary key column. The table trigger retrieves the value from env_seq and assigns that value to the column in the table. In this code, you're inserting four rows into the table.

Listing 8-15. *The insert_trigger Code*

```
private void insert_trigger(OracleConnection con)
{
  // this method will insert rows using the trigger
  // to get the values from the sequence

  // the sql statement to insert a row
  string sqlText = "insert into environment (env_desc) ";
  sqlText += "values (:p1)";

  // the command object associated with the sql statement
  OracleCommand cmd = new OracleCommand(sqlText, con);

  // the parameter object
  OracleParameter p1 = new OracleParameter();
  p1.Size = 32;
  p1.Value = "PROD";

  // add the parameter to the collection
  cmd.Parameters.Add(p1);
```

```
  // execute the command
  cmd.ExecuteNonQuery();

  // insert a row for stage
  p1.Value = "STAGE";
  cmd.ExecuteNonQuery();

  // insert a row for train
  p1.Value = "TRAIN";
  cmd.ExecuteNonQuery();

  // insert a row for test
  p1.Value = "TEST";
  cmd.ExecuteNonQuery();
}
```

The insert_notrigger Code

Like the code for the insert_trigger method, the code for the insert_notrigger method in
Listing 8-16 inserts four rows into the table. The code in this method explicitly references the
NEXTVAL pseudocolumn in the SQL statement associated with the command object. Because
you're using the same sequence from both methods, the values are consecutive.

Listing 8-16. *The insert_notrigger Code*

```
private void insert_notrigger(OracleConnection con)
{
  // this method will insert rows using sql
  // to get the values from the sequence

  // the sql statement to insert a row
  // notice how nextval is used
  string sqlText = "insert into environment (env_id, env_desc) ";
  sqlText += "values (env_seq.nextval, :p1)";

  // the command object associated with the sql statement
  OracleCommand cmd = new OracleCommand(sqlText, con);

  // the parameter object
  OracleParameter p1 = new OracleParameter();
  p1.Size = 32;
  p1.Value = "DEV";

  // add the parameter to the collection
  cmd.Parameters.Add(p1);

  // execute the command
  cmd.ExecuteNonQuery();
```

```
    // insert a row for sandbox
    p1.Value = "SAND";
    cmd.ExecuteNonQuery();

    // insert a row for evaluation
    p1.Value = "EVAL";
    cmd.ExecuteNonQuery();

    // insert a row for disaster recovery
    p1.Value = "DR";
    cmd.ExecuteNonQuery();
}
```

After running the sample code, you can query the table to verify that the values for the primary key column (env_id) were populated from the sequence as you expect. Listing 8-17 illustrates this process.

Listing 8-17. *Querying the Environment Table After Running the Sample*

```
SQL> select * from environment order by env_id;

    ENV_ID ENV_DESC
---------- --------------------------------
         1 PROD
         2 STAGE
         3 TRAIN
         4 TEST
         5 DEV
         6 SAND
         7 EVAL
         8 DR

8 rows selected.
```

Creating a Top-N Query

Frequently, you're required to report the *Top-N* values of a set of data. Often, this takes the form of a request to display the top salaries, sales amounts, and so on, across another dimension. For example, your report may need to show the top three employee salaries across each department. One of the easiest and most efficient ways to do this is to use the Analytic Functions provided by the database beginning with version 8.1.7.

■**NOTE** The Oracle Analytic Functions are a very large topic and therefore I won't be able to give them a full treatment in this text. I highly recommend that you consult the Oracle-supplied documentation, the "Database SQL Reference Guide" in particular, for details about these. In addition, another great resource is Tom Kyte's *Expert One-On-One Oracle* (Apress, 2003).

In order to illustrate creating a Top-N query, I'll use of the HR schema. The HR schema is installed as part of the database sample schemas and is shipped with version 9i and 10g of the database. The account is locked by default. When I installed the Oracle software, I elected to unlock this account and set the password. (See the installation walk-through in the Appendix for details about installing the sample schemas as part of the database installation procedure.) One of the tables in the HR schema is the EMPLOYEES table. This table is ideal for this sample; its structure is presented in Listing 8-18.

Listing 8-18. *The EMPLOYEES Table Structure*

```
C:\>sqlplus hr@oranet

SQL*Plus: Release 10.1.0.2.0 - Production on Mon Jul 19 14:15:32 2004

Copyright (c) 1982, 2004, Oracle.  All rights reserved.

Enter password:

Connected to:
Oracle Database 10g Enterprise Edition Release 10.1.0.2.0 - Production
With the Partitioning, OLAP and Data Mining options

SQL> desc employees
 Name                                      Null?    Type
 ----------------------------------------- -------- -------------------------
 EMPLOYEE_ID                               NOT NULL NUMBER(6)
 FIRST_NAME                                         VARCHAR2(20)
 LAST_NAME                                 NOT NULL VARCHAR2(25)
 EMAIL                                     NOT NULL VARCHAR2(25)
 PHONE_NUMBER                                       VARCHAR2(20)
 HIRE_DATE                                 NOT NULL DATE
 JOB_ID                                    NOT NULL VARCHAR2(10)
 SALARY                                             NUMBER(8,2)
 COMMISSION_PCT                                     NUMBER(2,2)
 MANAGER_ID                                         NUMBER(6)
 DEPARTMENT_ID                                      NUMBER(4)

SQL> exit
Disconnected from Oracle Database 10g Enterprise Edition↵
 Release 10.1.0.2.0 - Production
With the Partitioning, OLAP and Data Mining options

C:\>
```

For this sample, you display the top three employee salaries by department to the console window. You also display the department ID, the rank (1, 2, or 3), the employee name, and, finally, the employee salary. You use the dense_rank analytic function to accomplish this task. The reason for this is that the dense_rank function doesn't skip values. If two (or more) employees in a department have the same salary, the dense_rank function assigns contiguous ranking numbers. This is in contrast to the rank function. Although the rank function performs a similar task, it skips duplicate numbers resulting in noncontiguous ranking numbers. However, to accurately retrieve the Top-N values, you must have contiguous ranking numbers.

You can see how this works by using the EMPLOYEES table and performing both a dense_rank and a rank. To illustrate the difference between the functions, limit the query to department_id 60. As you'll see, department_id 60 has salaries that tie (i.e., are duplicates) making it easy to see the different results. Listing 8-19 contains the ranking query and the results of the query.

Listing 8-19. *The Difference in Results with dense_rank and rank Functions*

```
C:\>sqlplus hr/demo@oranet

SQL*Plus: Release 10.1.0.2.0 - Production on Fri Sep 3 11:52:12 2004

Copyright (c) 1982, 2004, Oracle.  All rights reserved.


Connected to:
Oracle Database 10g Enterprise Edition Release 10.1.0.2.0 - Production
With the Partitioning, Oracle Label Security, OLAP and Data Mining options

SQL> col employee format a16
SQL> select *
  2  from  (select department_id,
  3               dense_rank() over (partition by department_id
  4                                       order by salary desc) dense_rank,
  5               rank() over (partition by department_id
  6                                 order by salary desc) rank,
  7               first_name || ' ' || last_name EMPLOYEE,
  8               salary
  9         from   employees
 10         where  department_id = 60);

DEPARTMENT_ID DENSE_RANK       RANK EMPLOYEE             SALARY
------------- ----------  ---------- ---------------- ----------
           60          1           1 Alexander Hunold    9000
           60          2           2 Bruce Ernst         6000
           60          3           3 David Austin        4800
           60          3           3 Valli Pataballa     4800
           60          4           5 Diana Lorentz       4200

5 rows selected.

SQL> exit
Disconnected from Oracle Database 10g Enterprise Edition⍬
```

```
Release 10.1.0.2.0 - Production
With the Partitioning, Oracle Label Security, OLAP and Data Mining options

C:\>
```

In Listing 8-19, notice how for employee Diana Lorentz the dense_rank function assigned a rank value of 4 whereas the rank function assigned a value of 5. Since your example only looks at the top three salaries, this goes unnoticed. However, if your example looks at the top four salaries, this is an issue.

Listing 8-20 from the TopNQuery project (in this chapter's folder in the Downloads section of the Apress website) contains the single Main method you use to create and display the results of the Top-N query.

Listing 8-20. *The Top-N Query Main Method*

```
static void Main(string[] args)
{
  // create a connection to the HR schema
  string connStr = "User Id=hr; Password=demo; Data Source=oranet";
  OracleConnection oraConn = new OracleConnection(connStr);

  // the sql statement to get the top 3 salaries
  string sql = "select * ";
         sql += "from  (select department_id, ";
         sql += "                    dense_rank() over (partition by department_id ";
         sql += "                                       order by salary desc) rank, ";
         sql += "                    first_name || ' ' || last_name EMPLOYEE, ";
         sql += "                    salary ";
         sql += "         from    employees) ";
         sql += "where rank <= 3";

  // open the database connection
  oraConn.Open();

  // create a command object
  OracleCommand cmd = new OracleCommand(sql, oraConn);

  // create a data reader from the command object
  OracleDataReader dataReader = cmd.ExecuteReader();

  // the number of fields in the result set
  int fieldCount = dataReader.FieldCount;

  // output a header line
  Console.WriteLine("Department,Rank,Employee,Salary");

  // for each row in the result set
  // this is code that we used in chapter 2
  while (dataReader.Read())
```

```
{
  for (int i = 0; i < fieldCount; i++)
  {
    if (!dataReader.IsDBNull(i))
    {
      Console.Write(dataReader[i].ToString());
    }
    else
    {
      // null value
      Console.Write("(null)");
    }

    if (i < fieldCount - 1)
    {
      Console.Write(",");
    }
  }

  Console.WriteLine();
}

// explicitly close and dispose of objects
dataReader.Close();
dataReader.Dispose();
cmd.Dispose();
oraConn.Close();
oraConn.Dispose();
}
```

The code that is presented in Listing 8-20 is pretty much boilerplate code by now. The code to display the results to the console window is borrowed from the code you created in Chapter 2. The query that produces the result set is presented in Listing 8-21.

Listing 8-21. *The Top-N Query SQL Statement*

```
select *
from   (select department_id,
               dense_rank() over (partition by department_id
                                      order by salary desc) rank,
               first_name || ' ' || last_name EMPLOYEE,
               salary
        from   employees)
where rank <= 3
```

Like the SQL statement you use to retrieve data in row ranges, this SQL statement is really a composite of multiple statements. Although the overall query looks like two distinct queries, Oracle processes the statement as a single query.

What makes this statement special is the inclusion of the dense_rank analytic function discussed earlier. This function produces the consecutive ranking number for each row in the result set. In your case, you indicated that you want a ranking number for each department_id based on the salary sorted in descending order. You then alias the result of this function as rank. By limiting the rank to less than or equal to 3 in the outer query, you only retrieve the top three rows for the inner query.

■**TIP** For complete details of the Analytic Functions, see the supplied Oracle documentation.

You can see the results of running the sample in Listing 8-22. For some departments (such as department 10), there are less than three rows of data. There is one employee (Kimberly Grant) who isn't assigned to a department. You don't have to code anything special to handle these cases.

Listing 8-22. *The Top-N Query Sample Output*

```
C:\My Projects\ProOraNet\Oracle\C#\Chapter08\TopNQuery\bin\Debug>TopNQuery.exe
10,1,Jennifer Whalen,4400
20,1,Michael Hartstein,13000
20,2,Pat Fay,6000
30,1,Den Raphaely,11000
30,2,Alexander Khoo,3100
30,3,Shelli Baida,2900
40,1,Susan Mavris,6500
50,1,Adam Fripp,8200
50,2,Matthew Weiss,8000
50,3,Payam Kaufling,7900
60,1,Alexander Hunold,9000
60,2,Bruce Ernst,6000
60,3,David Austin,4800
60,3,Valli Pataballa,4800
70,1,Hermann Baer,10000
80,1,John Russell,14000
80,2,Karen Partners,13500
80,3,Alberto Errazuriz,12000
90,1,Steven King,24000
90,2,Neena Kochhar,17000
90,2,Lex De Haan,17000
100,1,Nancy Greenberg,12000
100,2,Daniel Faviet,9000
100,3,John Chen,8200
110,1,Shelley Higgins,12000
110,2,William Gietz,8300
(null),1,Kimberely Grant,7000

C:\My Projects\ProOraNet\Oracle\C#\Chapter08\TopNQuery\bin\Debug>
```

Chapter 8 Wrap-Up

It used to be that web applications were on the leading edge of application development; now, a web application is just another application. By its very nature, the Web operates in a disconnected manner. A browser sends a request, the server processes the request and returns data to the browser, and then the communication segment finishes. This model has implications for data access from a web forms page. Web forms pages must operate under a disconnected model. Fortunately, the .NET Framework takes this into account.

If you follow the good practices you've been developing, working with data in a web forms page isn't substantially different from working with data in a console application or a Windows Forms application. The primary consideration that you should take into account is the disconnected nature of the Web. By making sure that a database transaction doesn't span calls to the web server, you can handle this easily.

In this chapter, you examined the ASPNET user account and the permissions that account needs to use the Oracle software. In addition, you worked through a sample that illustrated how to use the ASPNET operating system account to permit anonymous access to the database via a web forms application. You also created a sample that illustrated one of the most commonly requested features in a web forms application that displays data—the ability to page through results. This sample highlighted a technique for retrieving the data in row ranges from the database rather than caching the data. Because no connection is maintained between the browser and the web server, this sample fits in nicely with the "request, process, retrieve, and close" model that is illustrative of the way in which the Web works.

Often, it isn't immediately obvious how the sequence object relates to performing a similar task in SQL Server. You use this object to achieve the functionality that an identity column in SQL Server provides, namely populating a primary key column with integer values. Here, you explored the various attributes of the sequence object and built a sample that illustrated the proper method of using the object from within a database trigger or external code.

I concluded the chapter by examining another commonly performed task in Oracle that isn't necessarily intuitive—creating a Top-N query. By using a feature of the Oracle database known as the Analytic Functions, you can easily create a query that returns the top n elements of a result set based on your criteria. The Analytic Functions are a powerful feature of the Oracle database, and I encourage you to continue to explore them as you develop your .NET programs.

SQL Tracing

In this chapter, you'll look at producing diagnostic or tracing data from the data provider, from the database, and from the .NET code you create. You can do this because the data provider and the database are both *instrumented*. I use the term instrumented here to mean code that has the ability to produce diagnostic information. An important distinction to keep in mind when you're discussing instrumented code and tracing is that it isn't error handling. It's information produced to indicate what actions are taking place, and frequently, it includes timing information as well. Of course, you may be able to use this information to troubleshoot why an error is happening, but code that creates trace information typically doesn't actually handle the error itself.

With the advent of modern development environments and tools, it's possible to step through code to see exactly what's happening. This is fine when you're working on the development phase of an application; however, what happens when the application goes into production or is at a remote location? If the end user of the application has the ability to enable trace output to be generated from within the application, you can determine exactly what is happening in a nonintrusive, hands-off manner.

Of course the act of generating a trace file isn't limited to a production situation only. Generating a trace file during the development phase of an application can be a valuable way to head off future problems. It's much easier to correct a potential issue you catch during development than it is once the application goes into production. A trace file is also a great learning experience because you can see directly how the data provider or the database processes code you write in an application.

Enabling Data Provider Tracing

The Oracle Data Provider for .NET has the capability to emit trace information into a file located in an operating system folder. This trace information details the activities that the data provider is undertaking to accomplish each task as it executes. You use three registry settings in conjunction with the data provider tracing mechanism. These registry settings are located under the `HKEY_LOCAL_MACHINE\SOFTWARE\ORACLE\ODP.NET` registry hive for the 9i data provider and under the `HKEY_LOCAL_MACHINE\SOFTWARE\ORACLE\KEY_%ORACLE_HOME%\ODP.NET` registry hive for the 10g provider. Here are the three settings:

`TraceFileName:` Determines the name of the trace file that is generated.

`TraceOption:` Determines if all tracing information is placed in a single file or if separate files are generated for each thread.

`TraceLevel:` Determines the amount or level of detail that is included in the trace file.

If these registry settings are missing from your machine, you can simply add them using the Registry Editor. Of course, you should be careful when you're editing the registry directly. Figure 9-1 illustrates what your registry might look like after you create the keys and assign default values.

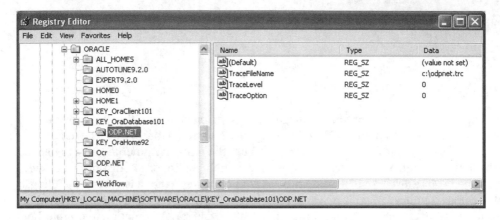

Figure 9-1. *The data provider registry entries for tracing*

The TraceFileName Registry Key

You use the TraceFileName registry key to indicate to the data provider the name of the folder and the file it should use to hold the trace output. If this file doesn't exist, the data provider creates it. However, the folder must exist, because the data provider won't create it.

The TraceOption Registry Key

The TraceOption registry key may have a value of either a 0 or a 1. It determines whether all trace information is stored in a single file or whether multiple files are generated. If this value is set to 0, then the file and folder, as defined by the TraceFileName registry key, are used with no modifications. If this key has a value of 1, then a thread identification value specified by the TraceFileName registry key is appended to the base name of the file. For example, if the Trace-FileName is left at the default value of odpnet.trc and the TraceOption is set to 0, the generated trace file is simply named odpnet.trc. On the other hand, if the TraceOption is set to 1, then the generated trace file name follows the form odpnet*ThreadID*.trc such as odpnet270.trc. In this example, 270 is the thread ID of the process being traced.

The TraceLevel Registry Key

You use the TraceLevel registry key to specify the level of trace output that should be generated. Currently, four levels of tracing are available:

- No tracing (Level 0)

- Method entry and exit as well as SQL information (Level 1)

- Connection pool information (Level 2)

- Distributed transaction information (Level 4)

To enable multiple levels of tracing, simply take the sum of the levels. For example, to trace method entry, exit, SQL information, and connection pool information, you would use a trace level of 3.

Creating a Data Provider Trace File

By setting the registry key values, as discussed, you're ready to create a trace file for the data provider. Figure 9-2 illustrates the registry settings you use to create a trace file that

- Is named c:\odpnet.trc

- Doesn't use multiple trace files for the output

- Produces entry, exit, SQL, and connection pool information

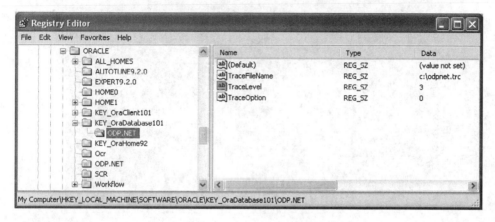

Figure 9-2. *The registry settings to create a sample trace file*

To create the trace file, you need to run some code that calls the data provider. Rather than create an application whose sole purpose is to call code for trace output, run the Top-N query code that you created in Chapter 8. Of course, you may use any code that calls the data provider for this activity. Listing 9-1 contains the results of running the code with tracing enabled.

Listing 9-1. *Running the Top-N Query Code to Create a Trace File*

```
C:\My Projects\ProOraNet\Oracle\C#\Chapter08\TopNQuery\bin\Debug>TopNQuery.exe

[ snipped output ]

C:\My Projects\ProOraNet\Oracle\C#\Chapter08\TopNQuery\bin\Debug>↵
dir c:\odpnet.trc
 Volume in drive C has no label.
 Volume Serial Number is 4847-2DDB

 Directory of c:\
```

```
07/20/2004  12:14 PM          129,533 odpnet.trc
              1 File(s)          129,533 bytes
              0 Dir(s)   48,599,035,904 bytes free
```

`C:\My Projects\ProOraNet\Oracle\C#\Chapter08\TopNQuery\bin\Debug>`

In Listing 9-1, you can see that the file was created based on the registry key settings. By opening the output file in an editor, as illustrated by Figure 9-3, you can easily trace the execution of the various steps that the data provider performed, see the connection pool created for the database connection, and see the SQL that the application submitted. In addition, the trace file contains timing information that allows you to determine how long each execution step took.

Figure 9-3. *Viewing the data provider trace file output*

Enabling Basic SQL Tracing

To view all the operations that Oracle performs with the SQL statements that you're submitting, enable SQL tracing. In addition to being able to see the actual operations that Oracle performs, when the TIMED_STATISTICS initialization parameter is set to True, you'll have access to timing information for those operations. In this section, we examine basic SQL tracing; in the next section, we examine extended SQL tracing.

To obtain the valuable timing information in the trace files, first set the TIMED_STATISTICS parameter, which determines whether the execution time for the various internal operations is measured, to True. In version 8i and earlier, this parameter has a default value of False, whereas in version 9i and later, it defaults to True. The DBA can set this parameter at the instance level by inserting the following line into the init or spfile file (see the section "Initialization Parameter Files and Server Parameter Files" in the Oracle concepts guide) and restarting the database:

`timed_statistics=true`

However, as developers, we can also set this parameter at the session level (see Listing 9-2), by issuing an `alter session` command from a SQL*Plus session with the database.

Listing 9-2. *Enabling SQL Trace*

```
C:\>sqlplus oranetuser@oranet

SQL*Plus: Release 10.1.0.2.0 - Production on Thu Sep 9 15:33:38 2004

Copyright (c) 1982, 2004, Oracle.  All rights reserved.

Enter password:

Connected to:
Oracle Database 10g Enterprise Edition Release 10.1.0.3.0 - Production
With the Partitioning, Oracle Label Security, OLAP and Data Mining options

SQL> alter session set sql_trace=true;

Session altered.

SQL>
```

Because end users enable SQL tracing, you aren't generally able to alter the location of the trace output. This is determined by a database initialization setting that the DBA configures. The `user_dump_dest` parameter determines the location of the file. In addition, Oracle names the file for you—you don't get a choice in the matter.

However, beginning with version 9i, you can ask Oracle to append an identifier to the name of the trace file, which makes it easier to identify the file name. In order to have Oracle append an identifier, simply issue an `alter session` statement similar to as the following:

```
alter session set tracefile_identifier=meaningful identifier;
```

For instance, if you wish to append the string ORANET to your trace files, you would issue a statement such as this:

```
alter session set tracefile_identifier=ORANET;
```

· You can then verify the values of these parameters in your session, as shown in Listing 9-3.

■NOTE If you aren't able to connect to the database with appropriate privileges, consult your database administrator about the values of these parameters.

Listing 9-3. *Viewing the Values of the user_dump_dest, timed_statistics, and tracefile_identifier Parameters*

```
C:\>sqlplus oranetadmin@oranet

SQL*Plus: Release 10.1.0.2.0 - Production on Thu Sep 9 15:47:55 2004

Copyright (c) 1982, 2004, Oracle.  All rights reserved.

Enter password:

Connected to:
Oracle Database 10g Enterprise Edition Release 10.1.0.3.0 - Production
With the Partitioning, Oracle Label Security, OLAP and Data Mining options

SQL> show parameter user_dump_dest

NAME                 TYPE        VALUE
-------------------- ----------- ---------------------------
user_dump_dest       string      C:\ORACLE\ADMIN\LT10G\UDUMP

SQL> show parameter timed_statistics

NAME                 TYPE        VALUE
-------------------- ----------- -----
timed_statistics     boolean     TRUE

SQL> show parameter tracefile_identifier

NAME                 TYPE        VALUE
-------------------- ----------- -----
tracefile_identifier string

SQL>
```

As you can see in this output, the value of the timed_statistics parameter is True, the value of the user_dump_dest parameter is C:\ORACLE\ADMIN\LT10G\UDUMP, and you haven't specified an identifier for your trace files. This means that trace files you generate will contain timing information, will be placed in the C:\ORACLE\ADMIN\LT10G\UDUMP directory, and won't have any identifiers appended to the end of the file name.

■**NOTE** Because the value of user_dump_dest is typically a directory on a server, you may not have rights to view files in that location. If this is the case, coordinate with your DBA to obtain access to the files you generate.

Tracing a SQL Statement

You can now go ahead and create a trace file with timing information for a simple query, as shown in Listing 9-4.

Listing 9-4. *Creating a SQL Trace File*

```
C:\>sqlplus oranetuser

SQL*Plus: Release 10.1.0.2.0 - Production on Tue Jul 20 12:56:48 2004

Copyright (c) 1982, 2004, Oracle.  All rights reserved.

Enter password:

Connected to:
Oracle Database 10g Enterprise Edition Release 10.1.0.2.0 - Production
With the Partitioning, OLAP and Data Mining options

SQL> alter session set sql_trace=true;

Session altered.

SQL> select * from environment order by env_id;

    ENV_ID ENV_DESC
---------- --------------------------------
         1 PROD
         2 STAGE
         3 TRAIN
         4 TEST
         5 DEV
         6 SAND
         7 EVAL
         8 DR

8 rows selected.

SQL> exit
Disconnected from Oracle Database 10g Enterprise Edition↵
 Release 10.1.0.2.0 - Production
With the Partitioning, OLAP and Data Mining options

C:\>
```

As you can see in Listing 9-4, issuing the `alter session set sql_trace=true;` statement enables SQL tracing in your session. If you want to disable SQL tracing, you simply issue a `alter session set sql_trace=false;` statement. When you're generating trace files, it's important to consider that in order to completely close the file, you need to disconnect from the database. Here you exited from your SQL*Plus session, which accomplishes the same result.

Now that you've created a trace file, you can see it in the directory specified by the user_dump_dest parameter as illustrated in Listing 9-5.

Listing 9-5. *Confirming the Trace File Creation*

```
C:\oracle\admin\lt10g\udump>dir
 Volume in drive C has no label.
 Volume Serial Number is 4847-2DDB

 Directory of C:\oracle\admin\lt10g\udump

07/20/2004  12:57 PM    <DIR>          .
07/20/2004  12:57 PM    <DIR>          ..
07/20/2004  12:58 PM             2,439 lt10g_ora_3404.trc
               1 File(s)          2,439 bytes
               2 Dir(s)  48,598,949,888 bytes free

C:\oracle\admin\lt10g\udump>
```

■**NOTE** On a multiuser system, there may be many trace files in the location specified by the user_dump_ dest parameter. Consult with your database administrator to obtain the correct trace file for your session. The naming convention of the trace files is both operating system and Oracle version dependent.

Formatting the Trace File Using tkprof

At this point, you can open the trace file in any text editor. You'll see that the trace file begins with header information that identifies the file, the database, and so forth. The main content follows the header information.

Because reading a raw trace file can be tedious, Oracle supplies a utility called tkprof, which can convert the raw trace file into a much more human-friendly format. This utility can accept many parameters and supports sorting output and other advanced features. The utility is documented in the "Database Performance Tuning Guide" in the Oracle documentation set. For your purposes here, you'll use the basic features of the utility and specify the following three parameters:

The input file name: The name of the raw trace file.

The output file name: The name that you wish to give to the file that tkprof produces.

The sys parameter: Indicates if you wish to include or exclude system information from the output file.

When Oracle processes SQL statements, it must make internal references many times (this is known as *recursive SQL*) to determine what type of object a name references. For example, in your sample, you specified a table name of ENVIRONMENT. Oracle has to consult its internal data dictionary to determine that the label "environment" refers to a table rather than a view. By specifying that you don't wish to see the SYS stats in your output file, you can filter out these internal activities from the resulting output file. Listing 9-6 illustrates using the tkprof utility in this manner. You now have a text file that is much easier to read than the raw trace file.

Listing 9-6. *Using the tkprof Utility on Your Raw Trace File*

```
C:\oracle\admin\lt10g\udump>tkprof lt10g_ora_3404.trc lt10g_ora_3404.txt sys=no

TKPROF: Release 10.1.0.2.0 - Production on Tue Jul 20 13:14:02 2004

Copyright (c) 1982, 2004, Oracle.  All rights reserved.



C:\oracle\admin\lt10g\udump>dir
 Volume in drive C has no label.
 Volume Serial Number is 4847-2DDB

 Directory of C:\oracle\admin\lt10g\udump

07/20/2004  01:14 PM    <DIR>          .
07/20/2004  01:14 PM    <DIR>          ..
07/20/2004  12:58 PM             2,439 lt10g_ora_3404.trc
07/20/2004  01:14 PM             5,347 lt10g_ora_3404.txt
               2 File(s)          7,786 bytes
               2 Dir(s)  48,598,667,264 bytes free

C:\oracle\admin\lt10g\udump>
```

Now that tkprof has formatted the raw trace file, you can see the SQL statement in the output file clearly:

```
select *
from
 environment order by env_id
```

call	count	cpu	elapsed	disk	query	current	rows
Parse	1	0.00	0.00	0	0	0	0
Execute	1	0.00	0.00	0	0	0	0
Fetch	2	0.00	0.00	0	4	0	8
total	4	0.00	0.00	0	4	0	8

```
Misses in library cache during parse: 1
Optimizer mode: ALL_ROWS
Parsing user id: 77

Rows    Row Source Operation
-------  --------------------------------------------------------
    8  TABLE ACCESS BY INDEX ROWID OBJ#(52216) (cr=4 pr=0 pw=0 time=86 us)
    8   INDEX FULL SCAN OBJ#(52217) (cr=2 pr=0 pw=0 time=228 us)(object id⤸
52217)
```

As reported in the tkprof output (the call column), an SQL statement may pass through three different phases. The statement is parsed and executed, and if it's a SELECT statement, results may be fetched. As you can see, this query was parsed and executed a single time. You need two fetch operations (indicated in the count column) to retrieve the rows from the database. In actuality, all the rows are returned by the first fetch operation and the second fetch operation only retrieves the "end of rows" marker.

The cpu column indicates how much time was spent on the CPU for each particular phase (or call).

The elapsed column indicates how much total time (i.e., wall clock time) each phase takes. Curiously, this output indicates each phase takes 0.00 seconds. Clearly the processing of each phase isn't instantaneous and doesn't consume just 0 seconds of time. What you see here is the effect of tkprof rounding the timing data to the nearest hundredth of a second. These operations simply consumed less than 1/100 of a second, and, therefore, they are reported as 0.00 time consumed. In the next section, you see that the real time is in the raw trace file.

The disk column indicates the number of disk reads Oracle requested from the operating system for each phase. Of course the read request may not actually result in a physical disk read if caching is implemented by the operating system or disk subsystem. However, Oracle issues a disk read call, and Oracle doesn't know how the operating system processes it. Again, for this sample query, you can see that the column contains the value 0. This just means a disk read request wasn't necessary because the data was cached in Oracle's memory.

The query column indicates the number of buffers Oracle retrieves in read consistent mode. Remember, I discussed Oracle's read consistency in Chapter 3. Here you can see that Oracle needs to read four buffers during the fetch phase.

Like the query column, the current column indicates the number of buffers Oracle retrieves. The difference between these two columns is that with current reads, the buffers are read based on the current point in time, not what the buffer looked like at the beginning of the query. You typically see buffers read in current mode in an UPDATE statement. In such a case, Oracle needs to read information from the buffer as it exists at the time of the read.

The final column, the rows column, simply indicates the actual number of rows processed during each phase. As expected, the sample query fetched all eight rows from the table since there was no where clause to limit the number of rows to be returned.

Enabling Extended SQL Tracing

It may surprise you to learn that the Oracle database code itself is highly instrumented. The interface to this instrumentation is known as the Oracle event system. You can use this system to activate these events for a particular session so the Oracle kernel records a variety of diagnostic trace information in your trace file.

■NOTE Using the event system to create trace files is a semisupported activity. Oracle support recommends that you only use the event system under Oracle support's direct guidance. If you use of the event system improperly, you can cause a database to be destroyed. However, using the event system to create SQL trace files is a well-known activity.

Each event in the Oracle event system is identified by a numeric value. From a performance diagnostics or tracing perspective, one of the most important events is the event known as 10046. There are several ways to set an event. You can set the event at the session level, using the alter session SQL statement. To do so, you'll use syntax that is slightly different from what you saw in the previous section. The syntax used to set the 10046 event looks like this:

```
alter session set events '10046 trace name context forever, level X';
```

Unlike basic SQL tracing which is either enabled or disabled, advanced SQL tracing has multiple levels available. The following are the levels of available tracing using the 10046 event:

Level 1: Basic SQL trace

Level 4: Basic SQL trace + bind variable values

Level 8: Basic SQL trace + wait information

Level 12: Basic SQL trace + bind variables + wait information

A Level 1 10046 trace is equivalent to the basic SQL trace you created in the previous section. As you can see, Level 4 and Level 12 traces include the values of bind variables used by the program. Recall that a trace file is simply a text file; therefore, you must be careful when you use trace files to avoid exposing sensitive or confidential information. For example, if you are working on a credit card processing system that uses bind variables (a good practice), and you enable a basic SQL trace of the application, the trace file doesn't include the actual values the system uses for the bind variables. You only see the placeholder. However, if you enable either a Level 4 or Level 12 10046 trace, these values are visible in the trace file.

■**CAUTION** Trace files are simple text files. Make sure you don't inadvertently expose sensitive information in a trace file.

To see how bind variable information is displayed in a trace file, you can declare a bind variable in an SQL*Plus session, assign it a value, and then use the bind variable in an SQL statement, creating a basic trace file of its execution, as shown in Listing 9-7. Then you can repeat the experiment using extended tracing, and you can compare the output and illustrate the presence of the bind variable value in the extended trace file. Setting sql_trace=true within a session is equivalent to setting event 10046 to Level 1.

Listing 9-7. *Creating a Trace File and Using a Bind Variable in SQL*Plus*

```
C:\>sqlplus oranetuser

SQL*Plus: Release 10.1.0.2.0 - Production on Tue Jul 20 14:01:32 2004

Copyright (c) 1982, 2004, Oracle.  All rights reserved.

Enter password:

Connected to:
Oracle Database 10g Enterprise Edition Release 10.1.0.2.0 - Production
With the Partitioning, OLAP and Data Mining options

SQL> variable v_env_id number
SQL> exec :v_env_id := 1;

PL/SQL procedure successfully completed.

SQL> alter session set sql_trace=true;

Session altered.

SQL> select env_desc from environment where env_id = :v_env_id;

ENV_DESC
--------------------------------
PROD

1 row selected.

SQL> exit
Disconnected from Oracle Database 10g Enterprise Edition⤶
 Release 10.1.0.2.0 - Production
With the Partitioning, OLAP and Data Mining options

C:\>
```

Here you create a bind variable and assign it a value of 1. You then enable basic SQL tracing and execute an SQL statement using the bind variable. After exiting your SQL*Plus session, you can examine the resulting trace file and verify that the value of the bind variable isn't present as illustrated here:

```
[ snipped content ]
PARSING IN CURSOR #1 len=57 dep=0 uid=64 oct=3 lid=64↵
 tim=8738935839 hv=3632398736 ad='6989f7d8'
select env_desc from environment where env_id = :v_env_id
END OF STMT
```

In the snipped portion of the trace file, you can plainly see the SQL statement and the fact that a bind variable (:v_env_id) is used. However, you can't see the value substituted into the bind variable when the statement was processed. In Listing 9-8, you repeat the process in Listing 9-7 except you enable a Level 4 10046 trace.

Listing 9-8. *Creating an Extended Trace File and Using a Bind Variable in SQL*Plus*

```
C:\>sqlplus oranetuser

SQL*Plus: Release 10.1.0.2.0 - Production on Tue Jul 20 14:10:16 2004

Copyright (c) 1982, 2004, Oracle.  All rights reserved.

Enter password:

Connected to:
Oracle Database 10g Enterprise Edition Release 10.1.0.2.0 - Production
With the Partitioning, OLAP and Data Mining options

SQL> variable v_env_id number
SQL> exec :v_env_id := 1;

PL/SQL procedure successfully completed.

SQL> alter session set events '10046 trace name context forever, level 4';

Session altered.

SQL> select env_desc from environment where env_id = :v_env_id;

ENV_DESC
--------------------------------
PROD

1 row selected.

SQL> exit
```

```
Disconnected from Oracle Database 10g Enterprise Edition↵
 Release 10.1.0.2.0 - Production
With the Partitioning, OLAP and Data Mining options

C:\>
```

Now when you look at the resulting trace file for the execution of the same statement with a Level 4 10046 trace active, you see a different situation. The following is the snipped output of the trace file.

```
[ snipped content ]
PARSING IN CURSOR #1 len=57 dep=0 uid=64 oct=3 lid=64↵
 tim=9134258609 hv=3632398736 ad='6989f7d8'
select env_desc from environment where env_id = :v_env_id
END OF STMT
BINDS #1:
 bind 0: dty=2 mxl=22(22) mal=00 scl=00 pre=00 oacflg=03↵
oacfl2=0000 size=24 offset=0
   bfp=05e4bc60 bln=22 avl=02 flg=05
   value=1
```

In this trace file, in the "BINDS #1" section, you can see that the value of the bind variable is clearly displayed as value=1. For a simple test like this, this isn't an issue. However, in an application that deals with sensitive data, making sure values of bind variables aren't exposed to unauthorized individuals could be a real concern.

Creating a Trace File from an Application

So far, you've been using SQL*Plus to create your trace files. In this section, you create a Windows Forms application that you use to generate a trace file from within the application. Figure 9-4 shows the design-time representation of the application's only form.

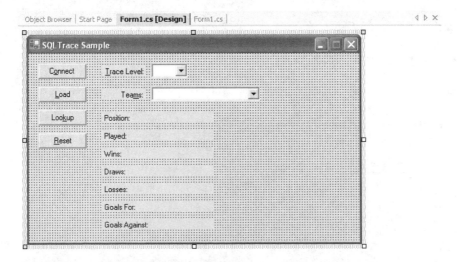

Figure 9-4. *The form used in the SQL trace application*

This form uses a form-level variable (or field, if you use the Add Field Wizard in Visual Studio) of type OracleConnection named oraConn that is initialized in the form's load event. Once the form loads, you can connect to the database using the code in Listing 9-9. This is the code behind the Connect button.

Listing 9-9. *The Connect Button Code*

```csharp
private void btnConnect_Click(object sender, System.EventArgs e)
{
  // create our standard connection string
  string connString = "User Id=oranetuser; Password=demo; Data Source=oranet";

  // only connect if we are not yet connected
  if (oraConn.State != ConnectionState.Open)
  {
    try
    {
      oraConn = new OracleConnection(connString);

      oraConn.Open();

      MessageBox.Show(oraConn.ConnectionString, "Successful Connection");
    }
    catch (Exception ex)
    {
      MessageBox.Show(ex.Message,"Exception Caught");
    }
  }
}
```

Once the database connection is established, you can load the teams from the LEAGUE_RESULTS table into the Teams drop-down list. The code to load the teams into this drop-down list is presented in Listing 9-10.

Listing 9-10. *The Load Button Code*

```csharp
private void btnLoadTeams_Click(object sender, System.EventArgs e)
{
  if (oraConn.State == ConnectionState.Open)
  {
    // remove any existing items
    cbTeams.Items.Clear();

    // get list of teams from database
    // and populate
    string sql = "select team from league_results order by team";

    OracleCommand cmd = new OracleCommand(sql, oraConn);
```

```
    OracleDataReader dataReader = cmd.ExecuteReader();

    while (dataReader.Read())
    {
      if (!dataReader.IsDBNull(0))
      {
        cbTeams.Items.Add(dataReader[0].ToString());
      }
    }

    if (cbTeams.Items.Count > 0)
    {
      // select the first item in the list box
      cbTeams.SelectedIndex = 0;
    }
  }
}
```

You entered the different trace levels that may be selected into the collection for the Trace Level drop-down list at design time. The valid values are depicted in Figure 9-5.

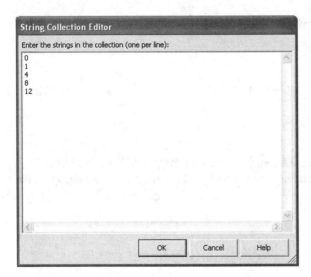

Figure 9-5. *The valid trace level values*

The values that are available in the Trace Level drop-down list represent the different levels you may assign to a 10046 event trace with the exception of the value 0. You're using the value 0 to indicate that tracing should be disabled. You can use the code in Listing 9-11 to populate the labels on the form with the value retrieved from the database.

Listing 9-11. *The Lookup Button Code*

```
private void btnLookup_Click(object sender, System.EventArgs e)
{
  if (oraConn.State == ConnectionState.Open)
  {
    string traceLevel = cbTraceLevel.SelectedItem.ToString();

    string traceSQL = "alter session set events ";

    if (traceLevel != "0")
    {
      // turn on tracing
      traceSQL += "'10046 trace name context forever, level " + traceLevel + "'";
    }
    else
    {
      // turn off tracing
      traceSQL += "'10046 trace name context off'";
    }

    string selectSQL = "select position, ";
    selectSQL += "played, ";
    selectSQL += "wins, ";
    selectSQL += "draws, ";
    selectSQL += "losses, ";
    selectSQL += "goals_for, ";
    selectSQL += "goals_against ";
    selectSQL += "from league_results ";
    selectSQL += "where team = :team";

    OracleParameter p_team = new OracleParameter();
    p_team.Size = 32;
    p_team.Value = cbTeams.SelectedItem.ToString();

    // create the oracle command object
    // and set the trace level
    OracleCommand cmd = new OracleCommand(traceSQL, oraConn);
    cmd.ExecuteNonQuery();

    // assign the text for selecting the data
    cmd.CommandText = selectSQL;

    // add the parameter to the collection
    cmd.Parameters.Add(p_team);
```

```
    // get a data reader object
    OracleDataReader dataReader = cmd.ExecuteReader();

    // populate labels with data from data reader
    if (dataReader.Read())
    {
      // position
      if (!dataReader.IsDBNull(0))
      {
        lblPosition.Text = "Position: " + dataReader[0].ToString();
      }

      // played
      if (!dataReader.IsDBNull(1))
      {
        lblPlayed.Text = "Played: " + dataReader[1].ToString();
      }

      // wins
      if (!dataReader.IsDBNull(2))
      {
        lblWins.Text = "Wins: " + dataReader[2].ToString();
      }

      // draws
      if (!dataReader.IsDBNull(3))
      {
        lblDraws.Text = "Draws: " + dataReader[3].ToString();
      }

      // losses
      if (!dataReader.IsDBNull(4))
      {
        lblLosses.Text = "Losses: " + dataReader[4].ToString();
      }

      // goals for
      if (!dataReader.IsDBNull(5))
      {
        lblGoalsFor.Text = "Goals For: " + dataReader[5].ToString();
      }

      // goals against
      if (!dataReader.IsDBNull(6))
      {
        lblGoalsAgainst.Text = "Goals Against: " + dataReader[6].ToString();
      }
    }
  }
}
```

The code behind the Lookup button begins by checking to see if the database connection is open. If it isn't, no further code executes. The code then builds an SQL statement to set the 10046 event to the appropriate level. If the value of the Trace Level drop-down list is 0, the code builds the appropriate command to turn off tracing. You next build a simple SQL statement to retrieve data from the LEAGUE_RESULTS table. This SQL statement uses a bind variable in place of the team name. You then create a parameter object and assign it the value of the team selected in the Teams drop-down list. Next, you execute the trace command to either enable or disable the 10046 trace output. You then simply execute the statement to retrieve data from the database and populate the various labels.

The simplistic Reset button code in Listing 9-12 does nothing more than clear the form labels.

Listing 9-12. *The Reset Button Code*

```
private void btnReset_Click(object sender, System.EventArgs e)
{
  lblPosition.Text = "Position:";
  lblPlayed.Text = "Played:";
  lblWins.Text = "Wins:";
  lblDraws.Text = "Draws:";
  lblLosses.Text = "Losses:";
  lblGoalsFor.Text = "Goals For:";
  lblGoalsAgainst.Text = "Goals Against:";
}
```

Figure 9-6 shows the form at run-time. I've selected a Level 12 (full) trace and have retrieved data for the Liverpool team.

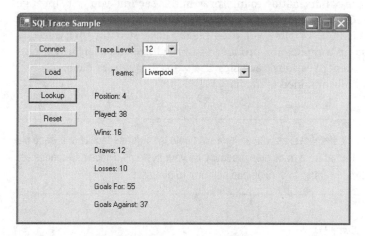

Figure 9-6. *The SQLTrace form at run-time*

After you close the form, the complete trace file is located in the user_dump_dest directory as illustrated in Listing 9-13. Note that I've removed the trace files that were previously generated for the sake of clarity. Of course, the actual name of your trace file is almost certainly going to differ.

Listing 9-13. *The SQLTrace Trace File*

```
C:\>cd C:\oracle\admin\lt10g\udump

C:\oracle\admin\lt10g\udump>dir
 Volume in drive C has no label.
 Volume Serial Number is 4847-2DDB

 Directory of C:\oracle\admin\lt10g\udump

07/20/2004  04:00 PM    <DIR>          .
07/20/2004  04:00 PM    <DIR>          ..
07/20/2004  04:01 PM             1,842 lt10g_ora_3480.trc
               1 File(s)          1,842 bytes
               2 Dir(s)  48,595,615,744 bytes free

C:\oracle\admin\lt10g\udump>
```

Interpreting the Trace File

Depending on the complexity of the application and the level of tracing you enable, a trace file can be a fairly unwieldy piece of information to interpret. In this section, you walk through the trace file generated by the SQLTrace sample application in the previous section. The complete trace file is contained in Listing 9-14. Here, you examine the basic structure of a trace file and the contents that the sample application produces. Although you are likely to see variations in the format and content of various trace files, this walk-through should give you a good idea of the information contained in the files.

■**NOTE** Due to platform and version differences, as well as improvements in the trace facility, the trace file I use here may differ in content and format from trace files produced on your systems. These differences are usually minor and easily translated from version to version and platform to platform.

Listing 9-14. *The SQLTrace Raw Trace File*

```
Dump file c:\oracle\admin\lt10g\udump\lt10g_ora_3480.trc
Tue Jul 20 16:13:37 2004
ORACLE V10.1.0.2.0 - Production vsnsta=0
vsnsql=13 vsnxtr=3
Oracle Database 10g Enterprise Edition Release 10.1.0.2.0 - Production
```

With the Partitioning, OLAP and Data Mining options
Windows XP Version V5.1 Service Pack 1
CPU   : 1 - type 586
Process Affinity: 0x00000000
Memory (A/P)   : PH:461M/1022M, PG:1867M/2462M, VA:1748M/2047M
Instance name: lt10g

Redo thread mounted by this instance: 1

Oracle process number: 18

Windows thread id: 3480, image: ORACLE.EXE (SHAD)


```
*** 2004-07-20 16:13:37.985
*** SERVICE NAME:(LT10G.SAND) 2004-07-20 16:13:37.934
*** SESSION ID:(145.65) 2004-07-20 16:13:37.934
=====================
PARSING IN CURSOR #1 len=69 dep=0 uid=64 oct=42 lid=64↵
 tim=16492332515 hv=3164292706 ad='698efb3c'
alter session set events '10046 trace name context forever, level 12'
END OF STMT
EXEC #1:c=0,e=150,p=0,cr=0,cu=0,mis=0,r=0,dep=0,og=1,tim=16492332502
XCTEND rlbk=0, rd_only=1
WAIT #1: nam='SQL*Net message to client' ela= 6 p1=1413697536 p2=1 p3=0
WAIT #1: nam='SQL*Net message from client' ela= 21295 p1=1413697536 p2=1 p3=0
=====================
PARSING IN CURSOR #1 len=118 dep=0 uid=64 oct=3 lid=64↵
 tim=16492434461 hv=4278431253 ad='697b75d0'
select position , played , wins , draws , losses , goals_for ,↵
 goals_against  from league_results where  team = :team
END OF STMT
PARSE #1:c=0,e=103,p=0,cr=0,cu=0,mis=0,r=0,dep=0,og=1,tim=16492434449
BINDS #1:
 bind 0: dty=1 mxl=32(18) mal=00 scl=00 pre=00 oacflg=03↵
 oacfl2=0010 size=32 offset=0
   bfp=05a6bcf4 bln=32 avl=09 flg=05
   value="Liverpool"
EXEC #1:c=20029,e=17724,p=0,cr=0,cu=0,mis=0,r=0,dep=0,og=1,tim=16492468301
WAIT #1: nam='SQL*Net message to client' ela= 6 p1=1413697536 p2=1 p3=0
WAIT #1: nam='SQL*Net message from client' ela= 4959 p1=1413697536 p2=1 p3=0
WAIT #1: nam='SQL*Net message to client' ela= 4 p1=1413697536 p2=1 p3=0
FETCH #1:c=0,e=3961,p=0,cr=7,cu=0,mis=0,r=1,dep=0,og=1,tim=16492489324
*** 2004-07-20 16:13:53.927
WAIT #1: nam='SQL*Net message from client' ela= 15831789 p1=1413697536 p2=1 p3=0
XCTEND rlbk=1, rd_only=1
WAIT #0: nam='SQL*Net message to client' ela= 5 p1=1413697536 p2=1 p3=0
```

```
WAIT #0: nam='SQL*Net message from client' ela= 8590 p1=1413697536 p2=1 p3=0
XCTEND rlbk=0, rd_only=1
STAT #1 id=1 cnt=1 pid=0 pos=1 obj=50727 op='TABLE ACCESS FULL⤶
 OBJ#(50727) (cr=7 pr=0 pw=0 time=164 us)'
```

The Trace File Header

All trace files generated by either the 10046 event facility, or by setting sql_trace=true, begin with a header. The header contains general information about the trace file and the system such as the location of the file, the database version, and so forth. The header differs slightly from version to version. Here is the header from the SQLTrace trace file:

```
Dump file c:\oracle\admin\lt10g\udump\lt10g_ora_3480.trc
Tue Jul 20 16:13:37 2004
ORACLE V10.1.0.2.0 - Production vsnsta=0
vsnsql=13 vsnxtr=3
Oracle Database 10g Enterprise Edition Release 10.1.0.2.0 - Production
With the Partitioning, OLAP and Data Mining options
Windows XP Version V5.1 Service Pack 1
CPU             : 1 - type 586
Process Affinity: 0x00000000
Memory (A/P)    : PH:461M/1022M, PG:1867M/2462M, VA:1748M/2047M
Instance name: lt10g

Redo thread mounted by this instance: 1

Oracle process number: 18

Windows thread id: 3480, image: ORACLE.EXE (SHAD)
```

The Session Section

Immediately following the header is the session section. This section contains information about the specific database session contained in the trace file. The session section may include an APPNAME entry. An application can call the supplied DBMS_APPLICATION_INFO PL/SQL package and set the application name in the database. I haven't done this in the sample application, so you won't see this in the following code excerpt from Listing 9-14. As you can see, the session section contains basic information but can help when you attempt to identify "your" trace file from among many.

```
*** 2004-07-20 16:13:37.985
*** SERVICE NAME:(LT10G.SAND) 2004-07-20 16:13:37.934
*** SESSION ID:(145.65) 2004-07-20 16:13:37.934
```

The First Parsing Section

The parsing section contains the SQL statement submitted to the database. The parsing section always contains information about the cursor associated with the SQL statement currently being processed. The following parsing section from the SQLTrace sample trace file illustrates this:

```
PARSING IN CURSOR #1 len=69 dep=0 uid=64 oct=42 lid=64⤸
 tim=16492332515 hv=3164292706 ad='698efb3c'
alter session set events '10046 trace name context forever, level 12'
END OF STMT
EXEC #1:c=0,e=150,p=0,cr=0,cu=0,mis=0,r=0,dep=0,og=1,tim=16492332502
XCTEND rlbk=0, rd_only=1
WAIT #1: nam='SQL*Net message to client' ela= 6 p1=1413697536 p2=1 p3=0
WAIT #1: nam='SQL*Net message from client' ela= 21295 p1=1413697536 p2=1 p3=0
```

The CURSOR Record

You can see that the first parsing section is for the SQL statement to enable tracing. The cursor information included in this section is as follows:

len=69: The length of the SQL statement.

dep=0: The recursive depth of the statement. Recursive SQL is SQL that Oracle must perform on your behalf, such as looking up the object type in the data dictionary. A value of 0 as you see here indicates that this statement is not a recursive statement.

uid=64: The user ID in the database of the user. For example, you can find this value in the user_users, all_users, and dba_users database views.

oct=42: The Oracle Command Type. This is an internal code you can use to identify the type of statement being processed.

lid=64: The privilege user ID. This is typically the same as the uid. However, when you're using stored code in the database that executes under the rights of the creator (definer's rights) rather than the user who is calling the procedure, this can be different.

tim=16492332515: A time stamp value. This value can be represented differently from platform to platform and version to version. In this case, it is represented in microseconds. You must set the timed_statistics parameter to True to populate this value.

hv=3164292706: A hash ID used to represent the SQL statement.

ad='698efb3c': The address of the SQL statement as represented in the v$sqlarea view.

The EXEC Record

After the SQL statement in parsing section, you see exec information. Typically, there are three stages in the overall processing of an SQL statement: parsing, executing, and fetching. These stages are represented by the PARSE, EXEC, and FETCH records in the trace file. Each of these records contains the same information. The EXEC record contains the following information:

c=0: The CPU time used for this operation. This is expressed in microseconds in your trace file, but it may also be expressed in centiseconds (as in version 9i). This can vary from version to version and platform to platform.

e=150: The elapsed time used for this operation. Think of elapsed time as wall clock time. This is expressed in the same units as CPU time.

p=0: The number of physical I/O calls for this operation.

cr=0: The number of database blocks retrieved from Oracle's buffer cache in memory in consistent mode. *Consistent mode* means the block must be consistent with the time that the statement started. This relates to Oracle's read consistency that we discussed earlier in the book.

cu=0: The number of database blocks retrieved from Oracle's buffer cache in memory in current mode. *Current mode* means what the block looks like right at this point in time, not what it looked like at the beginning of the statement.

mis=0: The number of times that Oracle didn't locate this statement in the library cache.

r=0: The number of rows returned for the statement.

dep=0: The recursive depth for this statement. This is the same as for the cursor record discussed earlier.

og=1: The optimizer goal used when the statement was submitted. The values are as follows: 1 means All Rows, 2 means First Rows, 3 means Rule, 4 means Choose. Consult with your database administrator for more information about how the optimizer is configured on your system.

tim=16492332502: The time stamp value for this step in the overall execution.

The XCTEND Record

After the EXEC record, you see a record of type XCTEND. This is the end of transaction marker and, as such, it only appears after a committed or rolled back transaction. Two fields are associated with the XCTEND record:

rlbk=0: Indicates if a rollback operation occurred. 0 means no rollback occurred and 1 means that a rollback did occur.

rd_only=1: Indicates if the transaction is read-only. A value of 1 means the transaction is read-only. A value of 0 means the transaction modified data.

The WAIT Records

At the end of the parsing section, you have two WAIT records. These records are one of the prime reasons you use a 10046 trace. These records tell you how much time Oracle spends processing a particular timed event. For full details of the waits Oracle can inform you about, see the "Oracle Database Reference" in the Oracle documentation set. The appendix of that guide includes the wait information reference.

The WAIT record is followed by a number that indicates which cursor the record is associated with. In this case, it is cursor #1. Here are the fields in the WAIT record:

nam='SQL*Net message to client': The name of the event. This name is the name used in the "Oracle Database Reference" appendix in the Oracle documentation set. You can also find this in the v$event_name view in the database.

ela= 6: The elapsed time spent waiting on the event in the same resolution as the time stamps—6 microseconds in this case.

p1=1413697536: The P1 value for a given event. This is specific to each event and is included in the documentation.

p2=1: The P2 value for a given event. This is specific to each event and is included in the documentation.

p3=0: The P3 value for a given event. This is specific to each event and is included in the documentation.

The Second Parsing Section

The second parsing section of the trace file contains the same information as the first section. This section is for the real SQL statement that you're submitting to the database. This section contains two additional record types that weren't present in the first parsing section.

The BIND Record

The first record that wasn't present is the BIND record:

```
BINDS #1:
 bind 0: dty=1 mxl=32(18) mal=00 scl=00 pre=00 oacflg=03↲
oacfl2=0010 size=32 offset=0
  bfp=05a6bcf4 bln=32 avl=09 flg=05
  value="Liverpool"
```

Like the WAIT record, the BIND record contains a number that associates this record to a cursor. Here are the fields in the BIND record:

bind 0: Indicates the zero-based offset for the bind variable. Because you only have a single bind variable in your statement, this is the only entry.

dty=1: The data type of the bind variable. The data type values and the internal number associated with them can be found under the "Datatypes" section in the "Oracle Call Interface Programmer's Guide" included in the Oracle documentation set.

mxl=32(18): The maximum length of the data type for this bind variable. This is the length you specify for the parameter in your code. The number in parentheses is known as the private maximum length and is used internally.

mal=00: The length of the array. Because you aren't using an array, this is 0.

scl=00: The scale value of a numeric bind variable.

pre=00: The precision value of a numeric bind variable.

oacflg=03: An internal flag used for bind variable options.

oacfl2=0010: Continuation of the previous internal flag.

size=32: The size passed in from the client.

offset=0: The offset used when performing what is known as a piece-wise bind.

bfp=05a6bcf4: The memory address of the bind.

bln=32: The length of the buffer in memory for the bind.

avl=09: The length of the real value that was substituted into the bind variable.

flg=05: Another internal flag value.

The STAT Record

The second record type that was not present in the first parsing section is the STAT record. Here is the extracted STAT record from the trace file:

```
STAT #1 id=1 cnt=1 pid=0 pos=1 obj=50727 op='TABLE ACCESS FULL↵
 OBJ#(50727) (cr=7 pr=0 pw=0 time=164 us)'
```

The STAT record contains the execution plan for the statement and a numeric identifier that associates this record with a cursor. This is the manner in which Oracle goes about performing the requested operation. In your case, there is only one STAT record. The tkprof utility uses these records to create and format the execution plan in its output. For more complex statements, the STAT records can run to many lines.

The breakdown of the STAT record is as follows:

id=1: The line number in the plan. Because you only have a single access plan entry, this is the only id you see.

cnt=1: The number of rows associated with this step in the plan. Your query returns a single row and you see this value is 1 for your query.

pid=0: The parent for this particular row source. If you had a more complex query that contained multiple row sources, this value would indicate a valid parent. A value of 0 indicates you have no parent.

pos=1: The position that this operation holds in the overall plan.

obj=50727: The object ID for this row source for simple or base objects. This is the `object_id` column in the `all_object` and `user_objects` views.

op='TABLE ACCESS FULL OBJ#(50727) (cr=7 pr=0 pw=0 time=164 us)': The actual operation associated with this step and row source. Here you can see you're performing a full table scan on object ID 50727 (the LEAGUE_RESULTS table).

■**NOTE** If you're examining a trace file and there aren't any STAT records, it is usually because you haven't disconnected from the database or closed the application. Oracle writes these final records at this point.

Chapter 9 Wrap-Up

In this chapter, you use the data provider and the database in a slightly different manner than you have in previous chapters. Rather than concentrating on how to perform specific tasks such as data manipulation or which data provider classes perform what function, you use features of the database and the data provider to learn what is happening during processing.

When an application reaches the production phase of its lifecycle, having the ability to take advantage of the instrumented code in both the data provider and the database can have great advantages. By turning on a switch and generating trace data that details exactly what the data provider and the database are doing, you can troubleshoot issues that happen at runtime. For example, by using the advanced SQL tracing facility, you can see the values of bind variables. Although you must ensure that this doesn't create a security risk, you may find this method invaluable when you're working with bad data. You can see exactly what values are being substituted into bind variables.

Although this chapter won't make you an expert on Oracle internals or trace file analysis, it should give you a more-than-sufficient head-start on interpreting trace file output. This chapter also gives you the ability to embed SQL in your applications that enables or disables the tracing facility. This can be a powerful feature to add to your applications. The ability to create trace information is a distinguishing feature of a professional application.

■■■

Obtaining and Installing the Oracle Software

In this appendix, I walk you through the steps for installing the Oracle server and the Oracle client software on a laptop running the Windows XP Professional operating system. These steps should provide you with enough information so that you can make any necessary adjustments to your environment. This exercise is somewhat mechanical in nature with little narrative so it isn't very exciting; however, by following these steps, you create an exact replica of the environment you use throughout this book, so it is useful.

I'll guide you through detailed and complete setups of both the Oracle server and the Oracle client version 10g (10.1.0) software. The Oracle server software includes the Oracle client components, so if you intend to install the Oracle server software on the same machine as Visual Studio, you don't need to install the client software separately. However, if you wish to take advantage of Oracle's graphical management utility (Oracle Enterprise Manager Console), you do need to install the client software. That utility is part of the client software installation package in the Oracle 10g release. Although you'll use Oracle 10g as your reference base, I've designed the book's sample code to work with the 8i, 9i, and 10g database servers.

NOTE The steps I present in this appendix allow you to create an installation that mirrors the installation used throughout the book. It isn't strictly necessary to follow these steps. If you have access to a database that has the sample schemas installed, you don't need to follow these steps. Of course, if you wish to create an environment that exactly mirrors the environment used in the book, these steps do just that.

Obtaining the Oracle Software

You may acquire the Oracle software through a variety of channels. If you're already an Oracle customer, you probably already have the appropriate software media. If you aren't or if you want to obtain your own copy of the software, a couple of options are available to you.

First, you may subscribe to Oracle "Tech Tracks" and receive the media as a CD-ROM distribution package. One advantage of the "Tech Tracks" subscription is that, with it, you automatically receive software updates on CD-ROM (or other appropriate media) periodically. This can be very convenient if you don't wish to download 1GB or so of CD-ROM image data. The "Tech Tracks" subscription also includes access to the Microsoft Knowledge Base.

Second, you can download the Oracle software (including the documentation) free of charge from the Oracle Technology Network (OTN). The OTN offers complete, functional versions of the software under a development license. Under this license, you're free to use the software as long as you don't deploy it to a production environment.

■**NOTE** Please consult the license agreement on OTN for all details, including any changes to the agreement.

Both the "Tech Tracks" subscription and the software download option are available at `http://otn.oracle.com`. In addition, OTN is a great resource for a variety of Oracle topics. Registration on OTN is free and you're presented with the complete license agreement prior to downloading the software.

In this text, you work with the Enterprise Edition of the 10g version of the database software. You only need to download the database software to work with the samples in this book. If you have access to a database already and only need the client, downloading it alone is sufficient.

■**NOTE** In addition to the database software, Oracle makes available a wide range of products that are downloadable under the OTN license agreement.

About the Oracle Universal Installer

You don't install the Oracle software using the traditional Windows-based installer. This is because Oracle software is supported on such a wide variety of platforms. To provide a consistent installation experience from platform to platform, Oracle created its own installation mechanism named, appropriately enough, the Oracle Universal Installer (OUI). The OUI is a Java-based and fully functional installation utility. You can start the installer by either using the typical autorun feature from CD-ROM media or by simply running the `setup.exe` program. You'll work with the installer by allowing the autorun feature to kick off your installation process as you work through two installation scenarios.

■**TIP** The Windows account you're using for the install must be a member of the local Administrators group on the Windows machine where you're performing the install.

Installing the Oracle Database 10g Software

When you insert the Oracle Database 10g CD-ROM into your CD drive, the autorun process should automatically launch the Autorun window as shown in Figure A-1.

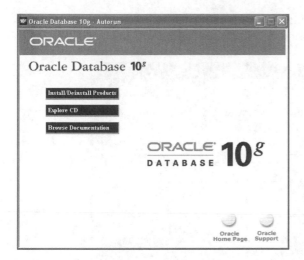

Figure A-1. *The Oracle Database 10g Autorun window*

The following steps will walk you through the process of installing the Oracle Database 10g software.

1. From the Autorun window, click the Install/Deinstall Products button.

    This starts the OUI initialization process as shown in Figure A-2.

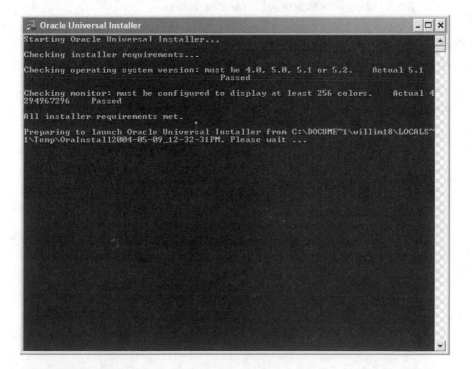

Figure A-2. *The OUI initialization process*

Once the installer completes the initialization process, you're presented with the
Oracle Database 10g Installation window as depicted in Figure A-3.

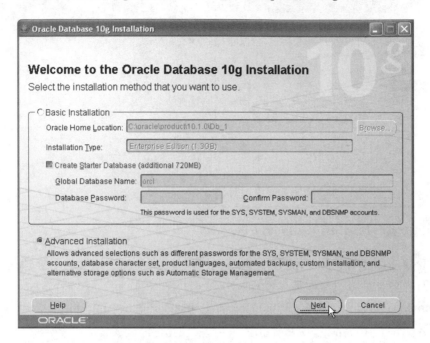

Figure A-3. *The Oracle Database 10g Installation window*

2. Select the Advanced Installation radio button and click Next to continue.

   This produces the Specify File Locations window shown in Figure A-4.

3. If this is the first Oracle product you've installed, accept the default values for the fields
   on this window or alter these values to suit your particular installation.

   As you can see, I've elected to change the values for both the Name and Path fields.

■**NOTE** You must install the Oracle Database software into its own directory. When you're using a
version prior to 10g, if you have at least one other Oracle product installed, the installer chooses
that Oracle Home by default.

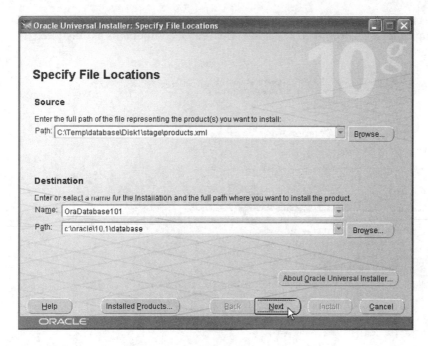

Figure A-4. *The Specify File Locations window*

4. Once you're satisfied with your selections in the Specify File Locations window, click Next to advance to the Select Installation Type window (see Figure A-5).

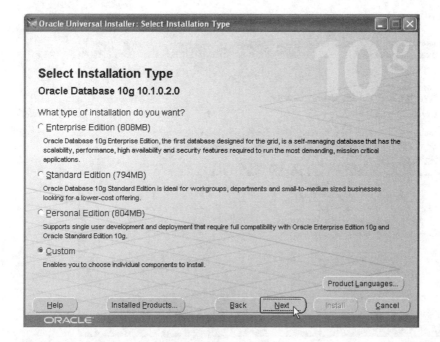

Figure A-5. *The Select Installation Type window*

5. Select the Custom radio button and click Next to advance to the Available Product Components window; then select the initial set of components as illustrated in Figure A-6.

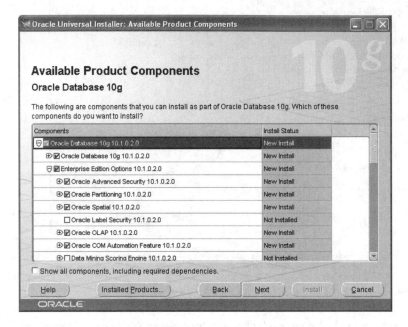

Figure A-6. *The Available Product Components window*

6. Continue to select the options as shown in Figure A-7.

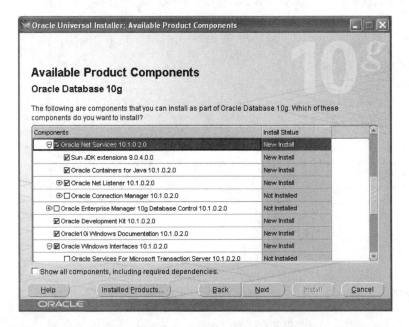

Figure A-7. *The Available Product Components window, continued*

7. Complete the selections as shown in Figure A-8.

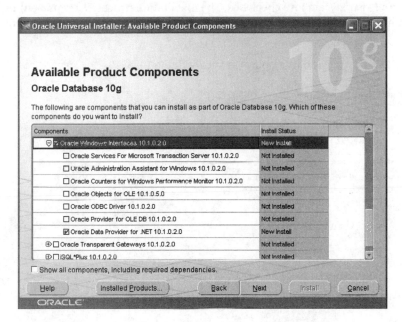

Figure A-8. *Completing the selections in the Available Product Components window*

8. Click Next to continue.

If you have an existing Oracle database on your machine, you'll now see the Upgrade an Existing Database window shown in Figure A-9.

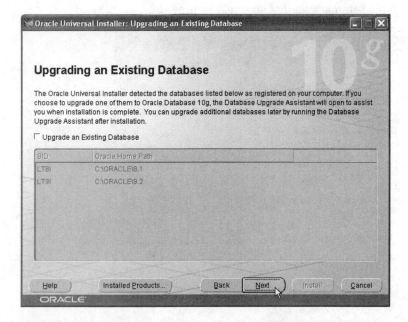

Figure A-9. *The Upgrade an Existing Database window*

9. If you're presented with the Upgrade an Existing Database window, don't select the Upgrade an Existing Database check box. The installation process I am presenting here creates a new database near the end of the process. Simply click Next to bypass this window.

The Create Database window displays as shown in Figure A-10.

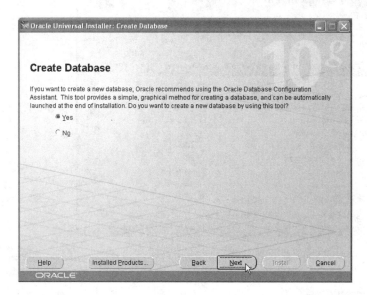

Figure A-10. *The Create Database window*

10. Click the Yes radio button on the Create Database window and then click Next to advance to the Summary window shown in Figure A-11.

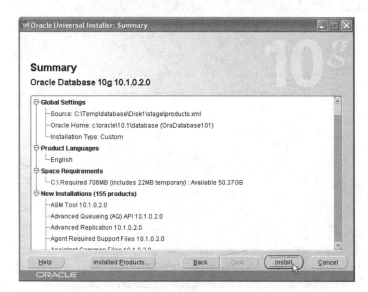

Figure A-11. *The Summary window*

11. Click Install to begin the installation process.

The install begins and displays the Install window as shown in Figure A-12.

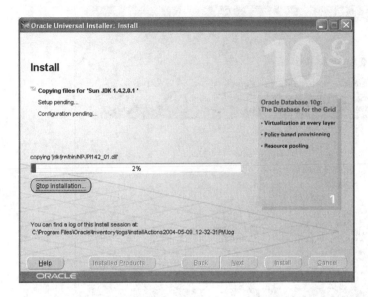

Figure A-12. *The Install window shortly after the installation process starts*

As the installation progresses, the installer updates the progress bar on the Install window. Once the selected components have been installed, the Install window resembles Figure A-13.

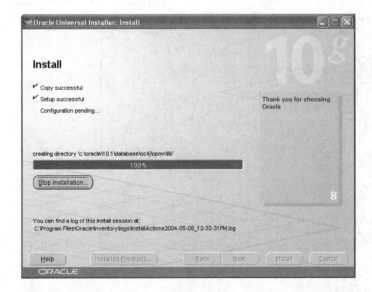

Figure A-13. *The Install window after components have been installed*

The installer automatically launches the necessary Configuration Assistants to configure the environment. The Configuration Assistants window resembles Figure A-14.

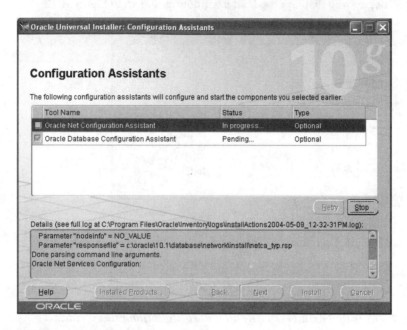

Figure A-14. *The Configuration Assistants window*

The installer automatically starts the Oracle Net Configuration Assistant as shown in Figure A-15.

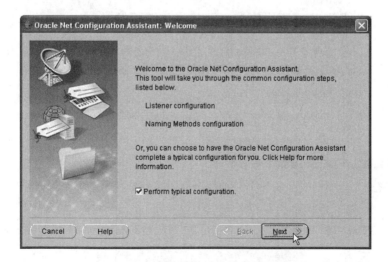

Figure A-15. *The Oracle Net Configuration Assistant Welcome window*

12. Click the Perform Typical Configuration check box and click Next to start the network configuration.

Doing so brings up the network configuration splash screen as shown in Figure A-16.

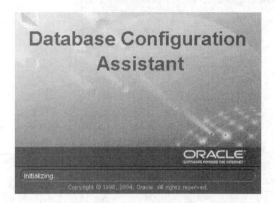

Figure A-16. *The Network Configuration splash screen*

Once the Network Configuration finishes, the installer automatically displays the Database Configuration Assistant window shown in Figure A-17.

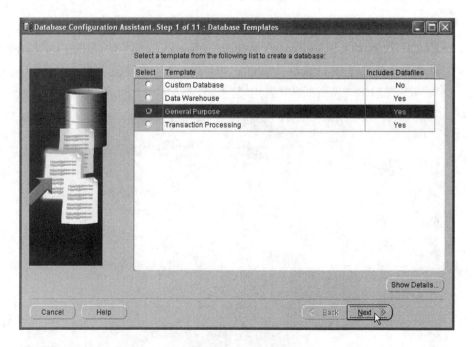

Figure A-17. *The Database Configuration Assistant initial window*

13. Select the General Purpose template and click Next to advance to step 2 of the Database Configuration Assistant (illustrated in Figure A-18).

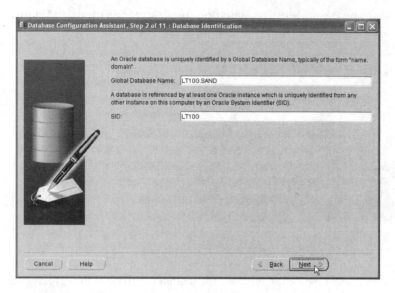

Figure A-18. *The Database Configuration Assistant, step 2*

14. Complete the Global Database Name field and accept the provided value for the SID field. (The name I selected for this install is a loose acronym for Laptop 10G Sandbox.)

15. Once you're satisfied with your choices, click Next to advance to step 3 of the Database Configuration Assistant, as shown in Figure A-19.

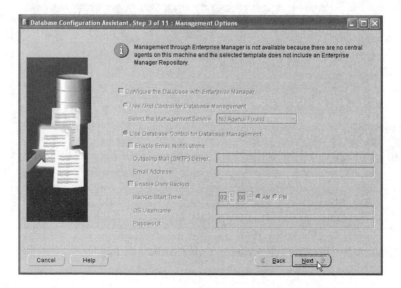

Figure A-19. *The Database Configuration Assistant, step 3*

Because you haven't installed the Grid Control software or the server-based version of the Enterprise Manager, the options on the Database Configuration, Step 3 window aren't available. These utilities are better suited to a server-based installation rather than a laptop that uses DHCP addressing.

16. In step 3 of the Database Configuration Assistant, click Next to display the step 4 window shown in Figure A-20.

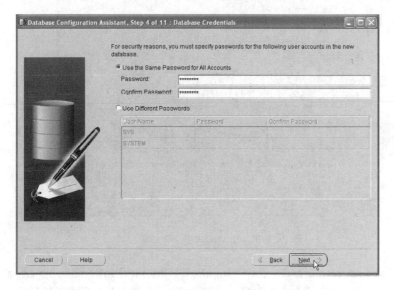

Figure A-20. *The Database Configuration Assistant, step 4*

17. Click the Use the Same Password for All Accounts radio button and enter a password. Click Next to advance to step 5 as depicted in Figure A-21.

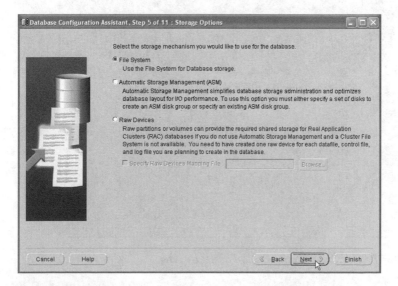

Figure A-21. *The Database Configuration Assistant, step 5*

18. Click the File System radio button and click Next to move on to step 6 as shown in Figure A-22.

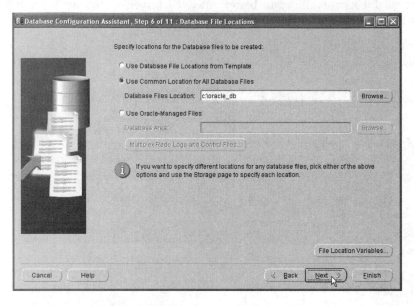

Figure A-22. *The Database Configuration Assistant, step 6*

19. Click the Use Common Location for All Database Files radio button and specify a directory to use. Once you've specified a directory, click Next to advance to step 7 as shown in Figure A-23.

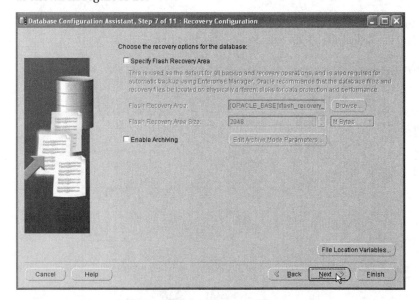

Figure A-23. *The Database Configuration Assistant, step 7*

20. Don't select any options from the step 7 window—the Flash Recovery and Enable Archiving options are related to backup and recovery operations, which I don't address. Just click Next to move on to step 8 shown in Figure A-24.

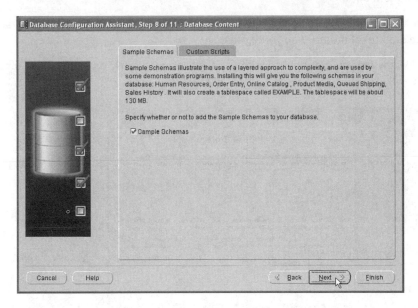

Figure A-24. *The Database Configuration Assistant, step 8*

21. Click the Sample Schemas check box and then click Next to advance to step 9, which is shown in Figure A-25.

Figure A-25. *The Database Configuration Assistant, step 9*

22. Click the Custom radio button.

   Doing so enables the Automatic and Manual radio buttons for the Shared Memory Management option.

23. Select Manual and complete the five memory fields with values that are appropriate for the amount of memory on your system.

24. Click Next when you are satisfied with your selections to move on to step 10 shown in Figure A-26.

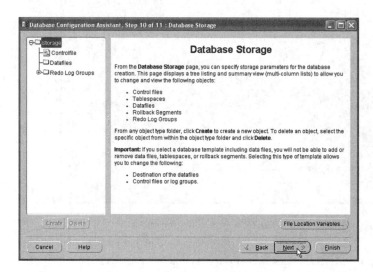

Figure A-26. *The Database Configuration Assistant, step 10*

25. Accept the values on the Database Storage window and click Next to move to the final step (see Figure A-27) before the database is created.

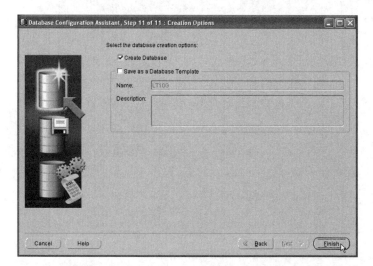

Figure A-27. *The Database Configuration Assistant, step 11*

26. Click Finish to complete the Database Configuration Assistant and display the Confirmation window shown in Figure A-28.

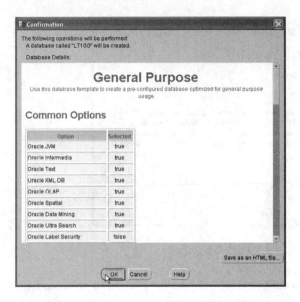

Figure A-28. *The Database Configuration Assistant Confirmation window*

27. Click OK on the Confirmation window to begin creating the database. The progress window displays as shown in Figure A-29.

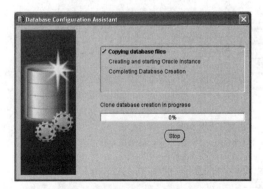

Figure A-29. *The Database Configuration Assistant Progress window*

Once it's finished creating the database, the assistant displays a task completed window as shown in Figure A-30.

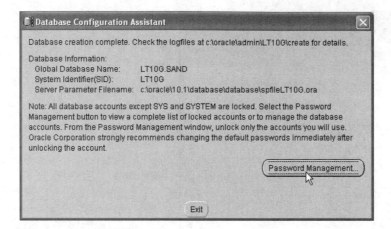

Figure A-30. *The database creation complete window*

28. Click the Password Management button to bring up the window depicted in Figure A-31.

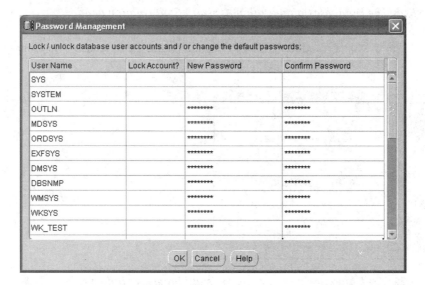

Figure A-31. *The Password Management window*

29. Choose and enter a password for each account in the database other than the SYS and SYSTEM accounts—you've already specified the password for those accounts. Be sure to remove the check mark from the Lock Account? column to unlock those accounts.

30. When you're satisfied with all you choices, click OK to return to the Database Configuration Assistant (see Figure A-32).

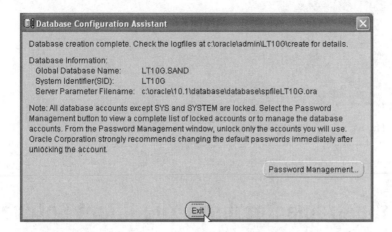

Figure A-32. *The database creation complete window*

31. Click Exit to leave the Database Configuration Assistant.

The End of Installation window displays (see Figure A-33).

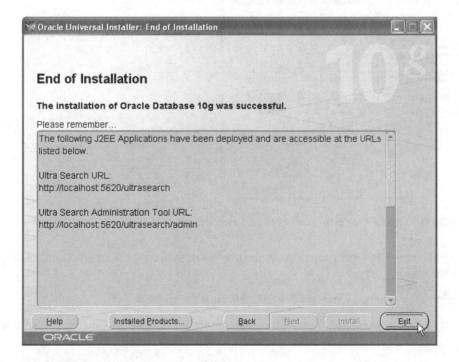

Figure A-33. *The End of Installation window*

32. Click Exit to display the confirmation window (see Figure A-34).

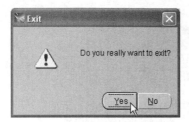

Figure A-34. *The Exit Confirmation window*

33. Click Yes to complete the installation.

Installing the Oracle Database 10g Client Software

When you insert the Oracle Database 10g Client CD-ROM into your CD drive, the autorun process should automatically launch the Autorun window shown in Figure A-35.

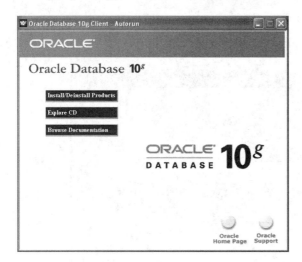

Figure A-35. *The Oracle Database 10g Client Autorun window*

The following steps walk you through the process of installing the Oracle Database 10g Client software.

1. From the Autorun window, click Install/Deinstall Products.

This starts the Oracle Universal Installer initialization process as shown in Figure A-36.

Figure A-36. *The Oracle Universal Installer initialization process*

Once the installer completes the initialization process, the Welcome window depicted in Figure A-37 appears.

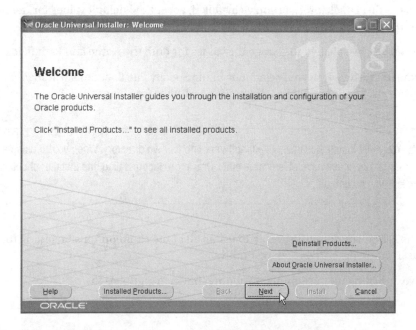

Figure A-37. *The Oracle Universal Installer Welcome window*

2. Click Next to advance to the Specify File Locations window shown in Figure A-38.

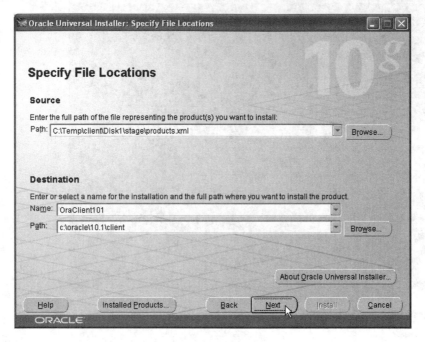

Figure A-38. *The Specify File Locations window*

3. If this is the first Oracle product you've installed, accept the default values for the fields on this window or alter these values to suit your particular installation.

   As you can see, I've elected to change the values for both the Name and Path fields.

4. Once you're satisfied with your selections in the Specify File Locations window, click Next to advance to the Select Installation Type window (see Figure A-39).

■**NOTE** You must install the Oracle Client software into its own directory. When you're using a version prior to 10g, if you have at least one other Oracle product installed, the installer chooses that Oracle Home by default.

---

5. Click the Administrator radio button to install all of the client options including the graphical Oracle Enterprise Manager utility.

6. Click Next to bring up the Summary window shown in Figure A-40.

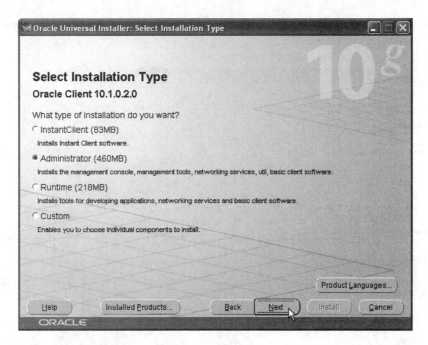

Figure A-39. *The Select Installation Type window*

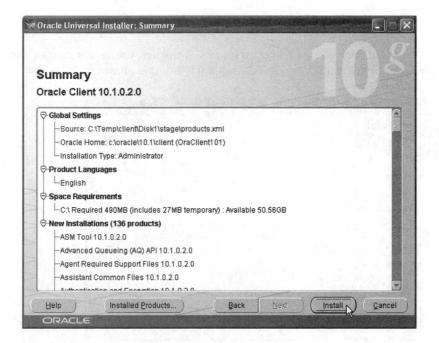

Figure A-40. *The Summary window*

7. Click the Install button to begin the installation process and display the progress window shown in Figure A-41.

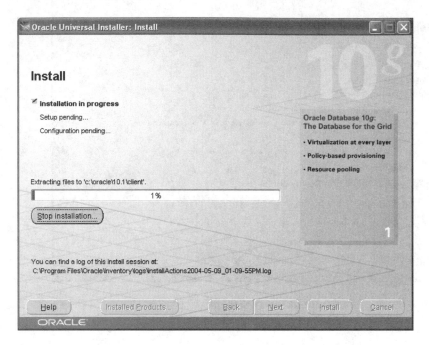

Figure A-41. *The client installation in progress*

Once the installation of the client components completes, the installer automatically displays the Oracle Net Configuration Assistant window as shown in Figure A-42.

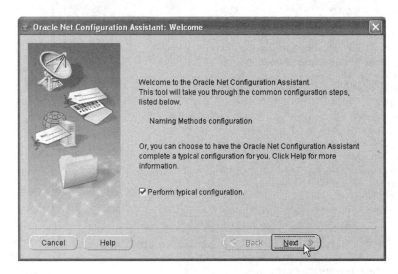

Figure A-42. *The Oracle Net Configuration Assistant, naming methods window*

8. Click the Perform typical configuration. check box and click Next to start the network configuration process as shown in Figure A-43.

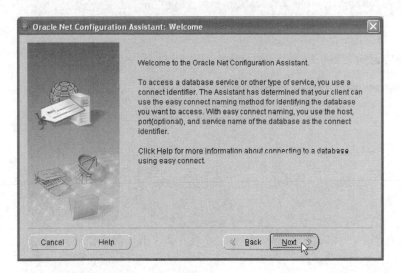

Figure A-43. *The Oracle Net Configuration Assistant, easy connect information window*

9. Click Next and the assistant begins configuration.

Once configuration is complete, the Done window appears (see Figure A-44).

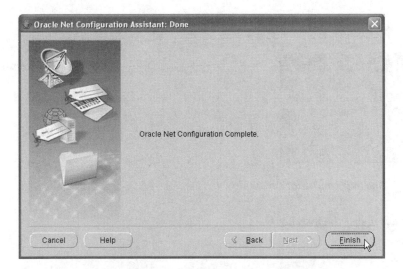

Figure A-44. *The Oracle Net Configuration Done window*

10. Click Finish to advance to the End of Installation window (see Figure A-45).

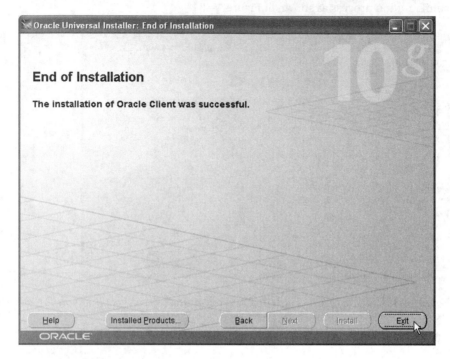

Figure A-45. *The End of Installation window*

11. Click Exit to bring up the confirmation window (see Figure A-46).

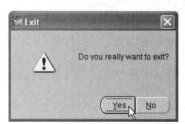

Figure A-46. *The Exit confirmation window*

12. Click the Yes to exit the installer.

Configuring the Registry to Use the Server Network Configuration

Because I've installed both the server and the client software on my laptop, I've created two distinct sets of network configuration files. However, I'd prefer not to have to maintain two separate network configurations.

Fortunately it is possible to configure the client software to use the server software network configuration files. If you've only installed the server or the client, but not both, you can safely skip these steps. You can also skip these steps if you intend to maintain separate configuration files for the client and the server if you have installed both on the same machine.

The manner in which you can configure the client software to use the server software configuration files is through a registry key. You also set the default database for the client software to be the database you created during the server software installation process.

The following steps walk you through the process of configuring the client software to use the server software configuration files.

1. Select the Oracle Home key in the left pane and create a new string value in the registry hive by right-clicking in the right pane and choosing New ➤ String Value, as shown in Figure A-47.

   The Edit String dialog appears.

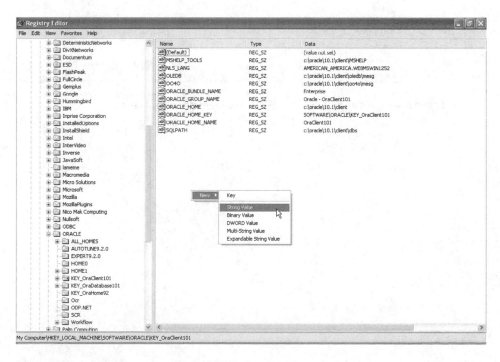

Figure A-47. *Creating a new string value in the client hive in the registry*

2. Complete the Value name and Value data fields as shown in Figure A-48.

Make sure the Value data entry points to the network\admin directory under the direc-tory where you installed the server software. This is the location where Oracle stores the network configuration files. You must use TNS_ADMIN for the Value name field.

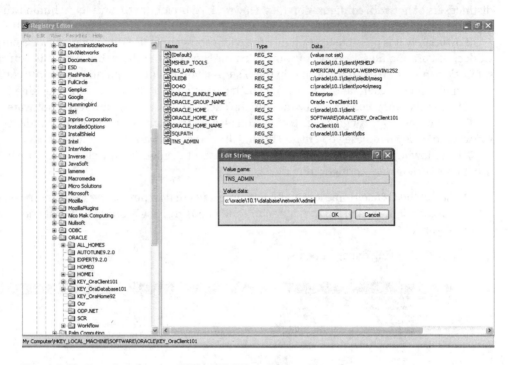

Figure A-48. *Creating the new TNS_ADMIN registry string value*

3. Once you've created the TNS_ADMIN entry, create another entry for the ORACLE_SID value by right-clicking in the right pane, selecting New ➤ String Value, and completing the fields (see Figure A-49).

This new entry represents the default database the client software will use. To fill out the fields in this dialog, use the SID value you used when you created the database earlier in the appendix.

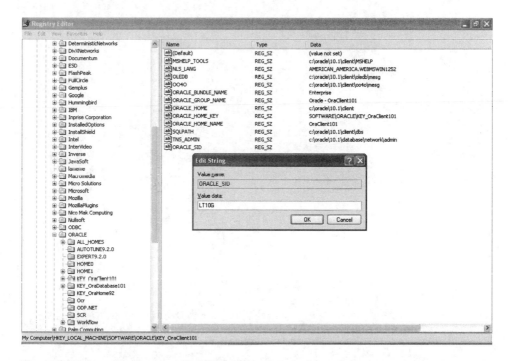

Figure A-49. *Creating the new ORACLE_SID registry string value*

Index

A

NOTE The ~ character is used to reduce the need to duplicate almost identical entries, which would otherwise follow one another in the index. For example, "bulk_/~insert/~select procedures" represents both the bulk_insert procedure and the bulk_select procedure. Similarly "GetOracleClob/~ForUpdate methods" represents both the GetOracleClob method and the GetOracleClobForUpdate method.

forums.apress.com

JOIN THE APRESS FORUMS AND BE PART OF OUR COMMUNITY. You'll find discussions that cover topics of interest to IT professionals, programmers, and enthusiasts just like you. If you post a query to one of our forums, you can expect that some of the best minds in the business—especially Apress authors, who all write with *The Expert's Voice*™—will chime in to help you. Why not aim to become one of our most valuable participants (MVPs) and win cool stuff? Here's a sampling of what you'll find:

DATABASES

Data drives everything.

Share information, exchange ideas, and discuss any database programming or administration issues.

INTERNET TECHNOLOGIES AND NETWORKING

Try living without plumbing (and eventually IPv6).

Talk about networking topics including protocols, design, administration, wireless, wired, storage, backup, certifications, trends, and new technologies.

JAVA

We've come a long way from the old Oak tree.

Hang out and discuss Java in whatever flavor you choose: J2SE, J2EE, J2ME, Jakarta, and so on.

MAC OS X

All about the Zen of OS X.

OS X is both the present and the future for Mac apps. Make suggestions, offer up ideas, or boast about your new hardware.

OPEN SOURCE

Source code is good; understanding (open) source is better.

Discuss open source technologies and related topics such as PHP, MySQL, Linux, Perl, Apache, Python, and more.

PROGRAMMING/BUSINESS

Unfortunately, it is.

Talk about the Apress line of books that cover software methodology, best practices, and how programmers interact with the "suits."

WEB DEVELOPMENT/DESIGN

Ugly doesn't cut it anymore, and CGI is absurd.

Help is in sight for your site. Find design solutions for your projects and get ideas for building an interactive Web site.

SECURITY

Lots of bad guys out there—the good guys need help.

Discuss computer and network security issues here. Just don't let anyone else know the answers!

TECHNOLOGY IN ACTION

Cool things. Fun things.

It's after hours. It's time to play. Whether you're into LEGO® MINDSTORMS™ or turning an old PC into a DVR, this is where technology turns into fun.

WINDOWS

No defenestration here.

Ask questions about all aspects of Windows programming, get help on Microsoft technologies covered in Apress books, or provide feedback on any Apress Windows book.

HOW TO PARTICIPATE:

Go to the Apress Forums site at **http://forums.apress.com/**.

Click the New User link.